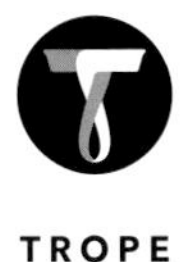

TROPE

ABOVE & ACROSS

ATLANTA

PHOTOGRAPHS BY

LUIS GAUD

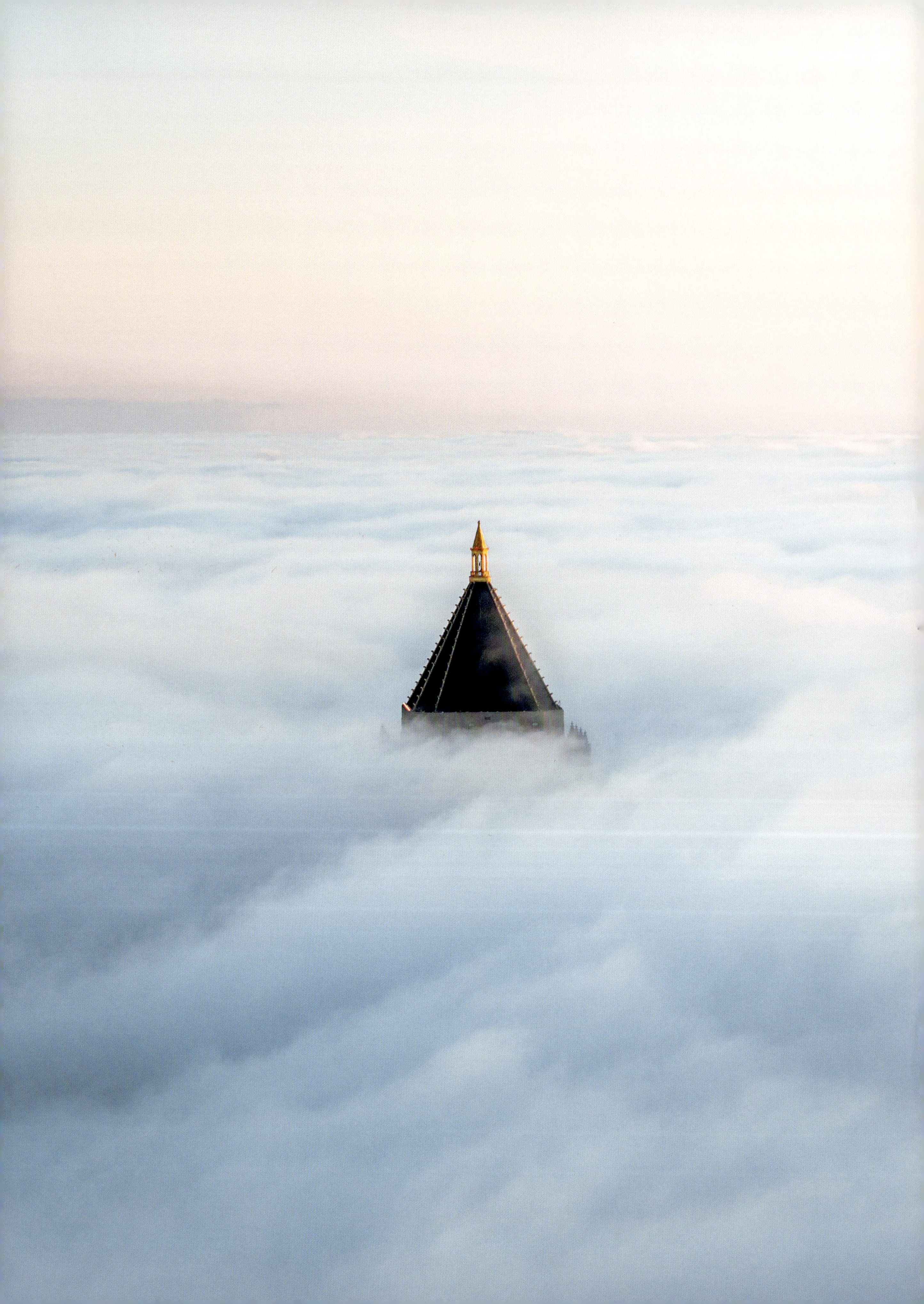

"Atlanta? I think it's the greatest city anywhere I know of."
—Ivan Allen, Jr., Former Mayor of Atlanta

Above & Across Atlanta is a curated collection of aerial photographs of Atlanta from photographer and Atlanta resident Luis Gaud.

A city on the rise, Atlanta is known for its welcoming charm, cultural diversity, and historical significance. Home to headquarters for such companies as CNN, Delta Air Lines, The Coca-Cola Company, and Home Depot, the city's strategic location, abundant and convenient transportation, and business-friendly environment make Atlanta an attractive destination for both corporations and entrepreneurs.

The images featured in *Above & Across Atlanta* represent a contemporary view of the city. Photographed in all seasons and at all times of day, from the glittering dome of the Georgia State Capitol building to the top of the Truist Plaza high rise that peeks above the clouds on a foggy day to the illuminated SkyView Atlanta Ferris wheel at night, each image captures a snapshot of the city's multifaceted character.

Atlanta is a city rooted in history, yet constantly progressing. The photographs in this collection, taken from observation decks and atop buildings, and with the use of drones, capture the juxtaposition of time—presenting Atlanta from fresh perspectives.

Featuring a variety of architectural styles, ranging from modern glass-and-steel skyscrapers to historic buildings with neoclassical and Art Deco influences, the city's skyline is both diverse and distinct. Set against the backdrop of the city's natural landscape, including rolling hills and forests, the city's skyline features skyscrapers like the Bank of America Plaza and the Georgia-Pacific Tower, as well as prominent thoroughfares like Peachtree Street, resulting in a look that is uniquely "Atlanta"—visually striking and also reflective of Atlanta's status as a major urban center.

Let *Above & Across Atlanta* transport you and experience the breathtaking beauty of Atlanta—from above & across.

Michelle Fitzgerald & Jack Van Boom
Editors

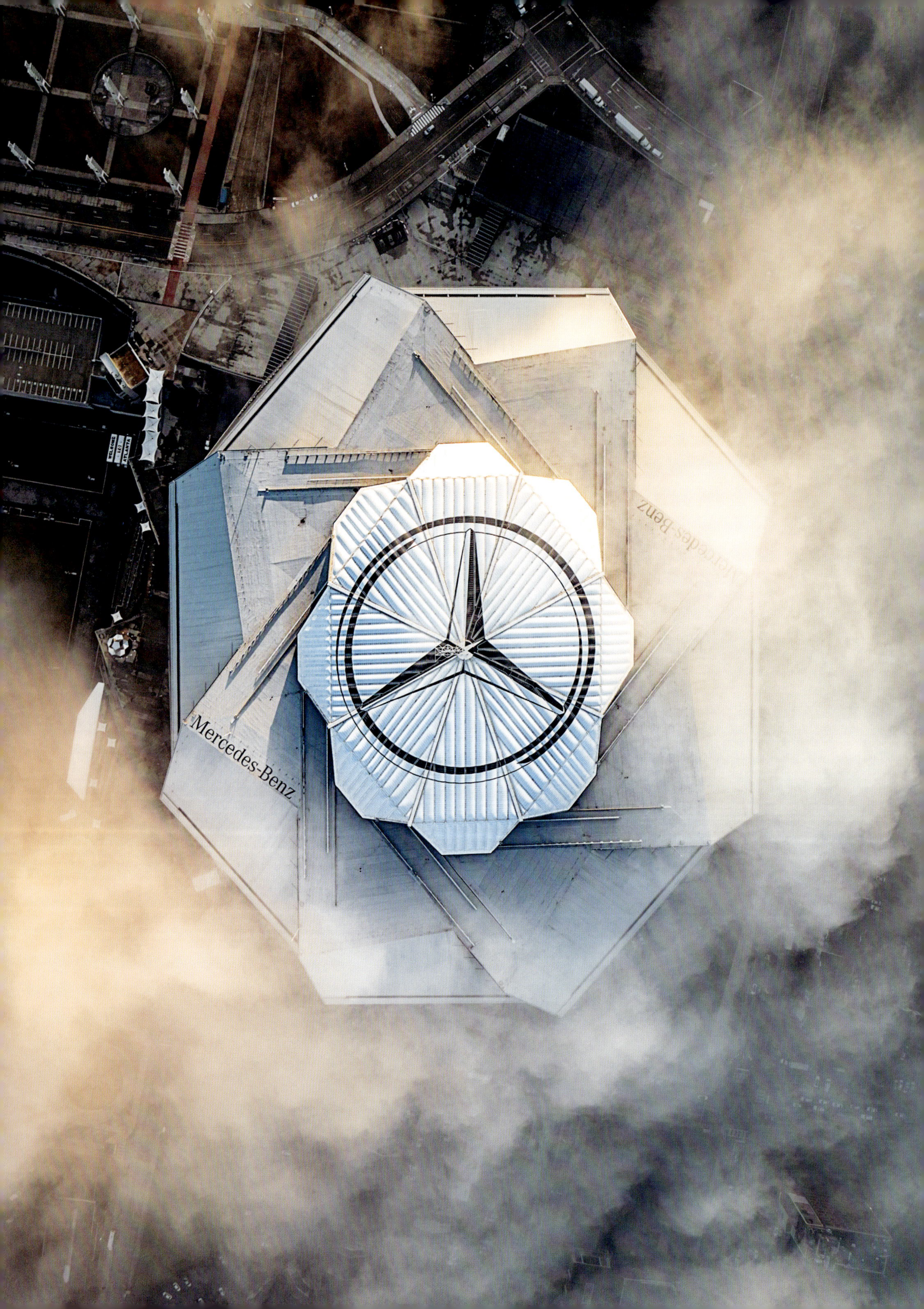

Mercedes-Benz
Mercedes-Benz

"I came to Atlanta before it started growing, so I grew with Atlanta. I made a contribution to Atlanta, but Atlanta made one hell of a contribution to me."
—Andrew Young, Former Mayor of Atlanta

Atlanta unfolds beneath Luis Gaud's lens like a mosaic — a vibrant tapestry woven from verdant green spaces and dynamic cityscapes. The breathtaking collection of aerial photography is more than just a bird's-eye view; it's an invitation to explore a city that pulsates with creativity and a rich history that extends far beyond its impressive skyline.

Atlanta wears the nickname "The City in the Forest" proudly. Lush parks and ancient trees intertwine with bustling streets, offering a unique blend of nature and urban energy. But beneath this flourishing canopy lies a resilient and luminous soul brimming with artistic expression and a past woven with pivotal moments including the ashes of the Civil War. The embers of the Civil War ignited the flames of civil rights leadership, a legacy that continues to inspire not only Atlanta, but the country as a whole. Or perhaps the 1996 Centennial Olympic Games, a moment that thrust Atlanta onto the international stage. These are just some of the brushstrokes on a canvas that have shaped Atlanta's spirit.

Atlanta's music scene embodies the city's innovative spirit. From the electrifying rhymes of local hip-hop legends like OutKast and Killer Mike to the soulful legacy of gospel, Atlanta's soundscape thrives on a vibrant fusion of rhythms. This openness to new influences is what makes Atlanta's music scene so dynamic. Vibrant concerts erupt in unexpected places, transforming landmarks like Hotel Clermont, Ponce City Market, and beloved parks into temporary music halls. The energy pulsates through these spaces, a testament to Atlanta's undeniable creative heartbeat.

Atlanta is a city that thrives on creativity, and the symphony of creativity of its diverse communities. Visitors are instantly struck by the inspiration that fuels its energy. This isn't just a place with a beautiful skyline; Atlanta is a cultural, historical, and political powerhouse. It's the birthplace of Martin Luther King Jr. and Spike Lee, the political home turf of Stacey Abrams and John Lewis, and a leading destination for film and television production. Its influence extends far beyond city limits, shaping not just the United States, but in many ways, the entire world. From music, culinary arts, fashion, and design to movie production and the ongoing fight for civil rights, Atlanta's legacy continues to influence the world stage.

Luis Gaud's *Above & Across Atlanta* offers a glimpse into this remarkable city from above and within. Prepare to be inspired by the beauty, energy, and stories that unfold on every page.

Andrew Clark
Atlanta-based Photographer

The Phoenix ♦ In Atlanta, amidst the bustling streets and vibrant culture, the phoenix reigns supreme as a potent symbol of resilience and revival. While the city may not boast an official emblem, the phoenix has woven itself into the very fabric of Atlanta's identity, embodying its remarkable history of rising from the ashes of adversity. ♦ The genesis of this association can be traced back to the days of the Civil War when General William Tecumseh Sherman's Union Army razed Atlanta to the ground in 1864. The devastating inferno left much of the city in ruins, its once-thriving infrastructure reduced to ash and rubble. ♦ Yet, from the ashes of destruction emerged a newfound spirit of determination and renewal. Atlanta began the arduous journey of rebuilding, spurred by an unwavering resolve to reclaim its former glory. In this rebirth, the city found resonance with the mythical phoenix of ancient Greek lore — a majestic bird known for its ability to rise from its own ashes. ♦ This powerful symbolism became deeply ingrained in Atlanta's ethos, epitomizing its spirit of resilience and progress. Today, the "phoenix" is omnipresent throughout the city, immortalized in its seal adorned with the Latin inscription "Resurgens," meaning "rising again." Depicted in the seal is the phoenix, soaring triumphantly from the flames of destruction, a poignant reminder of Atlanta's indomitable spirit. ♦ The phoenix also graces the landscape of Atlanta in various forms — from public artworks to architecture and the visual representations of local organizations. Each serves as a testament to the city's enduring ability to overcome adversity and emerge stronger than ever before. ♦ In Atlanta, the phoenix is more than just a mythical creature — it's a beacon of hope, a symbol of resilience, and a testament to the city's unwavering spirit in the face of adversity. As Atlanta continues to evolve and thrive with its remarkable population growth and bustling industry, the legend of the phoenix remains an enduring symbol of its journey from the ashes to new heights of prosperity.

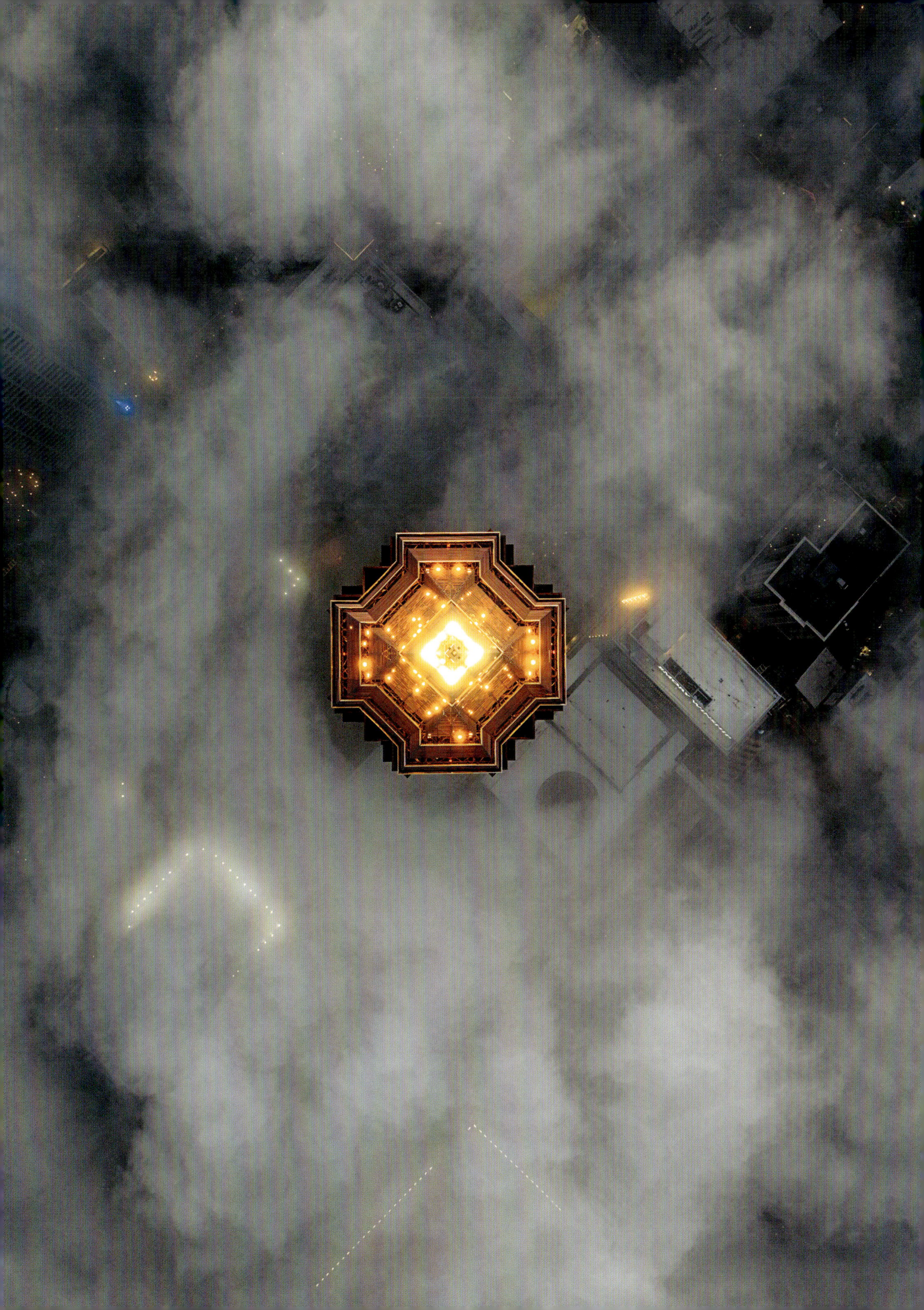

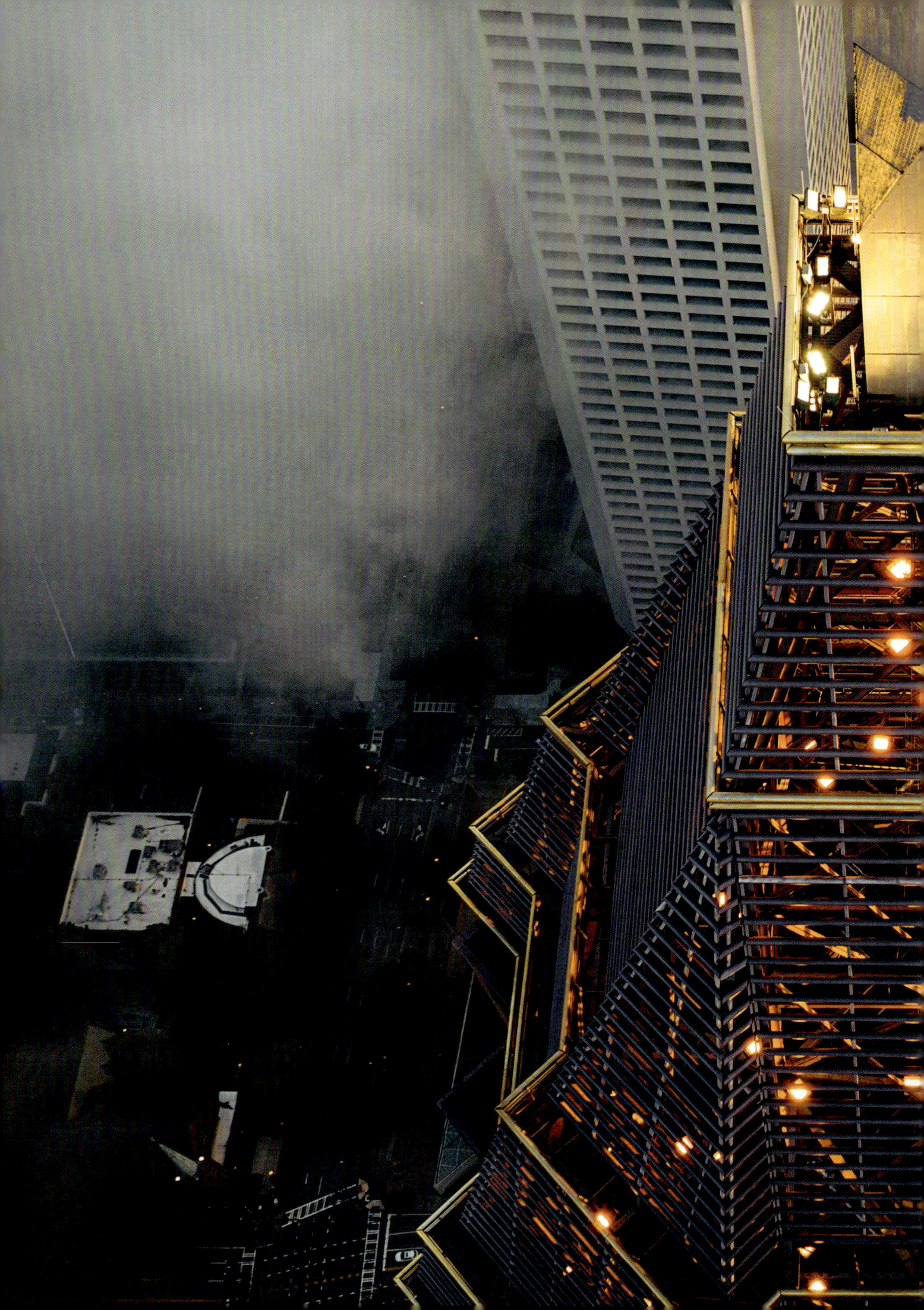

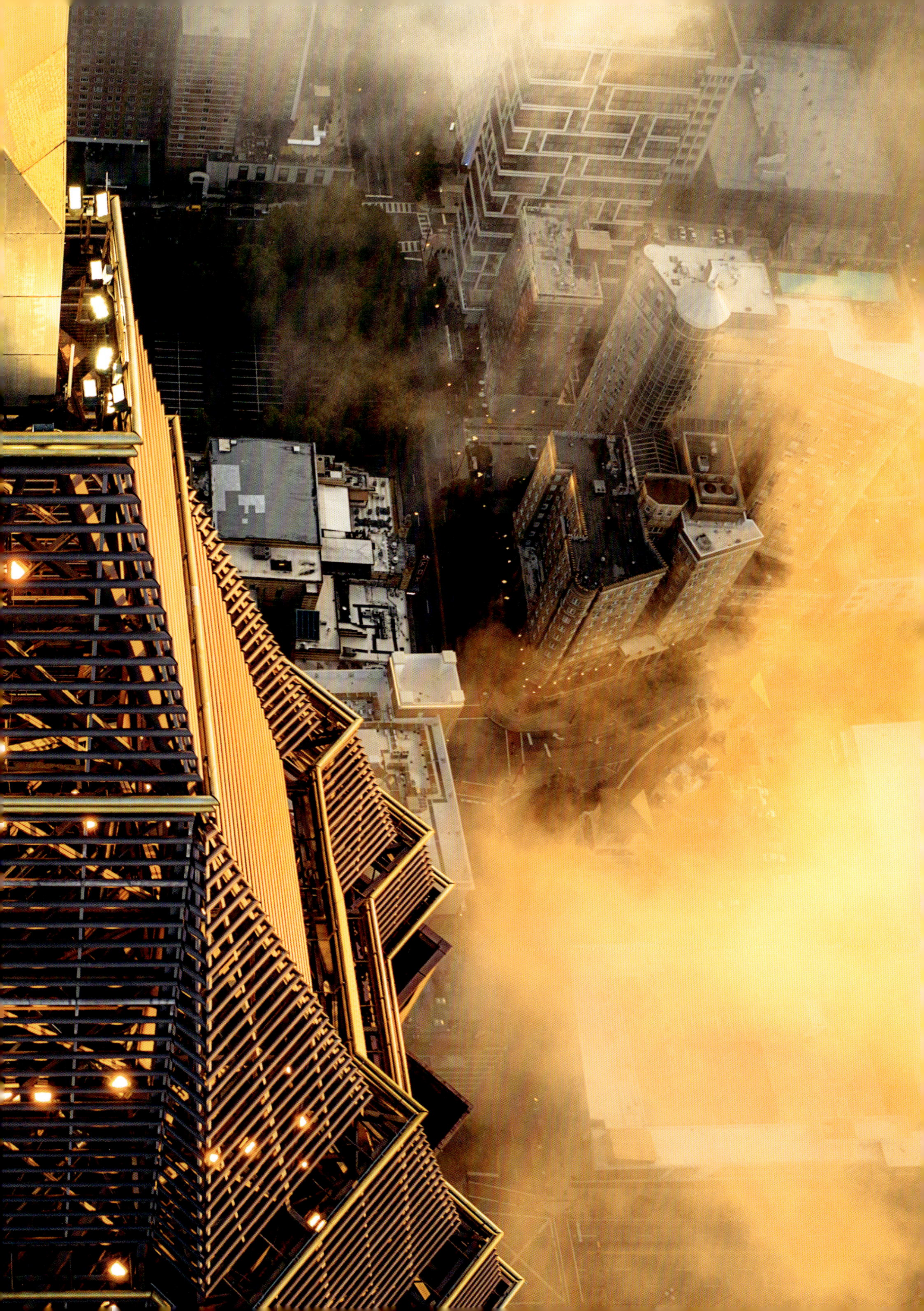

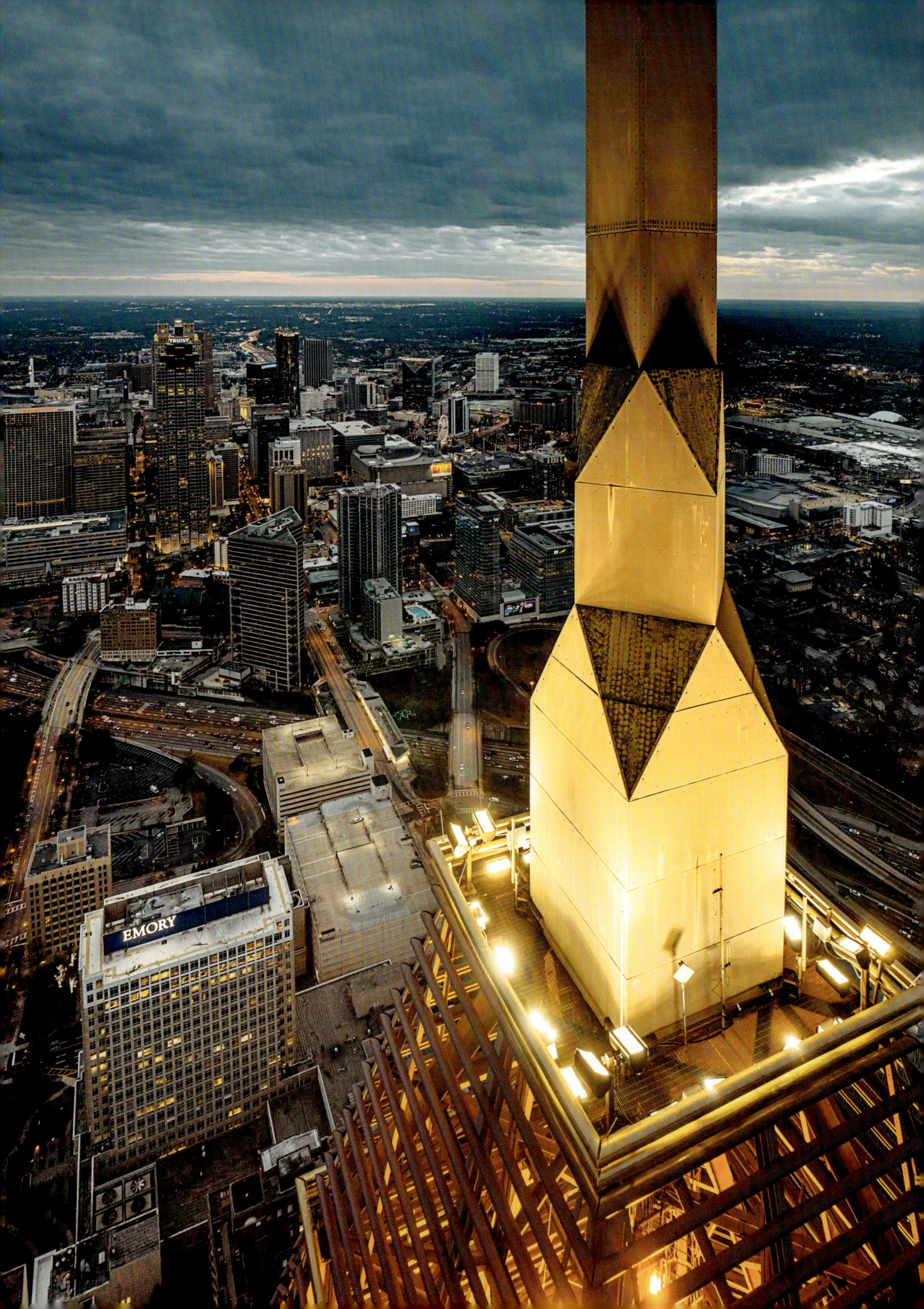
TRUIST
EMORY

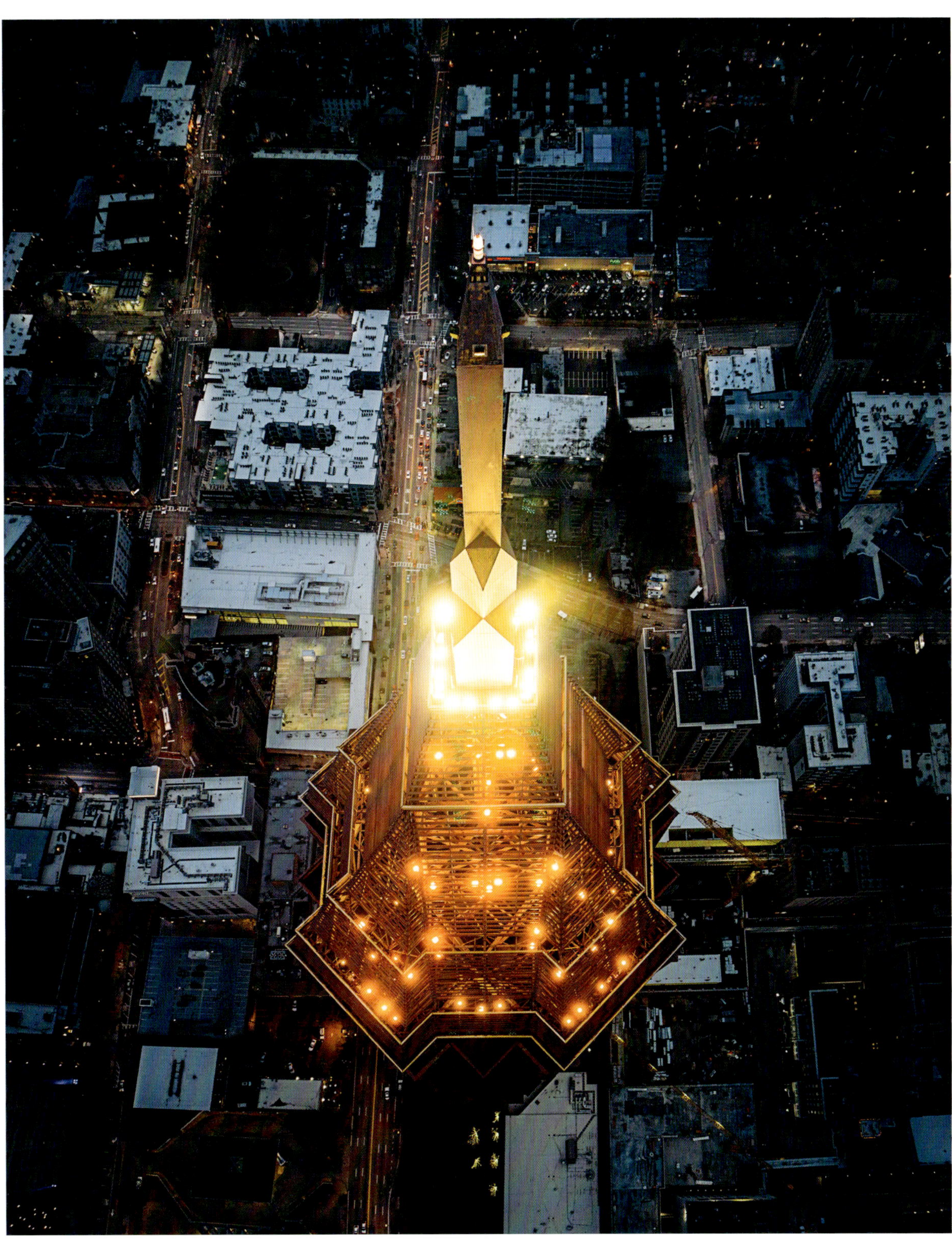

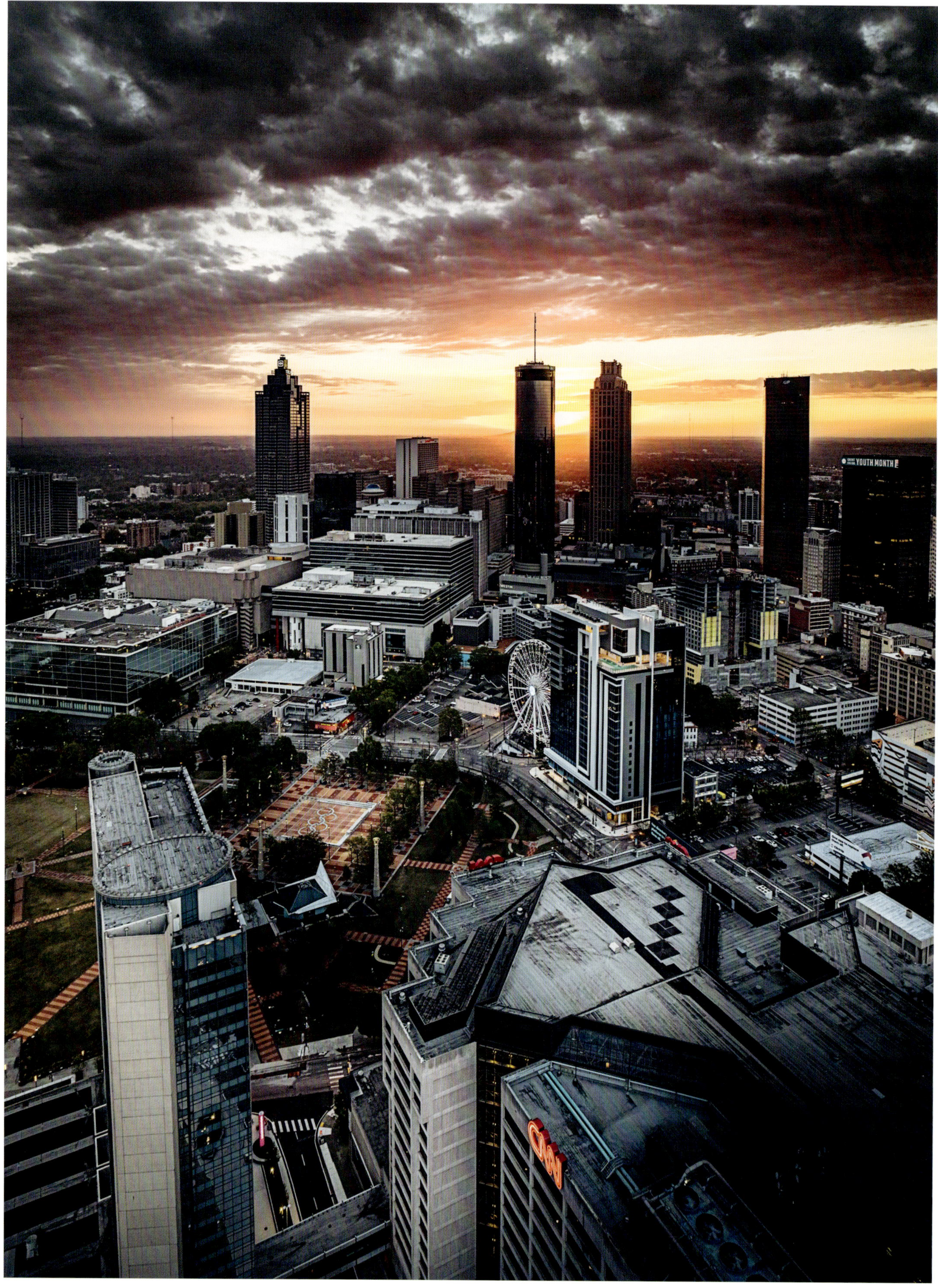

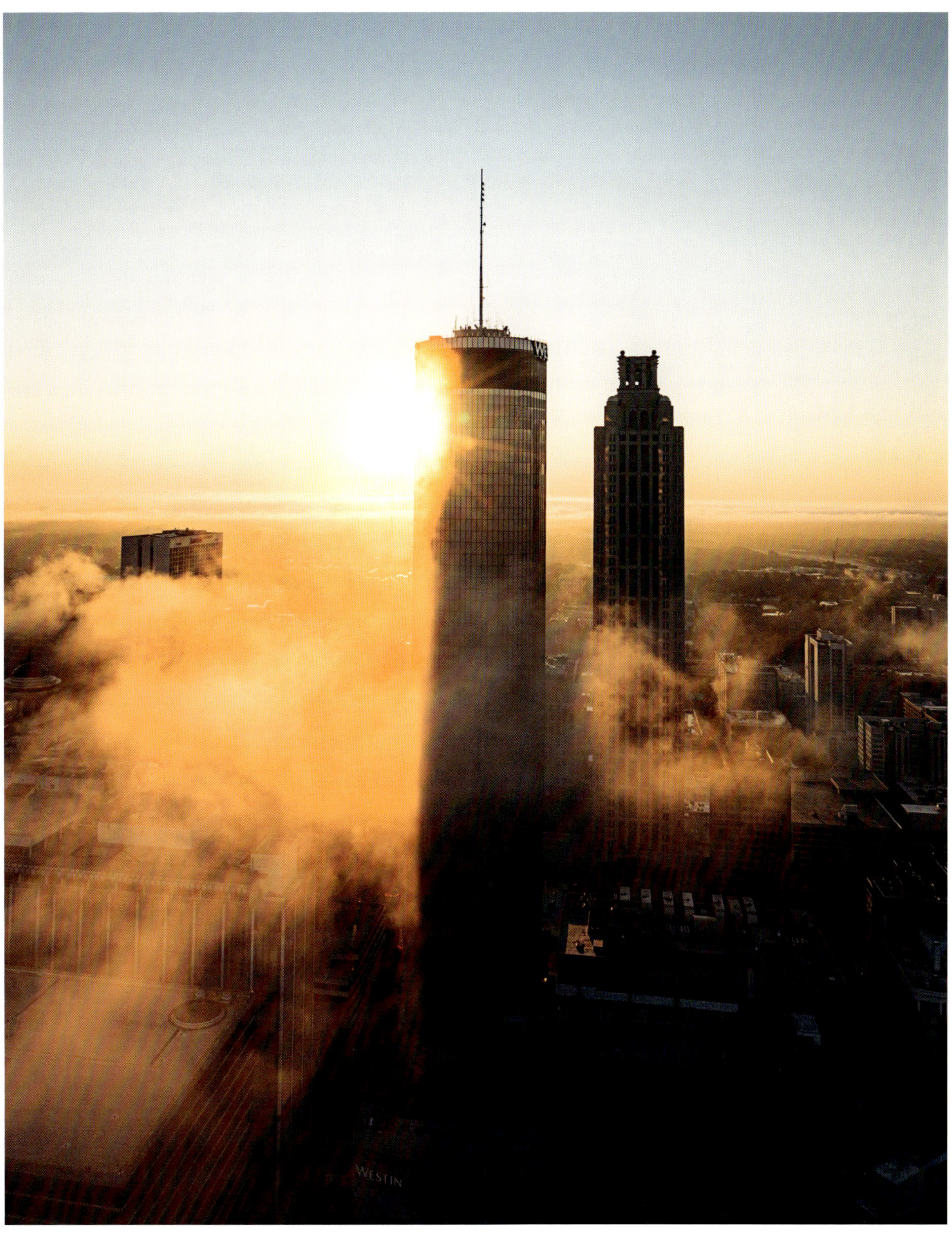

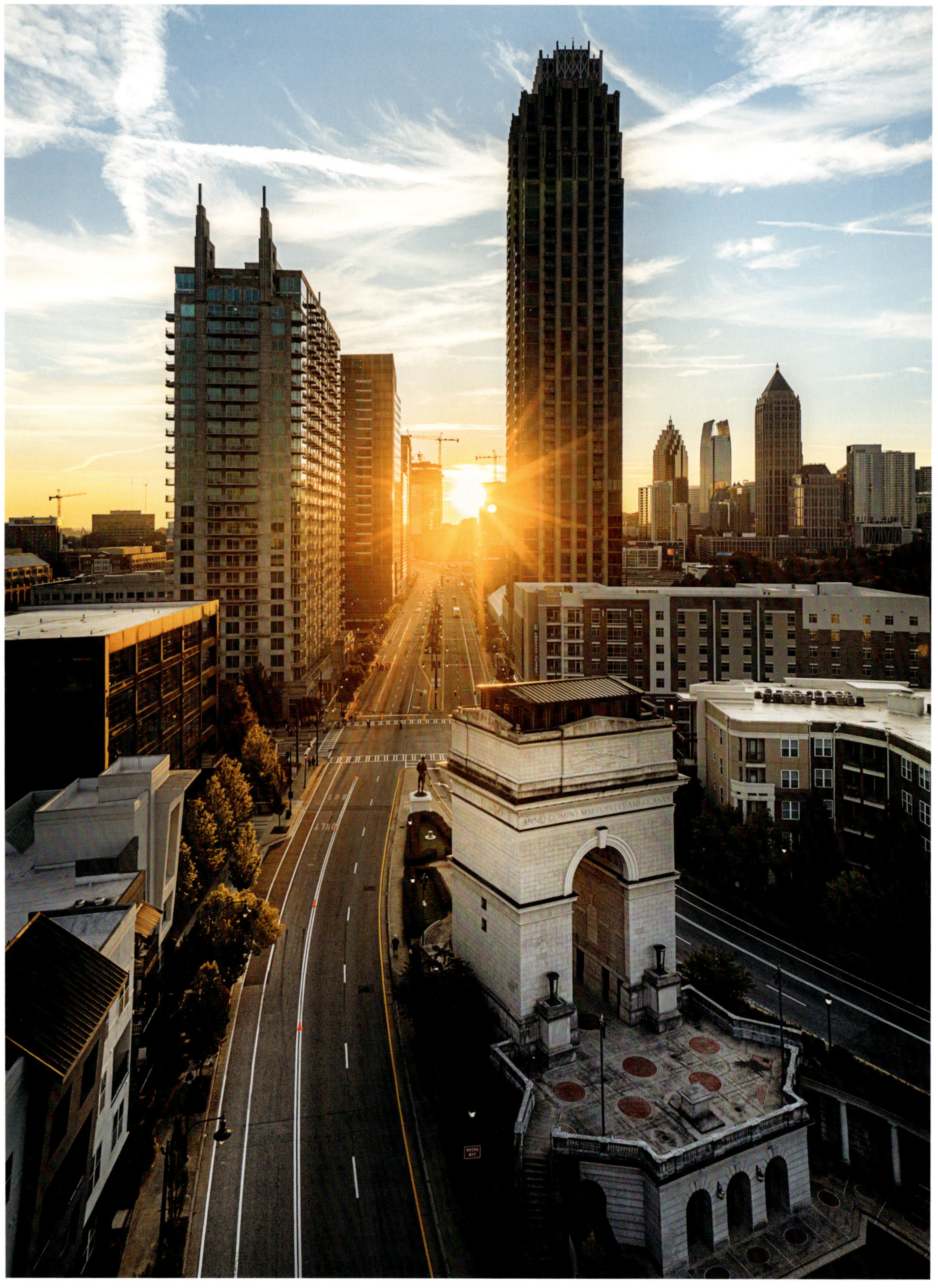
ANNO DOMINI MCMXCIV

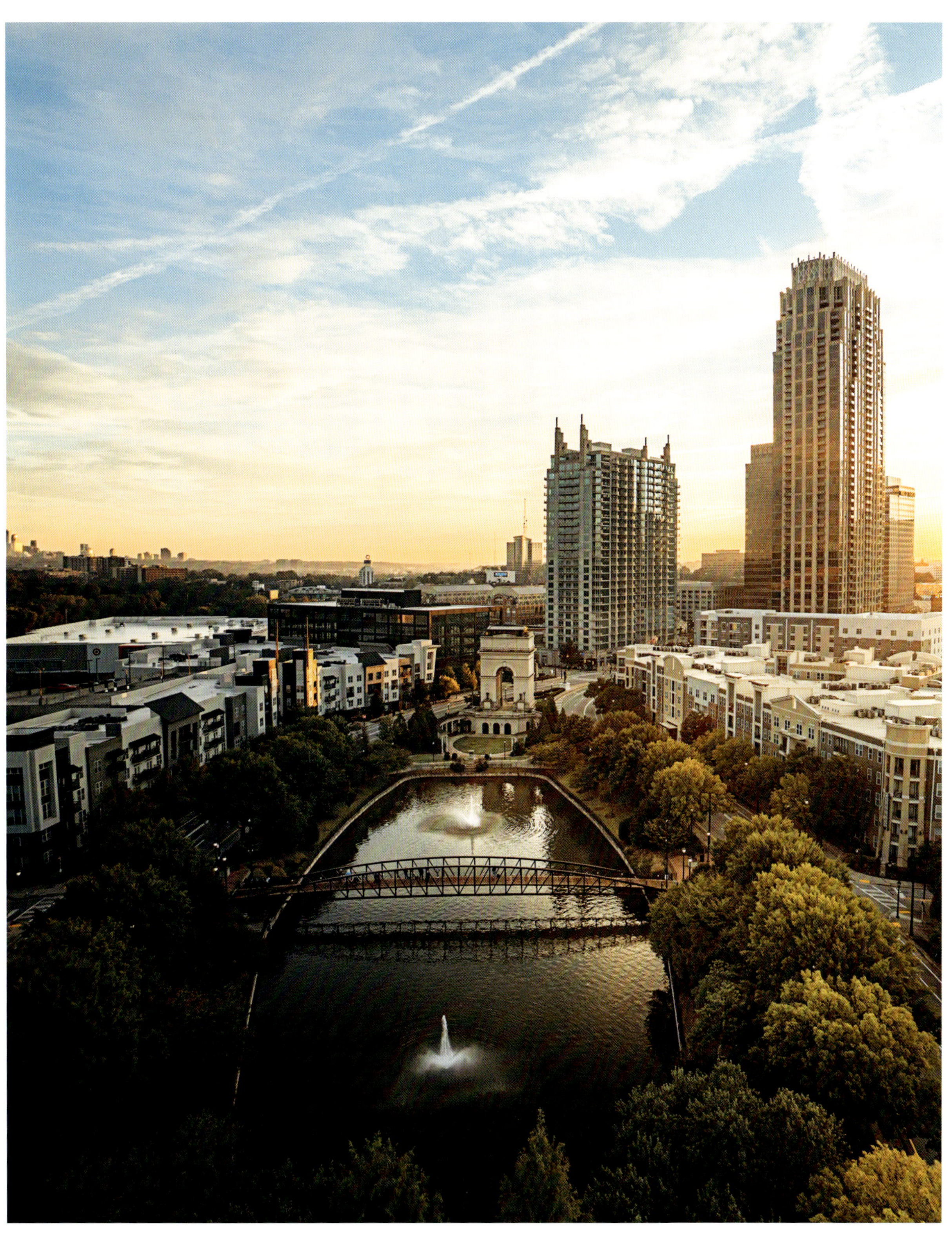

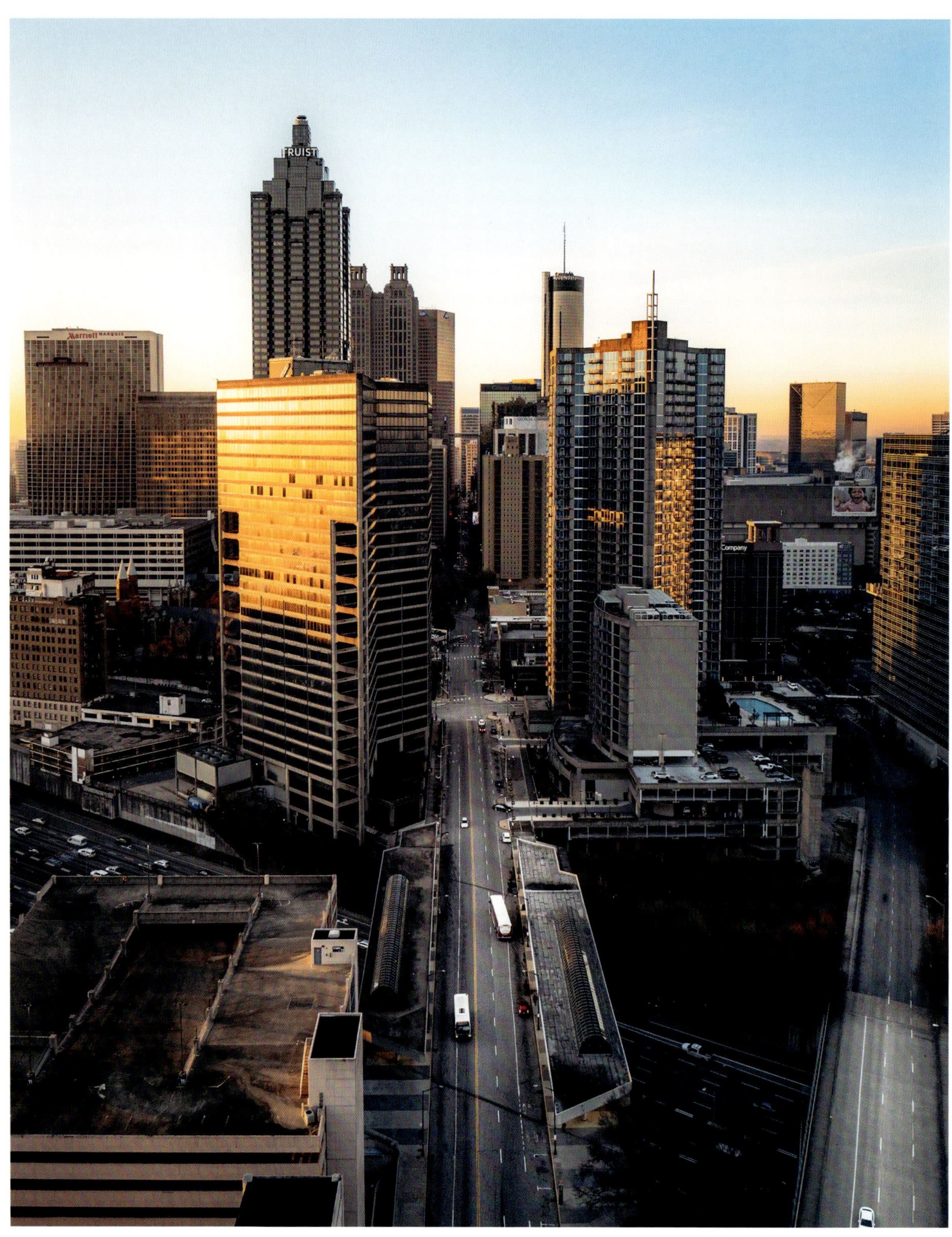

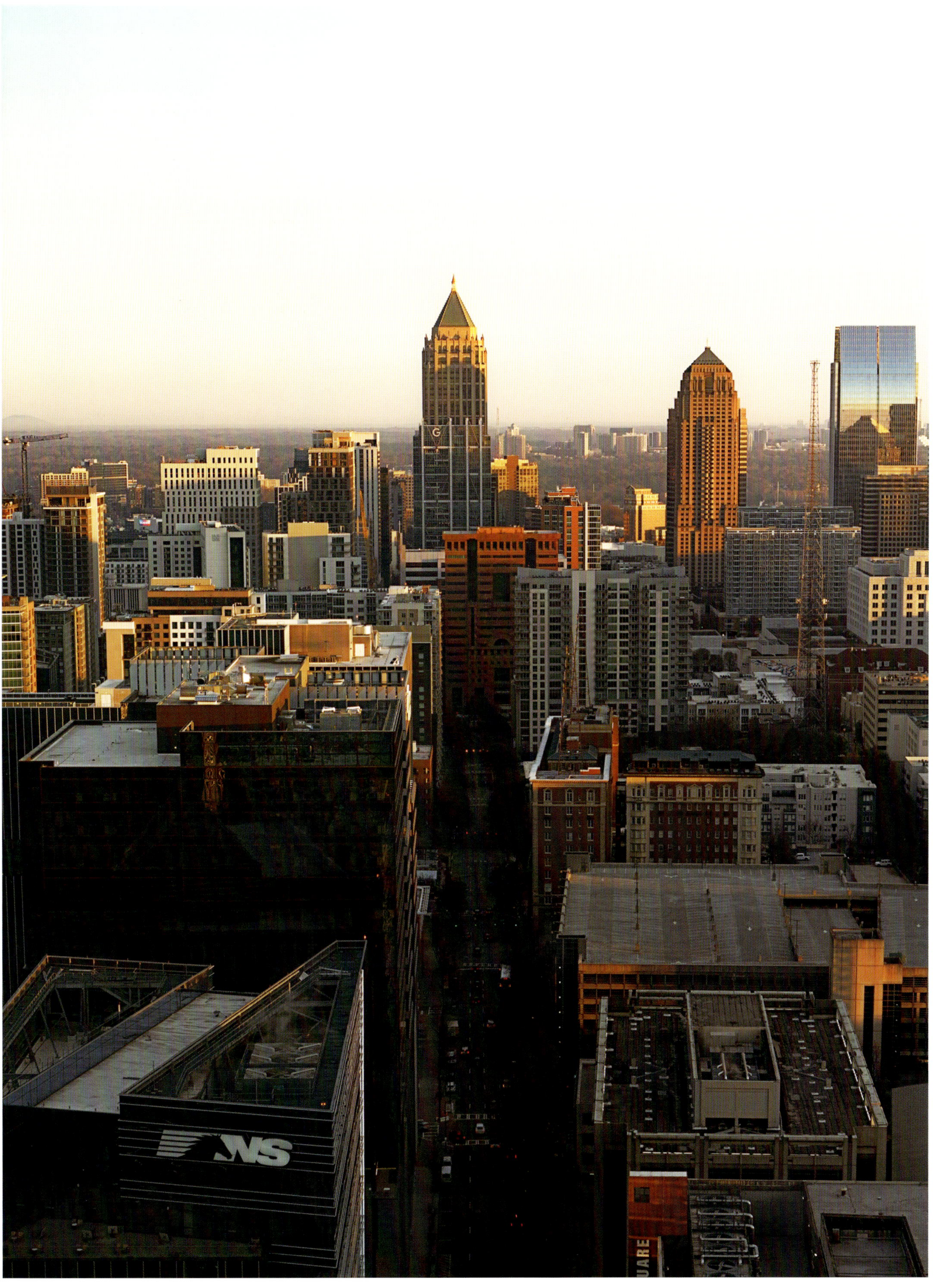

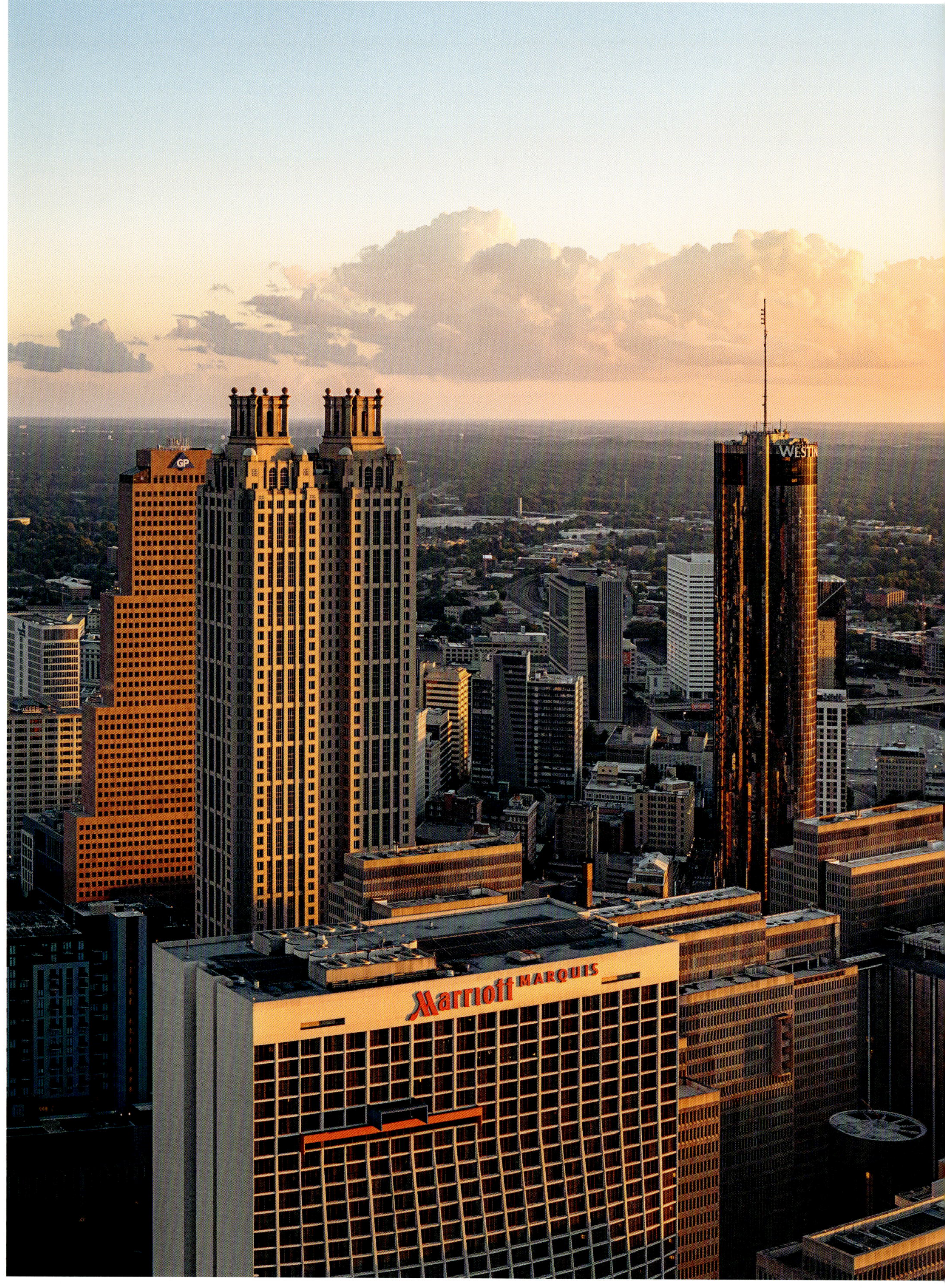

GP
WESTIN
Marriott MARQUIS

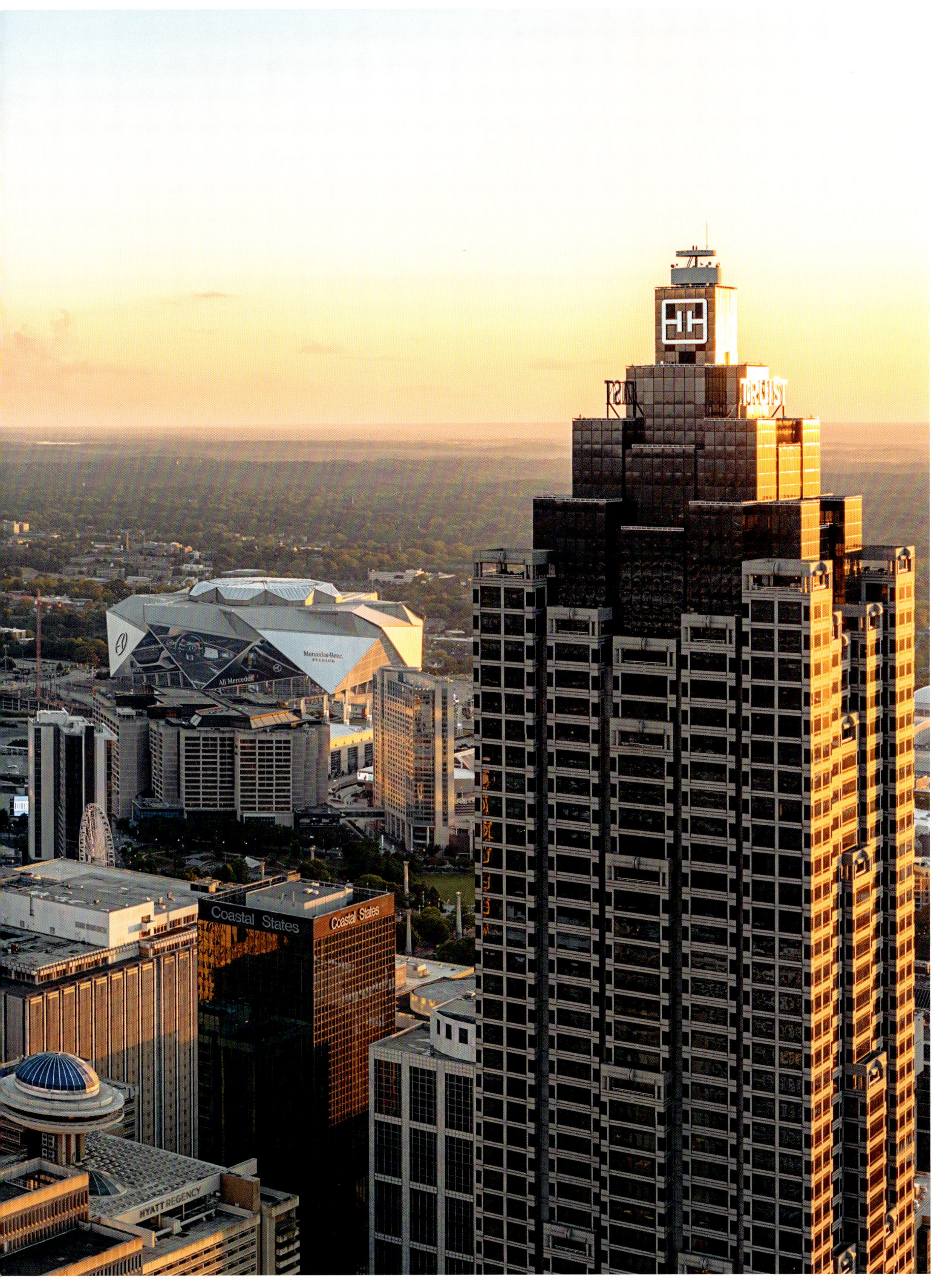

Mercedes-Benz
STADIUM
All Mercedes
Coastal States
Coastal States
HYATT REGENCY

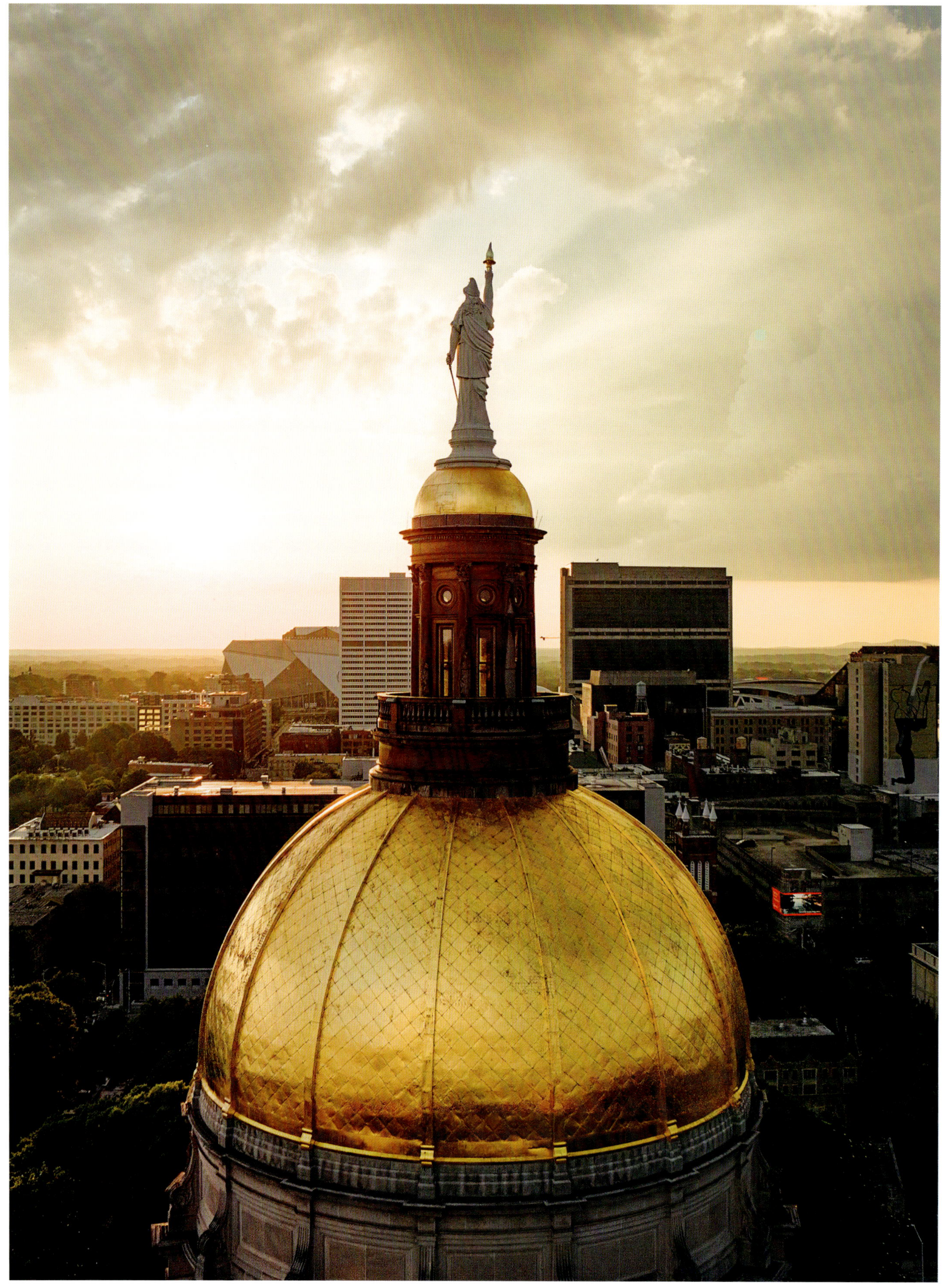

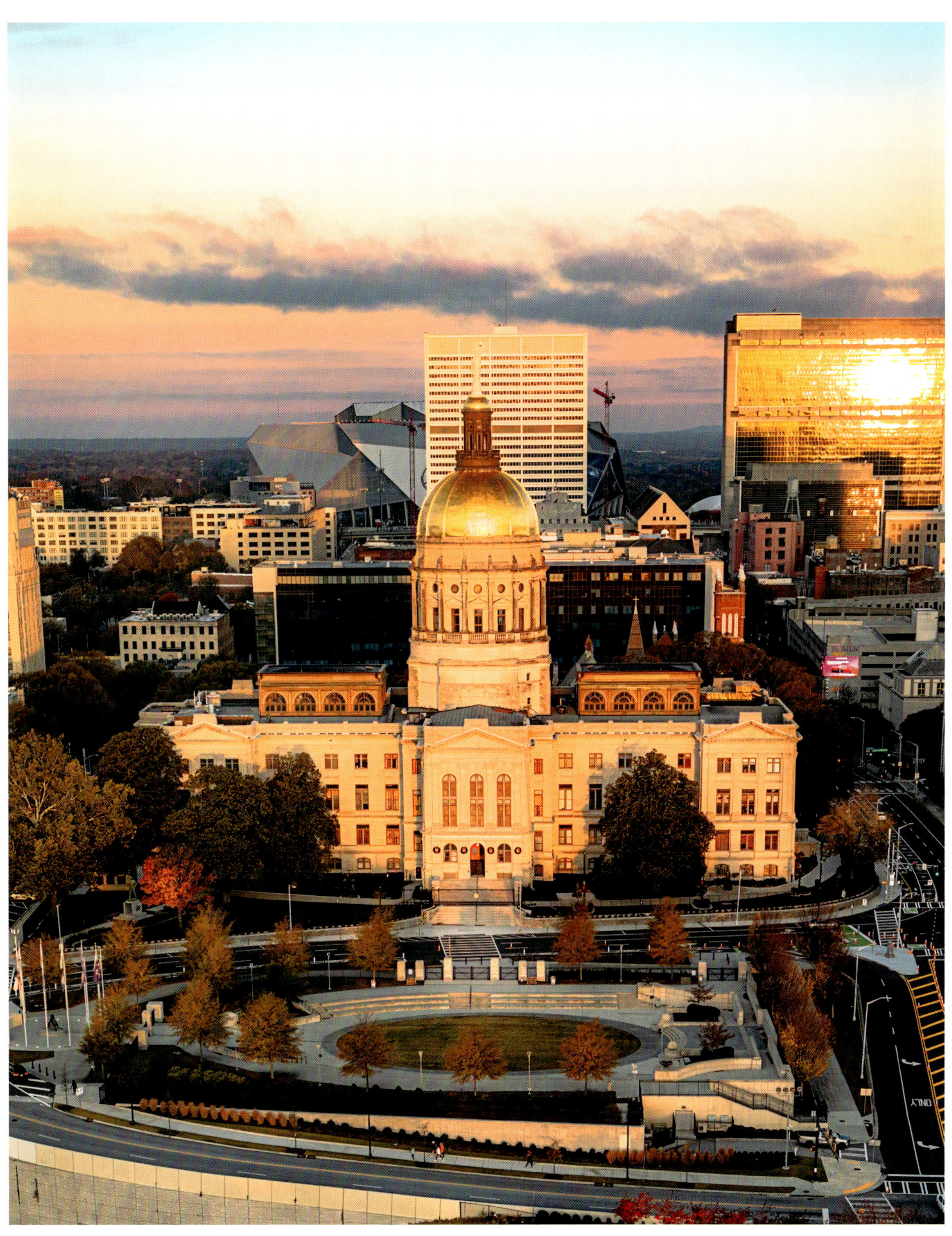

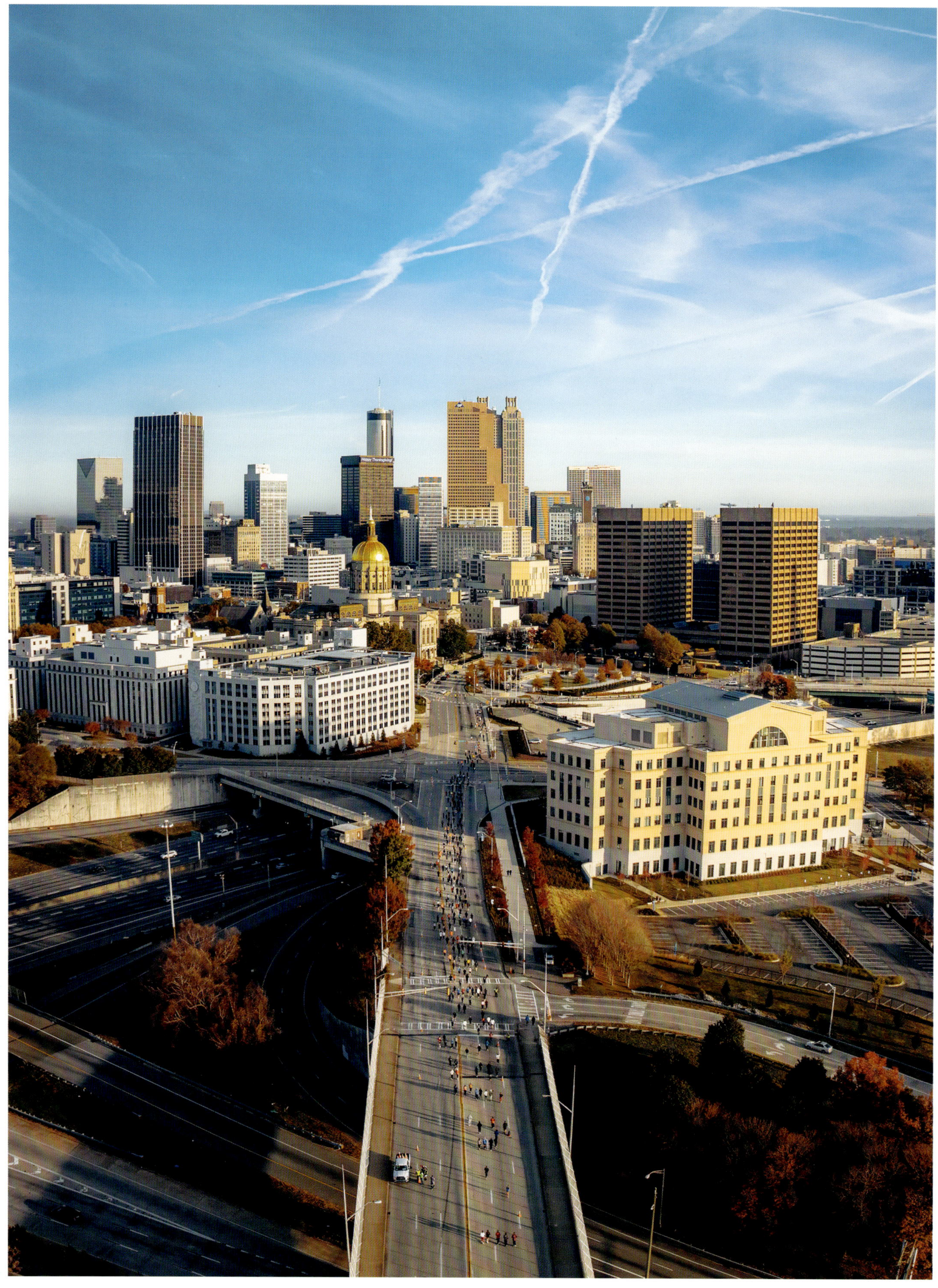

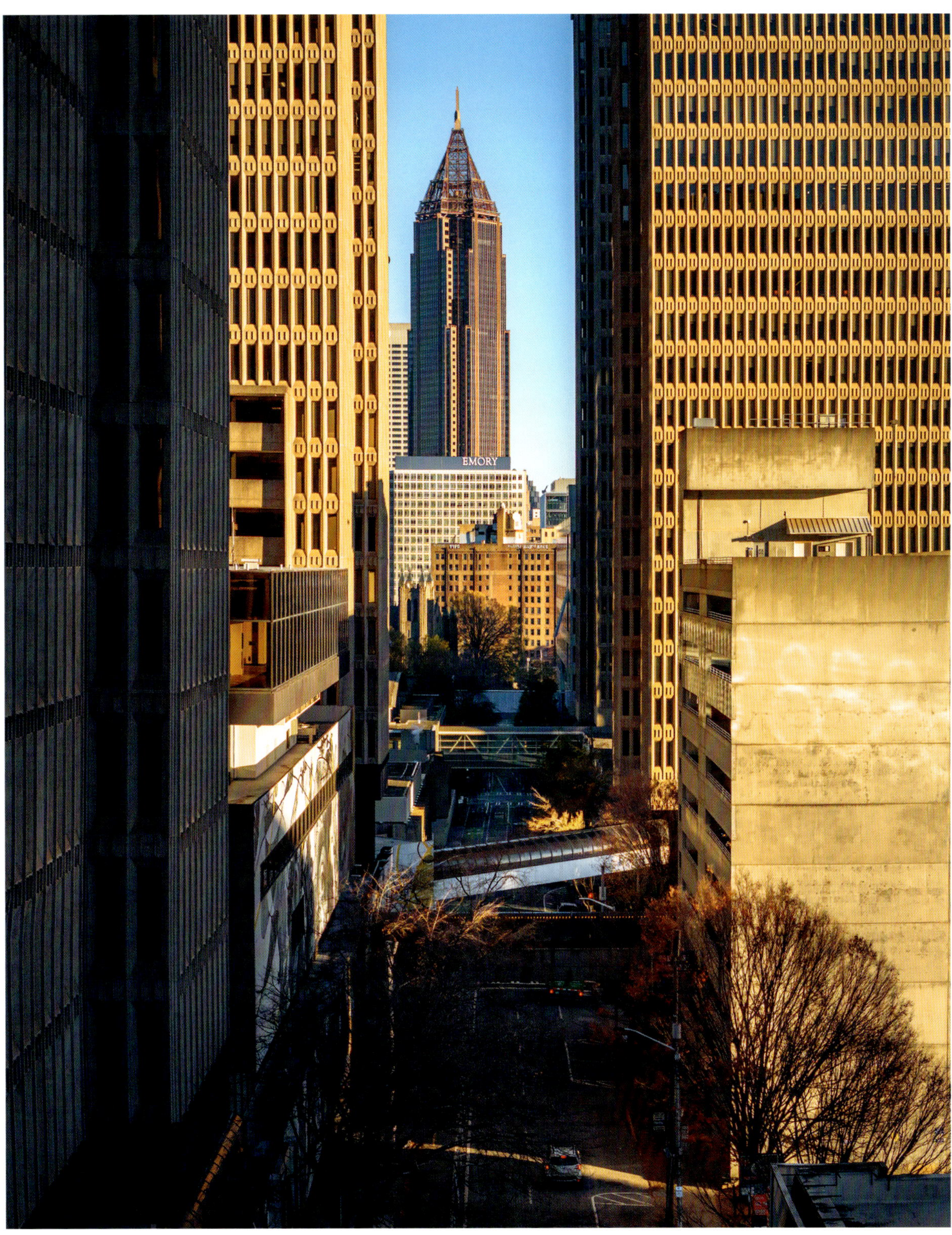

EMORY

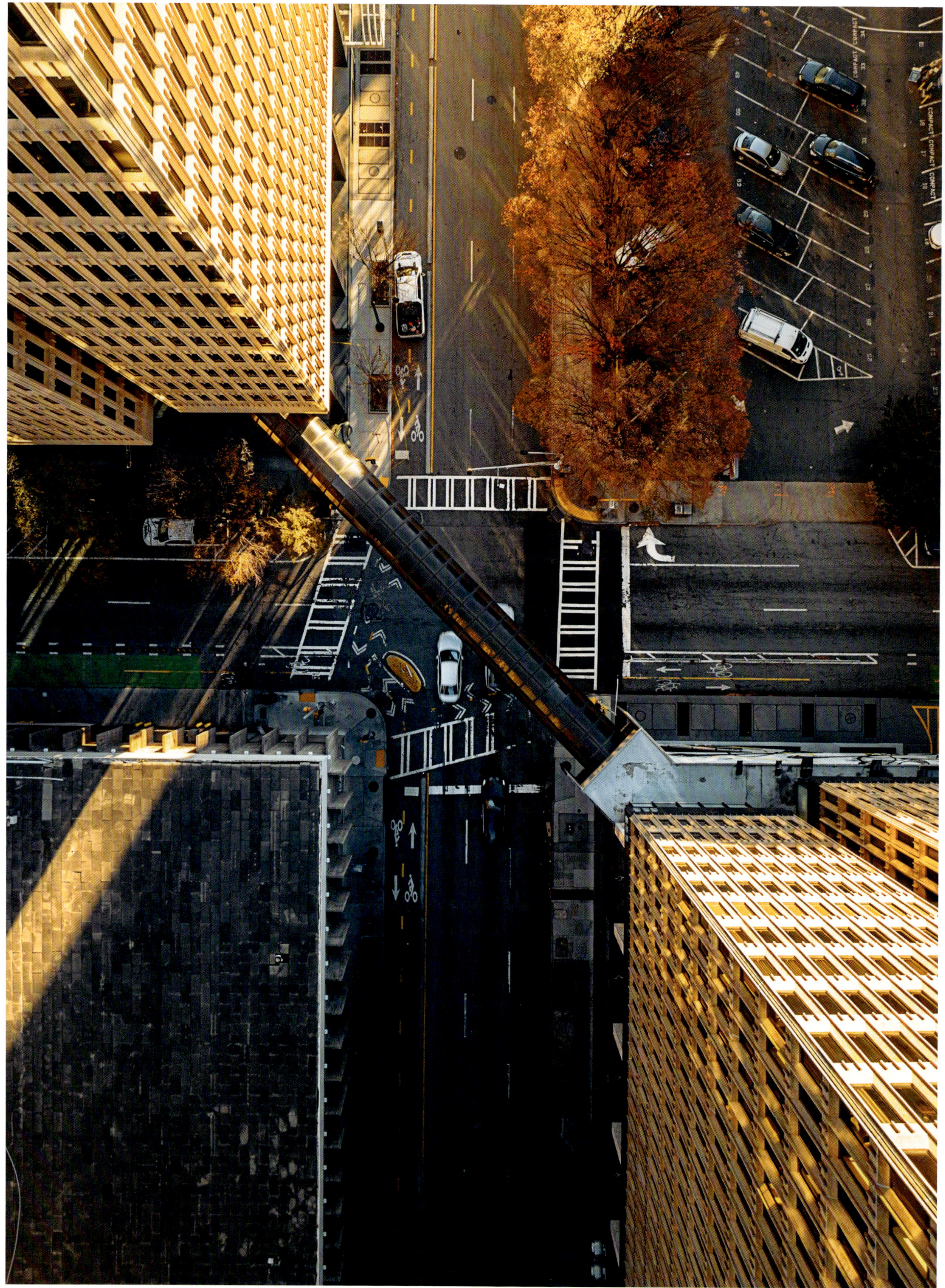

COMPACT

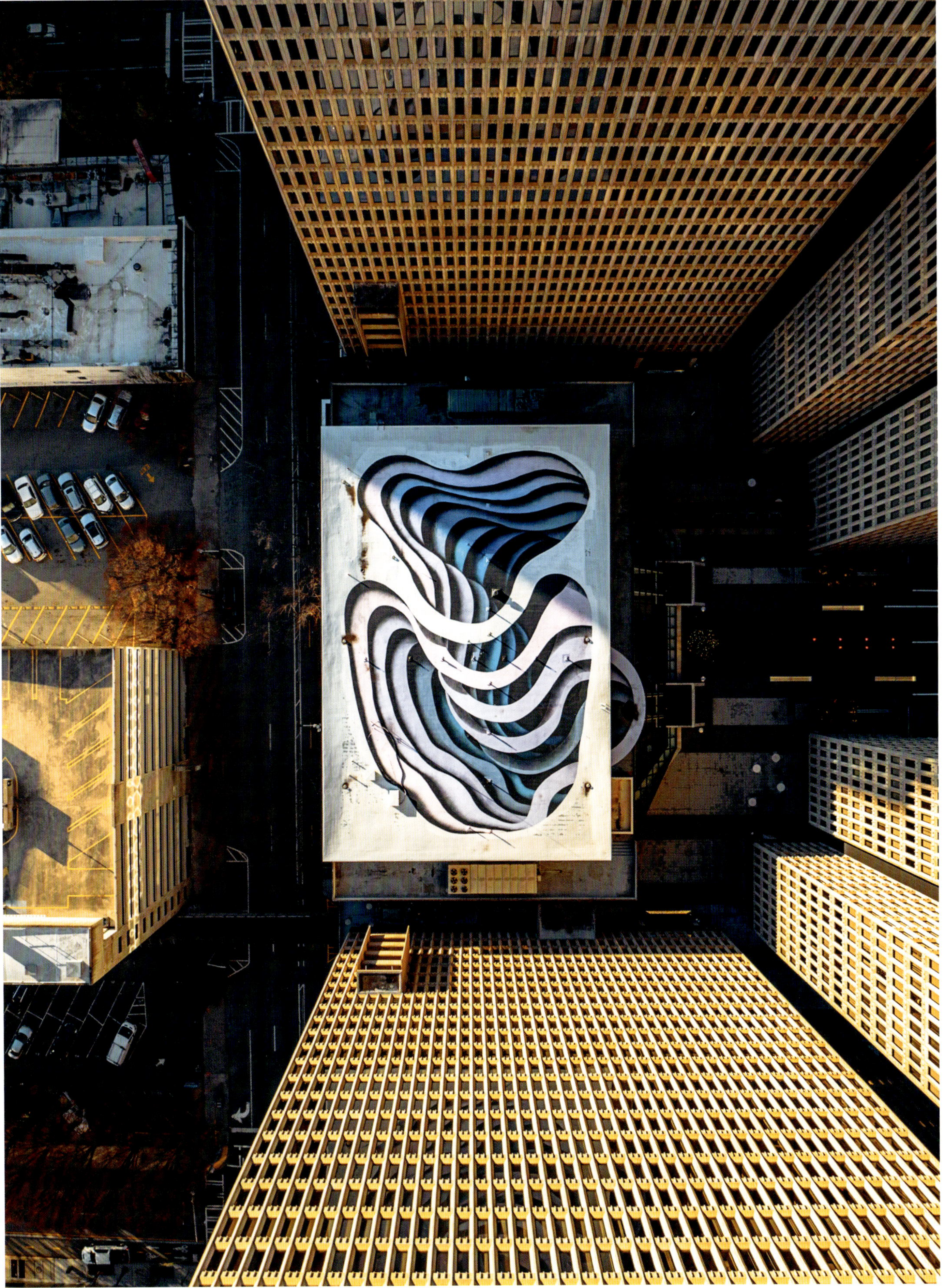

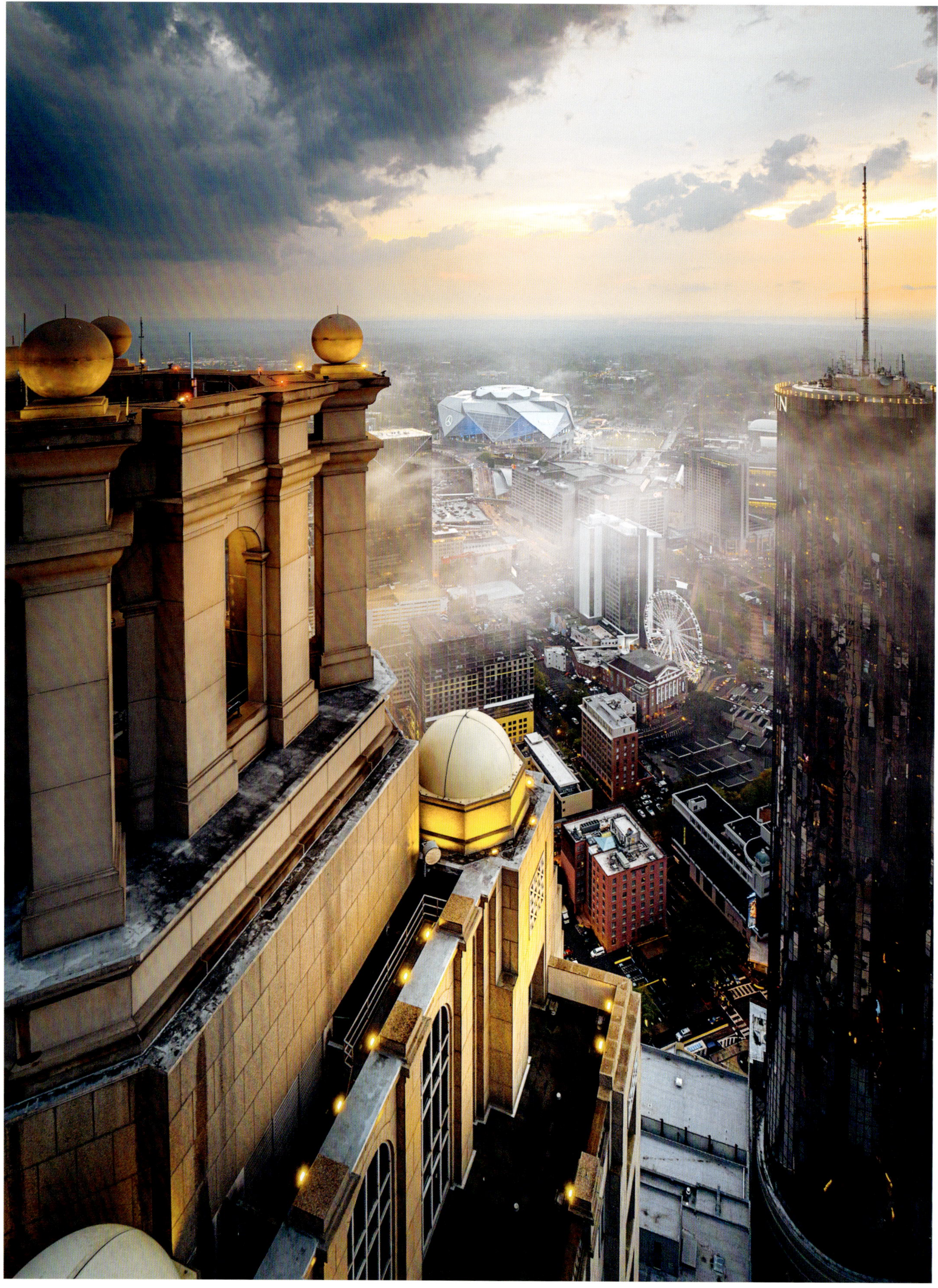

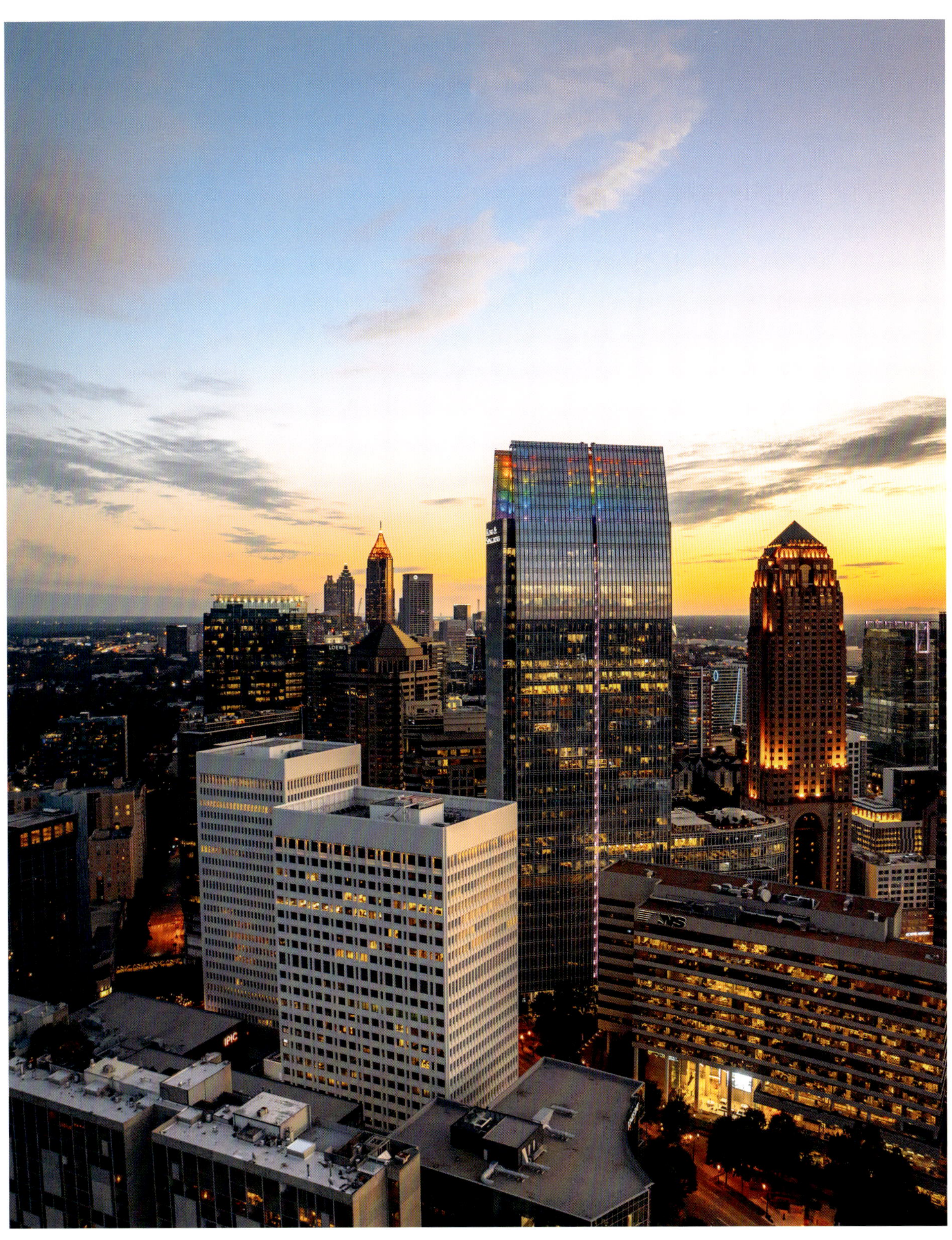

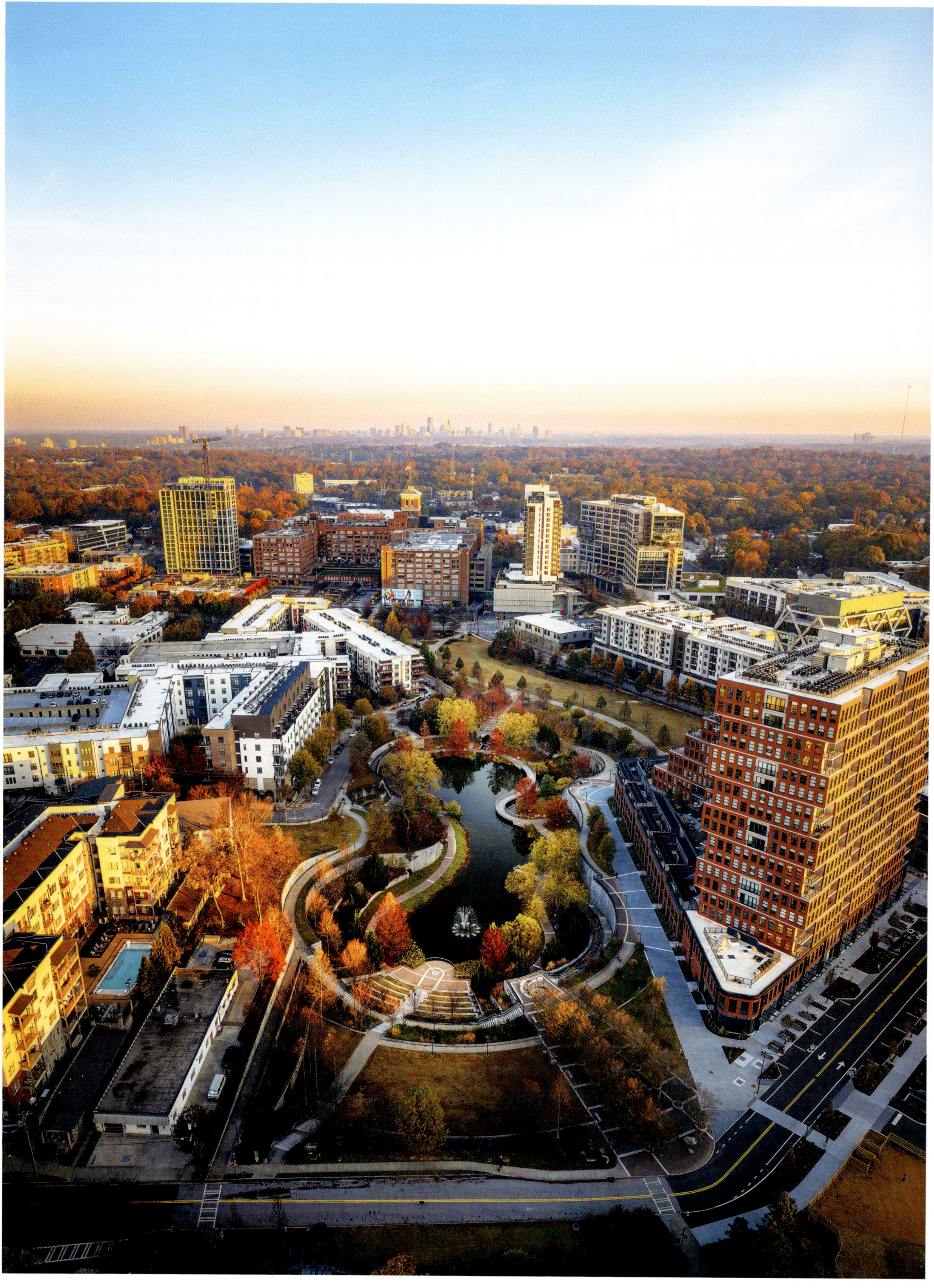

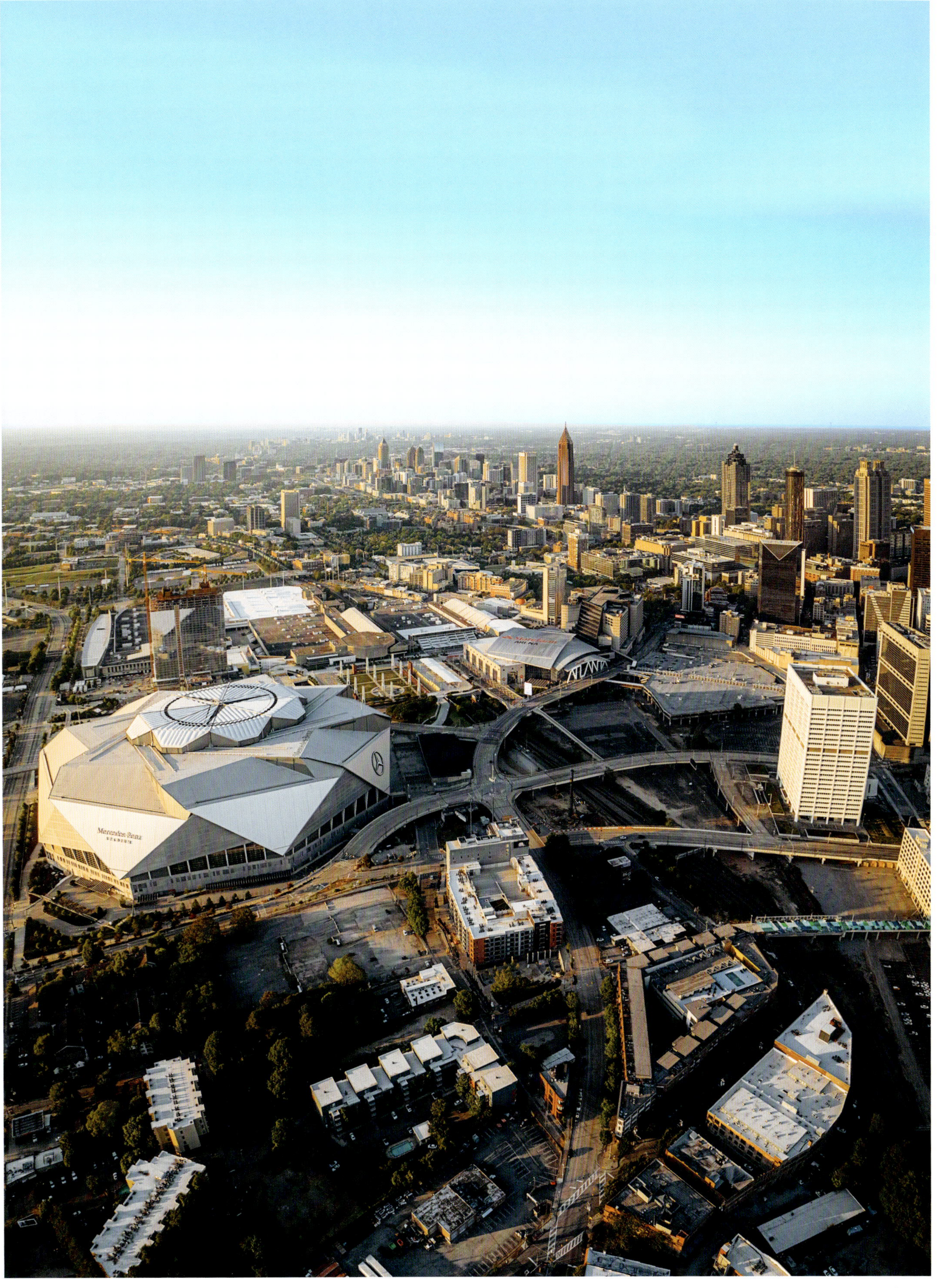

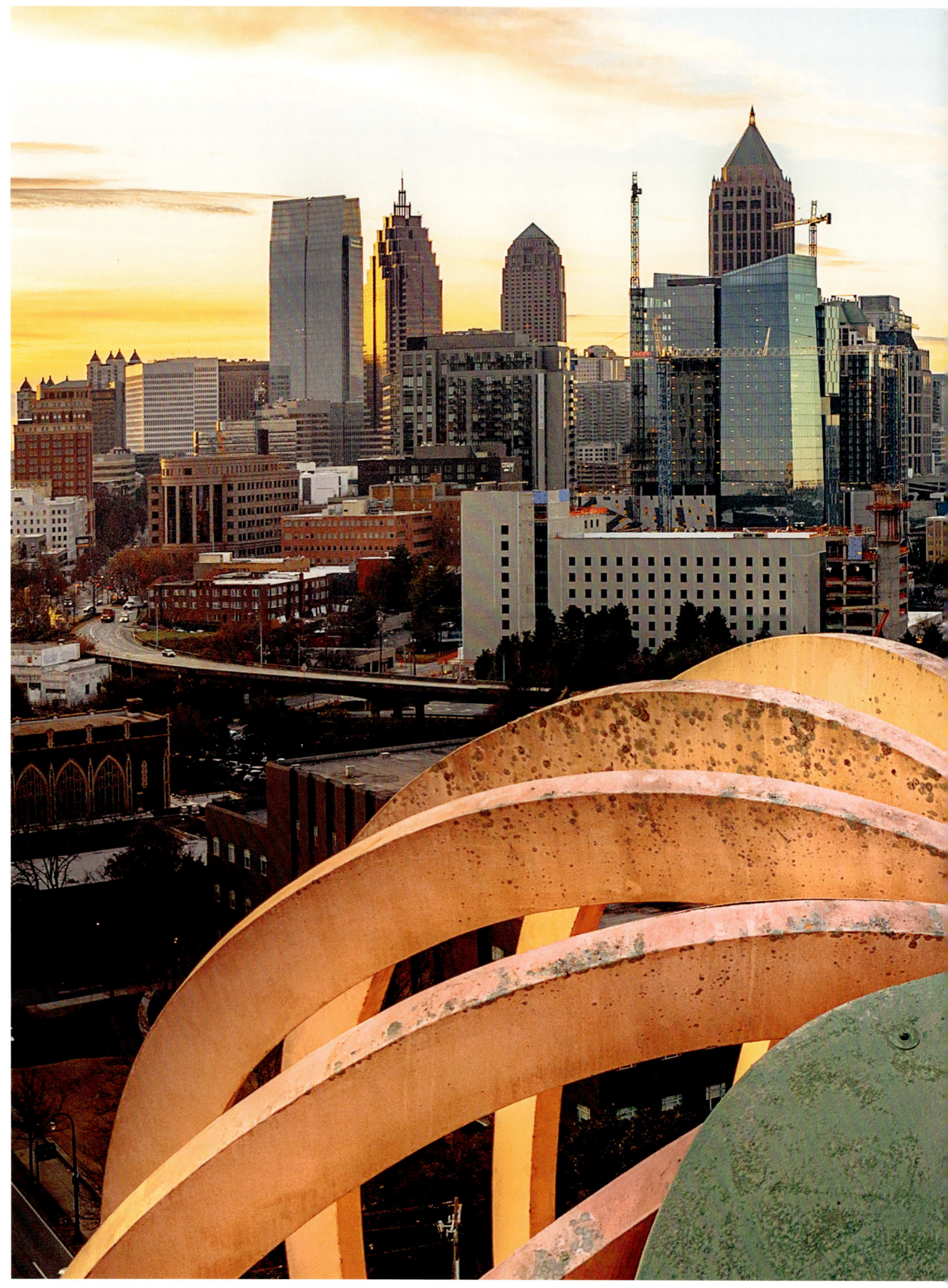

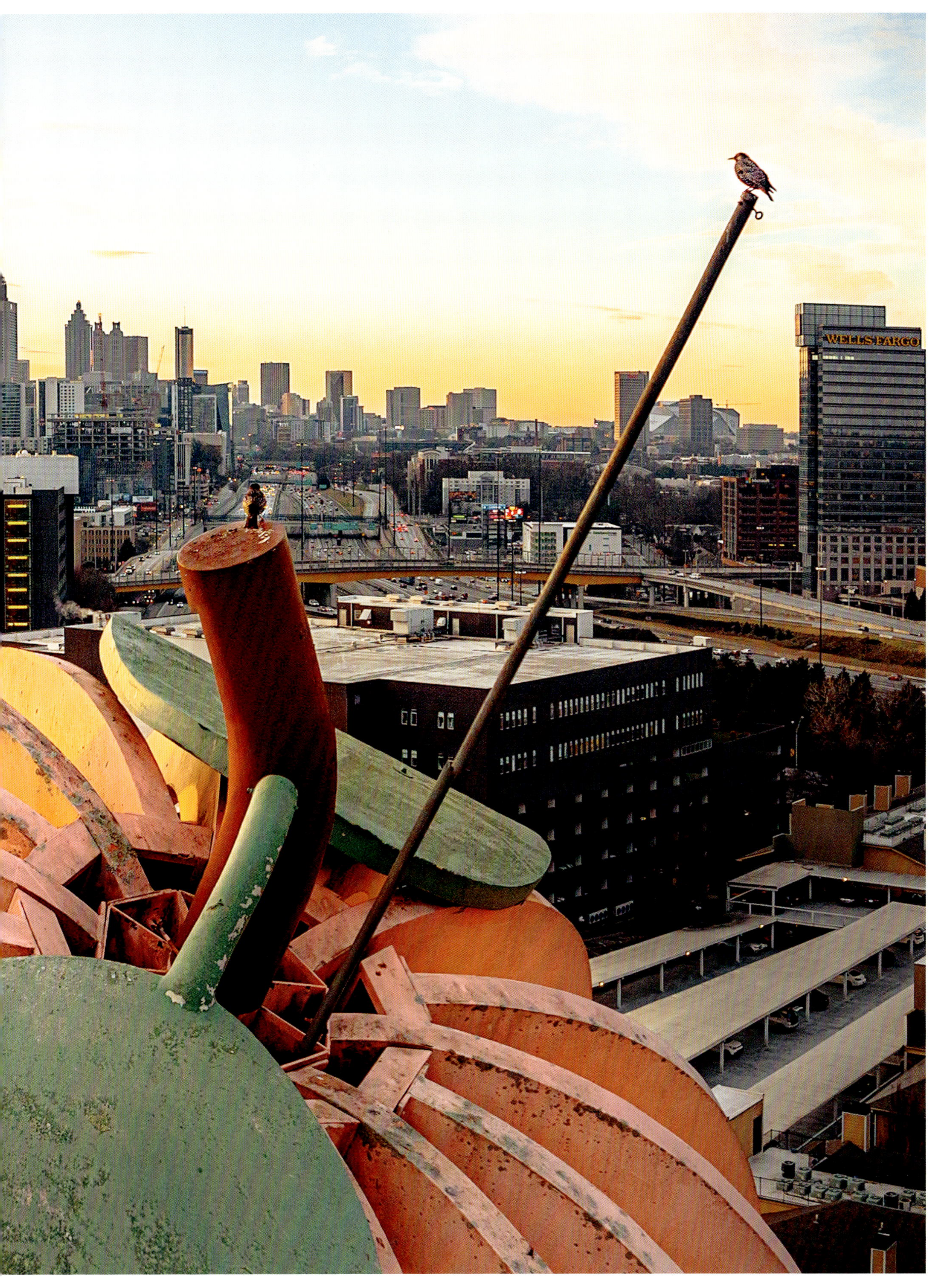
WELLS FARGO

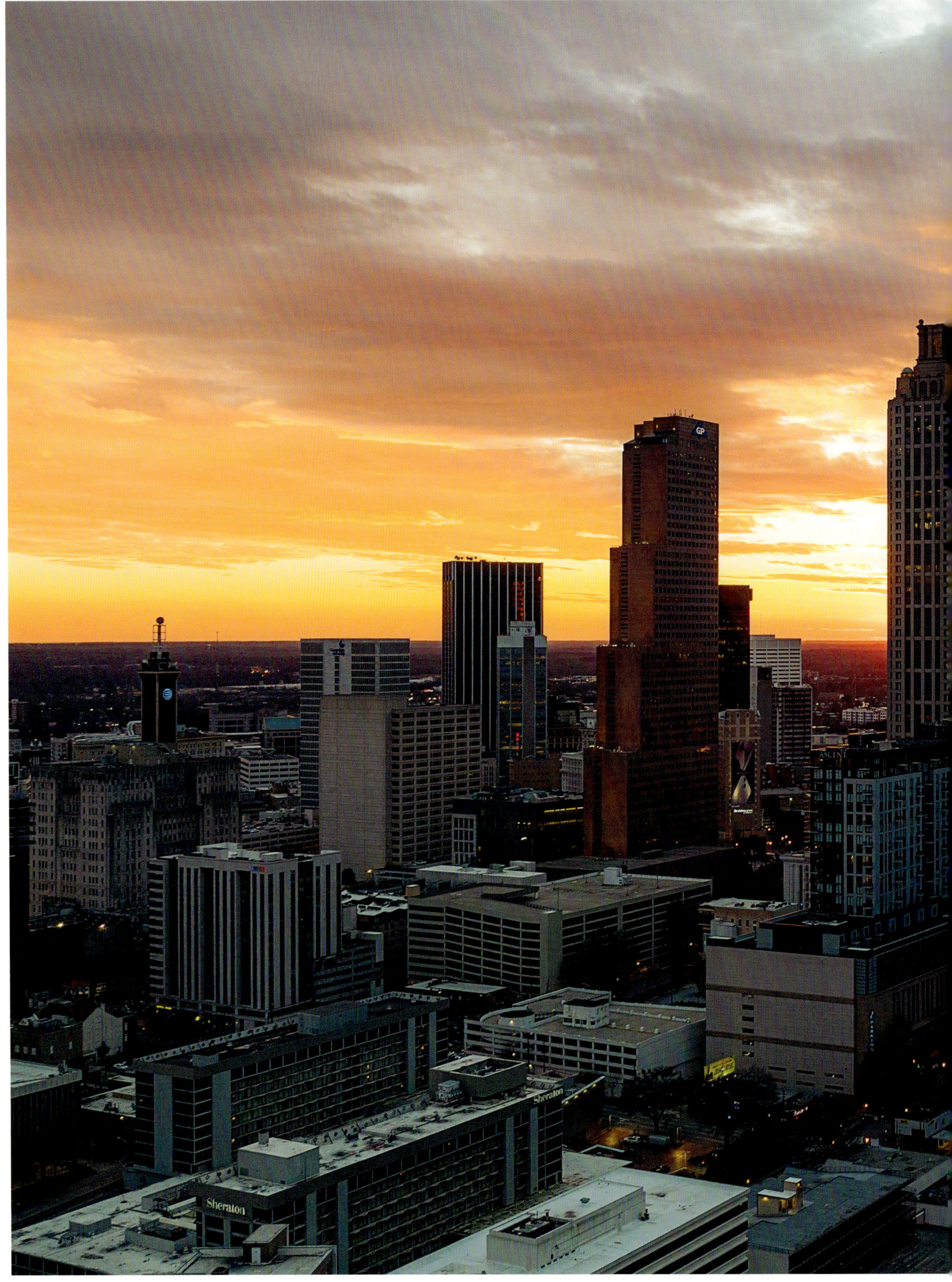

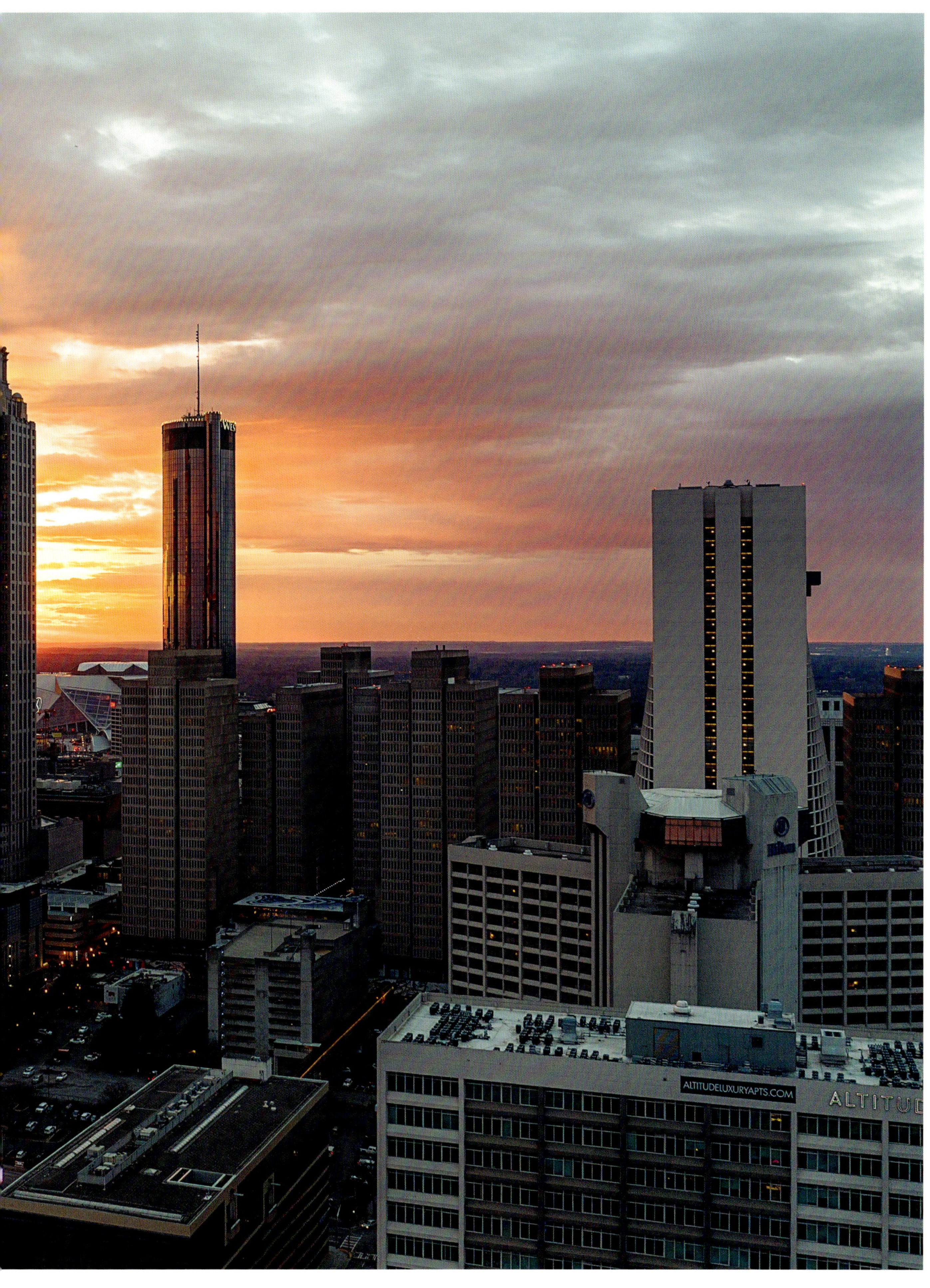

ALTITUDELUXURYAPTS.COM
ALTITUD

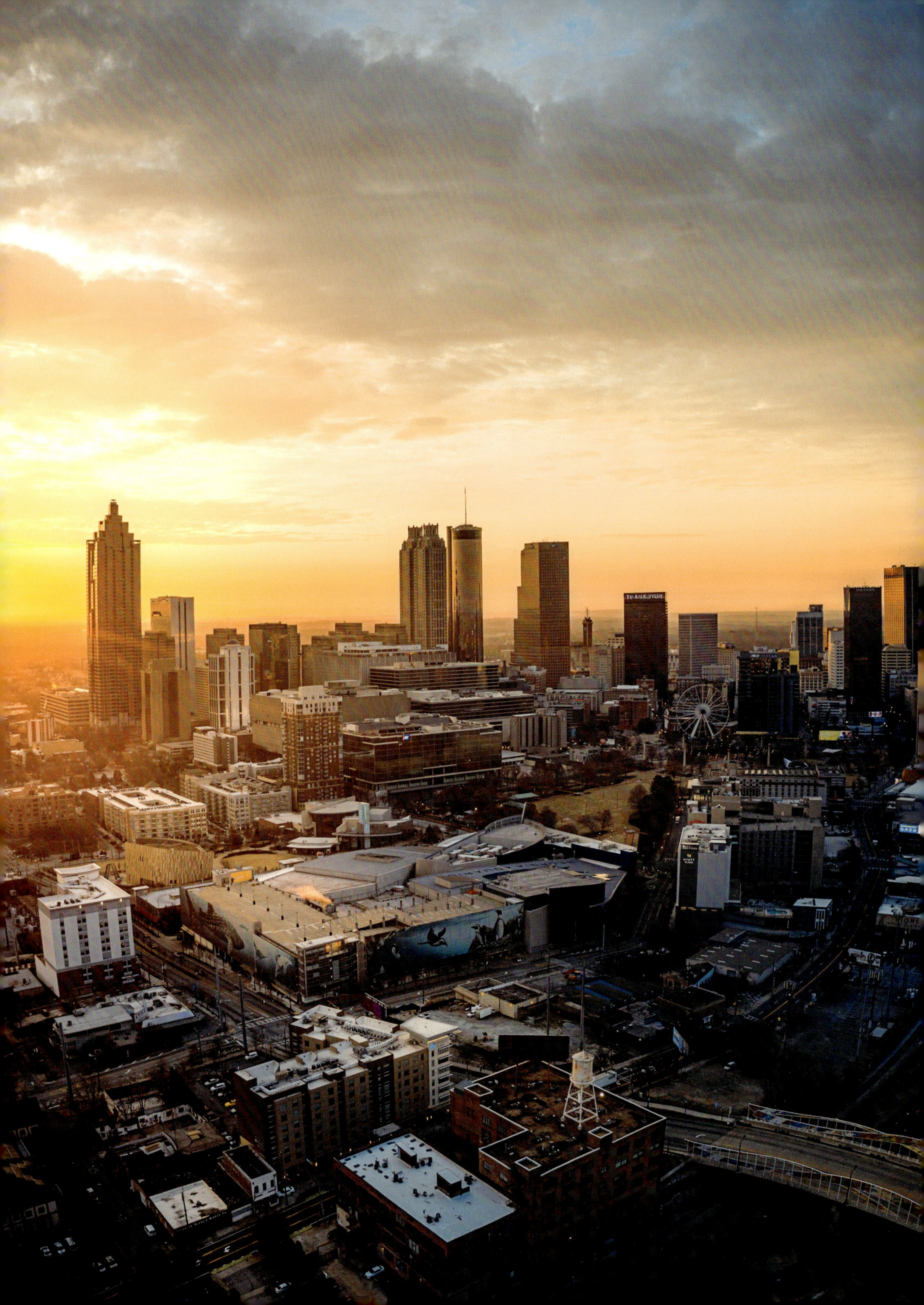

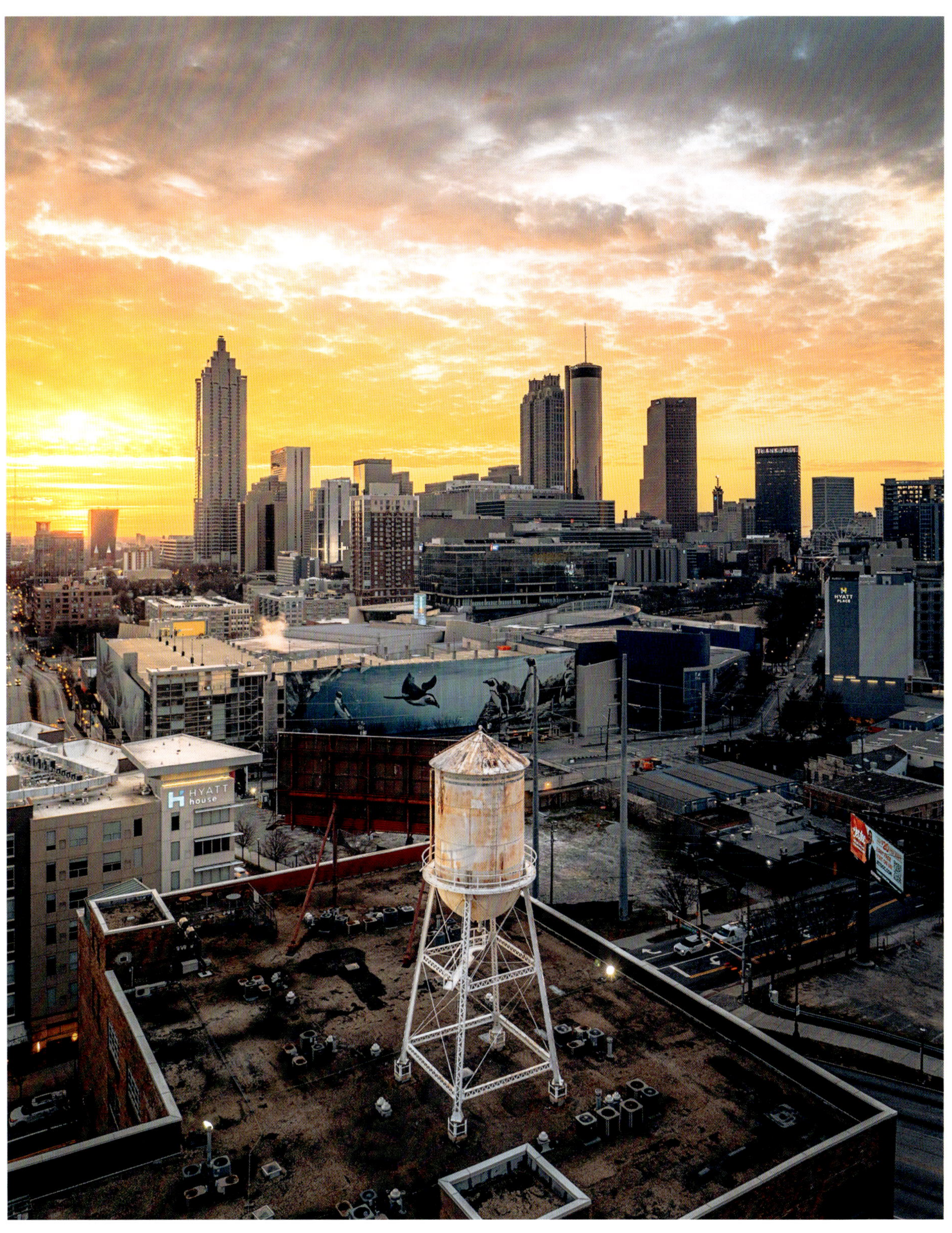

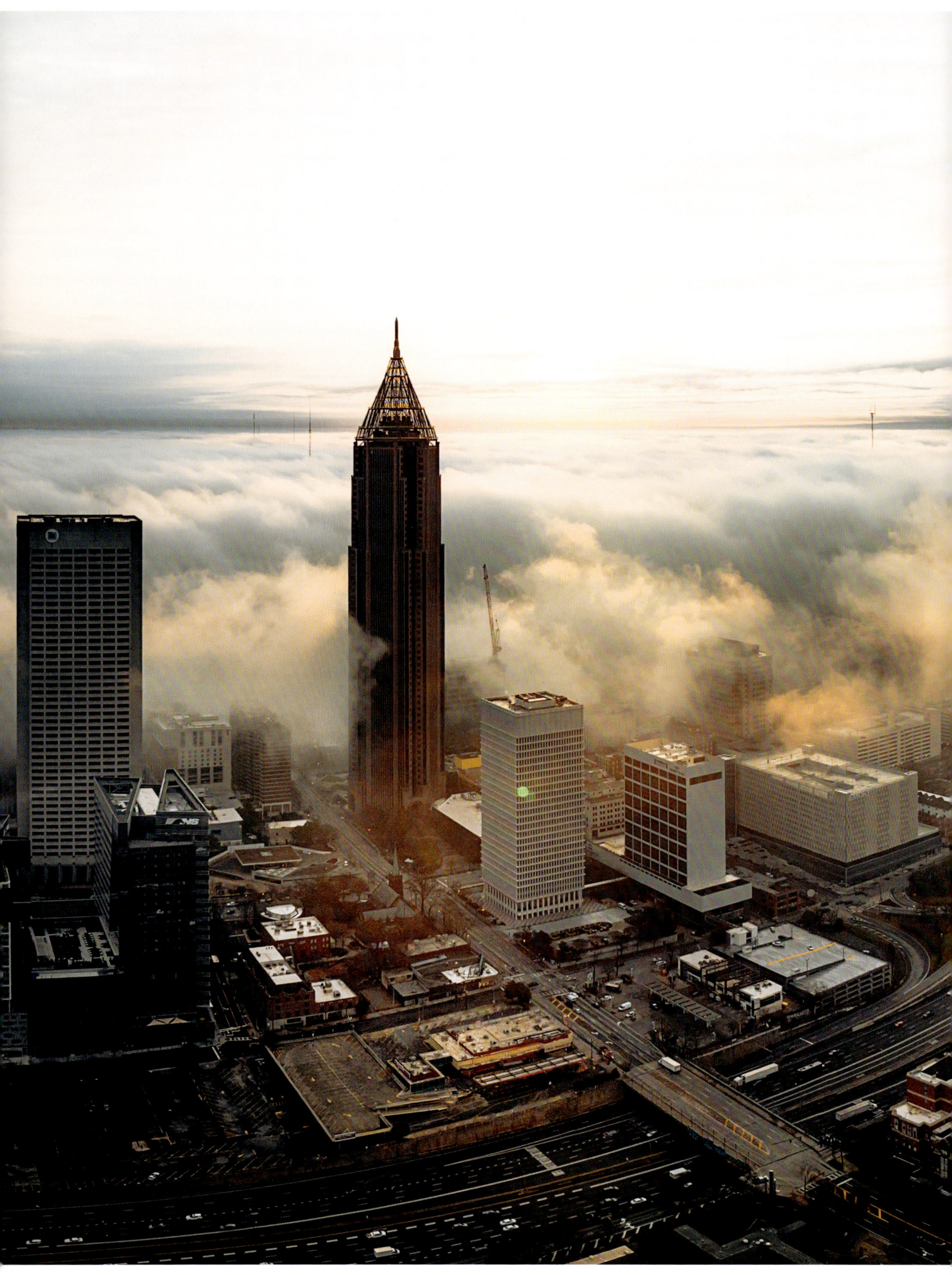

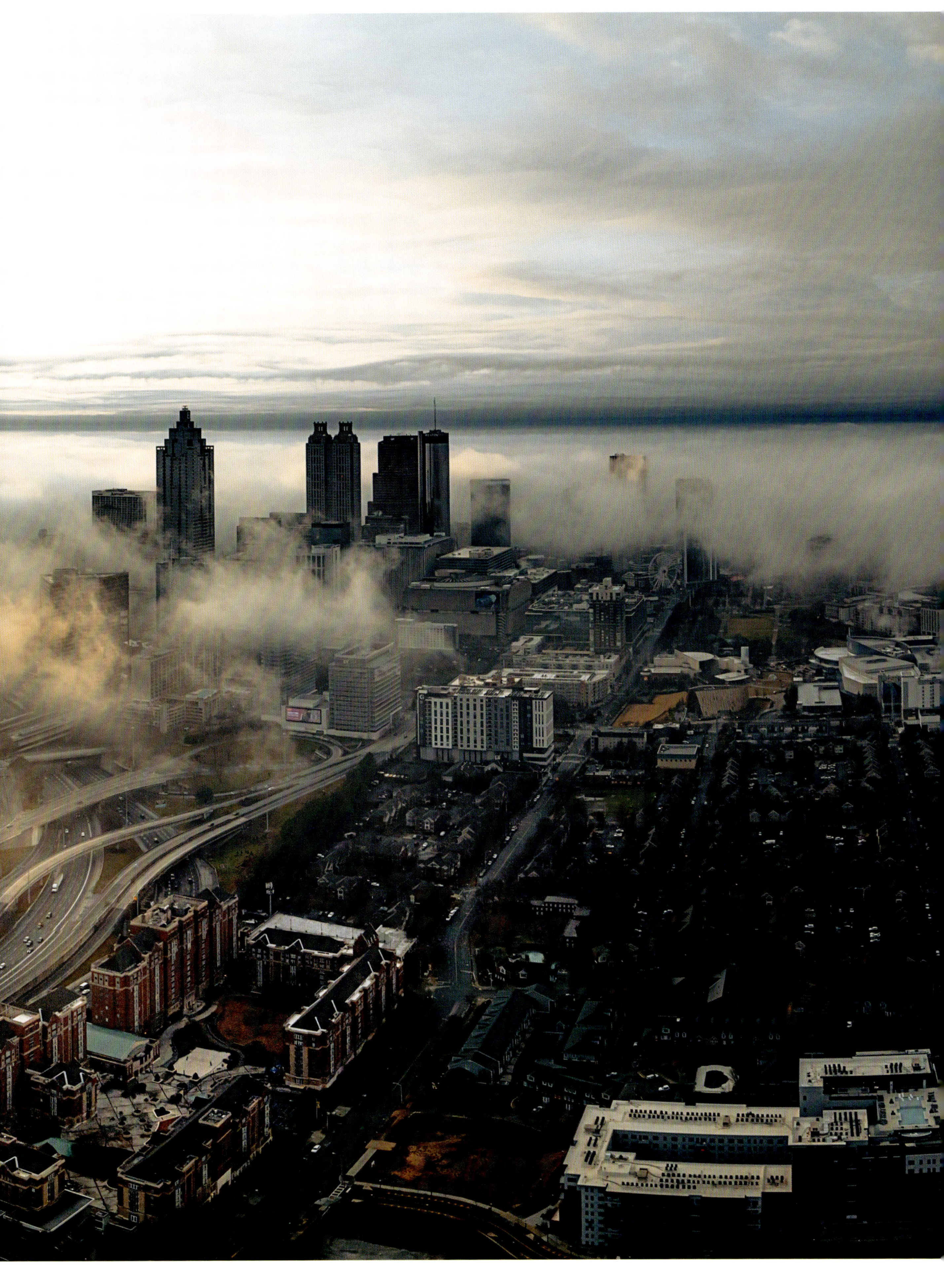

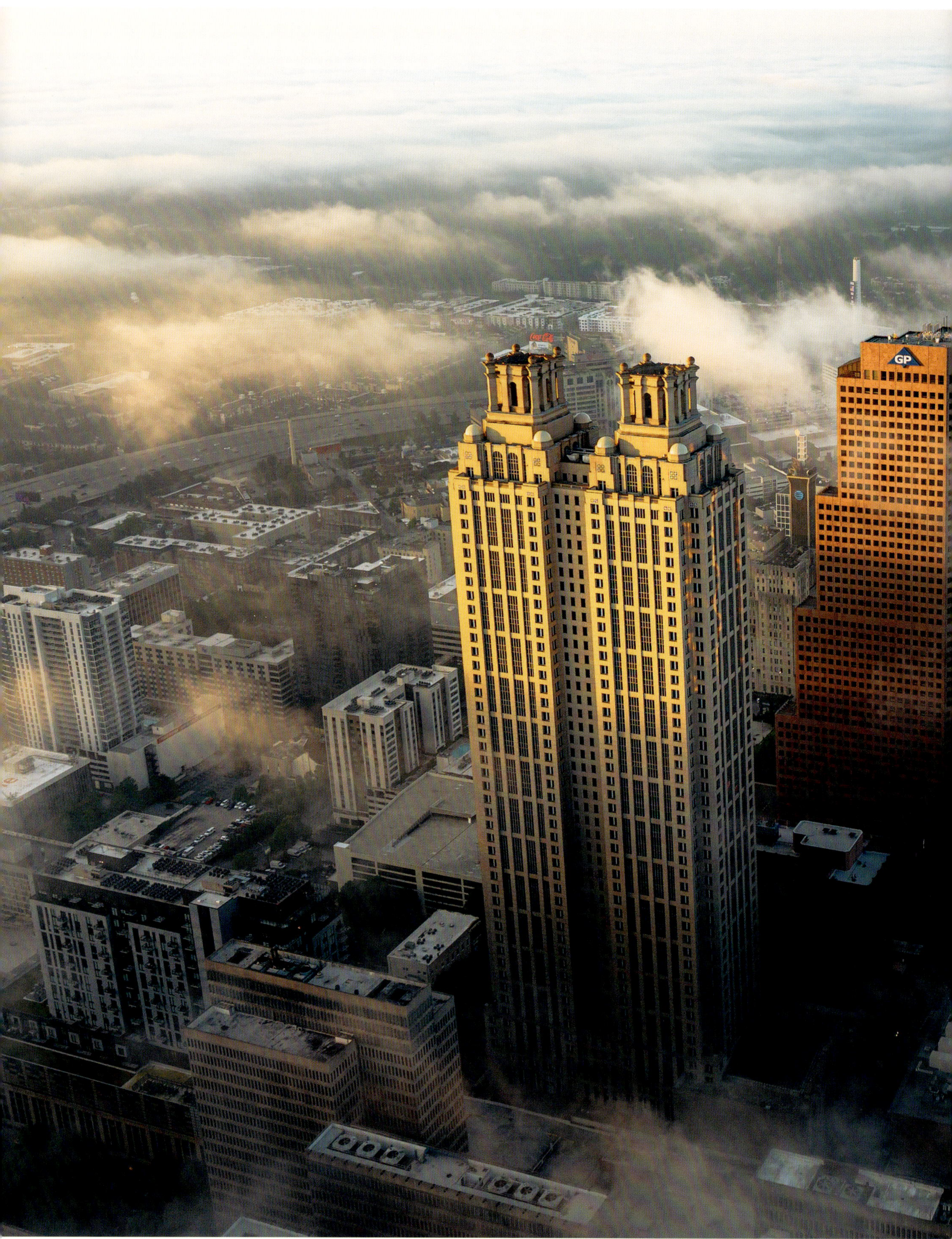

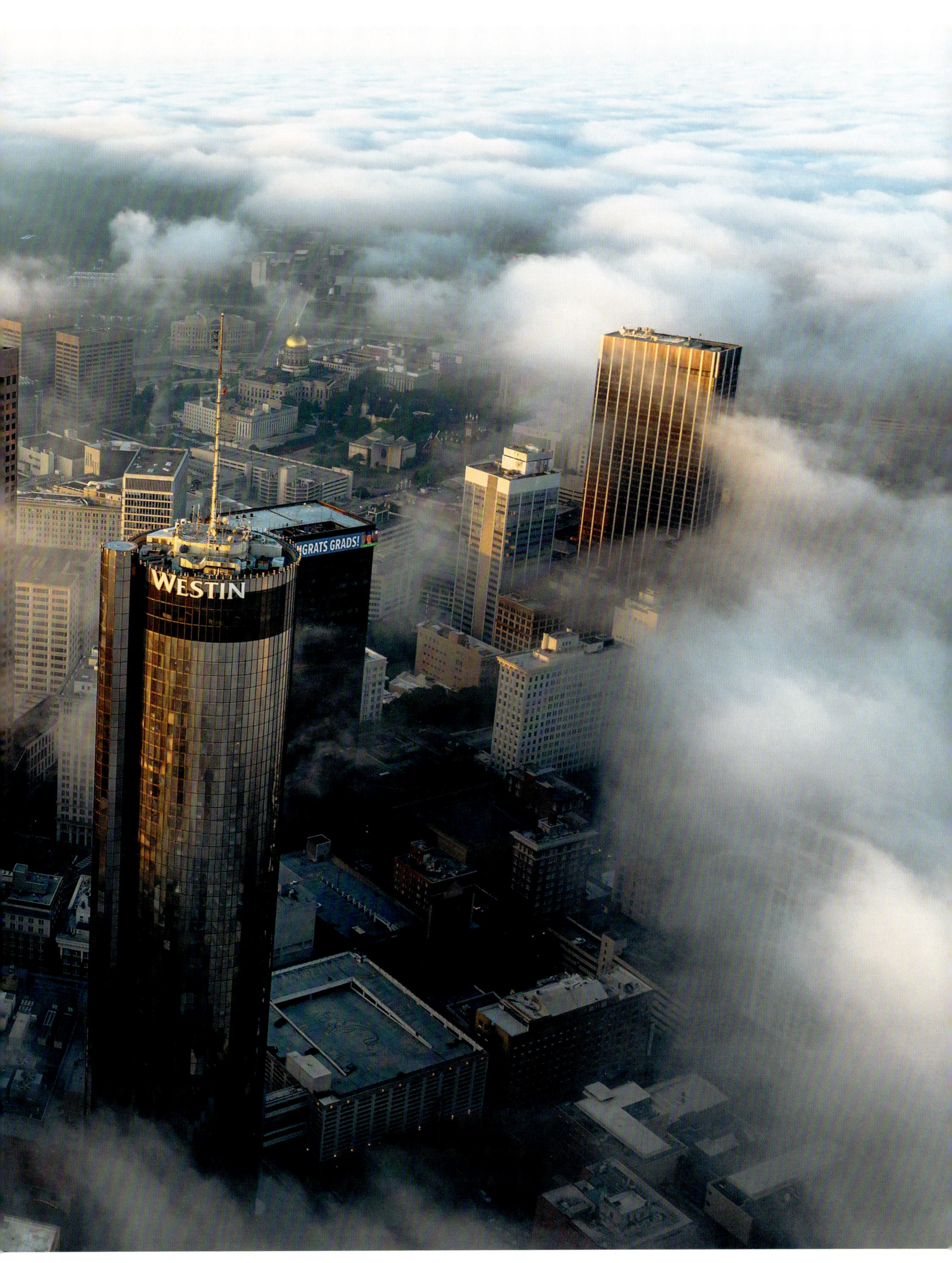

WESTIN
GRATS GRADS!

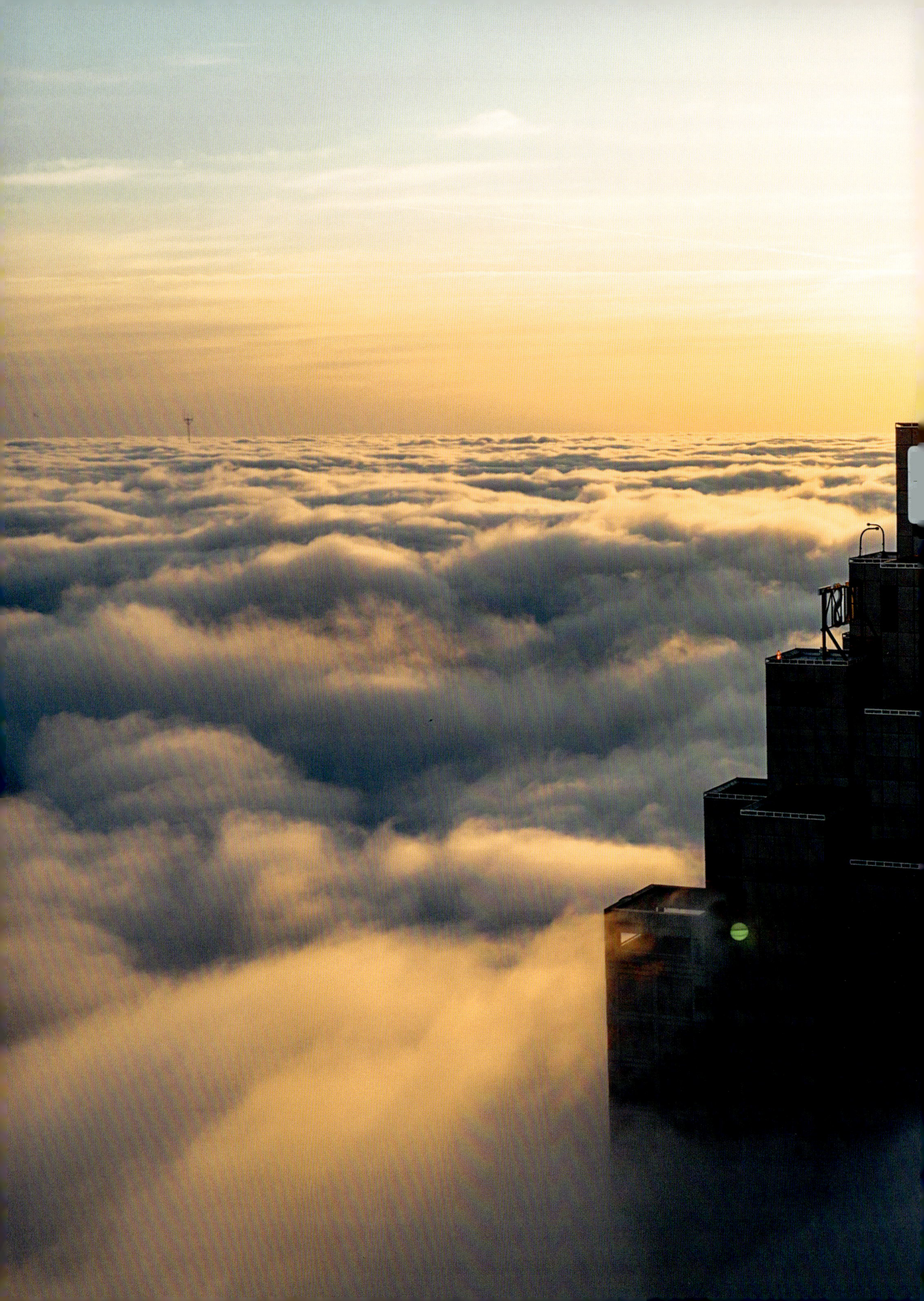

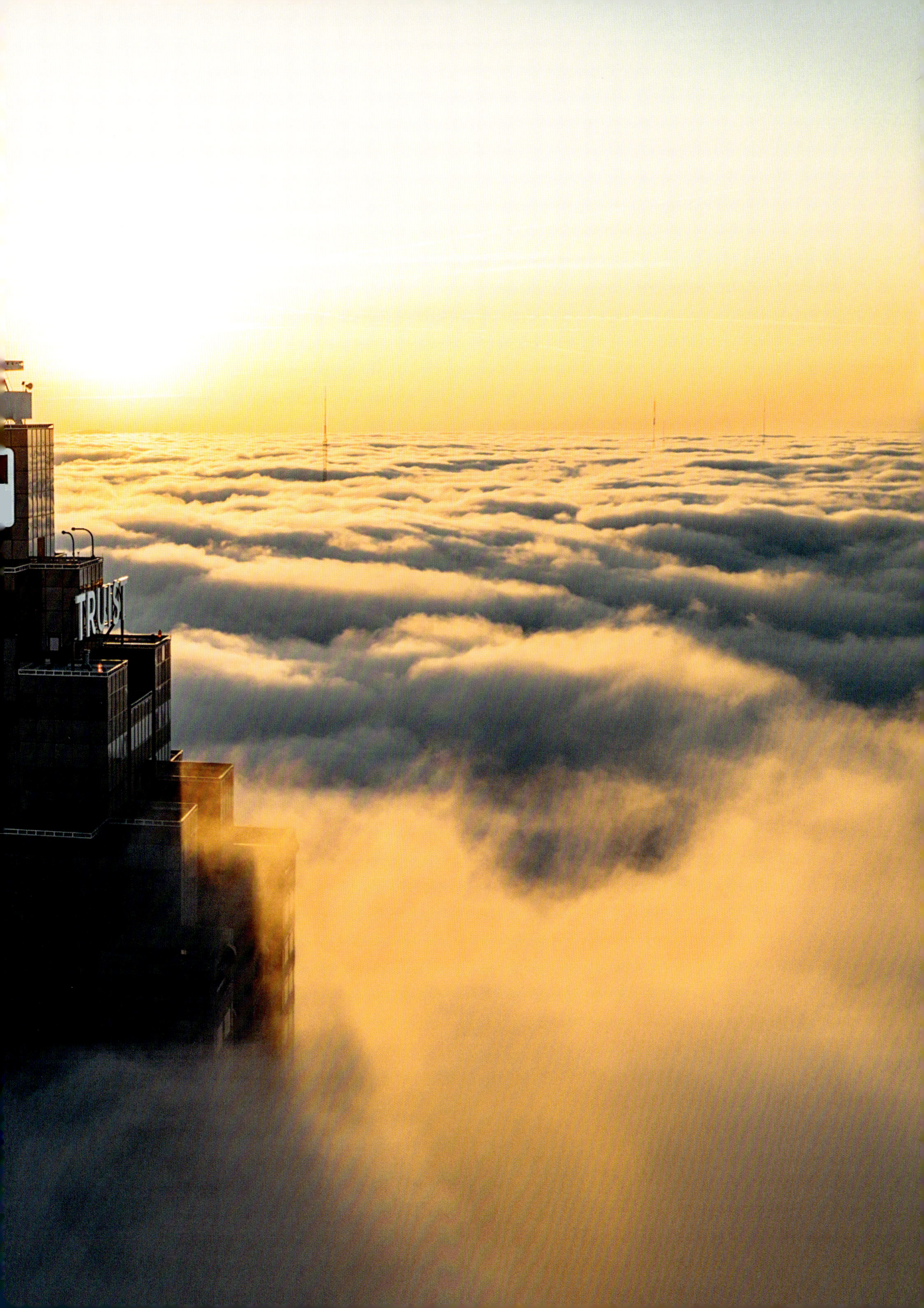

TRUST

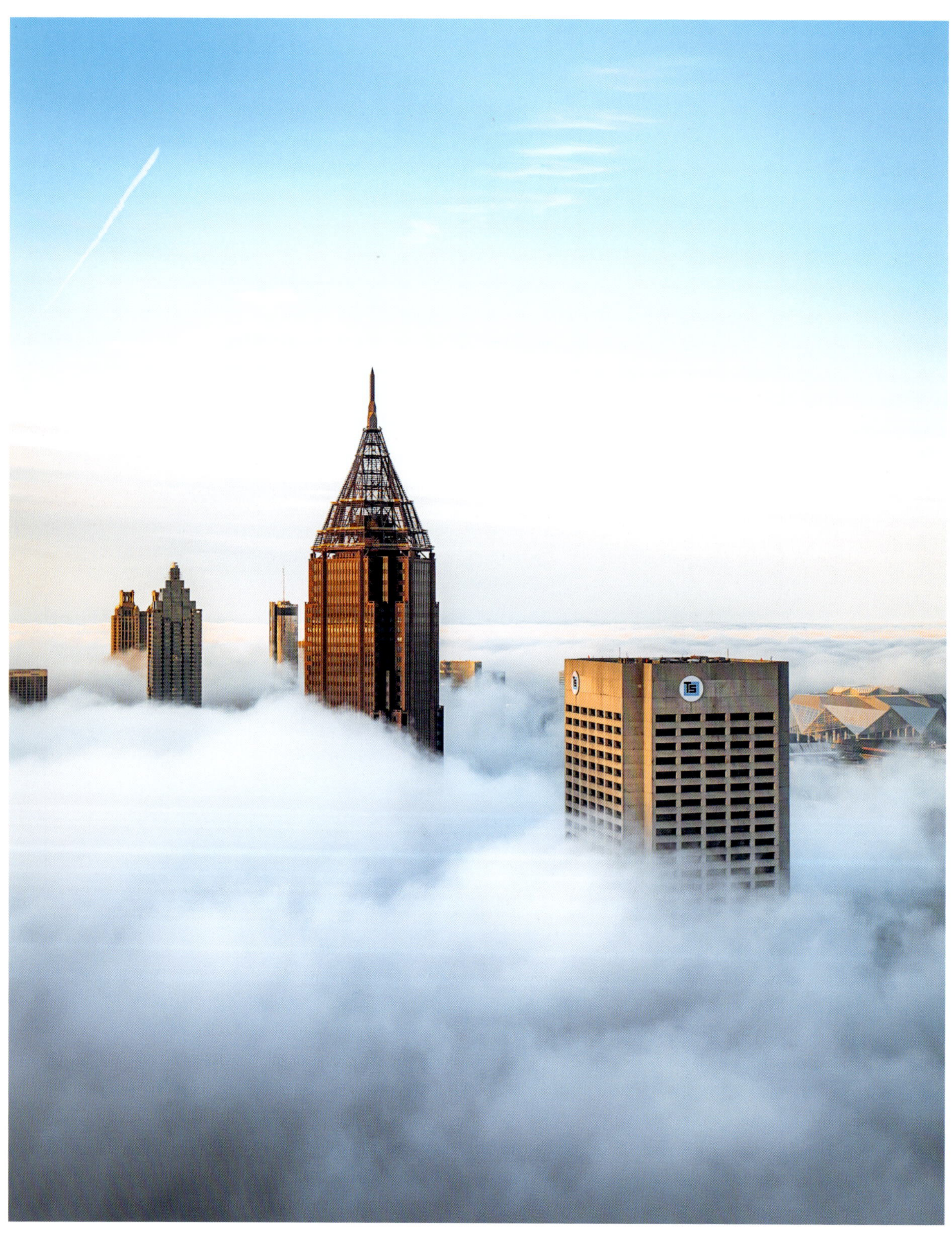

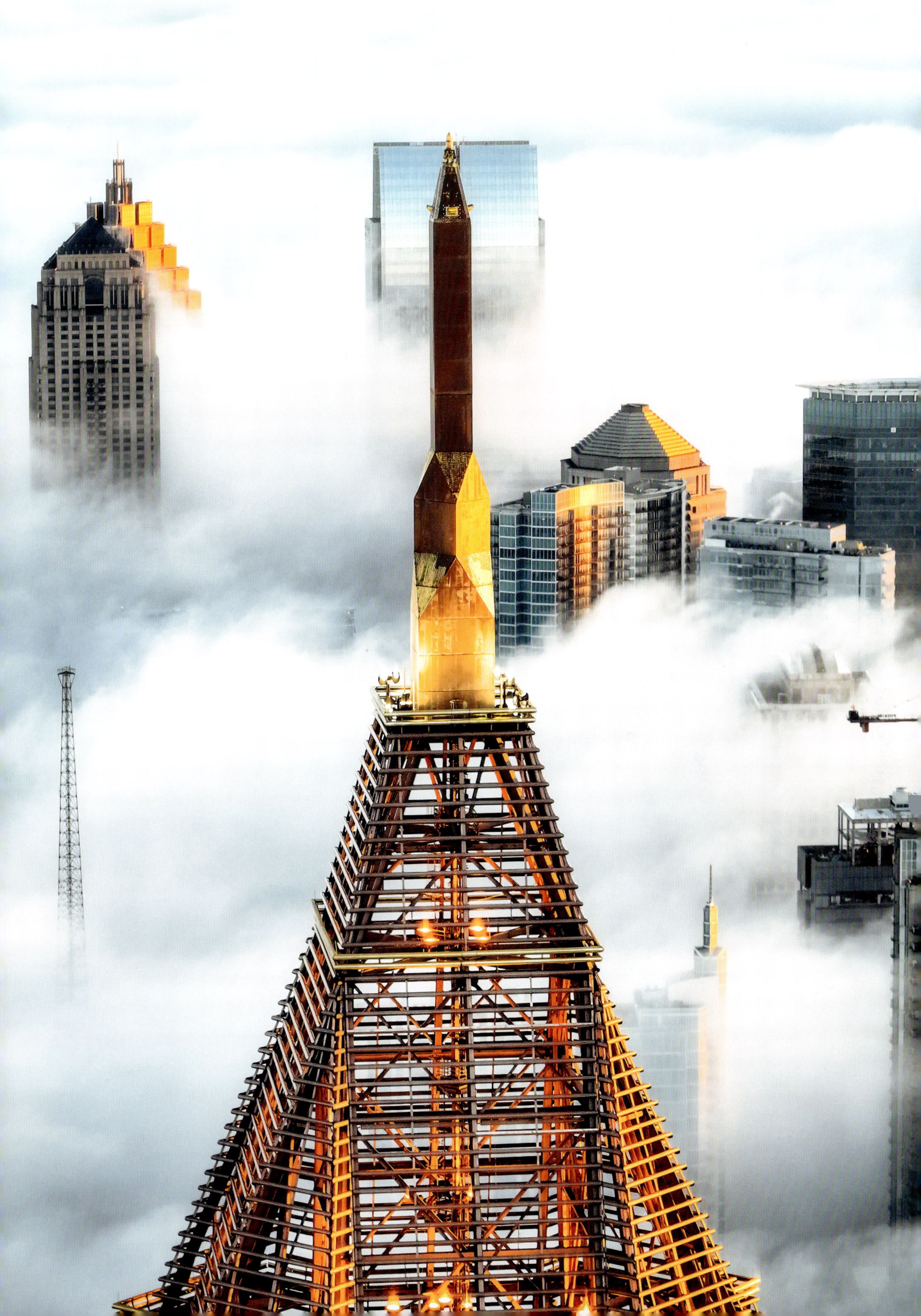

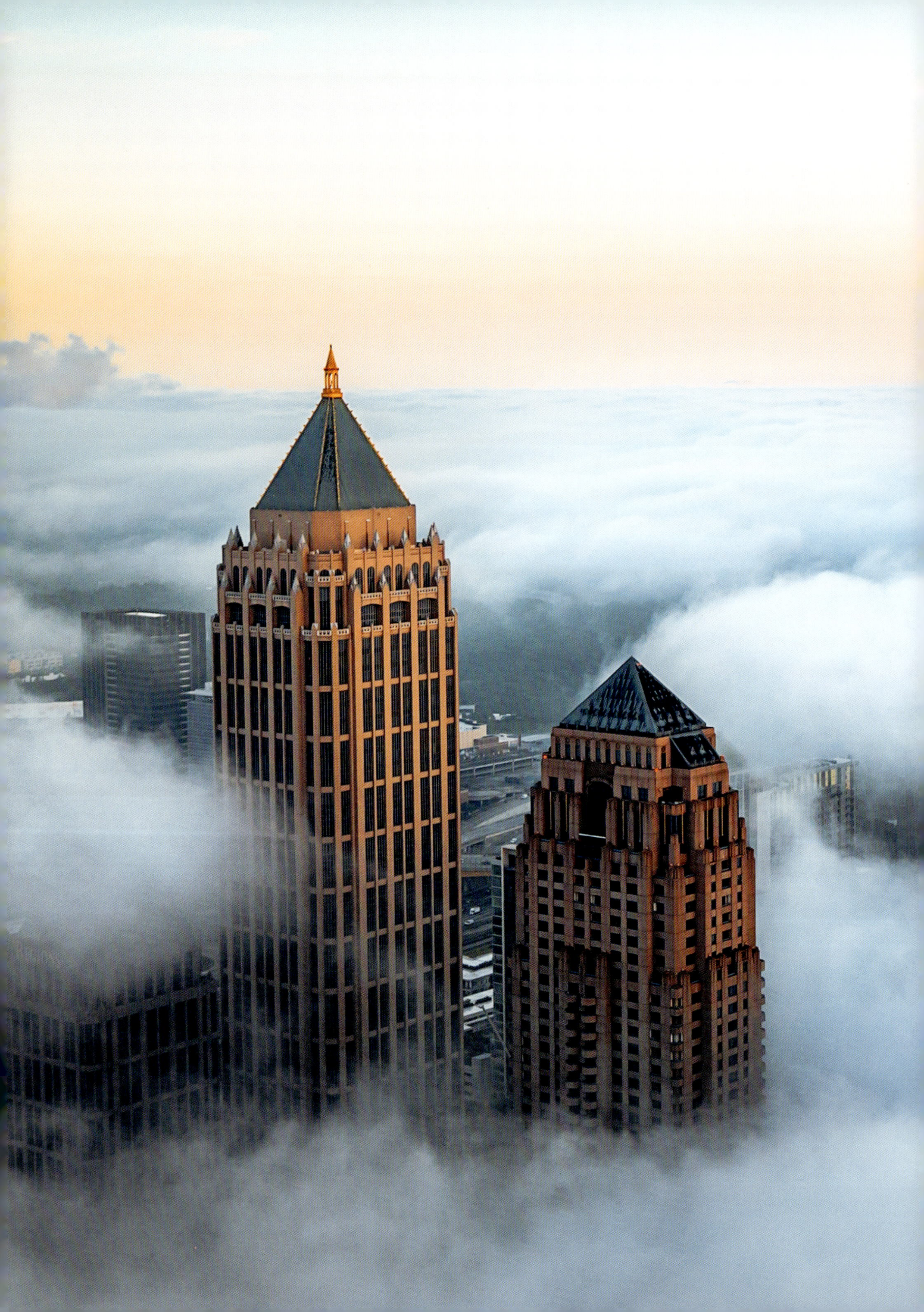

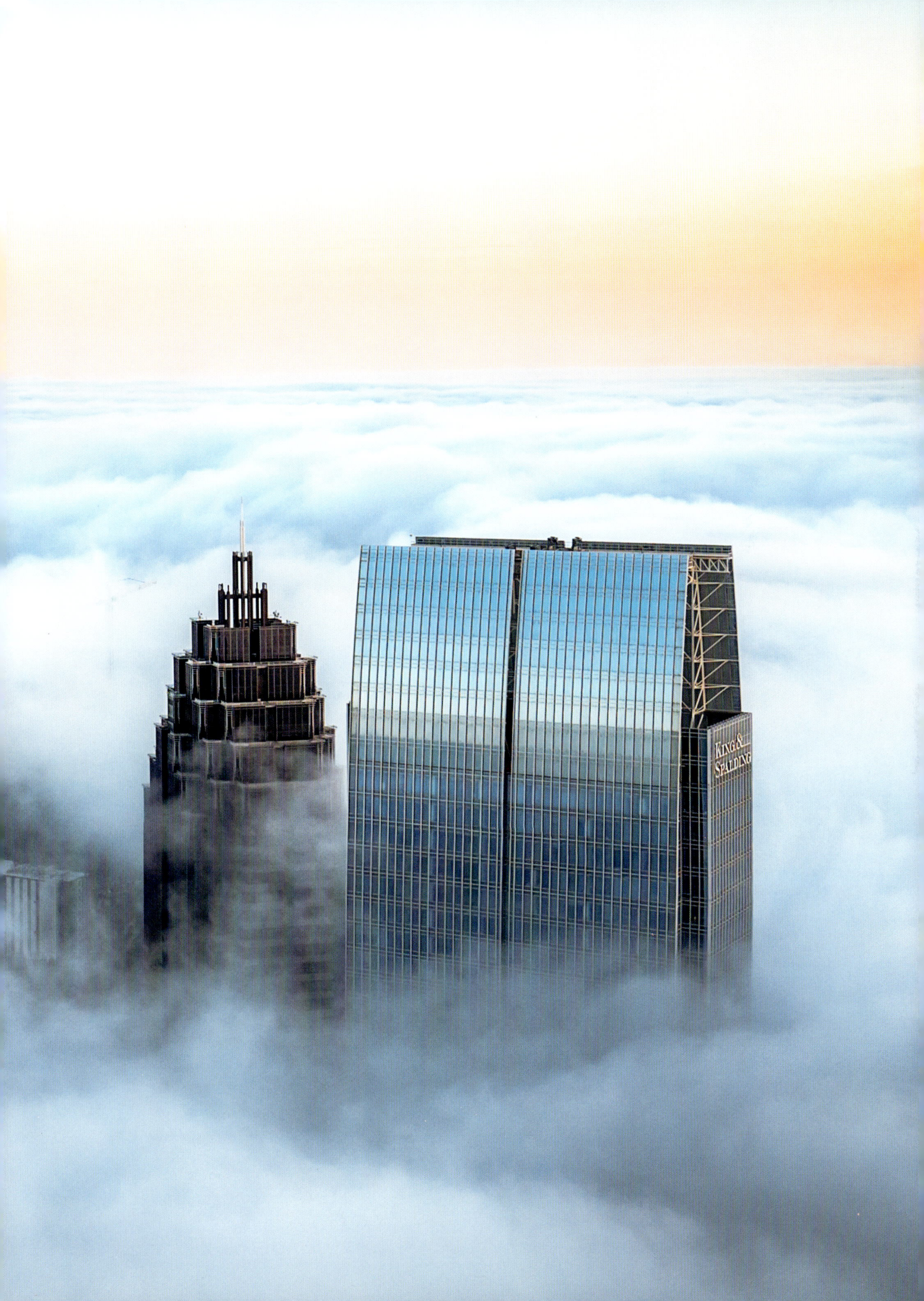

KING &
SPALDING

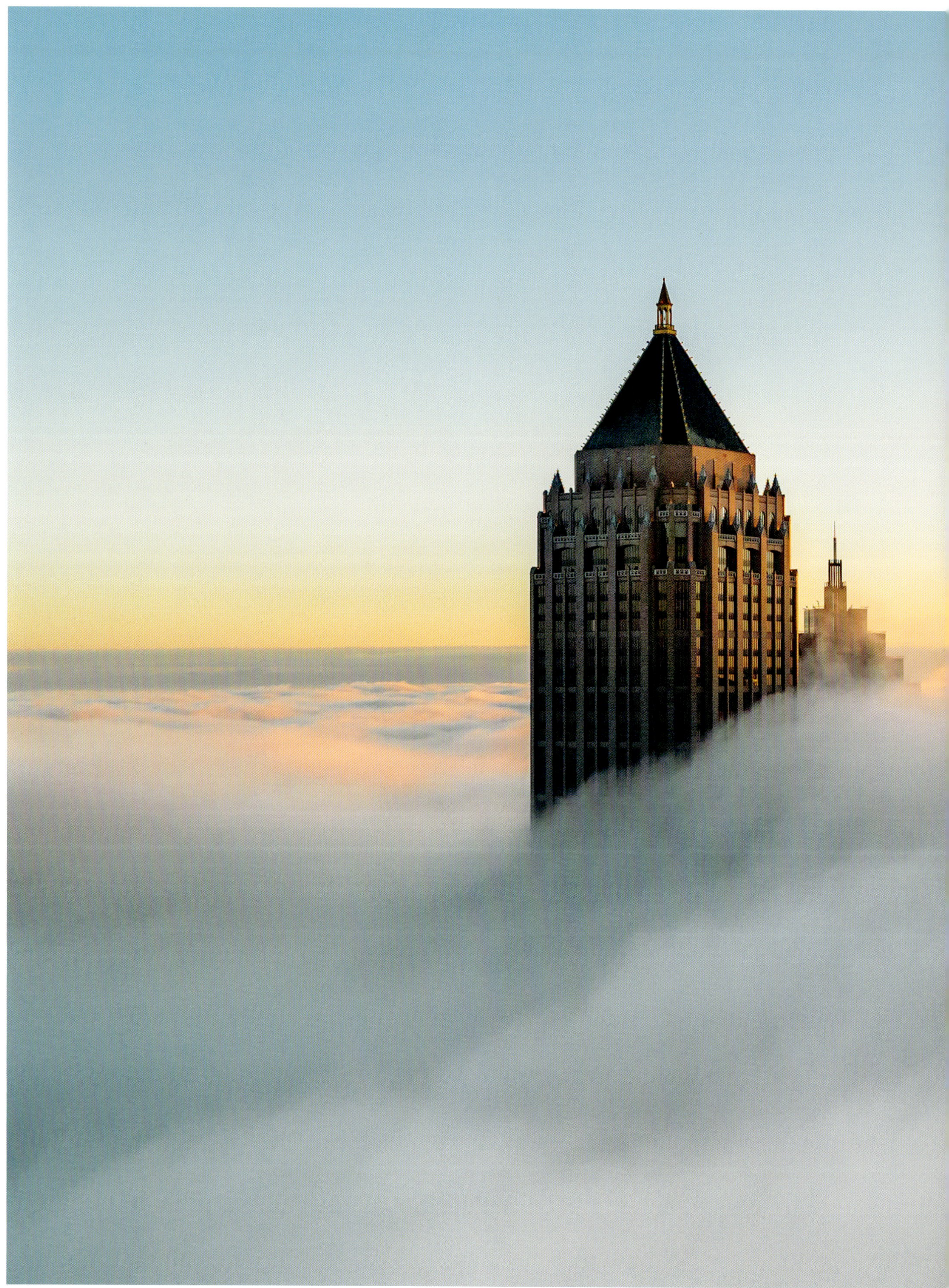

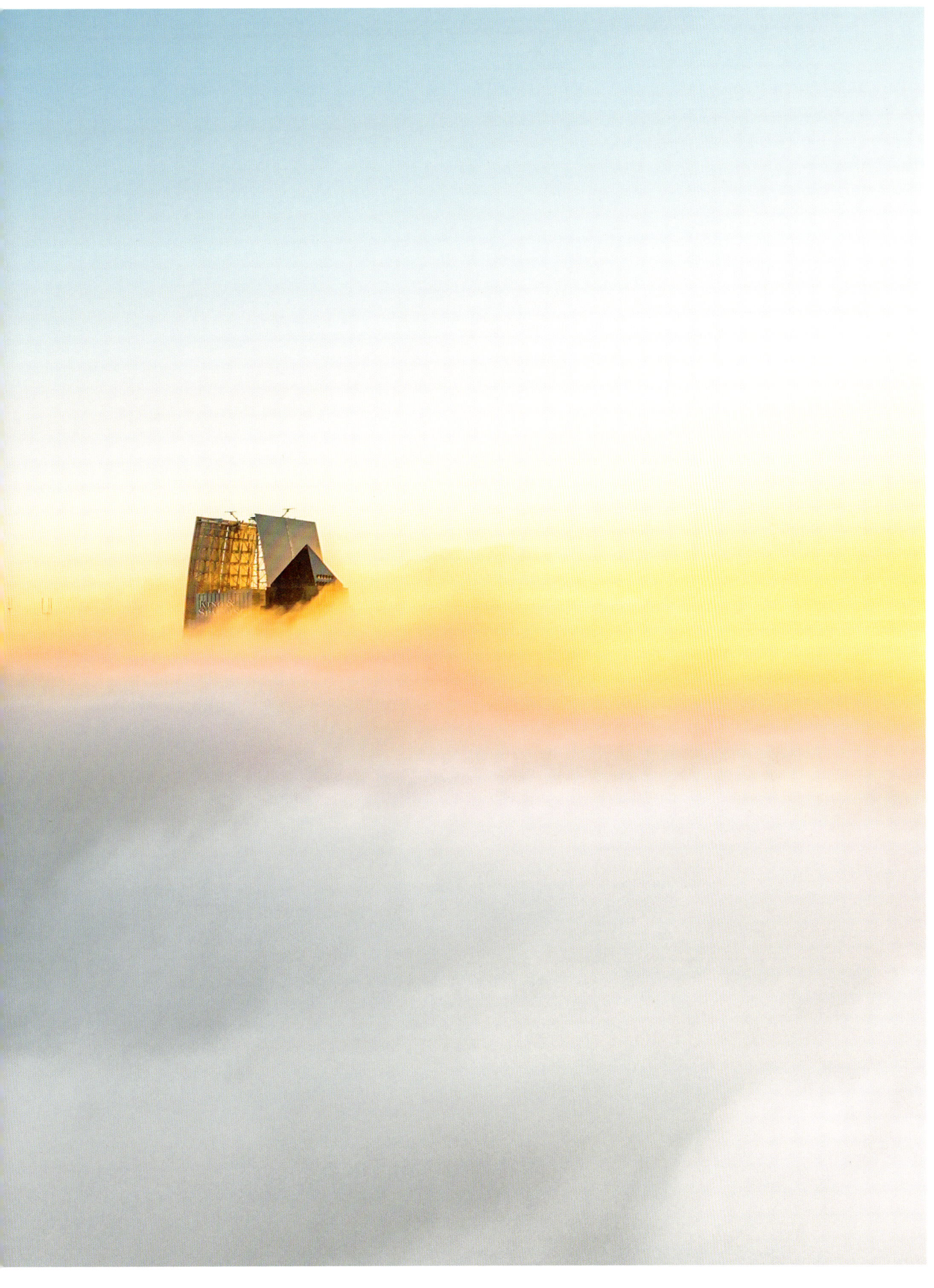

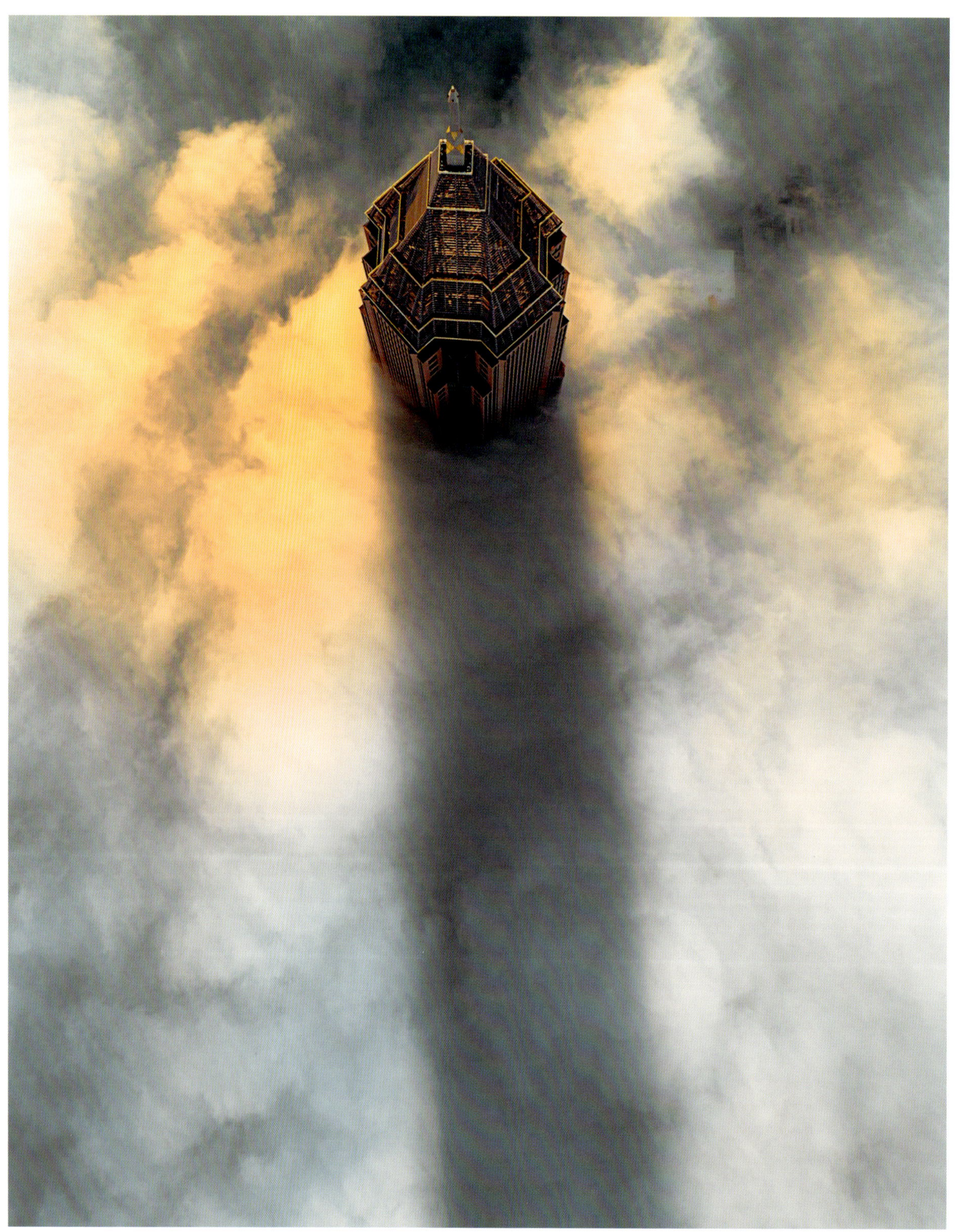

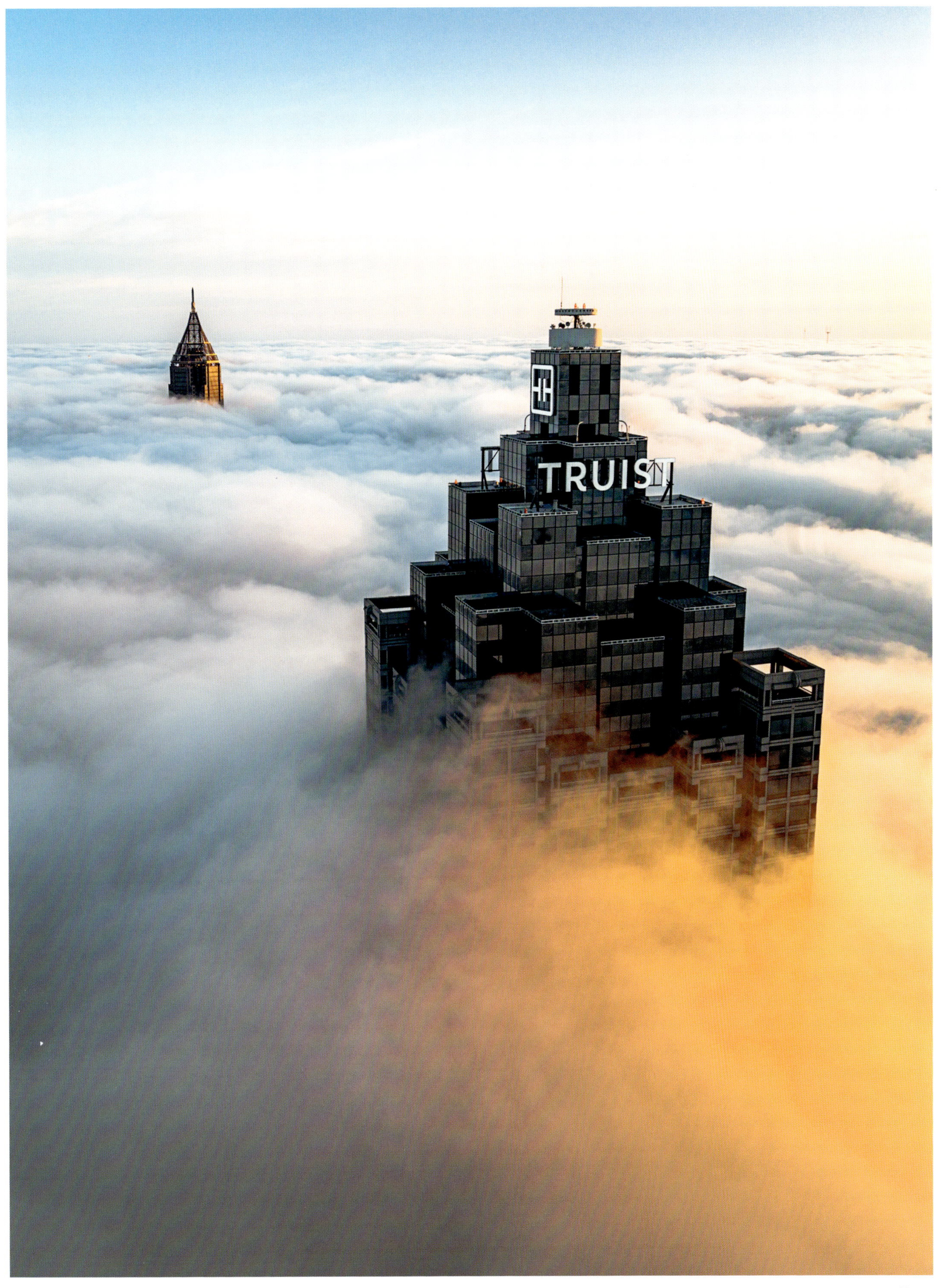

TRUIST

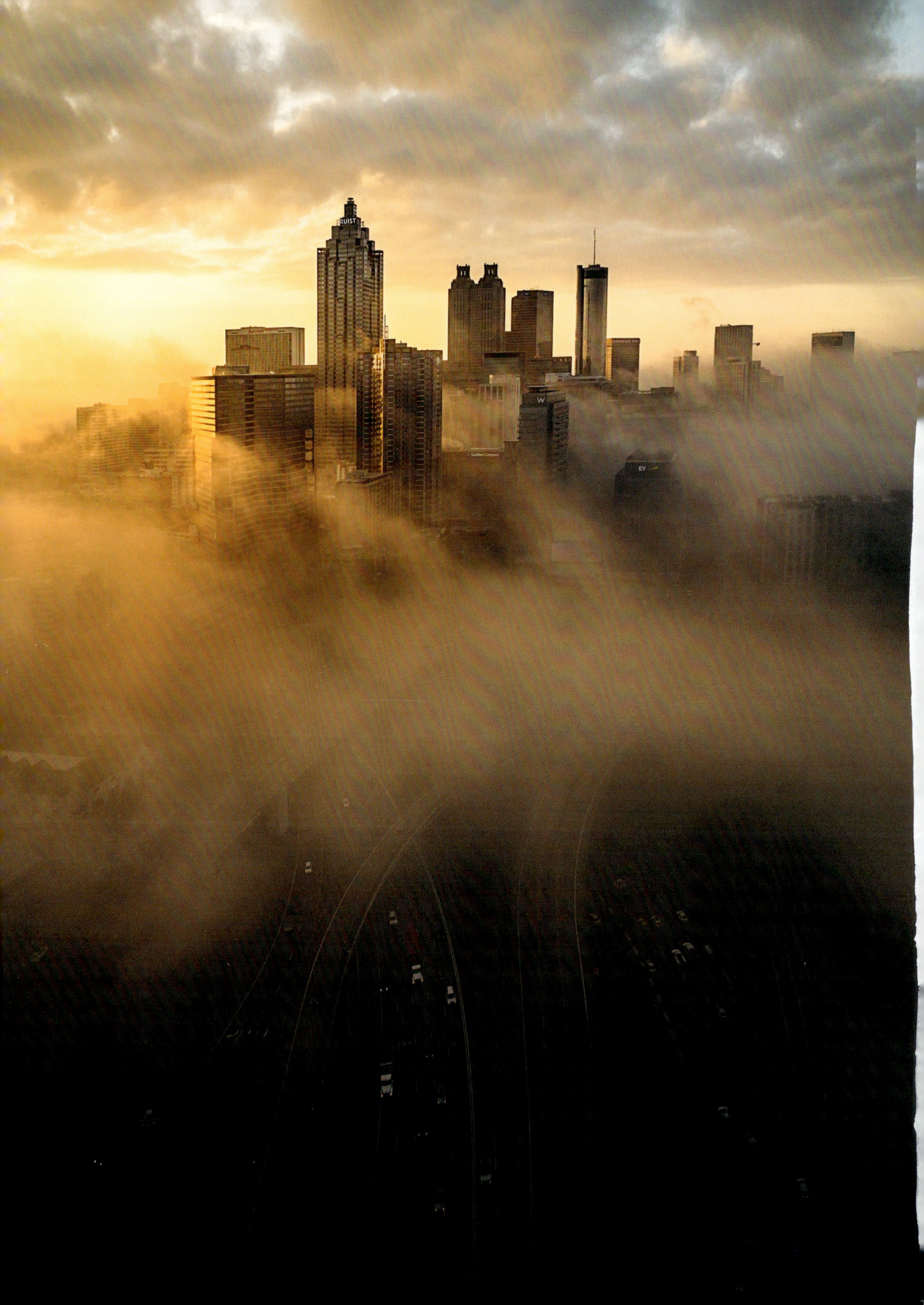

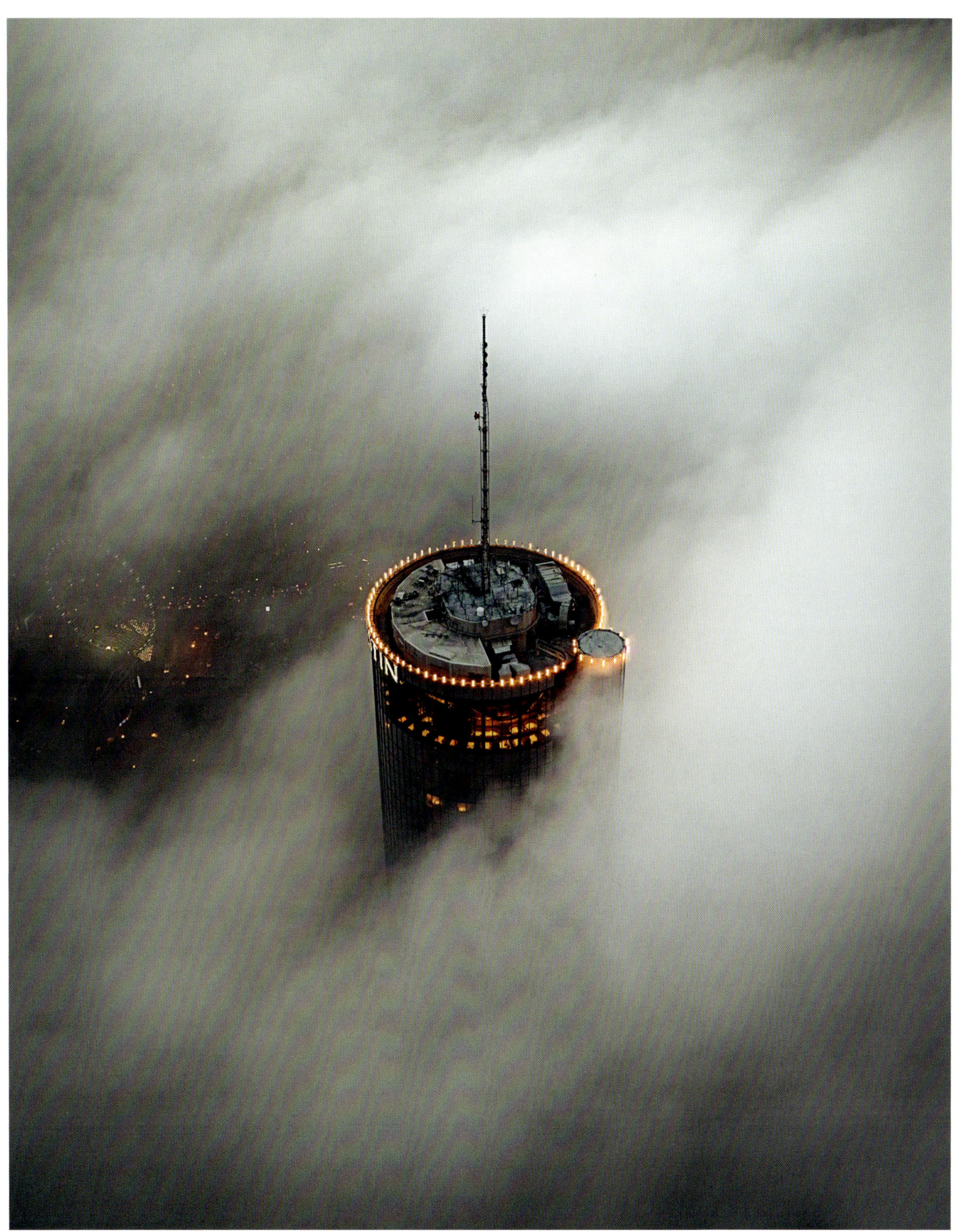

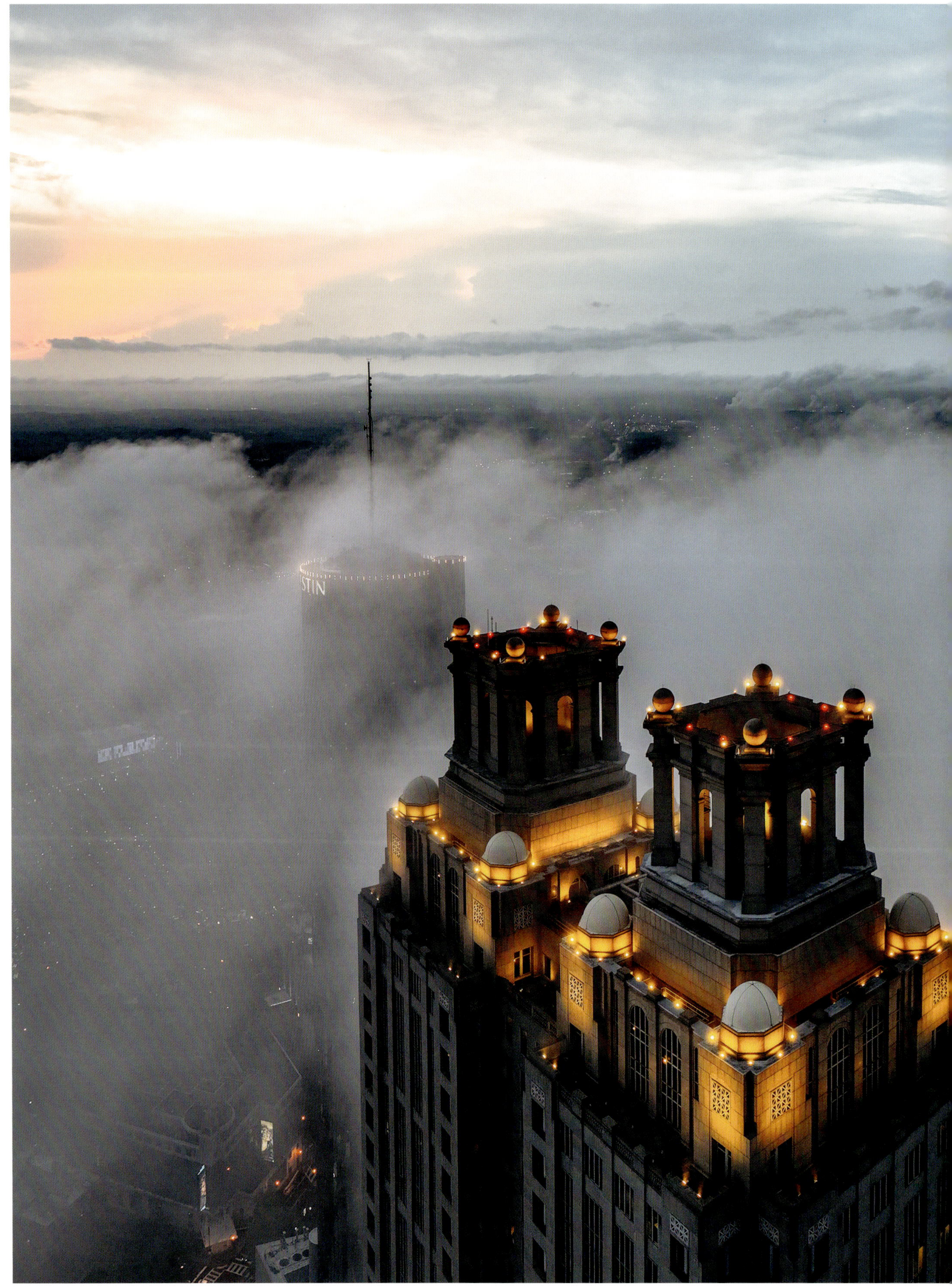

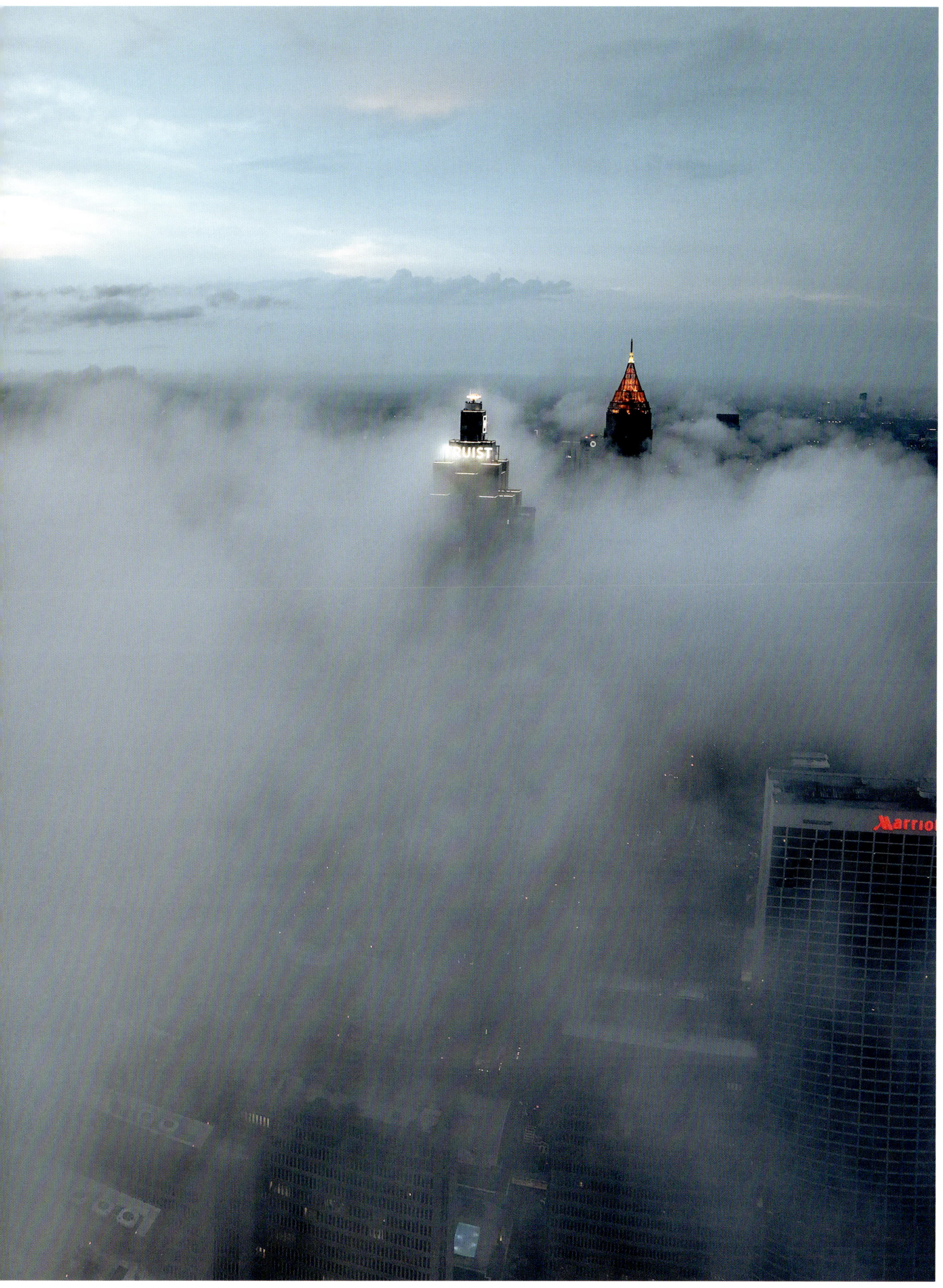
TRUIST
Marrio

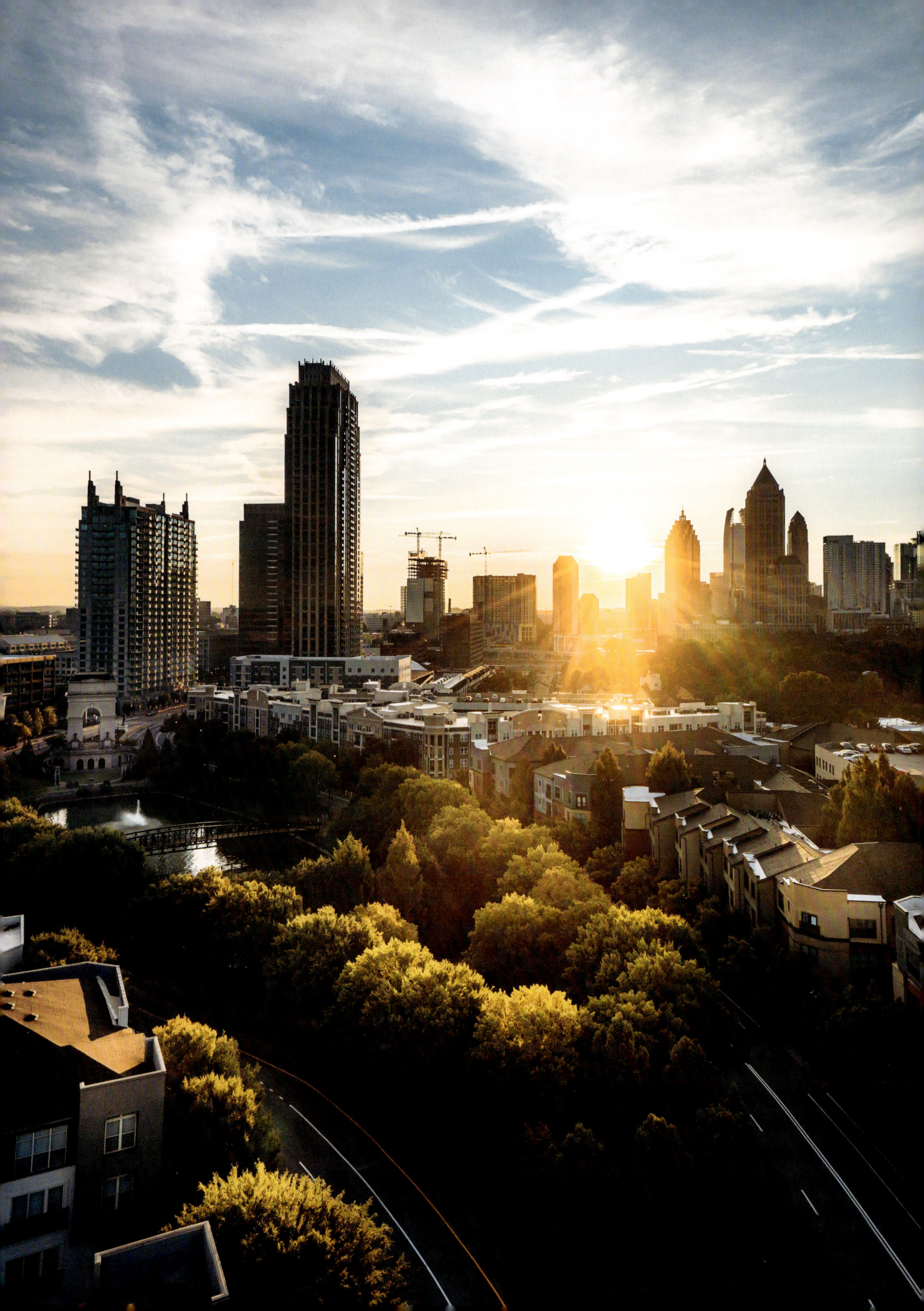

City in a Forest ♦ A bustling metropolis, Atlanta's abundance of trees and green spaces interspersed throughout the city have earned it the nickname "city in a forest." Atlanta's impressive tree canopy covers over 50% of the city, making it one of the most forested major cities in the country. This dense canopy provides much-needed shade, helping to cool against the city's heat, particularly in the hot and humid summer months. Atlanta's lush forests and wooded areas weave their way through neighborhoods, parks, and commercial districts, offering residents and visitors spaces to explore, unwind, and soak in the natural beauty. ♦ Piedmont Park is an iconic centerpiece of Atlanta's outdoor scene, a sprawling oasis spanning over 200 acres in the heart of Midtown. This lush space offers a wealth of activities, whether it's leisurely strolls along winding paths, picnics on expansive lawns, or engaging in a friendly game of soccer or volleyball. With stunning views of the city skyline as a backdrop, Piedmont Park is a beloved gathering place for people to relax, exercise, and connect with nature. ♦ Nestled within the bustling Midtown neighborhood, the Atlanta Botanical Garden provides a serene sanctuary, boasting an impressive collection of plants from around the world. Visitors can wander through the Japanese Garden and the fragrant Rose Garden or explore the enchanting Canopy Walk, a suspended walkway that offers breathtaking views of the garden below. ♦ Within Grant Park, Zoo Atlanta is home to over 1,000 animals representing more than 200 species from around the world. The oldest cultural institution in Atlanta, Zoo Atlanta offers visitors the opportunity to journey across continents without leaving the heart of the city. ♦ Atlanta's outdoor spaces aren't just limited to parks and gardens. The Atlanta BeltLine, a former railway corridor that has been transformed into a dynamic urban trail, has become a beloved gathering place where locals come to walk, bike, and socialize amidst public art installations and community events. ♦ Atlanta's outdoor spaces serve as vibrant hubs of culture and creativity. From free concerts and outdoor film screenings to yoga classes and food festivals, there's always something happening in Atlanta's parks and public spaces. Atlanta's outdoor spaces offer something for everyone.

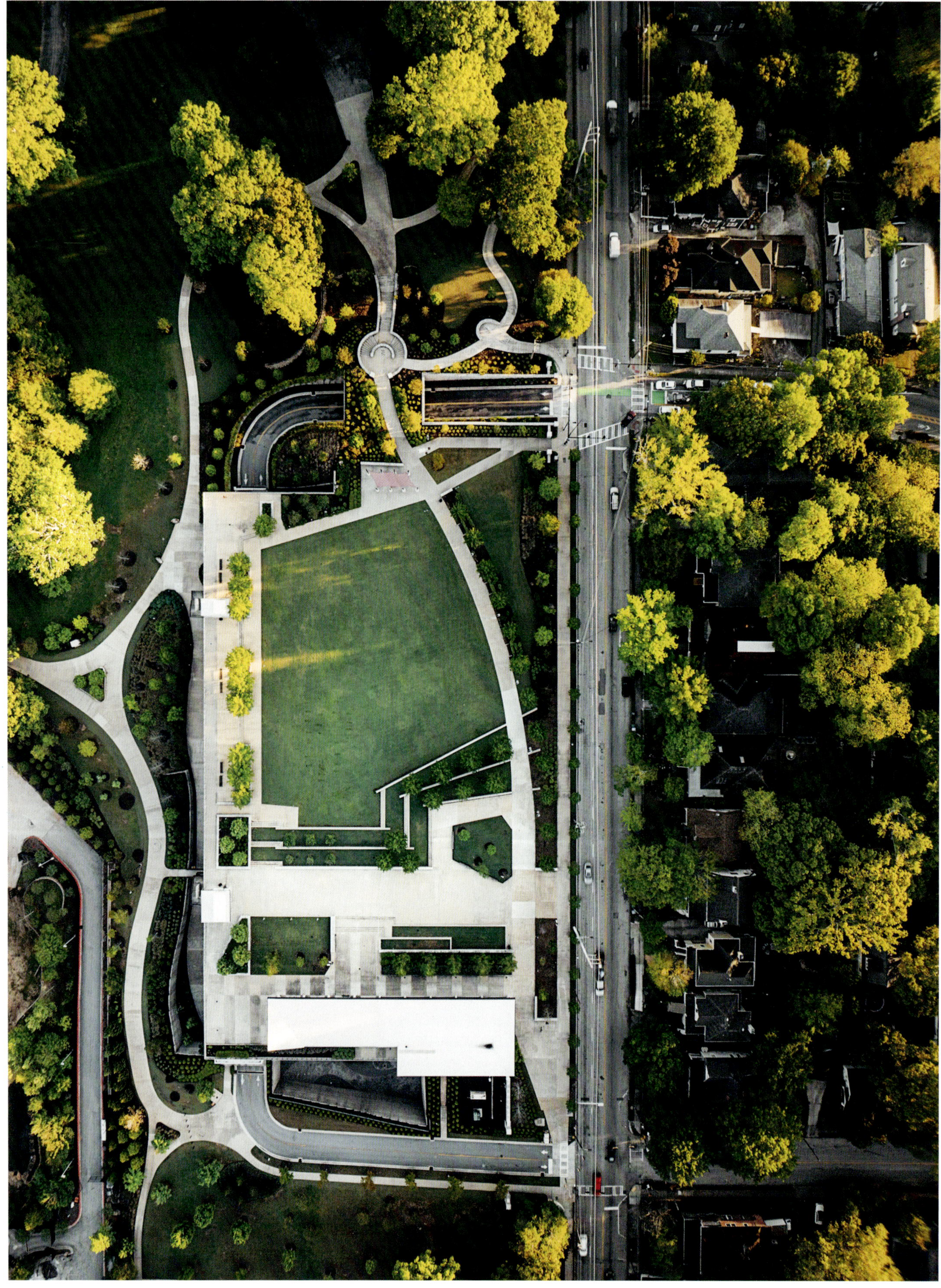

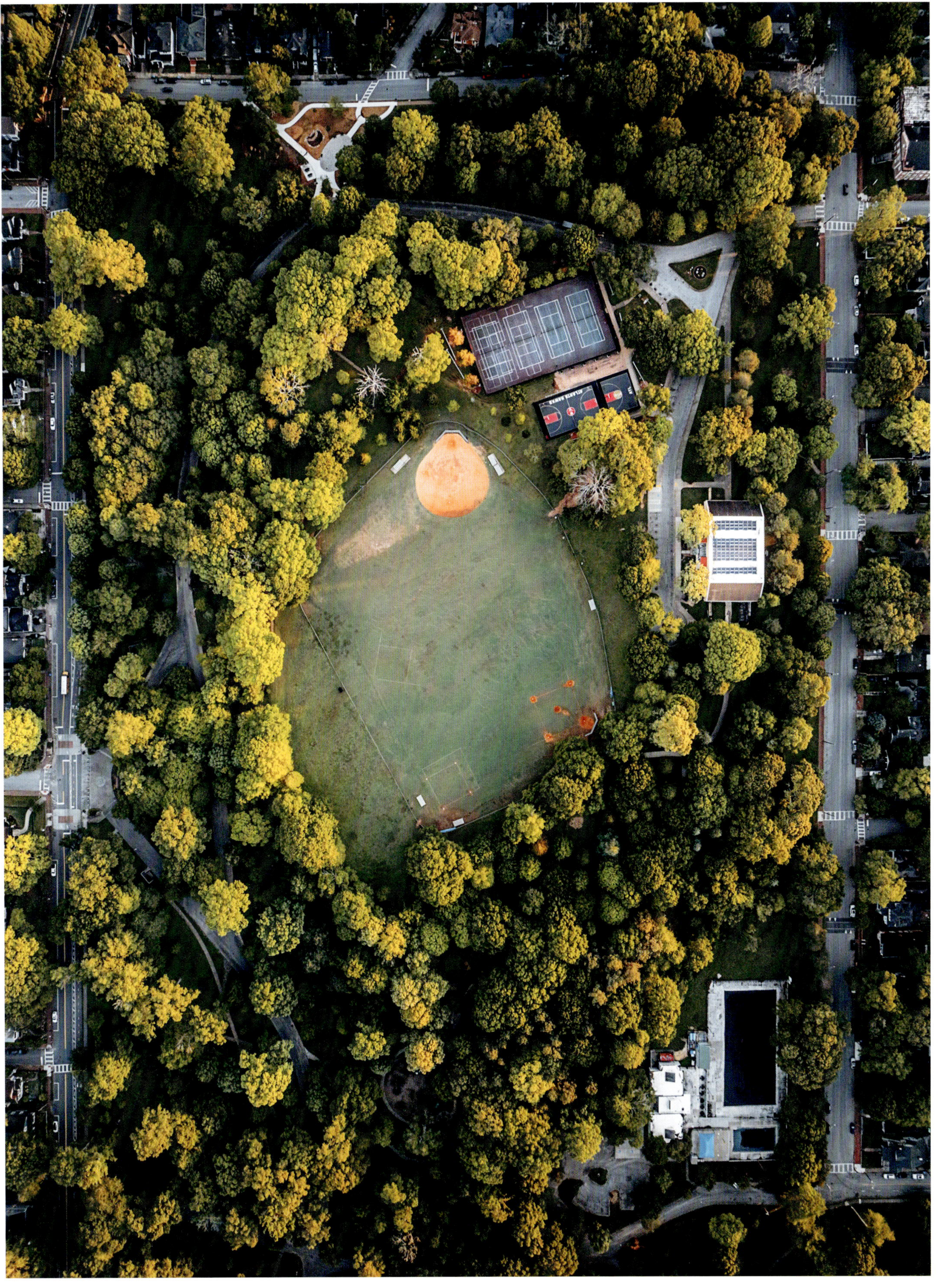

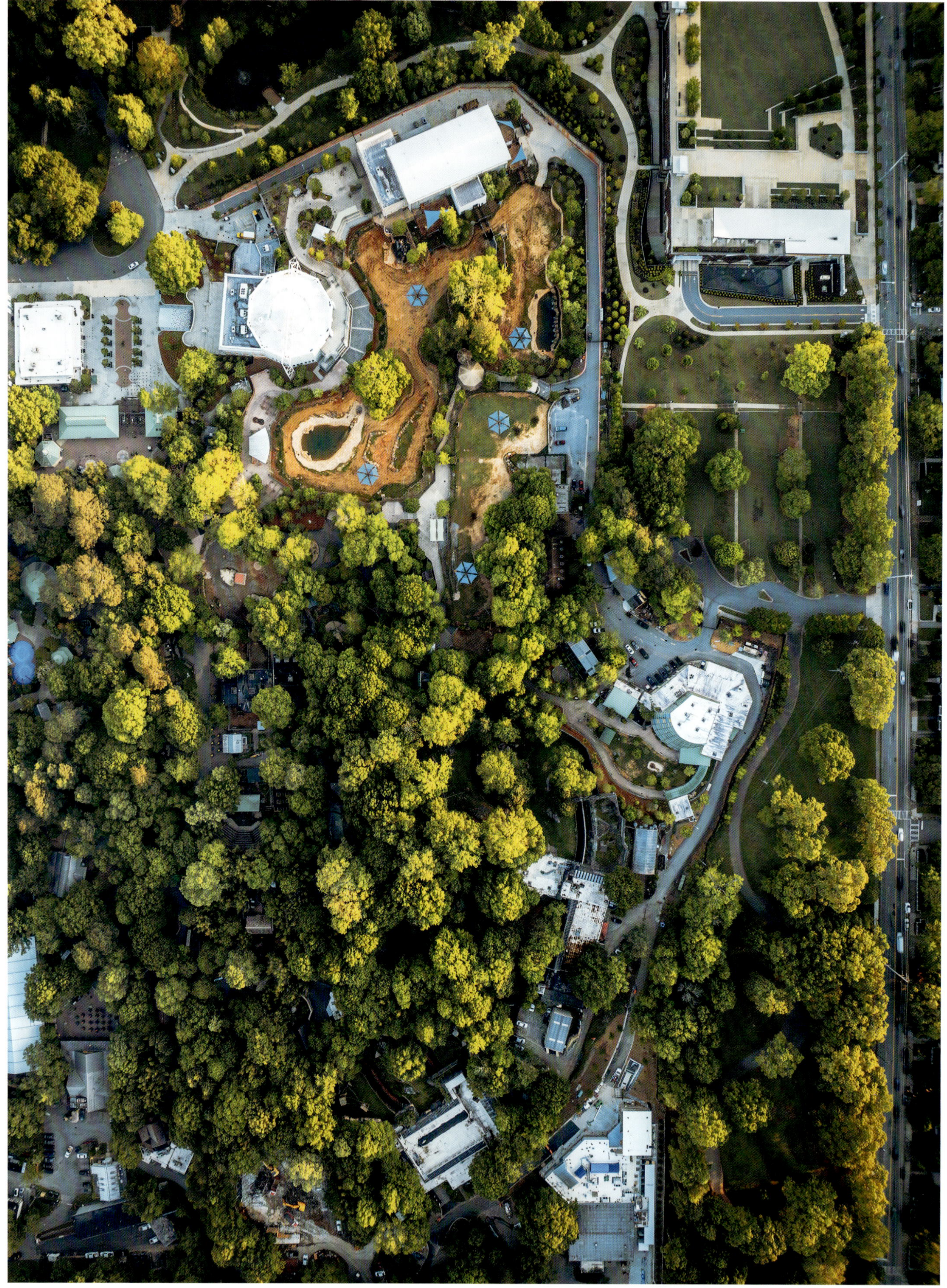

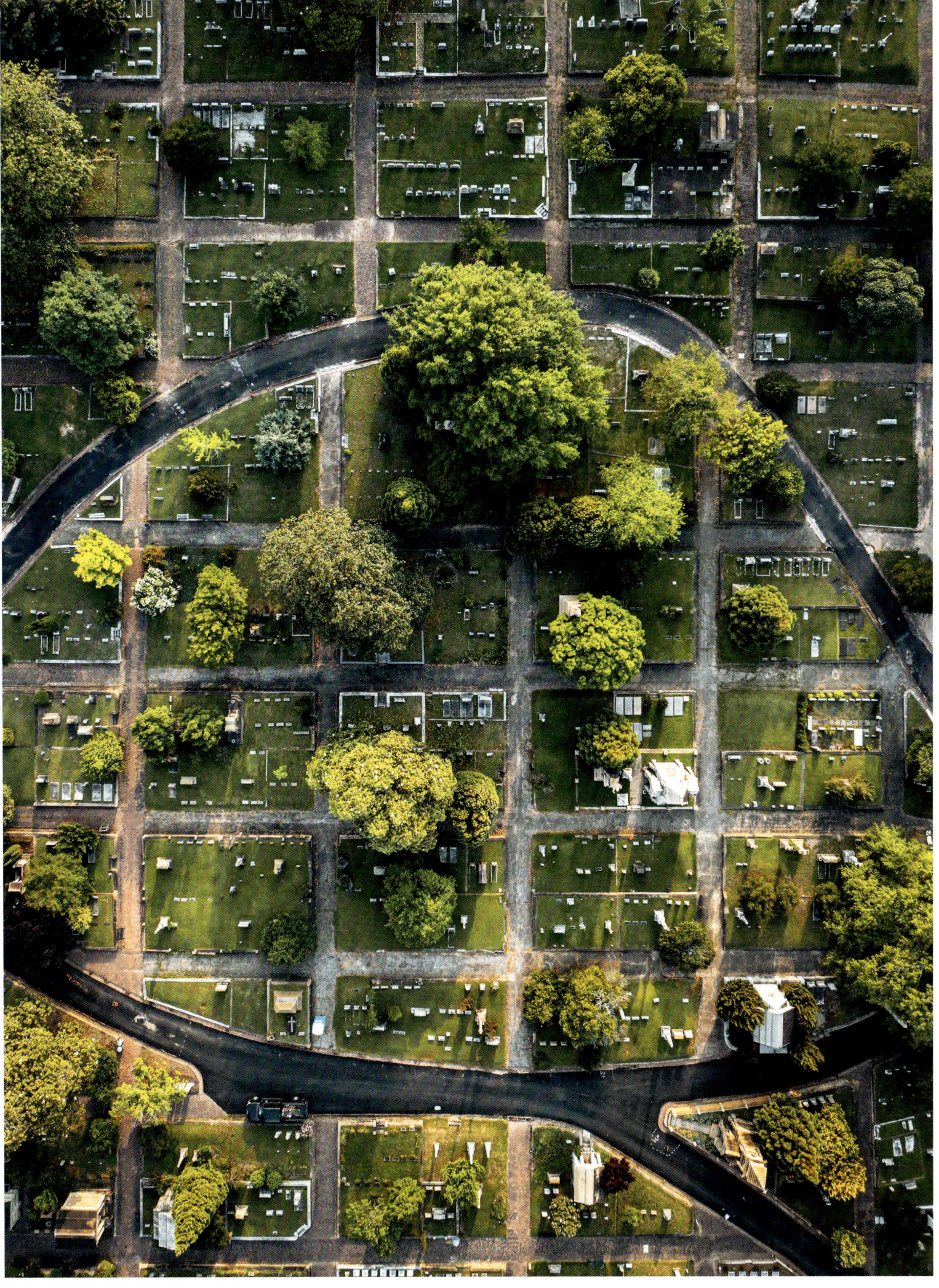

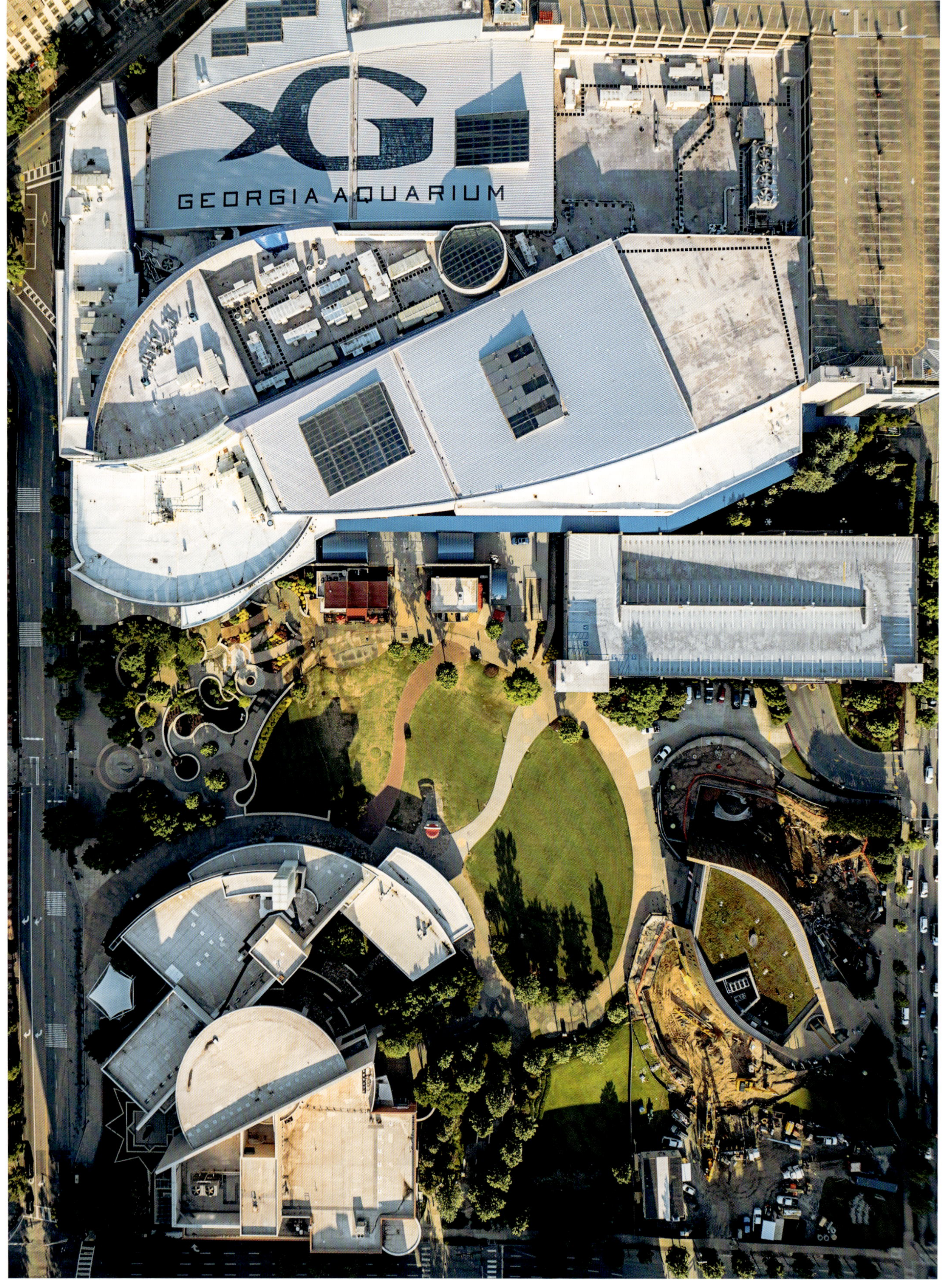

GEORGIA AQUARIUM

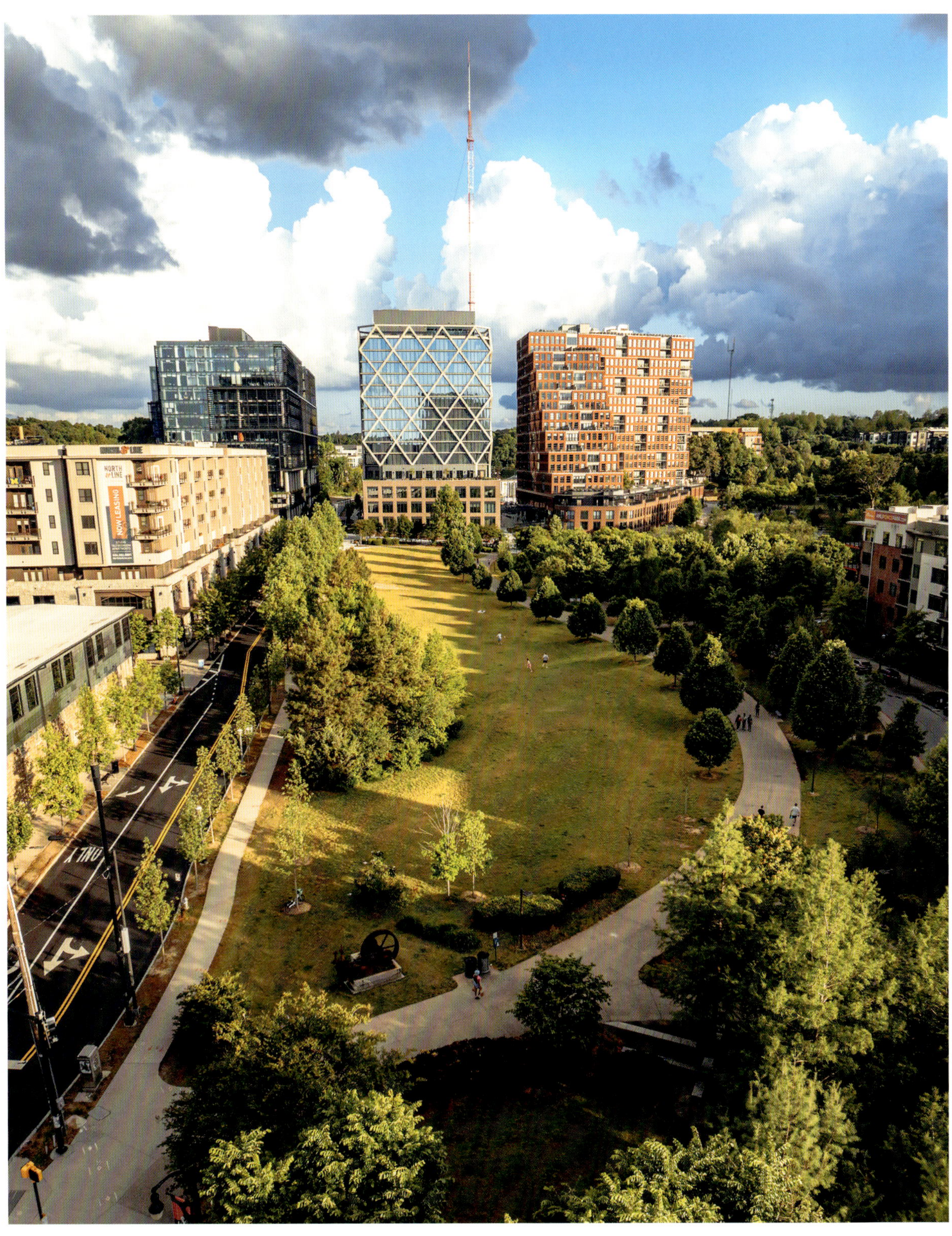

NORTH and LINE
NOW LEASING

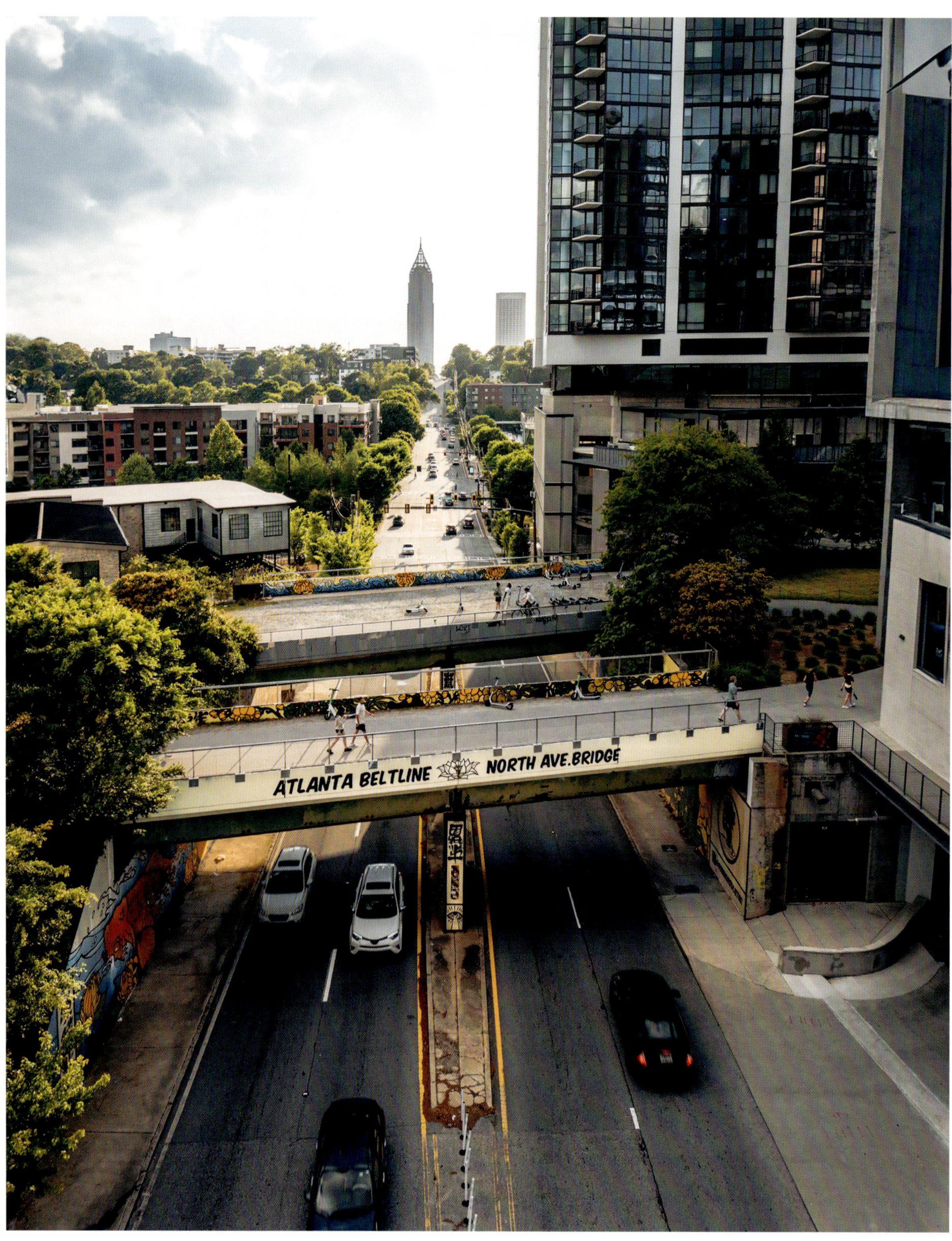

ATLANTA BELTLINE
NORTH AVE.BRIDGE

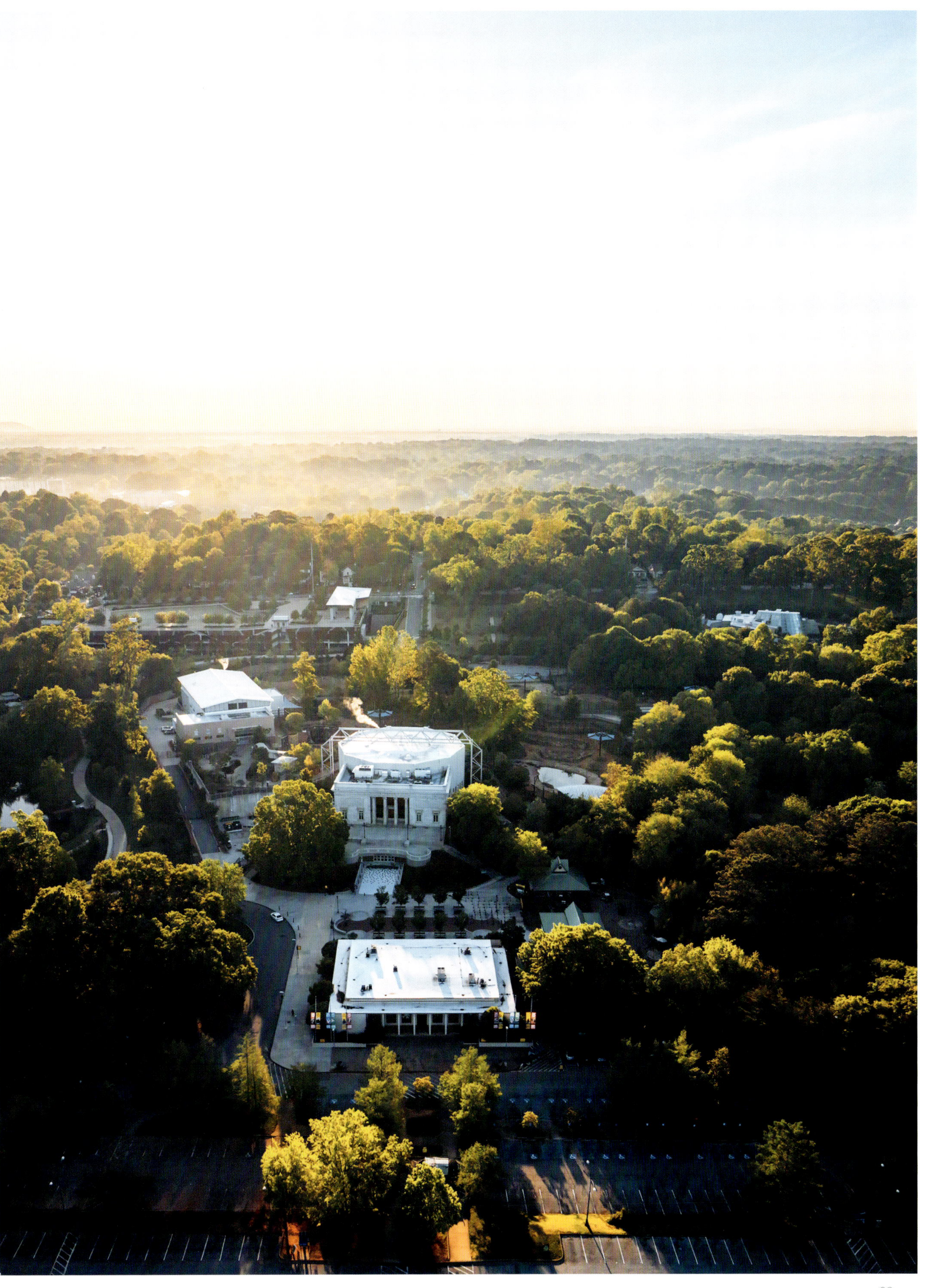

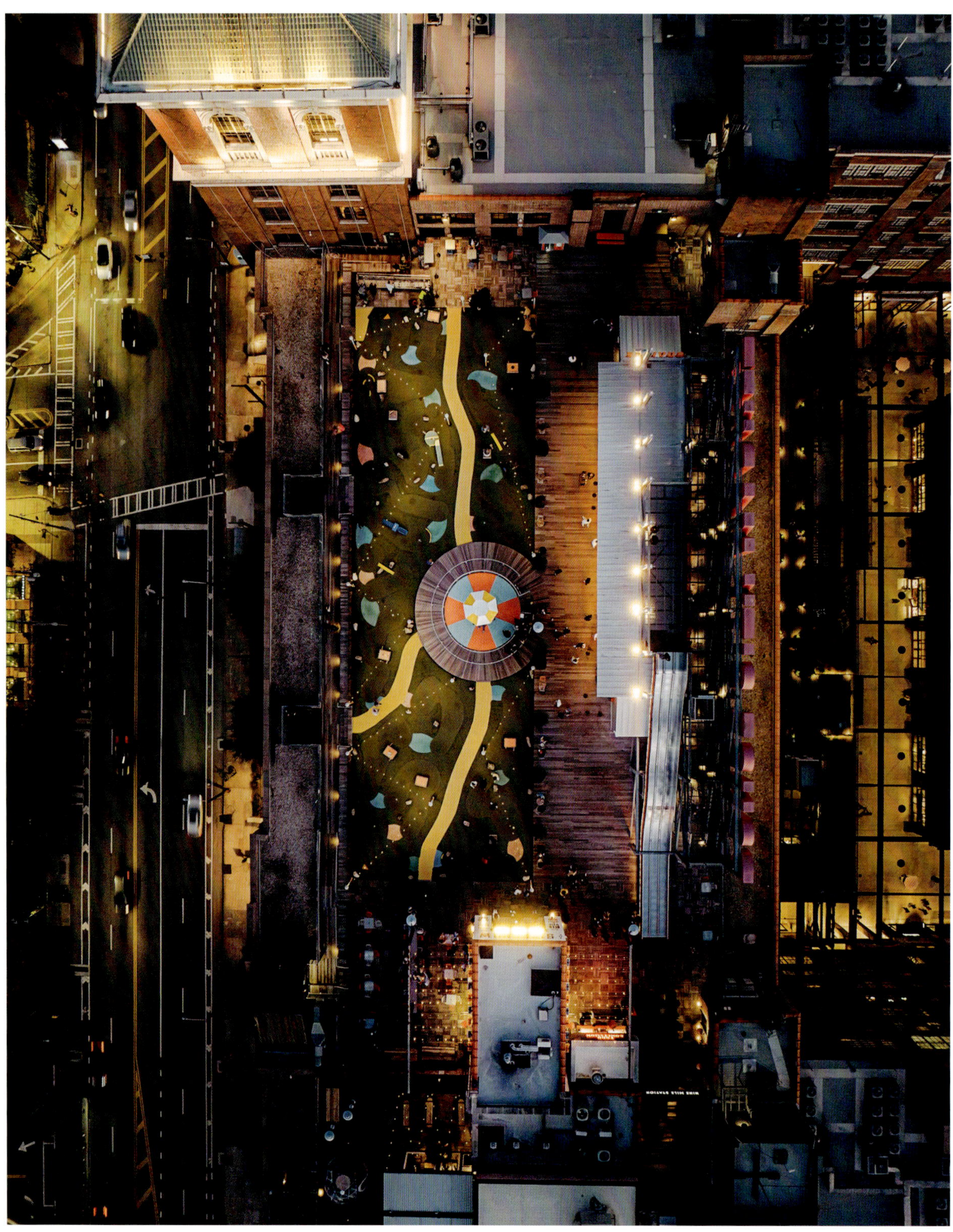

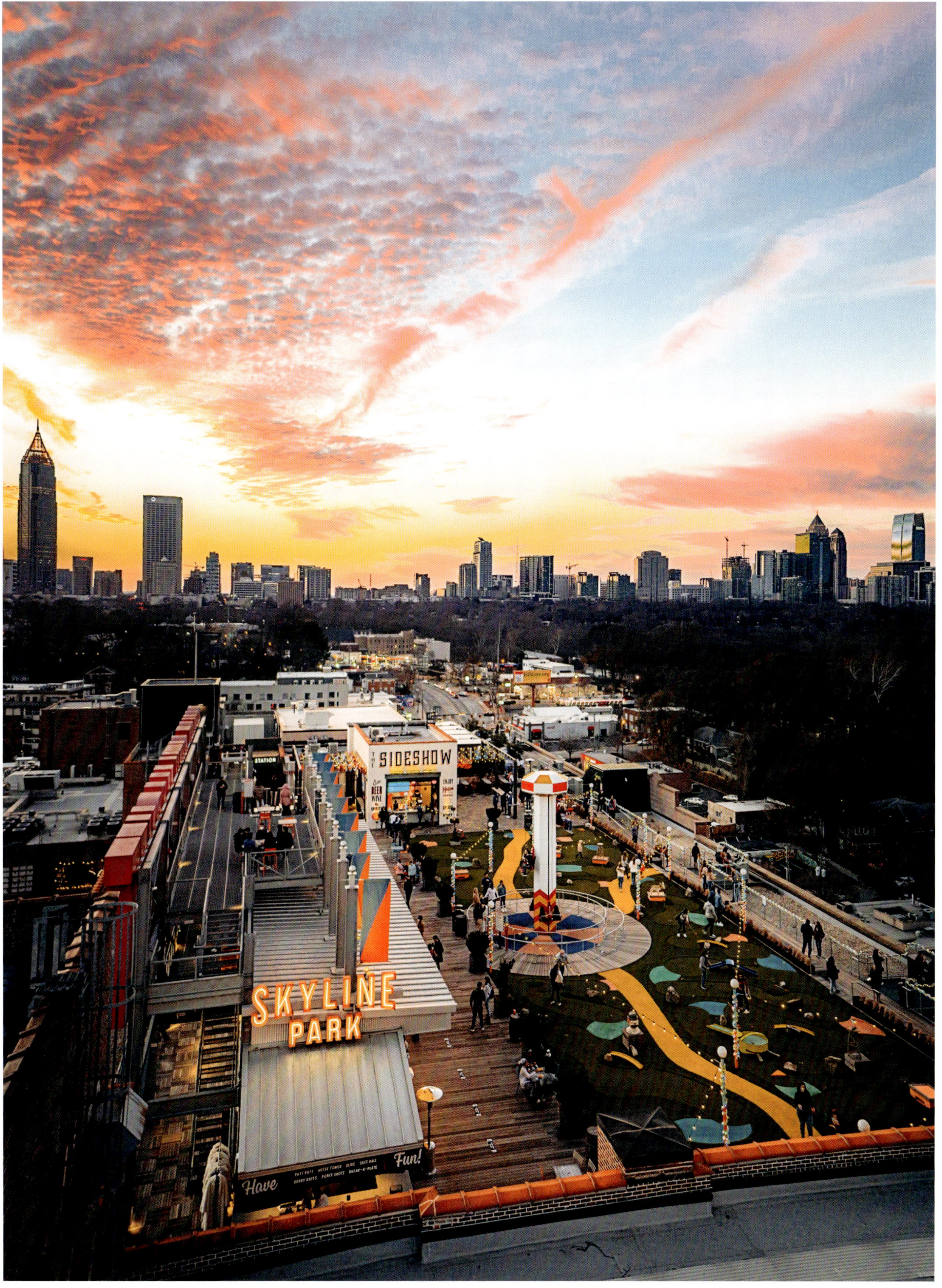
THE SIDESHOW
STATION
SKYLINE PARK
Have Fun!

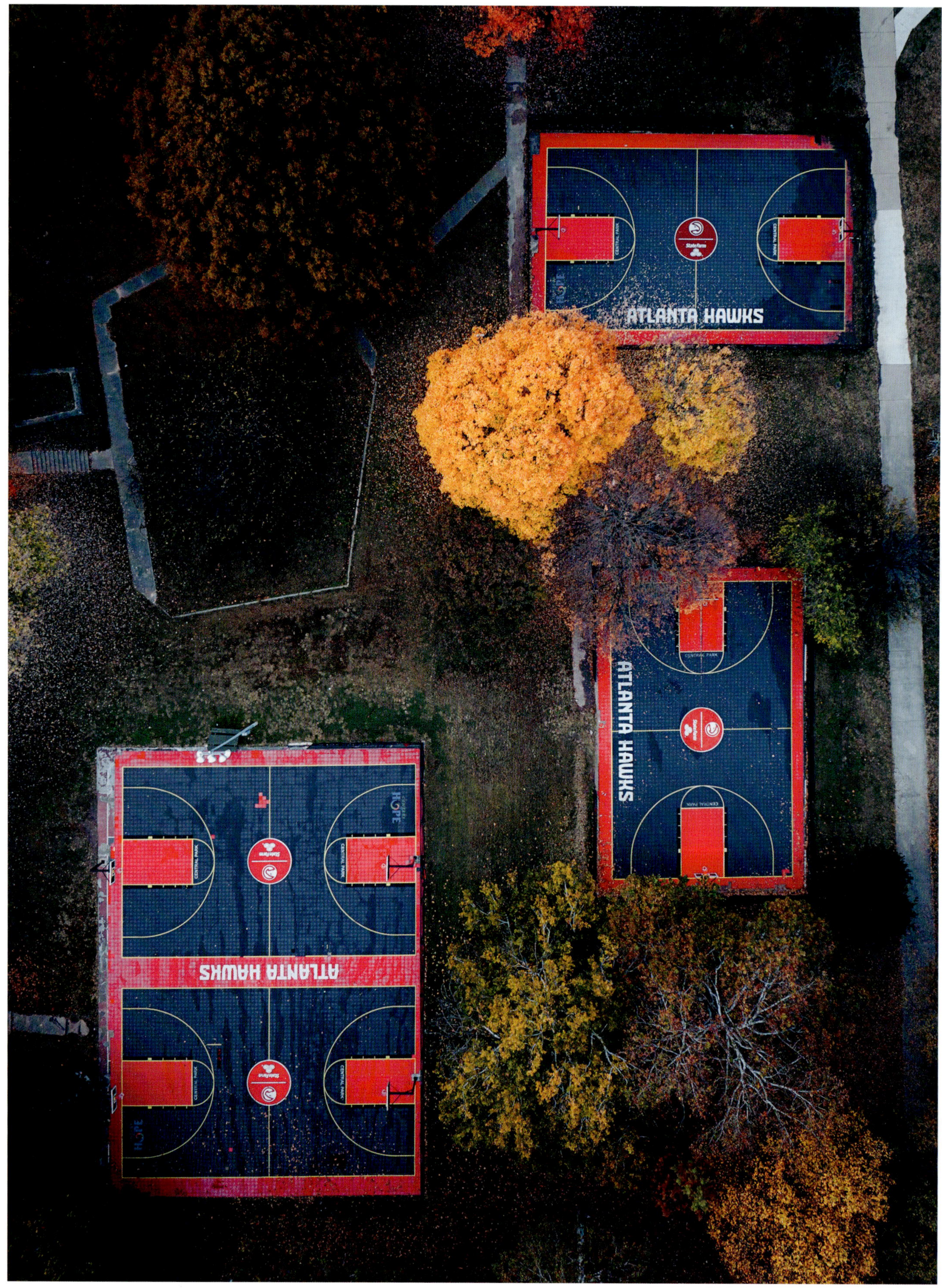
ATLANTA HAWKS
ATLANTA HAWKS
ATLANTA HAWKS
StateFarm
CENTRAL PARK
HOPE

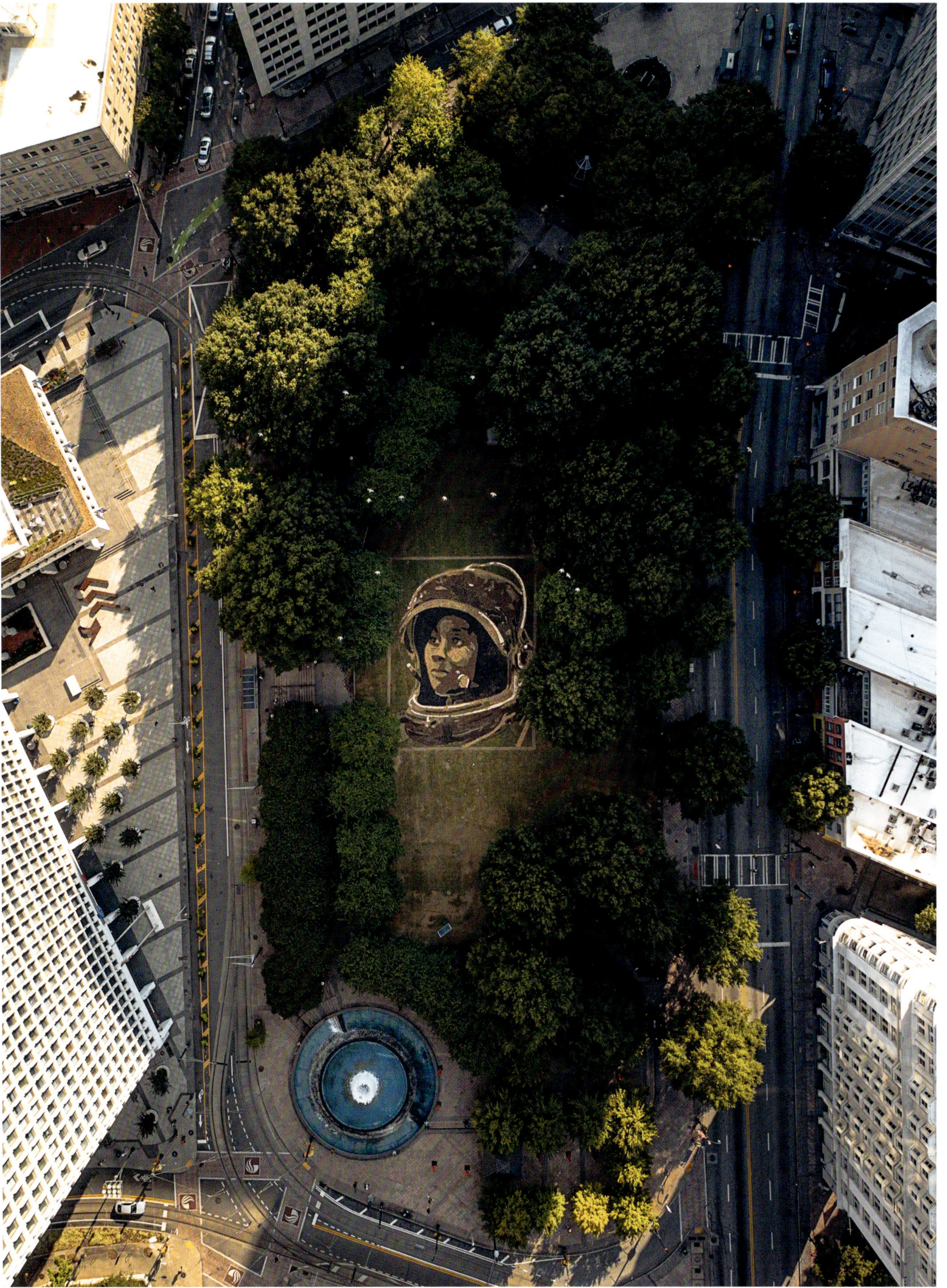

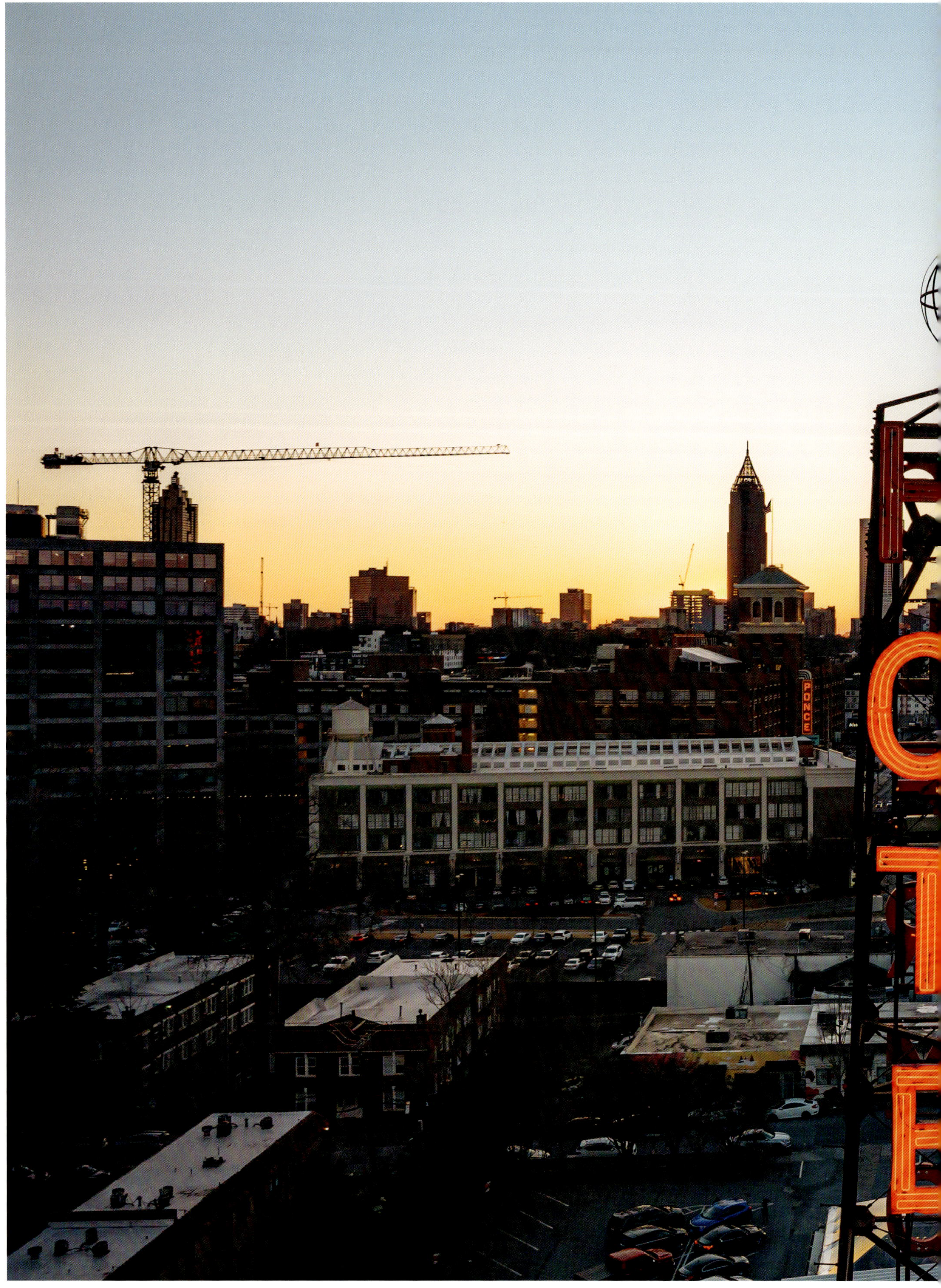
PONCE
HOTEL

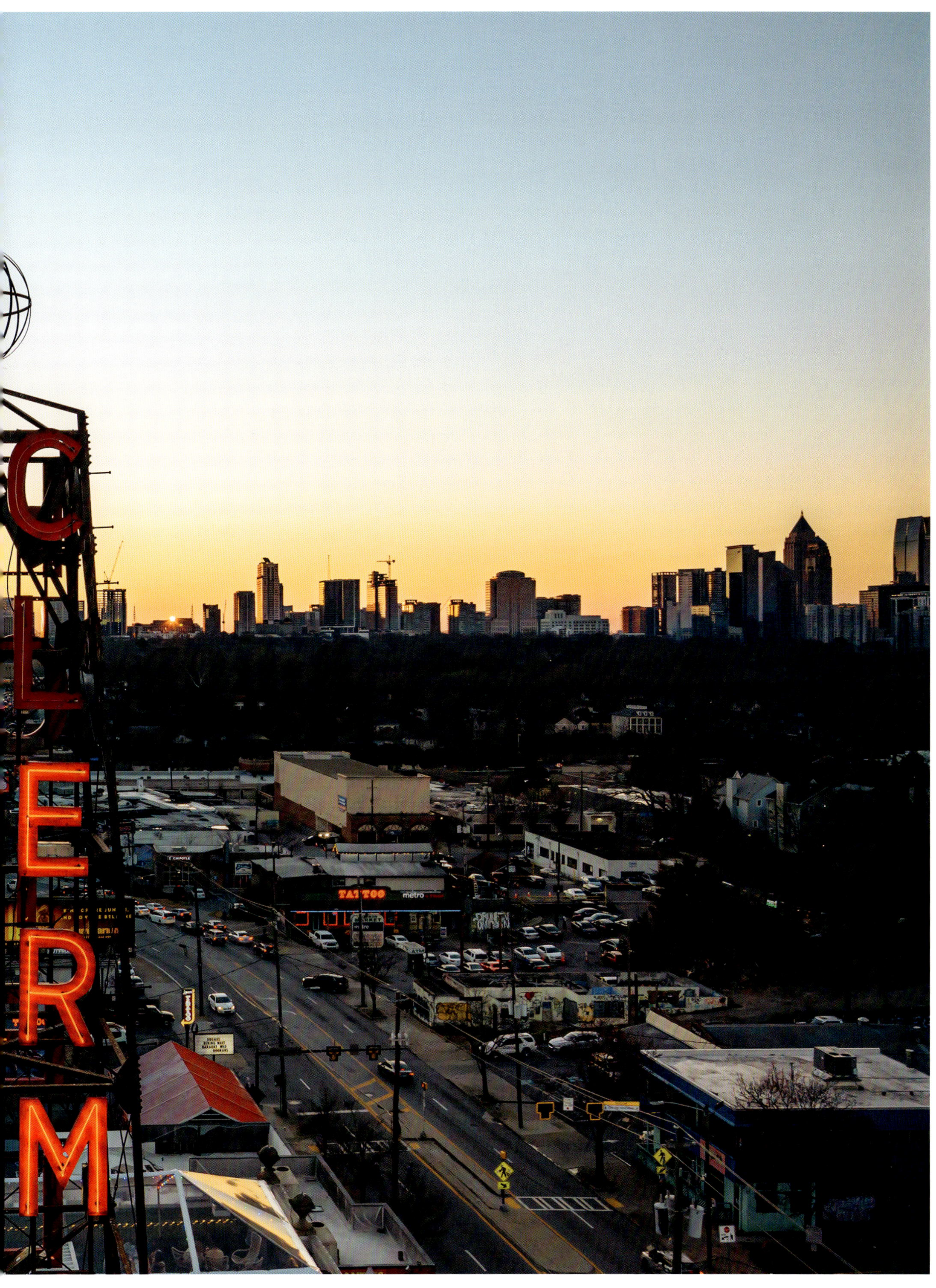

C
L
E
R
M
TATTOO
metro

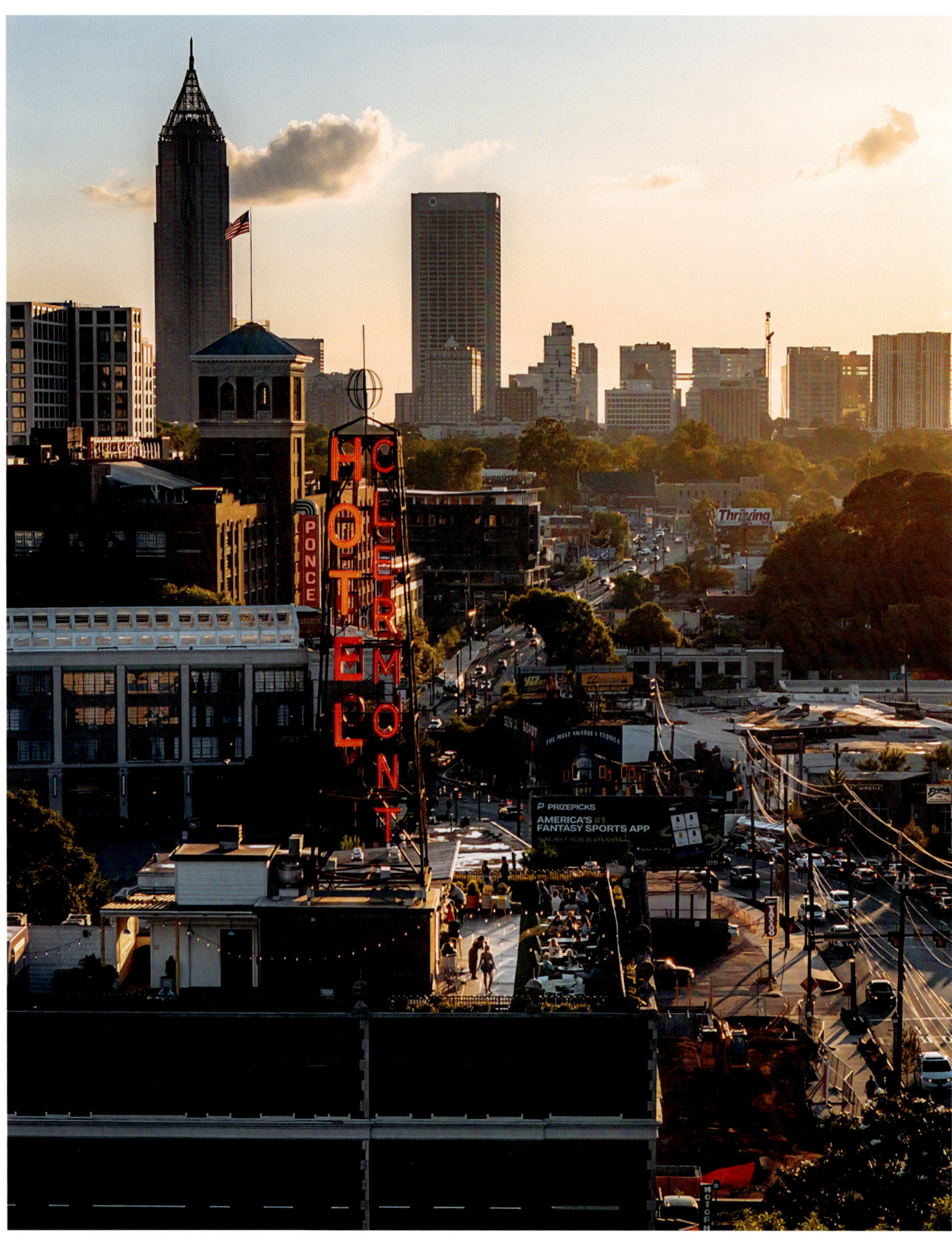

HOTEL
CLERMONT
PONCE
PRIZEPICKS
AMERICA'S #1
FANTASY SPORTS APP
Thriving

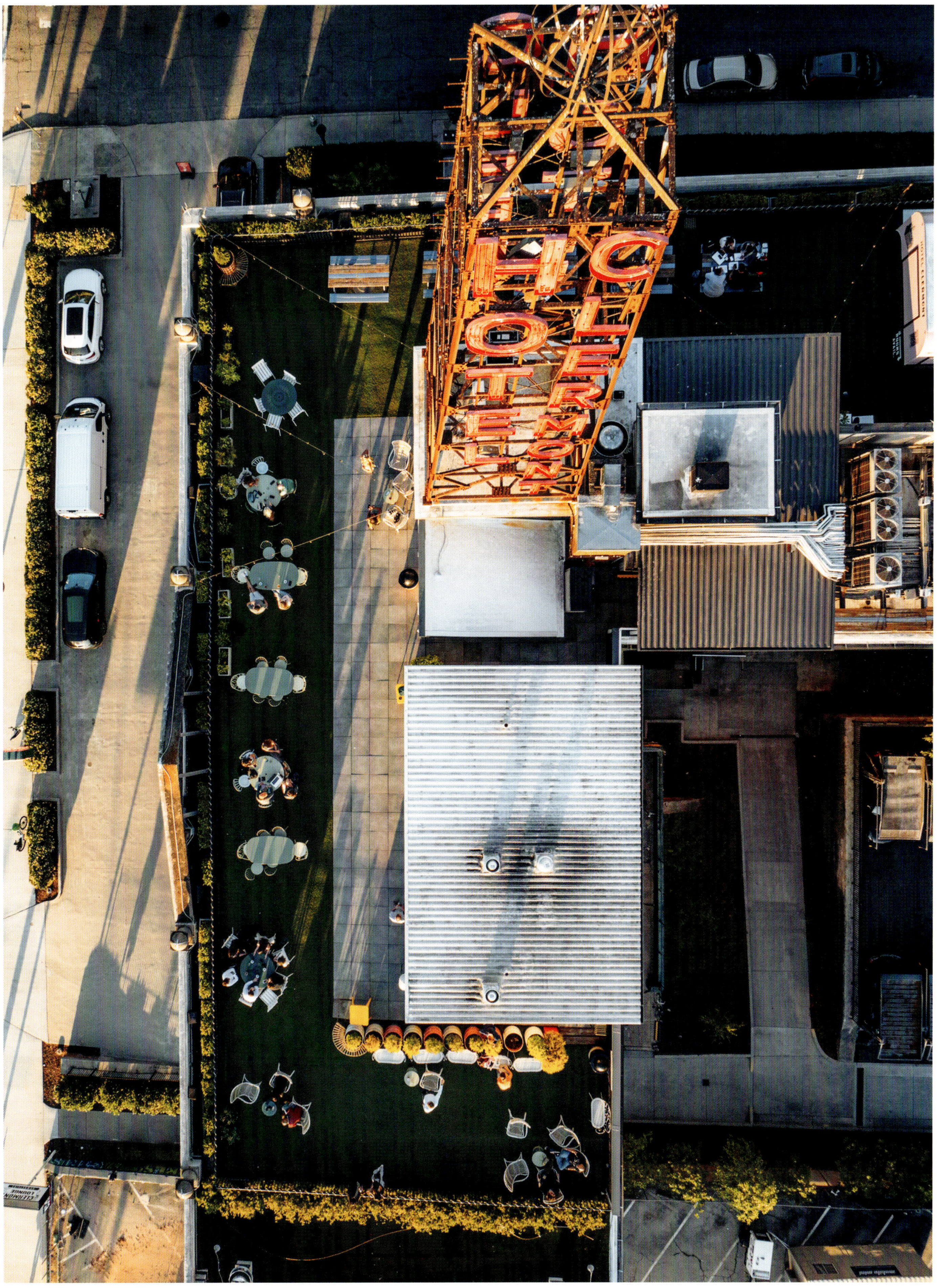
HOLLYWOOD
CLERMONT
HOTEL

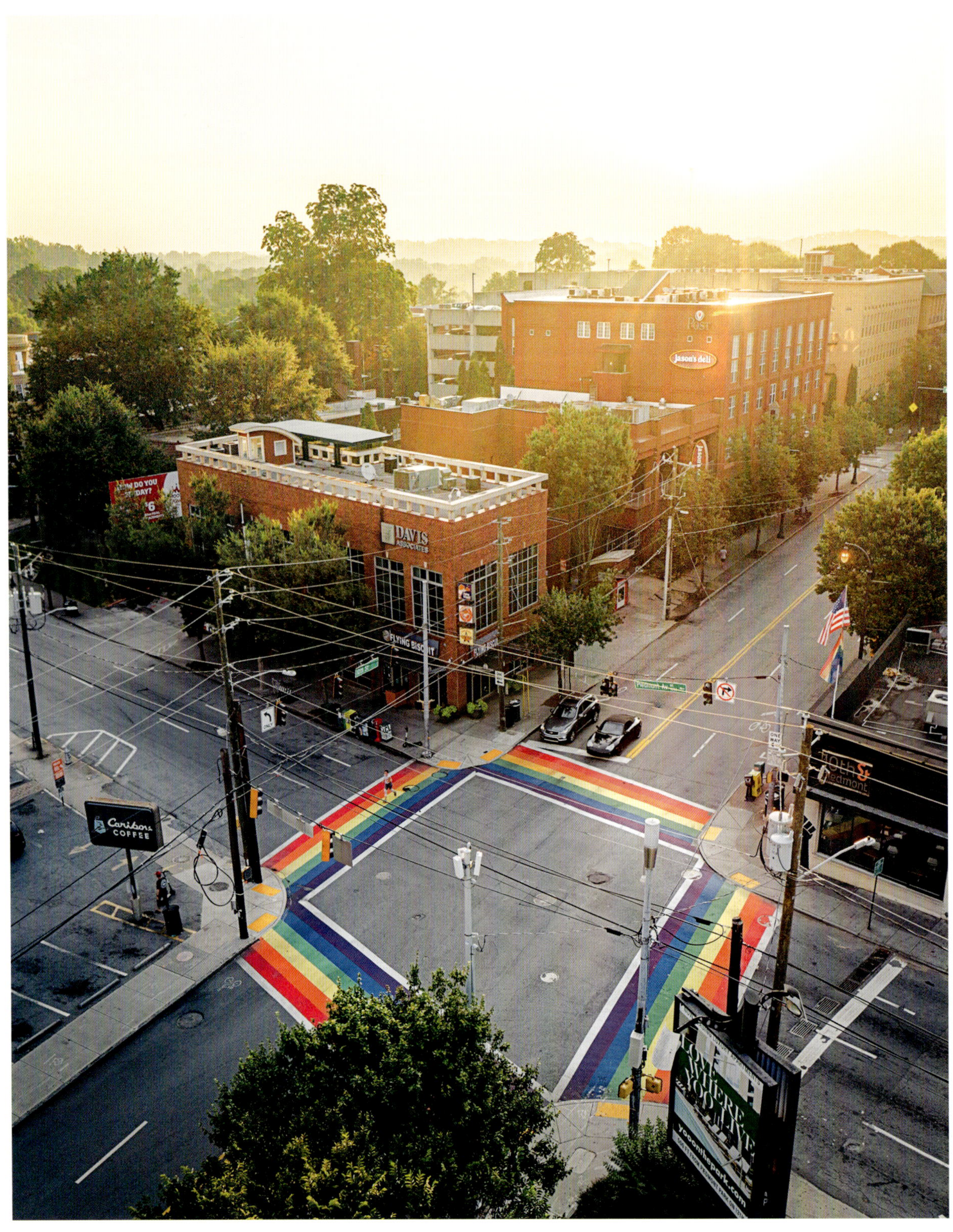
Post
jason's deli
DAVIS ASSOCIATES
HOW DO YOU
DAY?
$6
FLYING BISCUIT
Caribou COFFEE
10th & Piedmont
ONE WAY
LOVE WHERE YOU LIVE
yoco.intwnpark.com

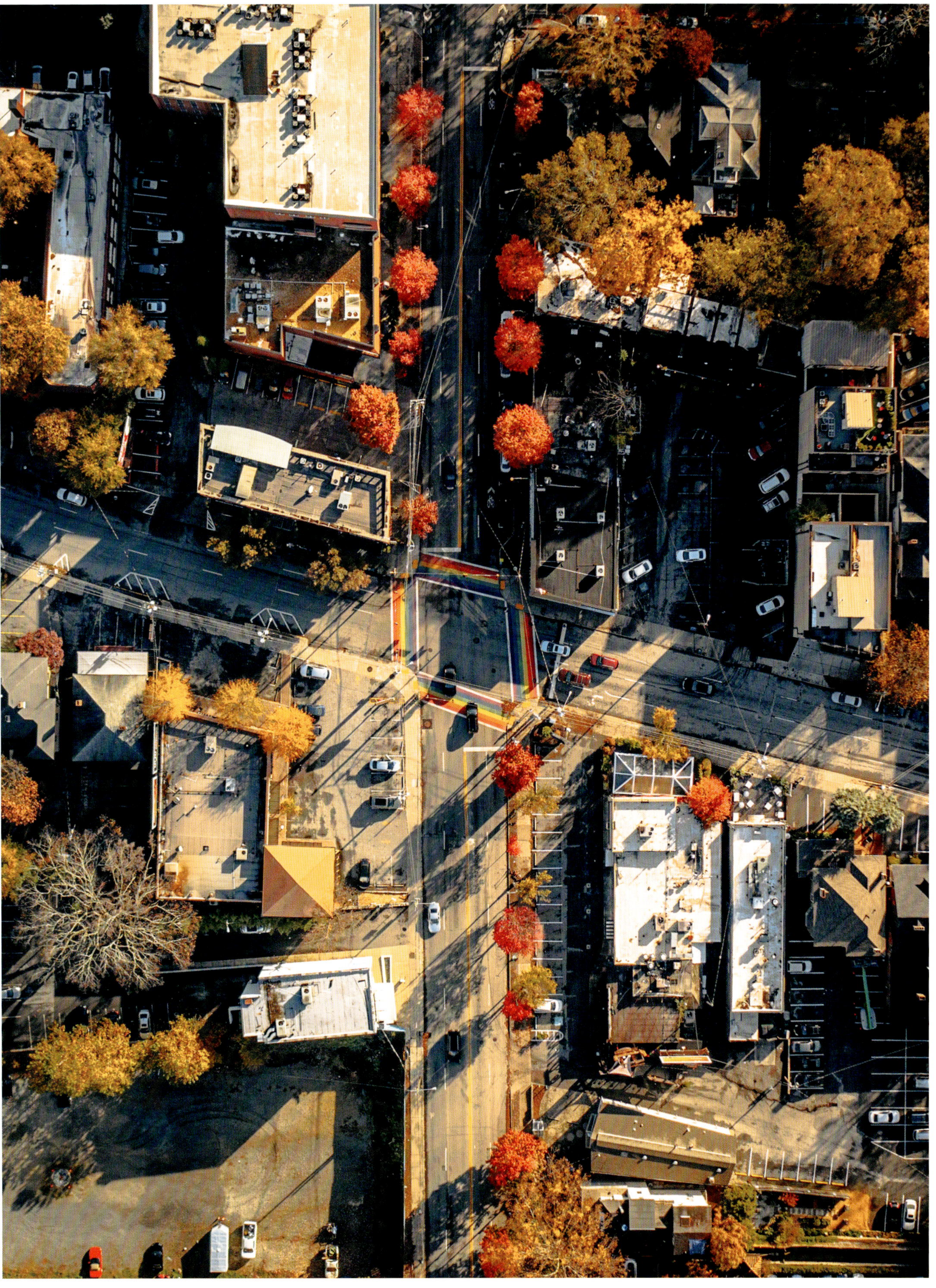

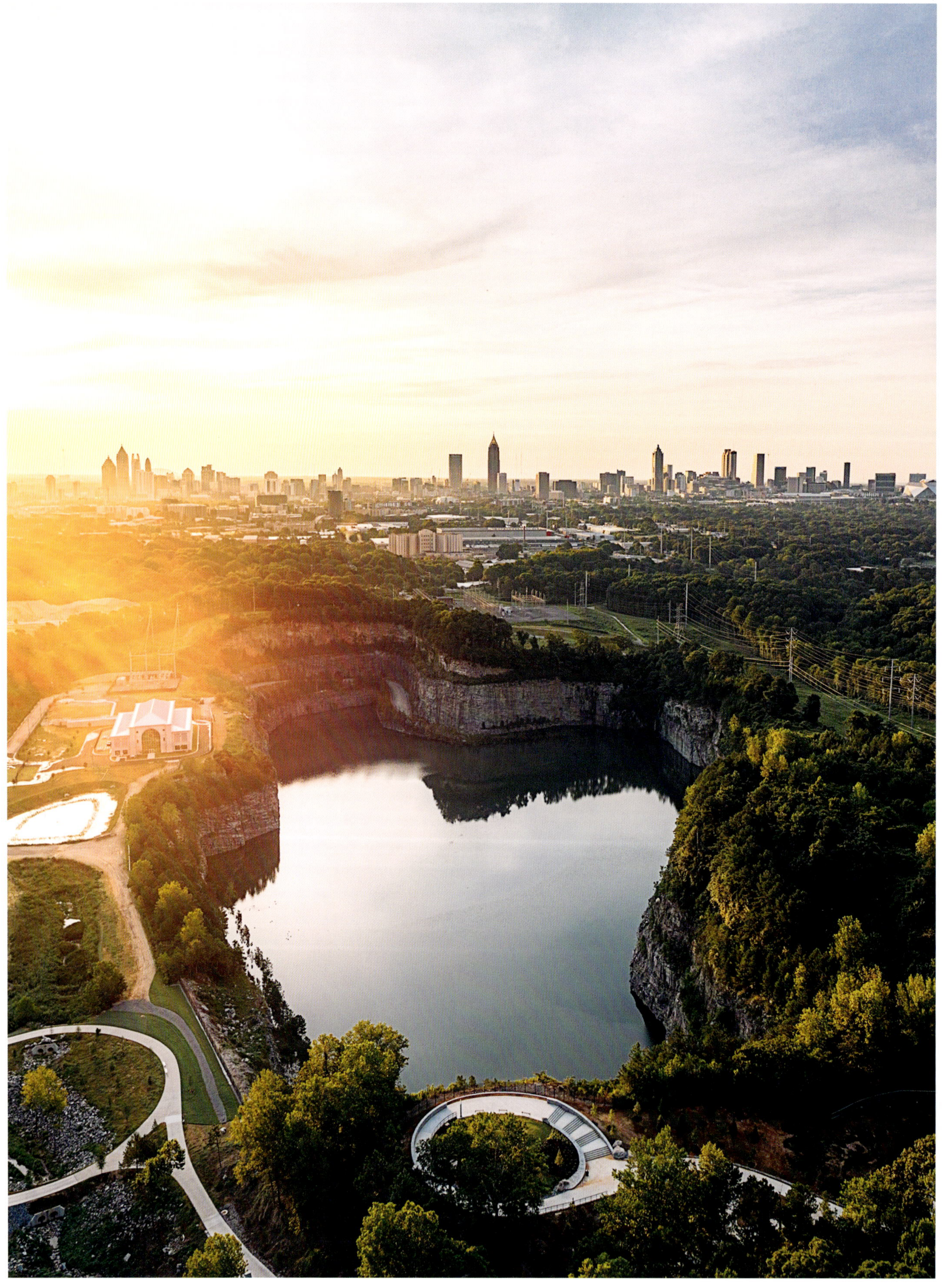

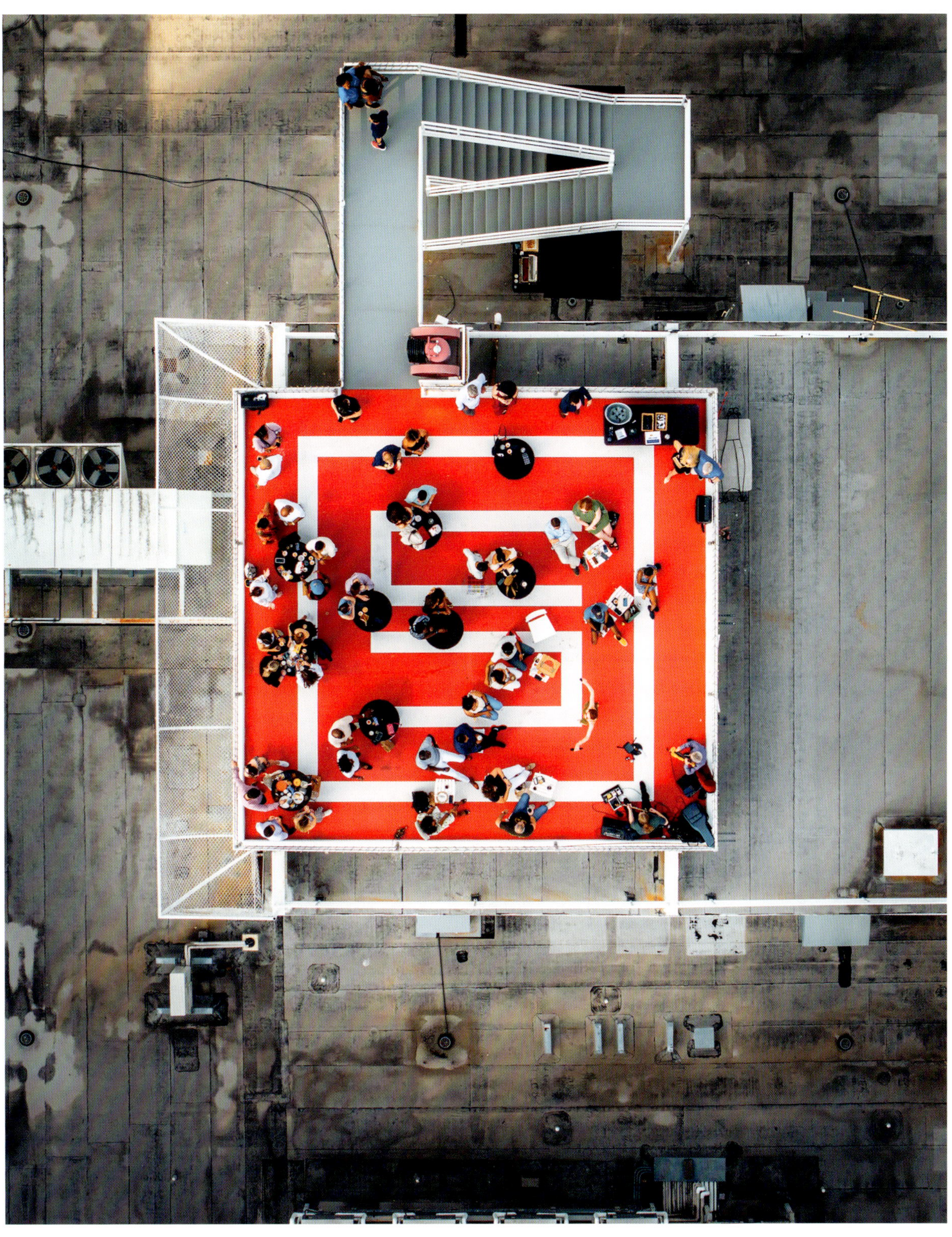

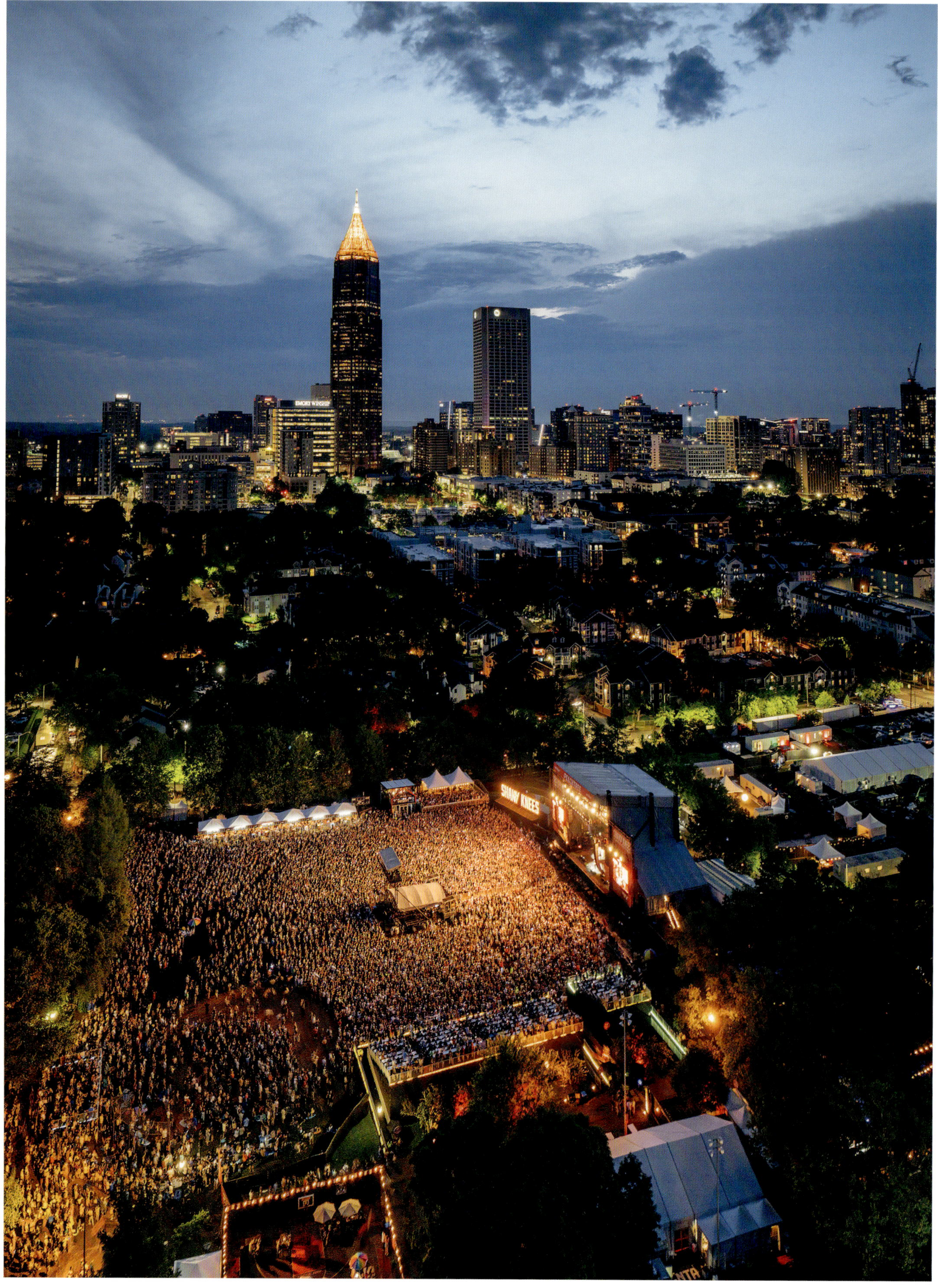
SHAKY KNEES

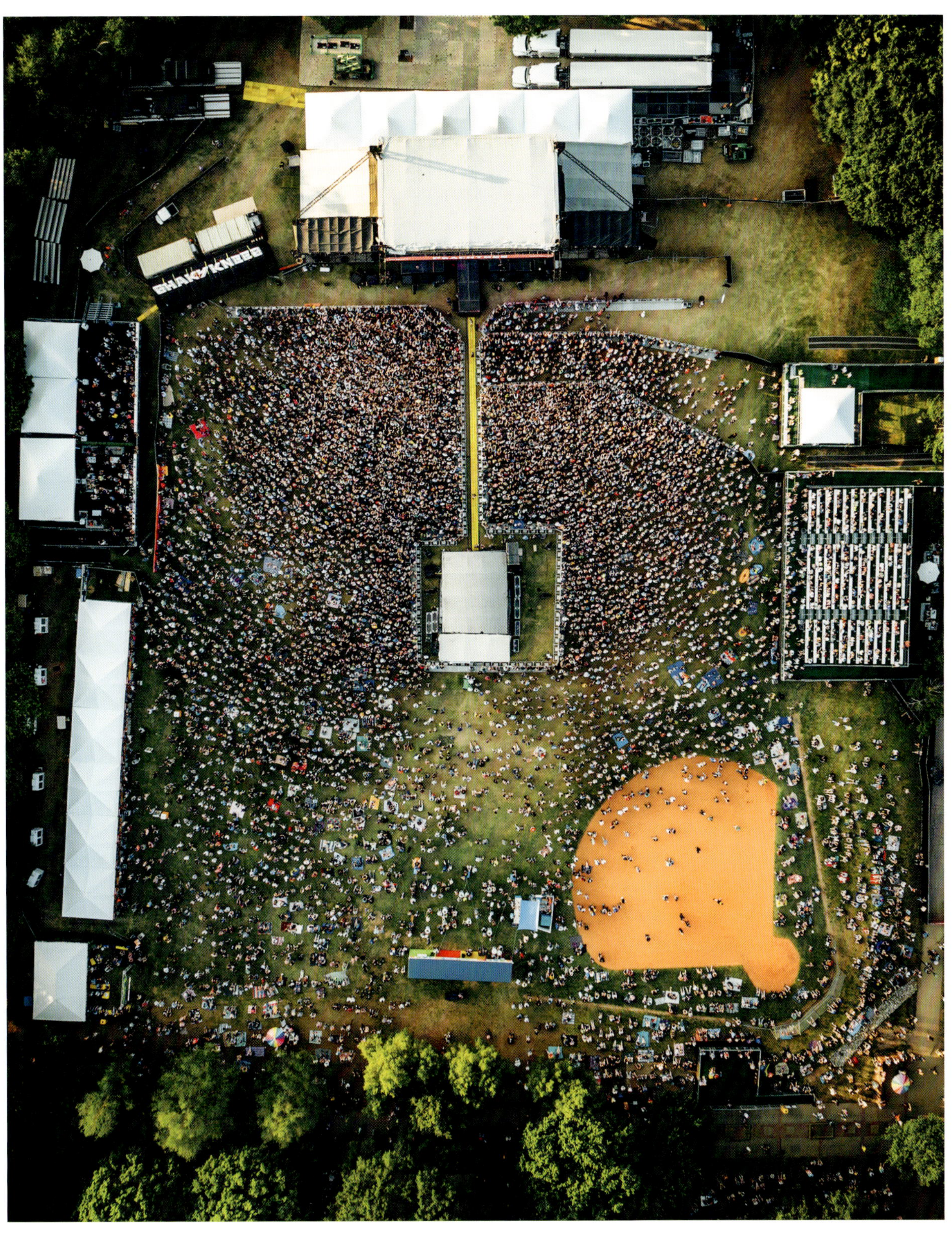
SHAKY KNEES

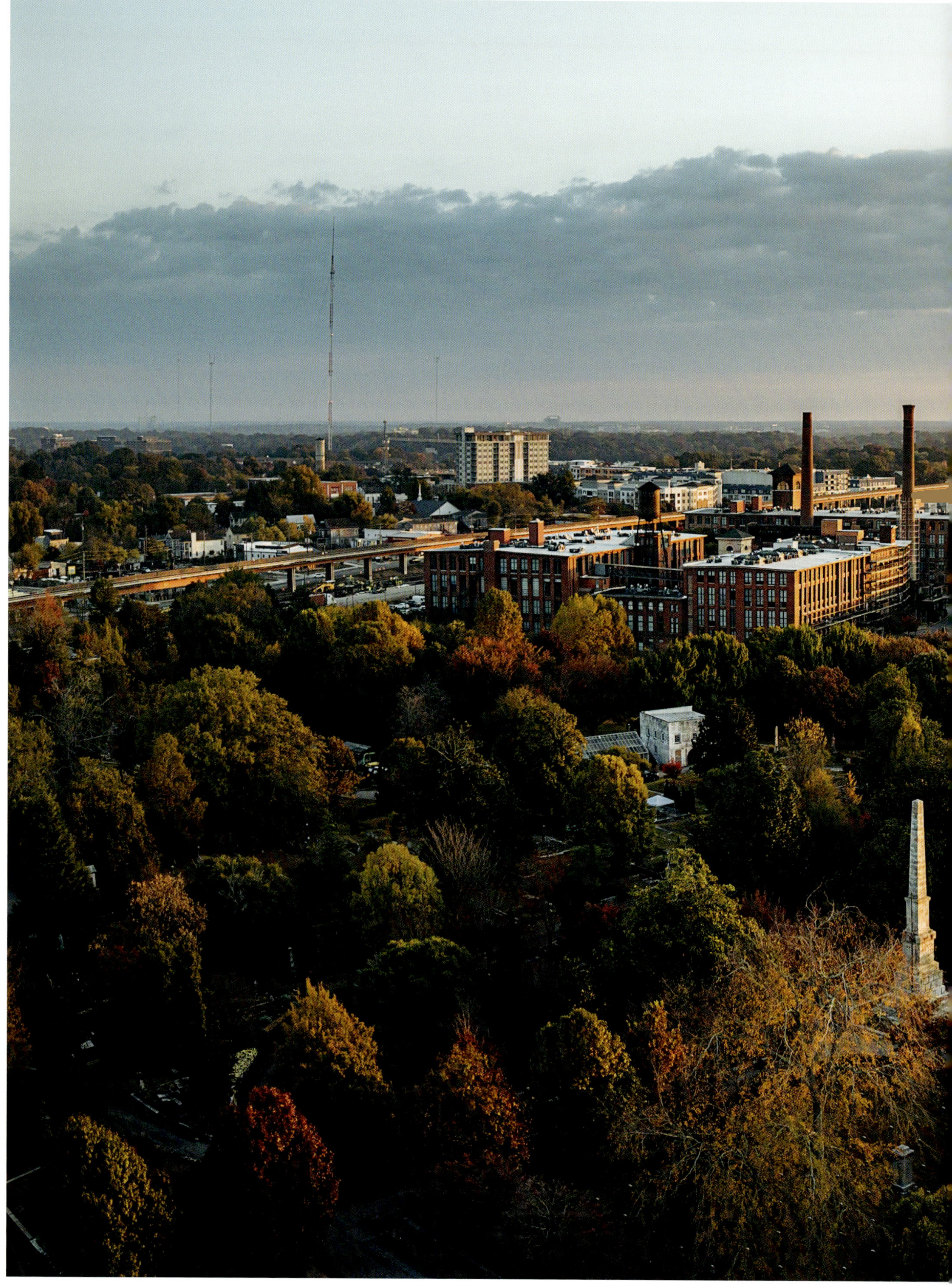

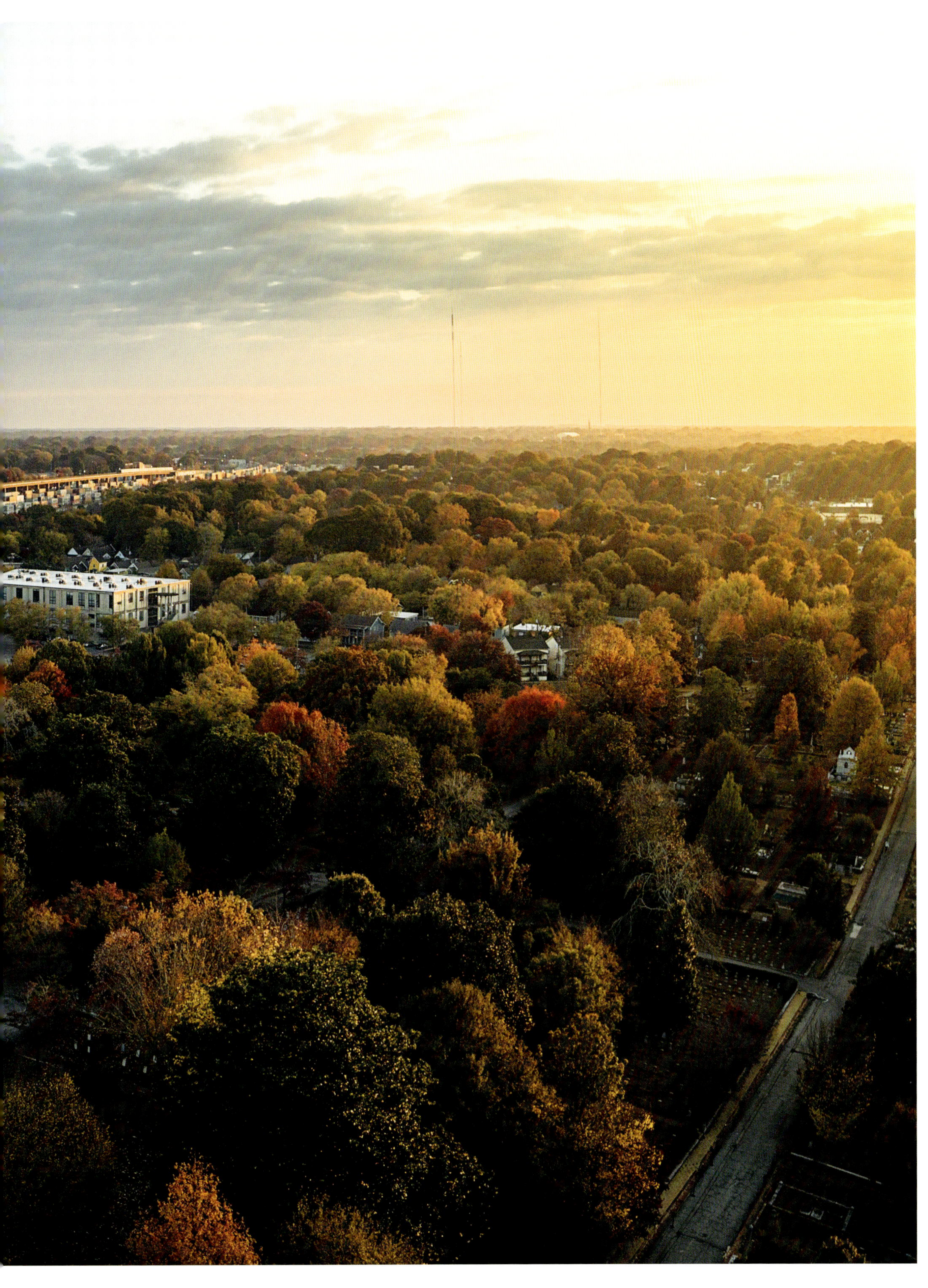

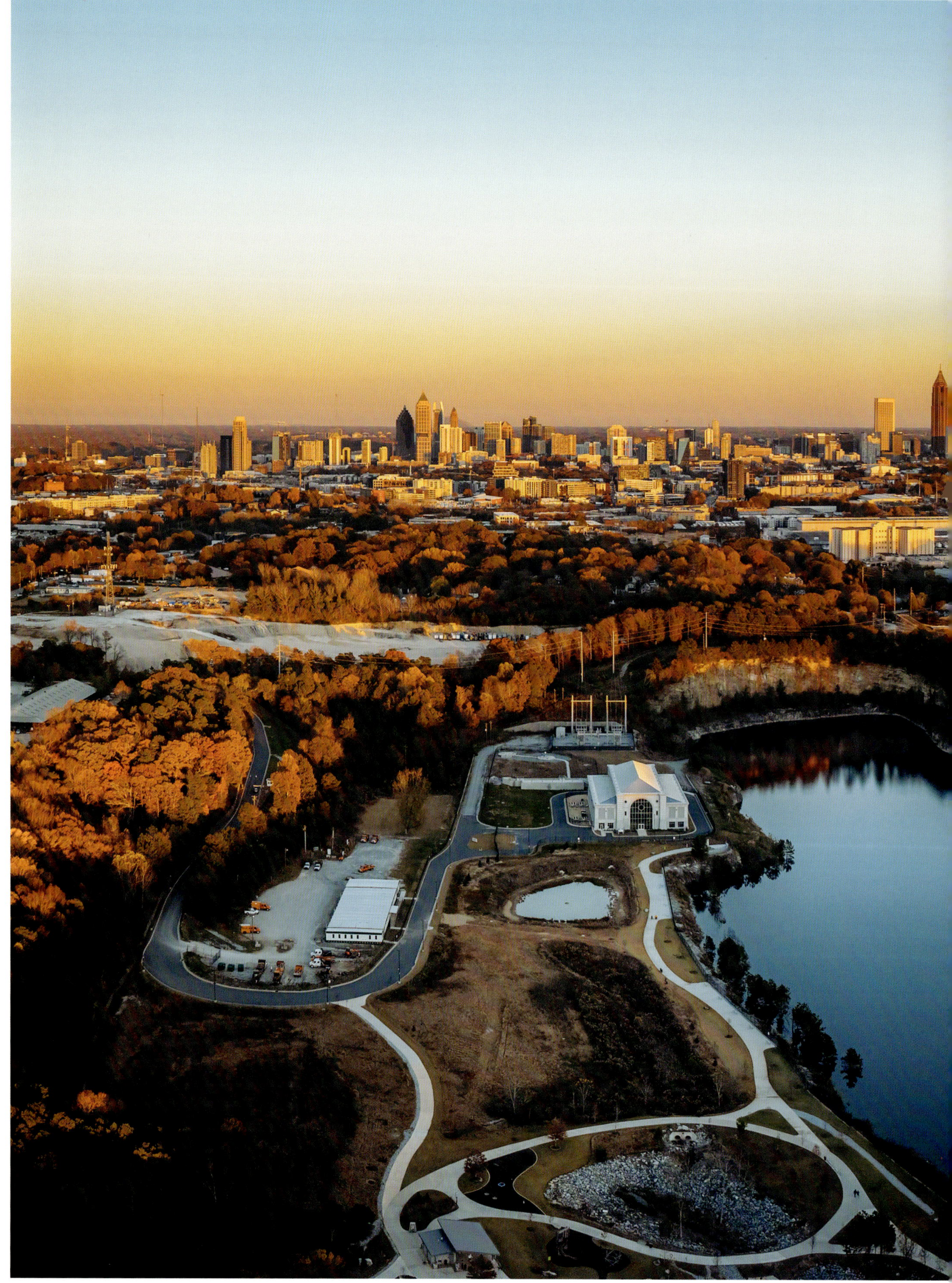

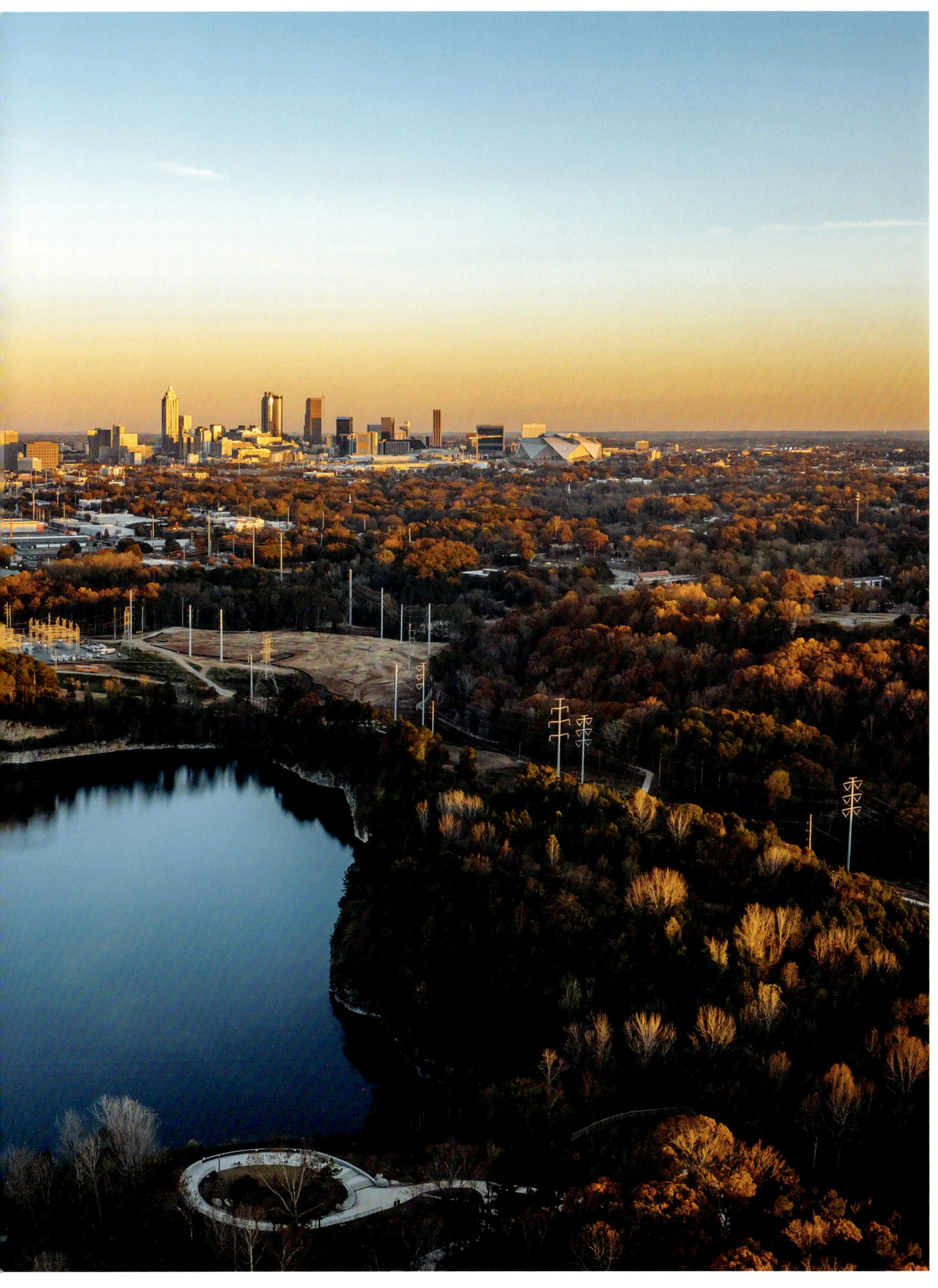

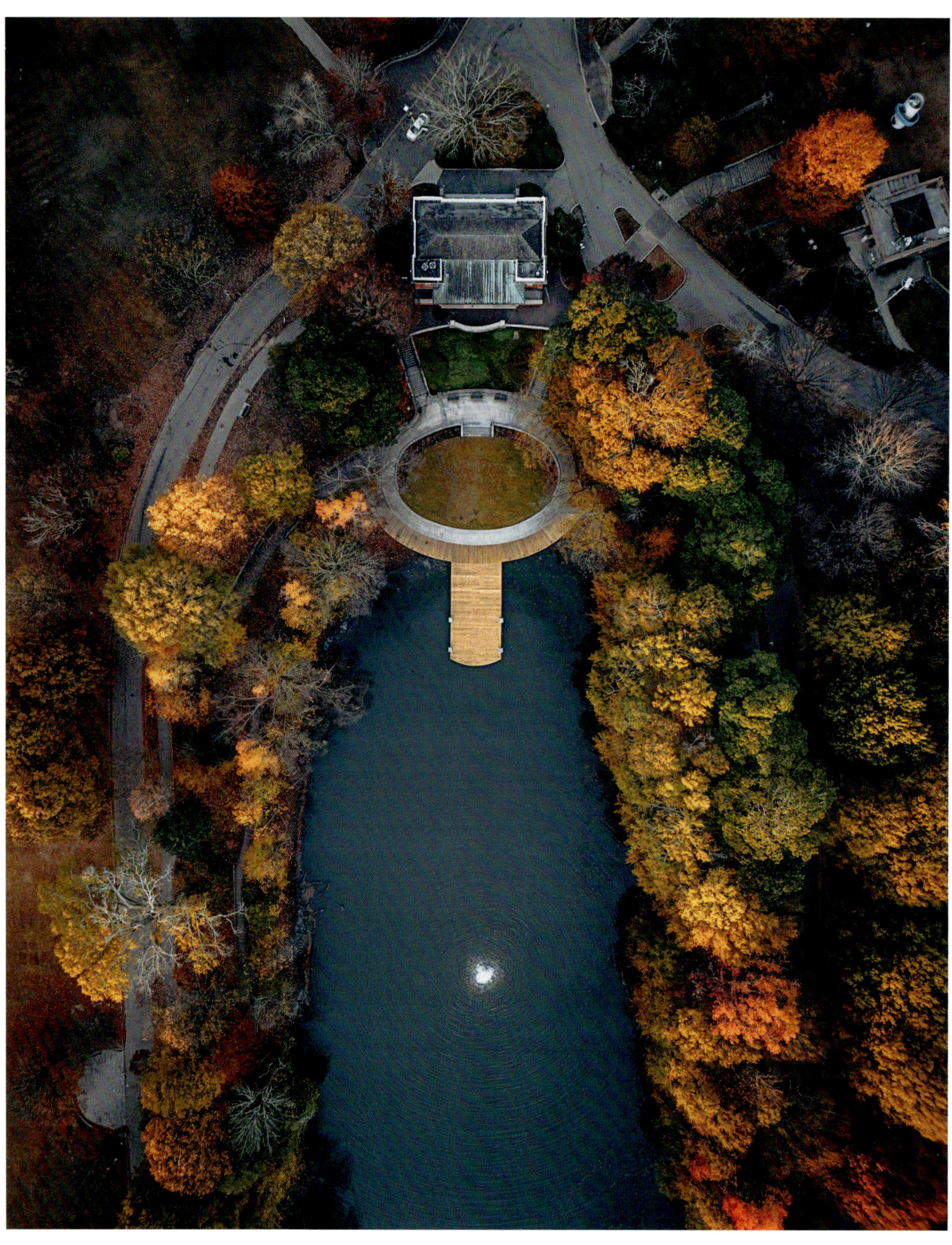

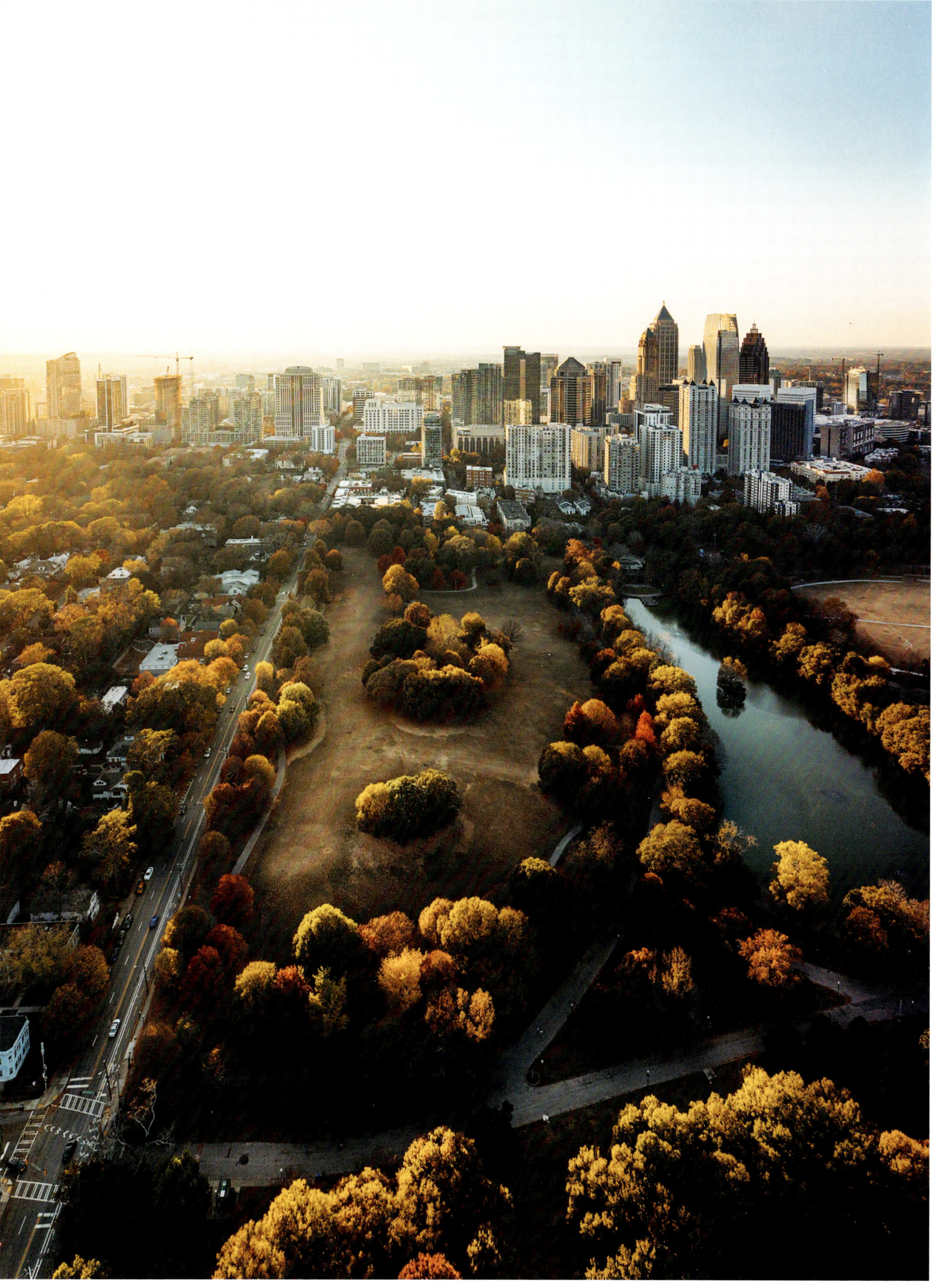

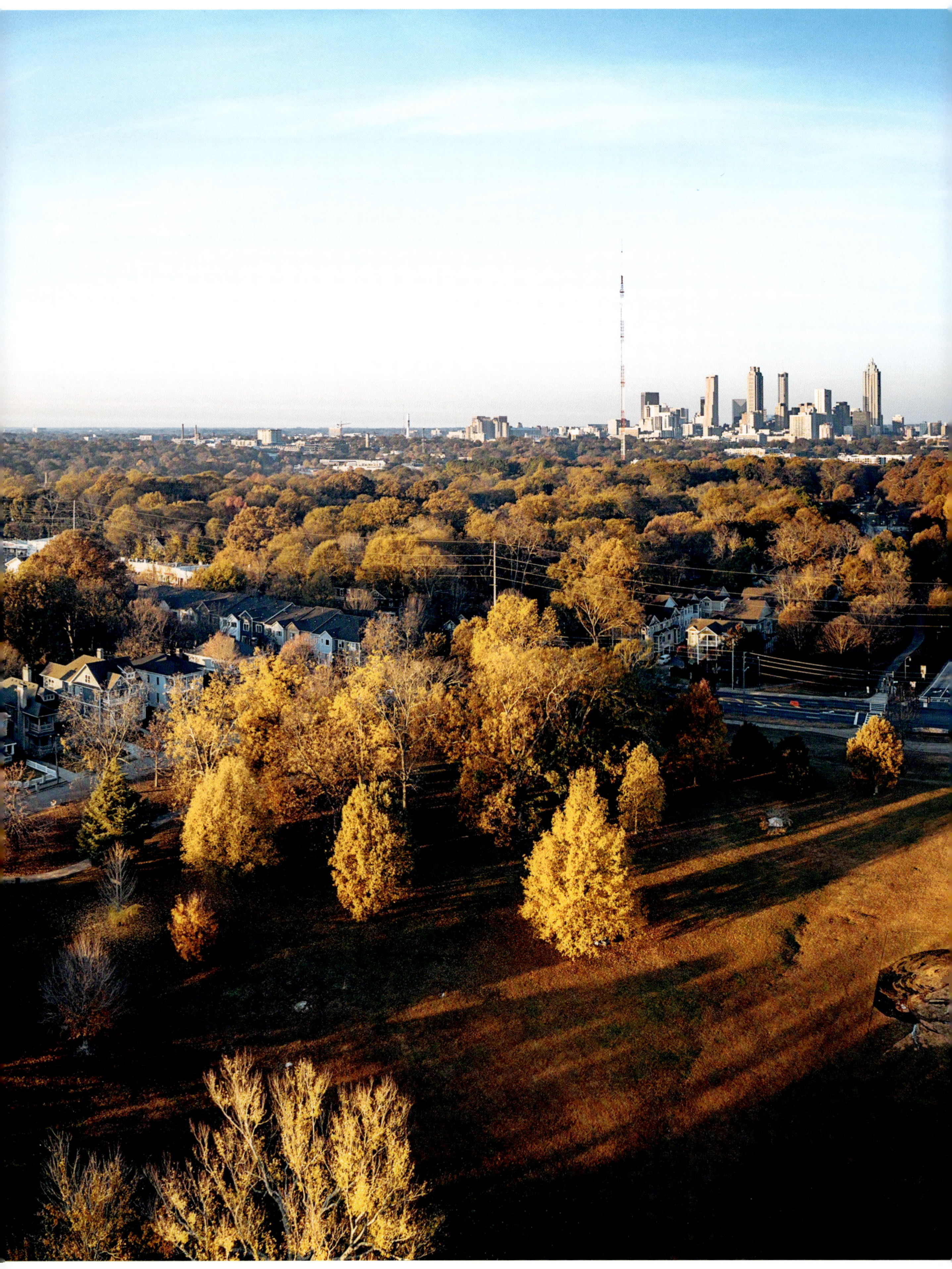

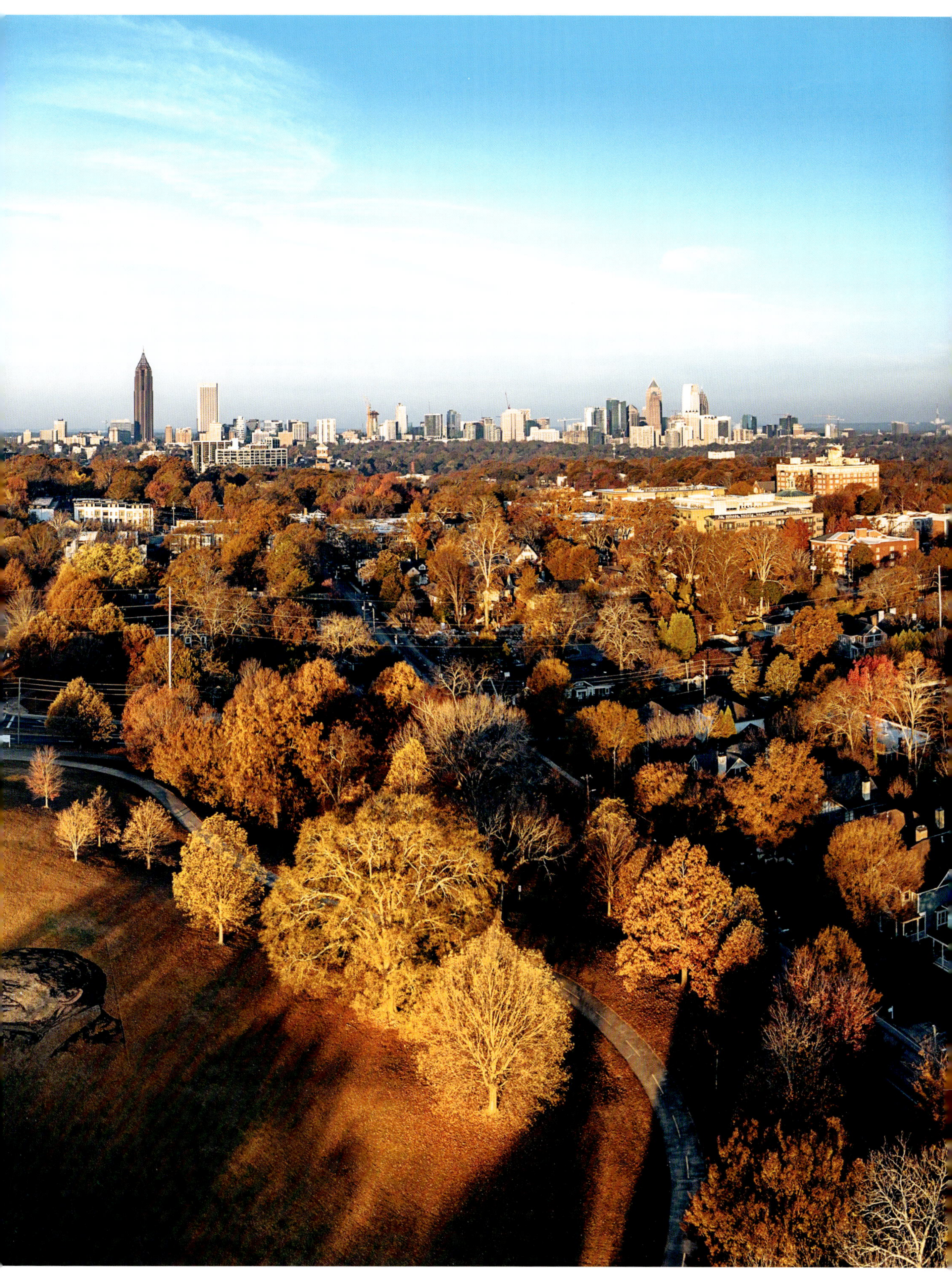

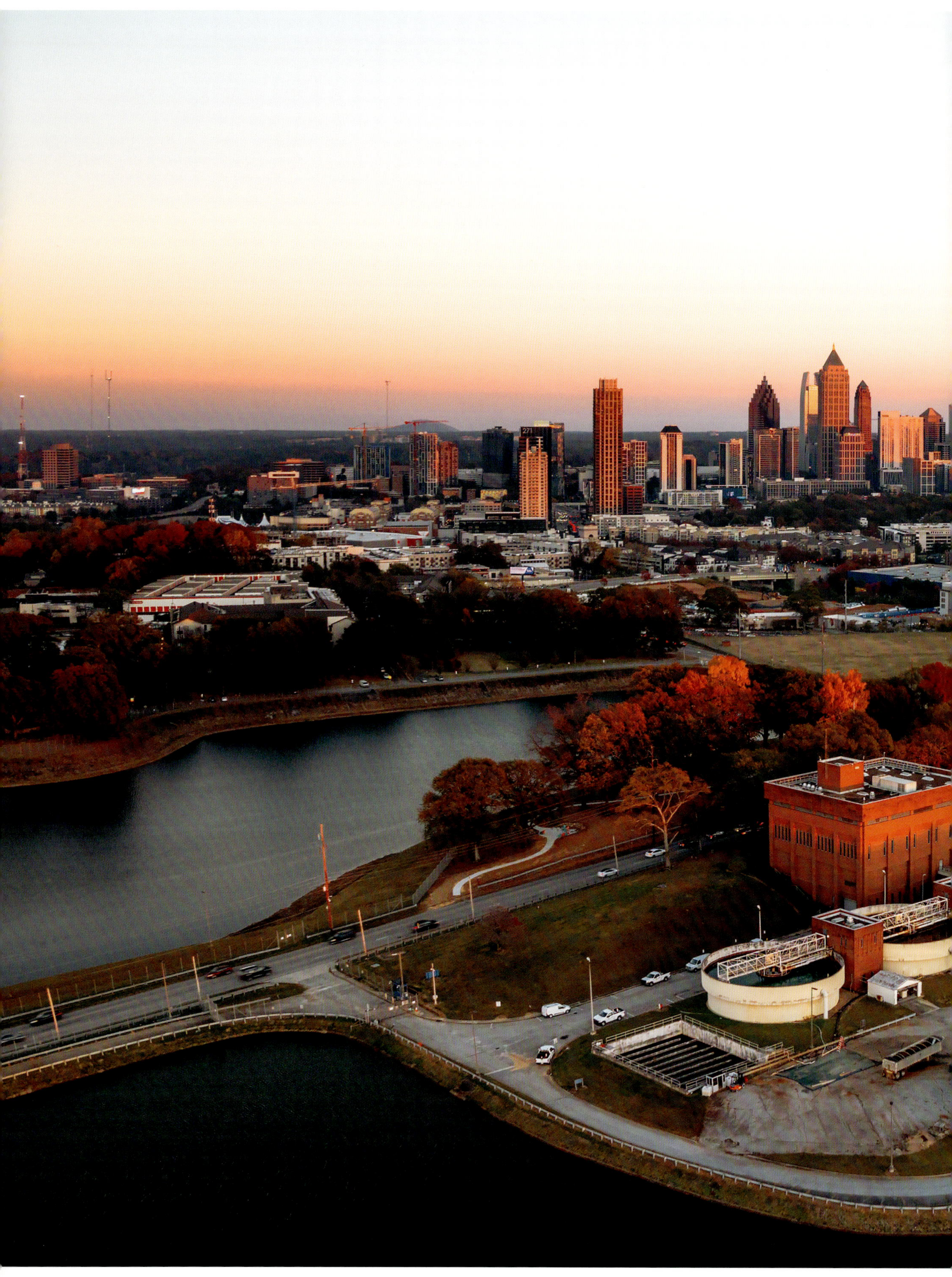

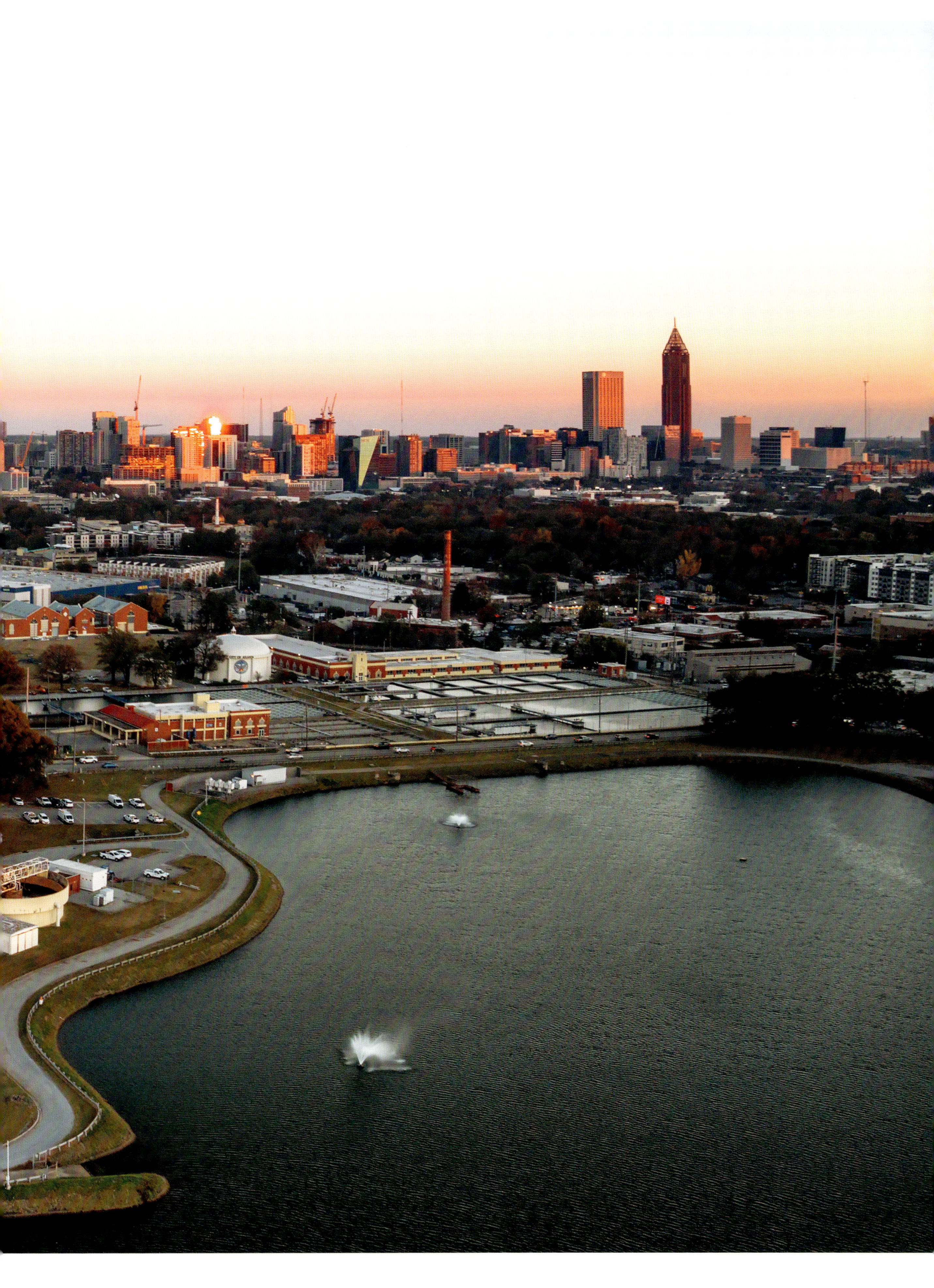

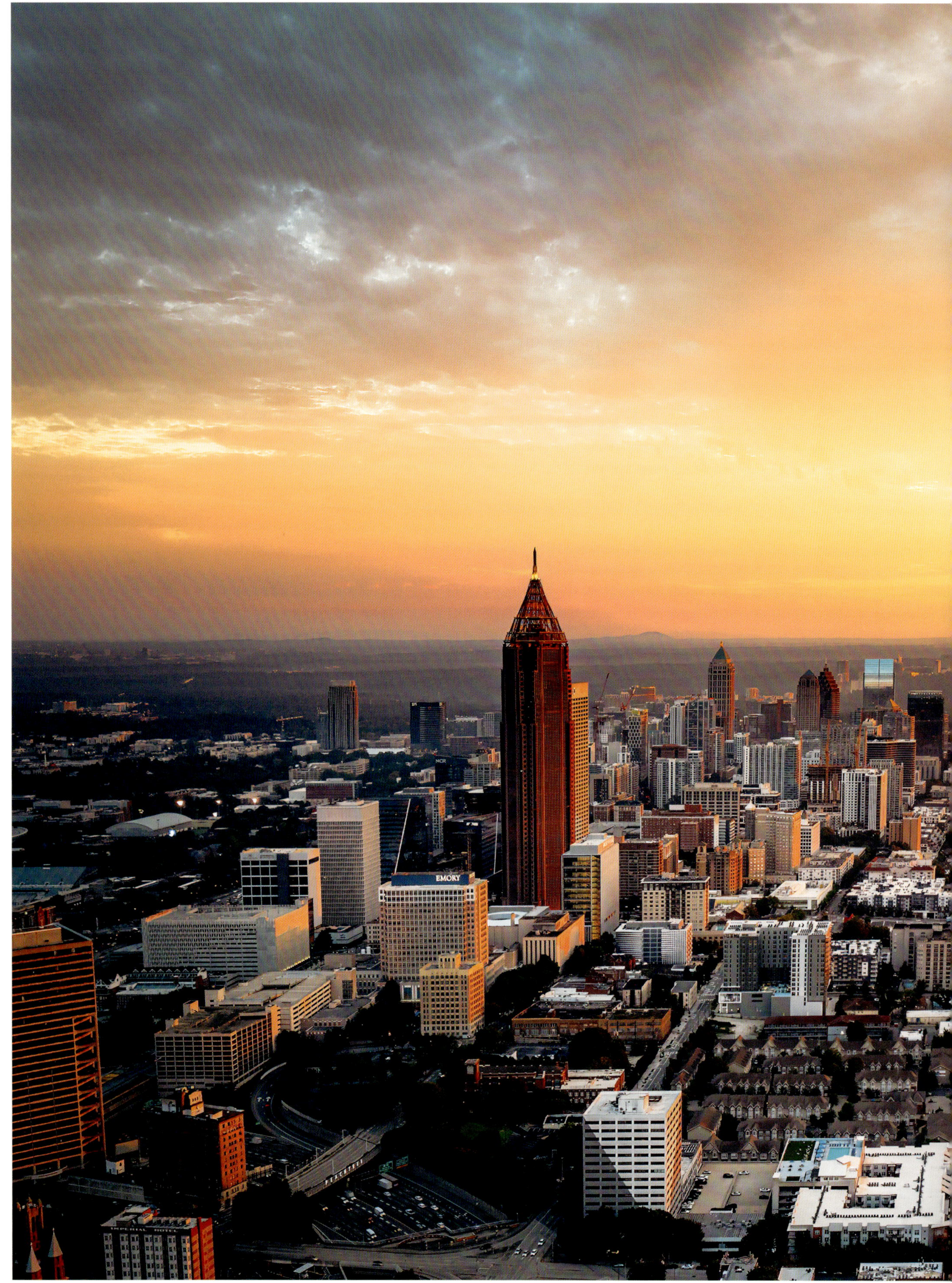

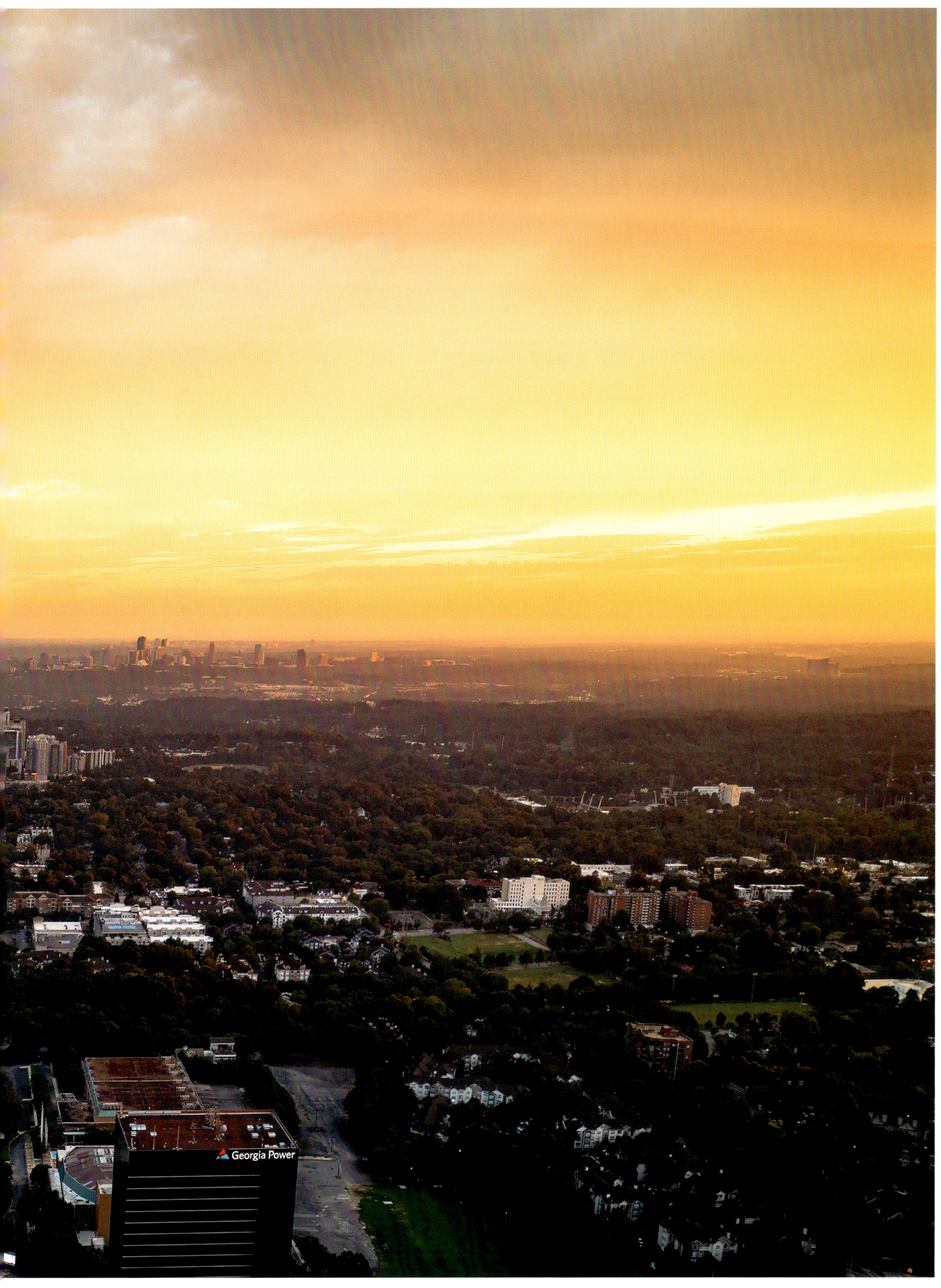
Georgia Power

A Hub for Business & Industry ◆ Renowned for its strategic location, world-class infrastructure, and dynamic economy, Atlanta has long been a magnet for entrepreneurs, innovators, and global corporations alike, making it a powerhouse of commerce and connectivity. A vibrant hub of business and transportation, a diverse array of companies spanning industries, including The Coca-Cola Company, Delta Air Lines, UPS, and Home Depot, all call Atlanta home. ◆ At the crossroads of major interstate highways and home to the world's busiest airport, Hartsfield-Jackson Atlanta International Airport, Atlanta boasts unparalleled accessibility and connectivity, serving as a vital gateway for both domestic and international travel. Hartsfield-Jackson connects Atlanta to every corner of the globe, facilitating seamless business transactions and fostering economic growth on a global scale. The city's extensive network of highways, railways, and public transit systems ensures efficient movement of goods and people throughout the region. ◆ Atlanta's public transportation system provides a network of buses and trains serving the city and surrounding areas. The MARTA Rail operates four rail lines, connecting various neighborhoods and suburbs to key destinations within the city limits, including downtown, Midtown, Buckhead, and the airport. The Atlanta Streetcar is a modern streetcar system that operates in downtown Atlanta, connecting key attractions such as the Martin Luther King Jr. National Historic Site, Centennial Olympic Park, and the Georgia State Capitol. ◆ Atlanta's business-friendly environment, coupled with its strategic location and world-class transportation infrastructure, has solidified its position as a leading center for commerce and connectivity in the Southeast. A city on the rise, Atlanta embodies the spirit of innovation, opportunity, and entrepreneurship.

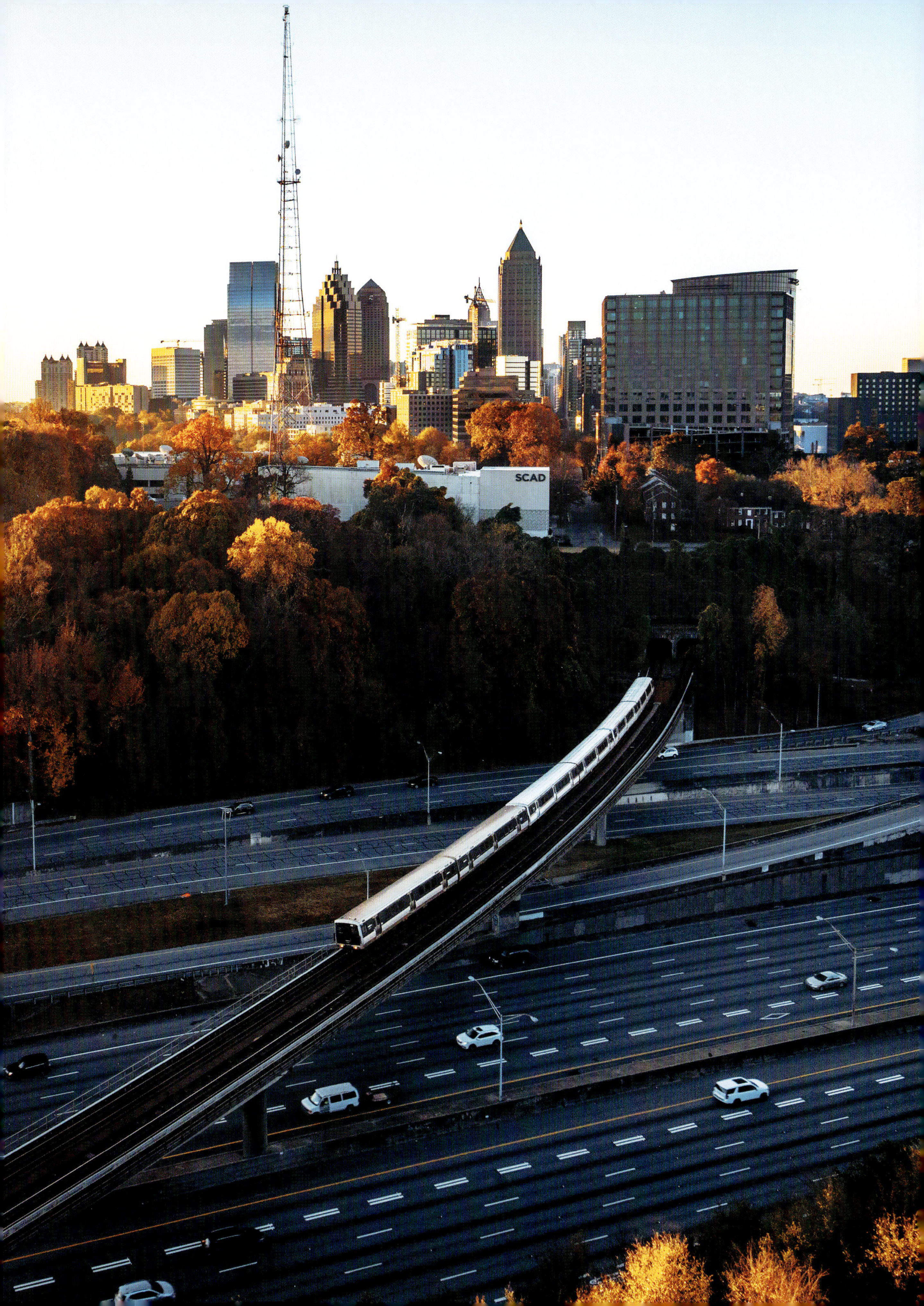

SCAD

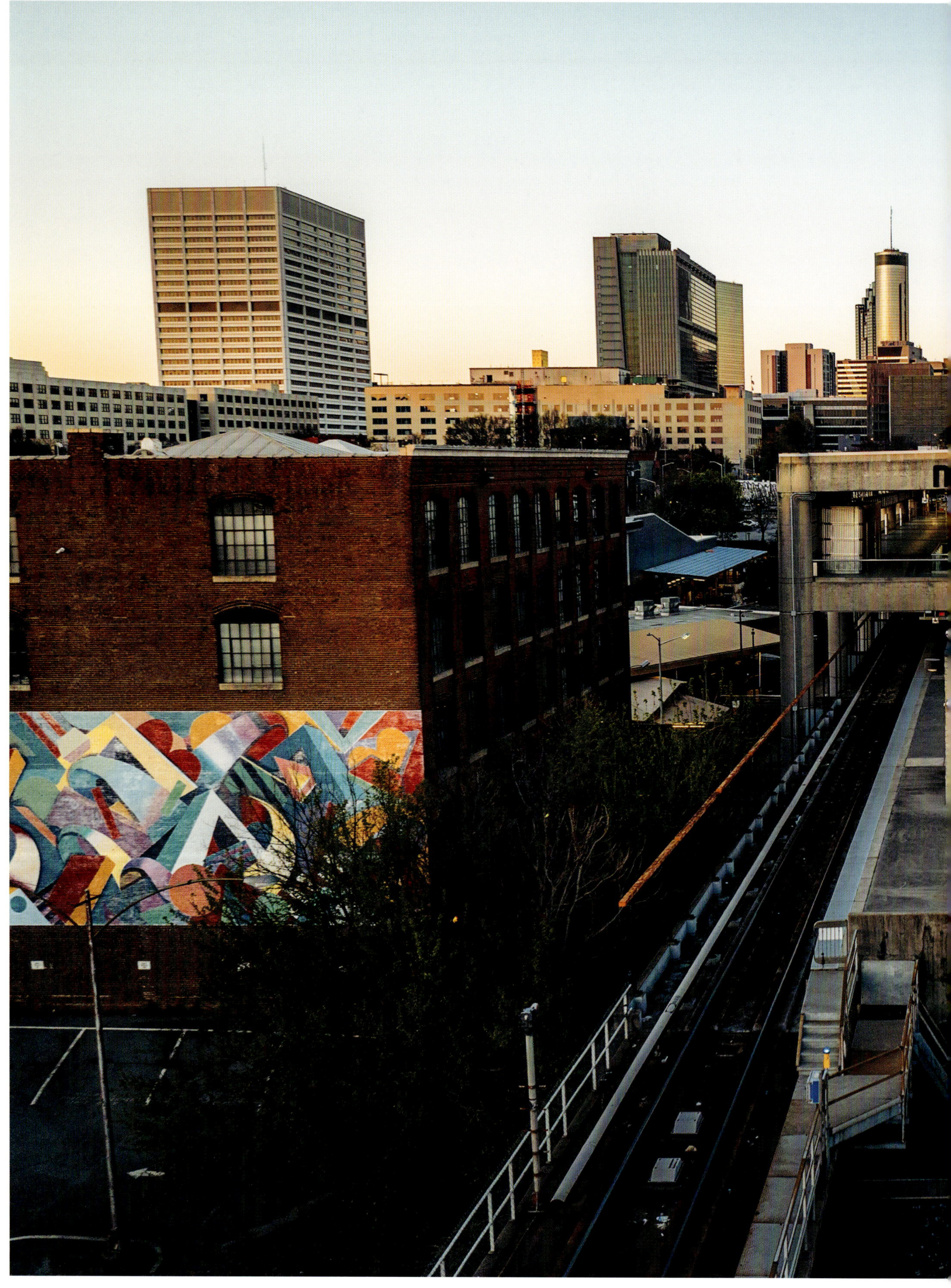

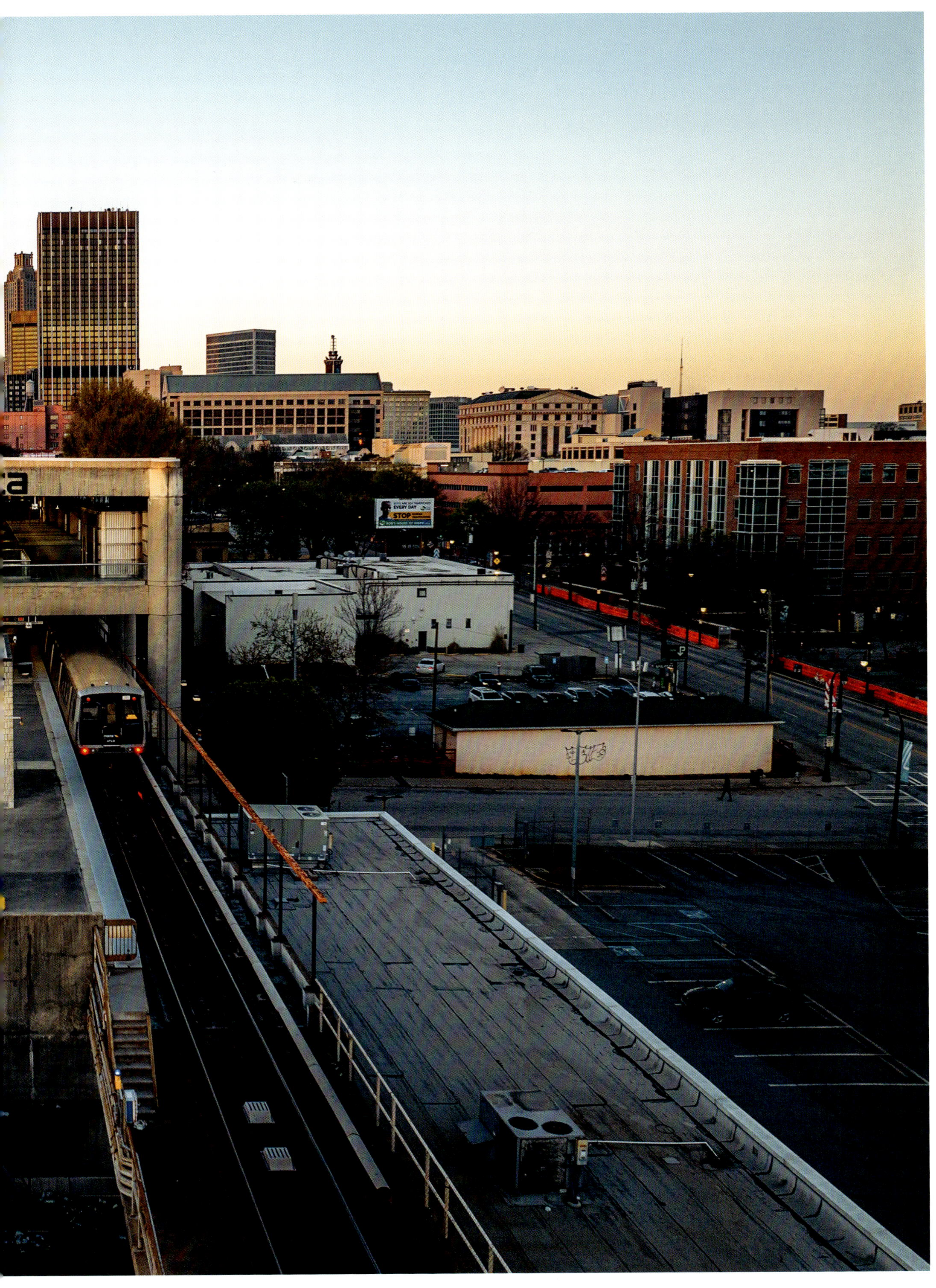

BOYS ARE SEX TRAFFICKED
EVERY DAY
STOP
BOB'S HOUSE OF HOPE

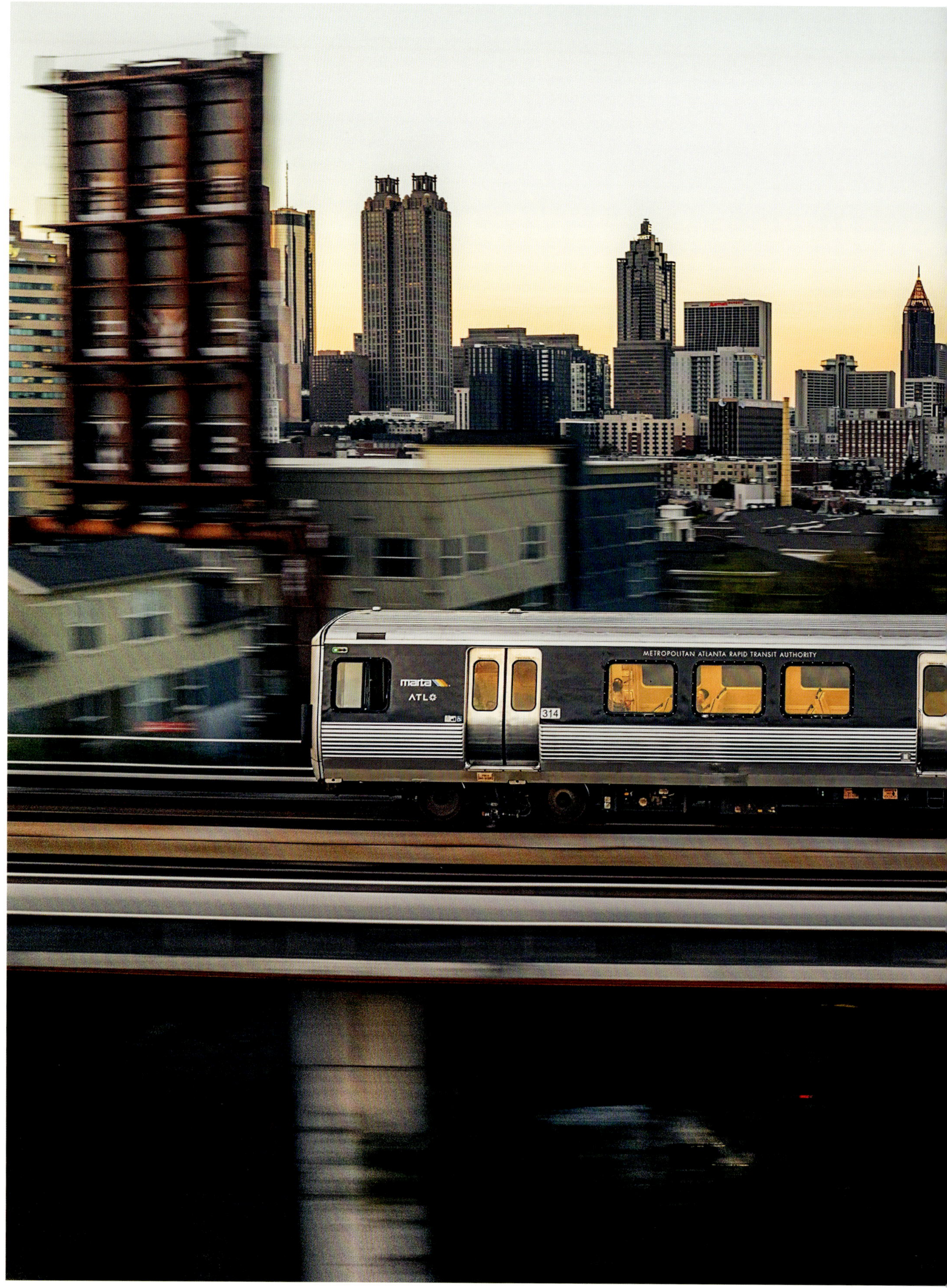

marta
ATL
314
METROPOLITAN ATLANTA RAPID TRANSIT AUTHORITY

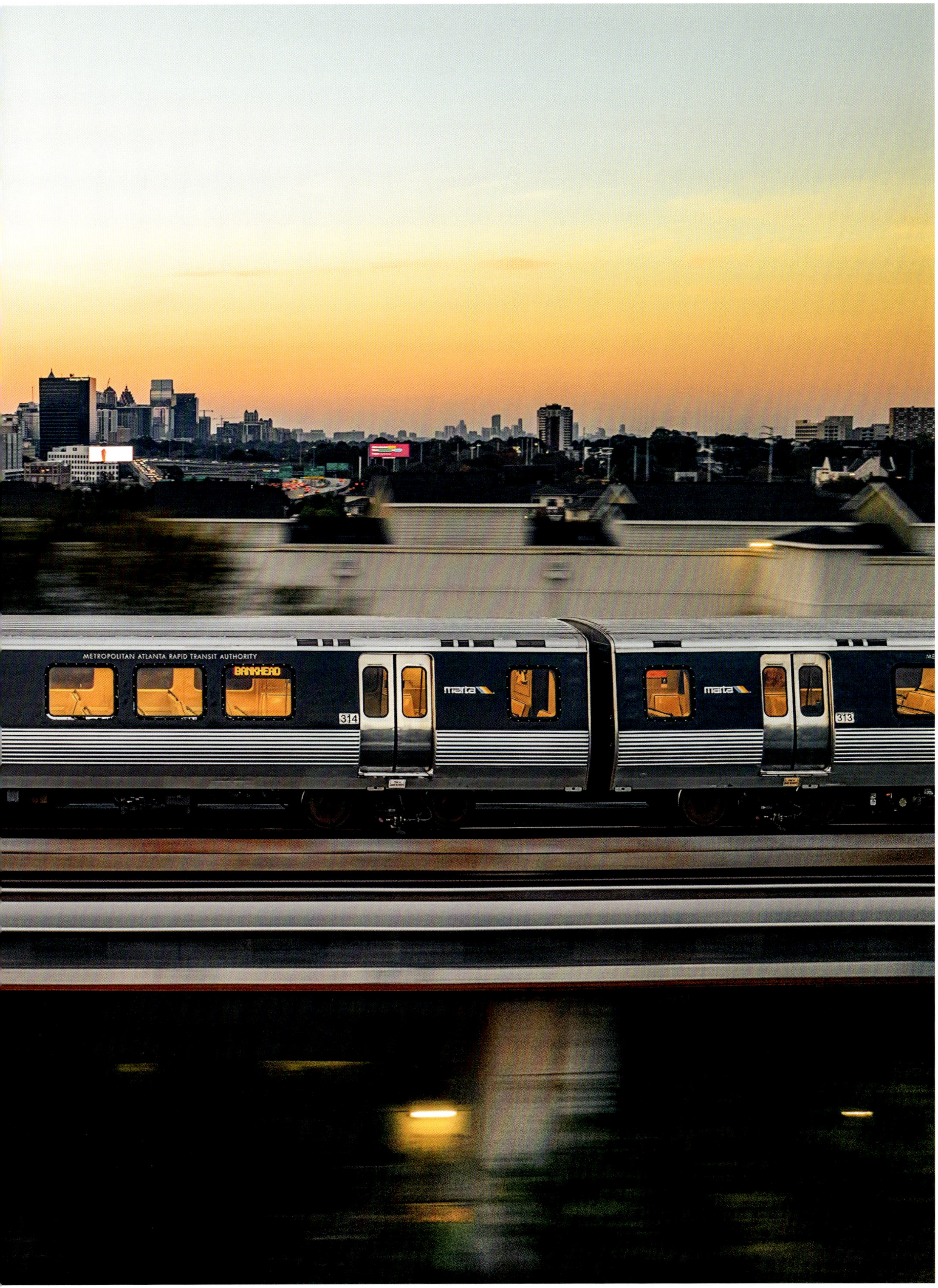

METROPOLITAN ATLANTA RAPID TRANSIT AUTHORITY
BANKHEAD
marta
314
marta
313

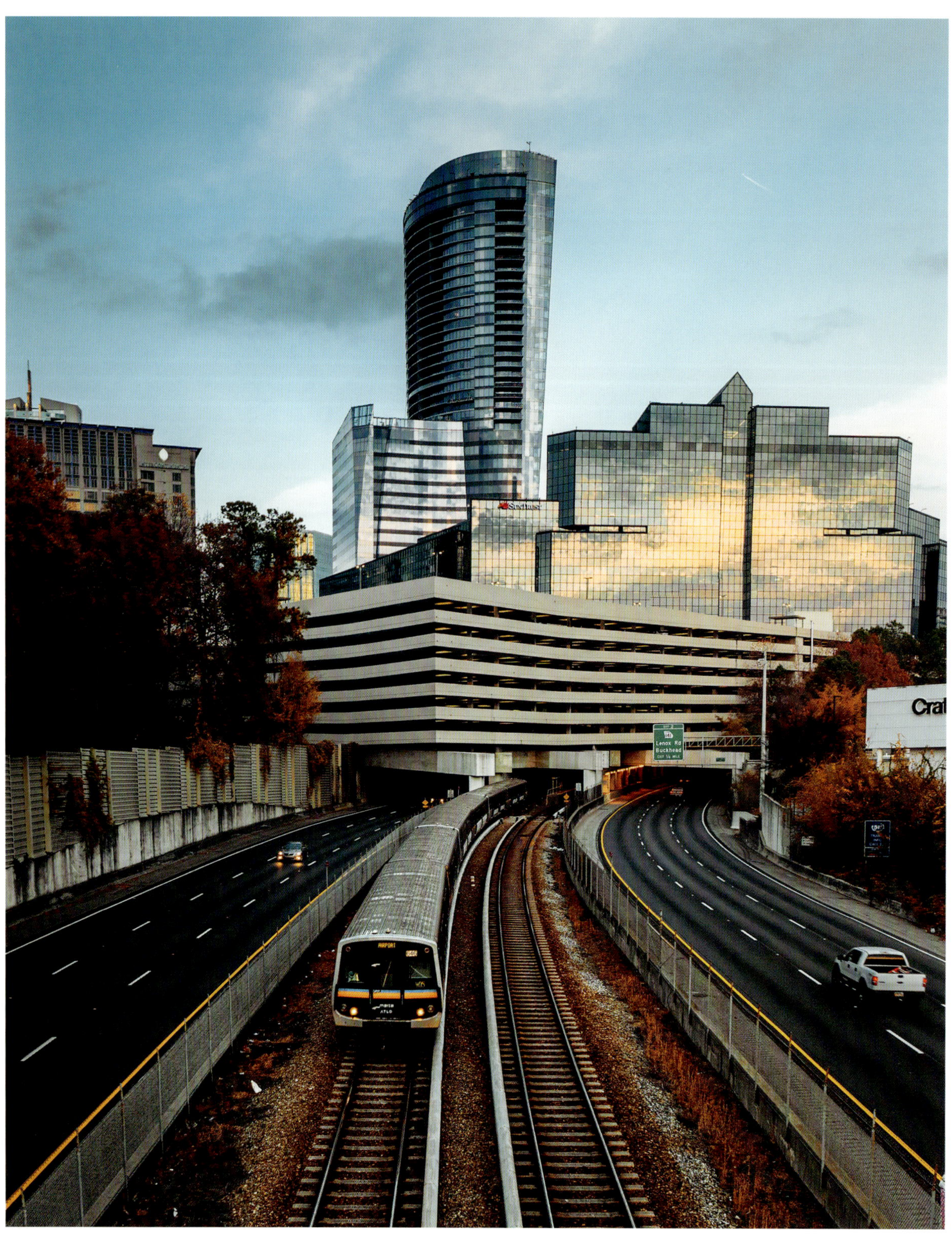
Lenox Rd
Buckhead
EXIT ½ MILE
AIRPORT
marta
ATL

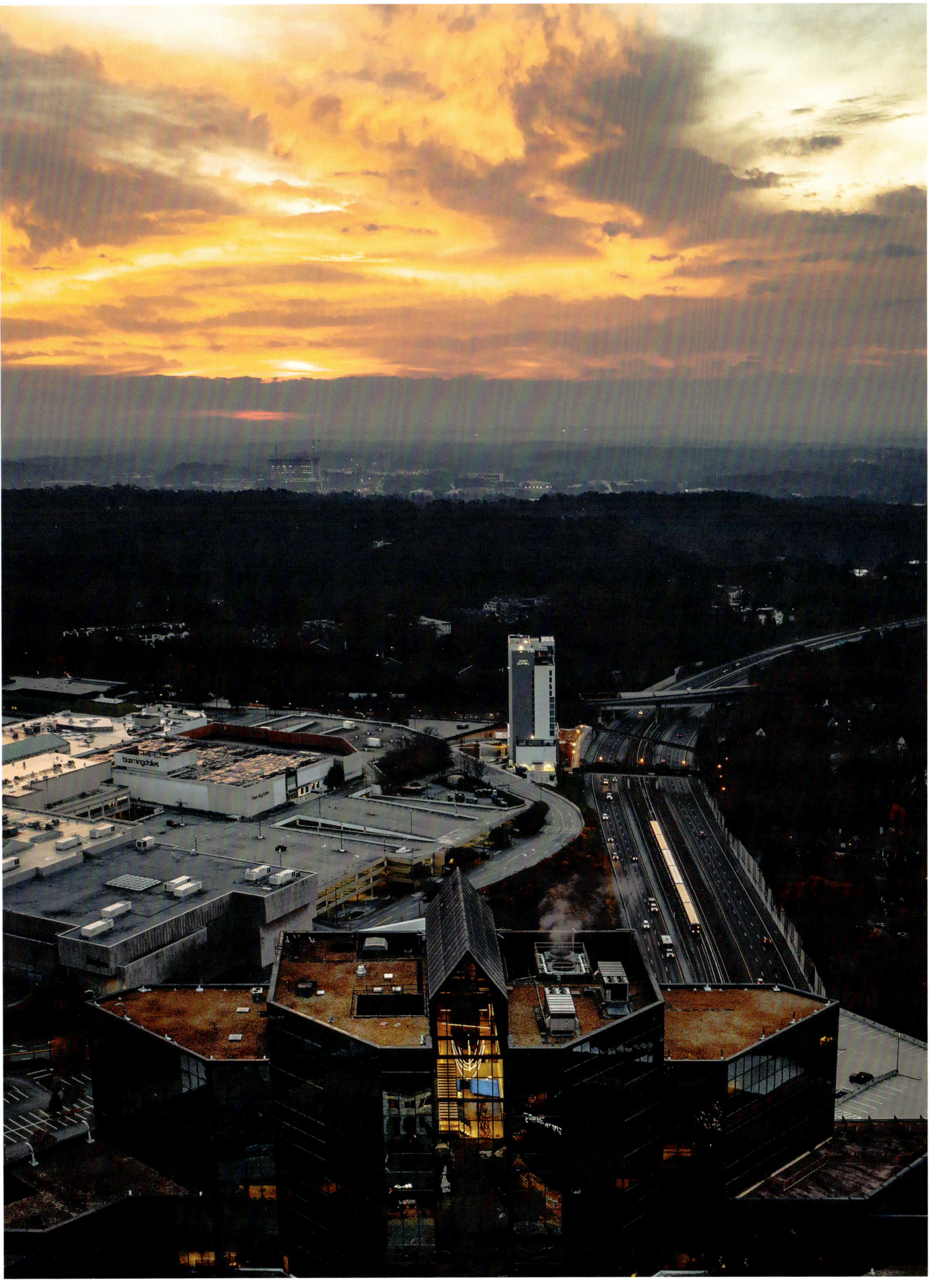

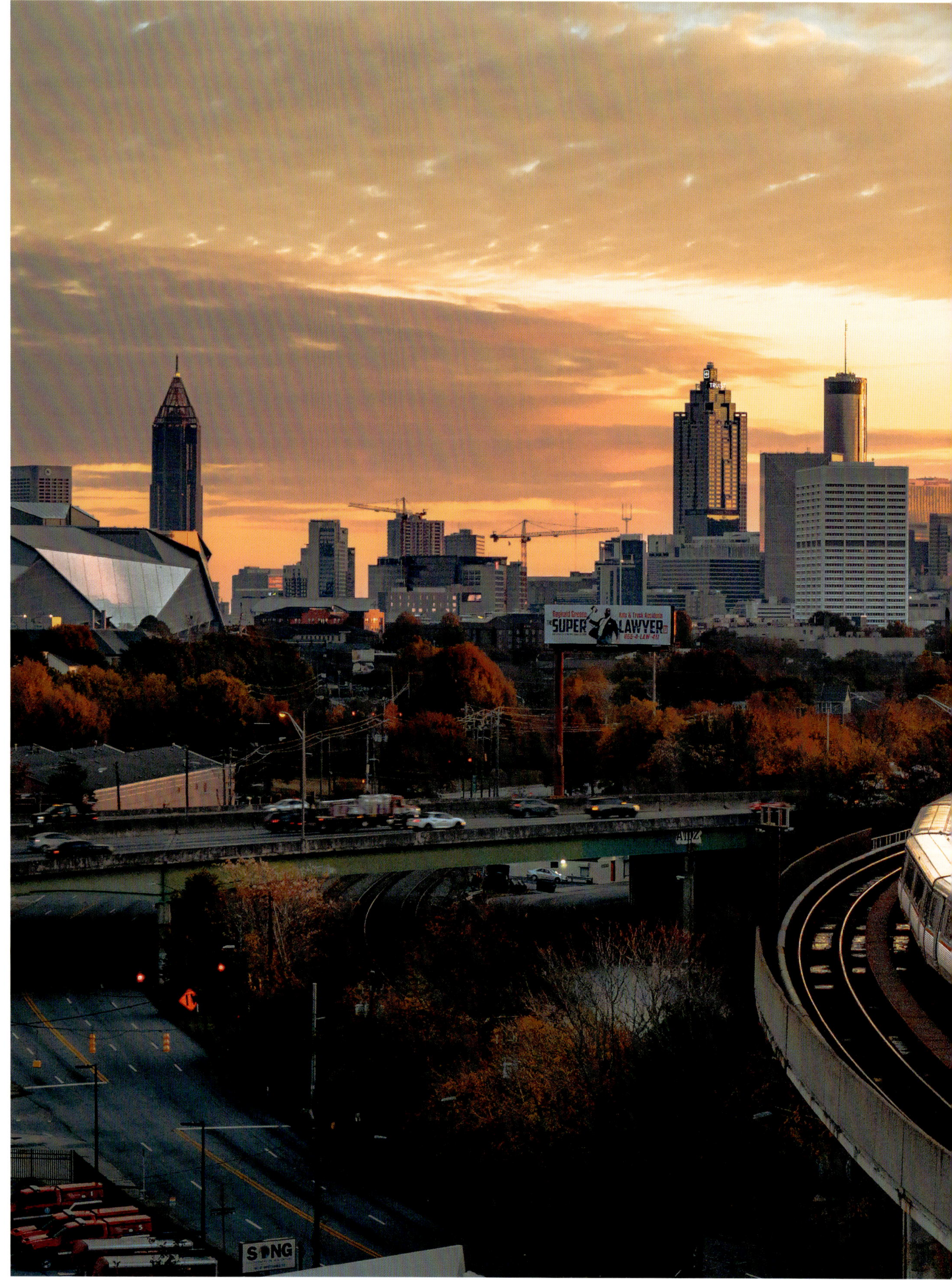

SUPER LAWYER

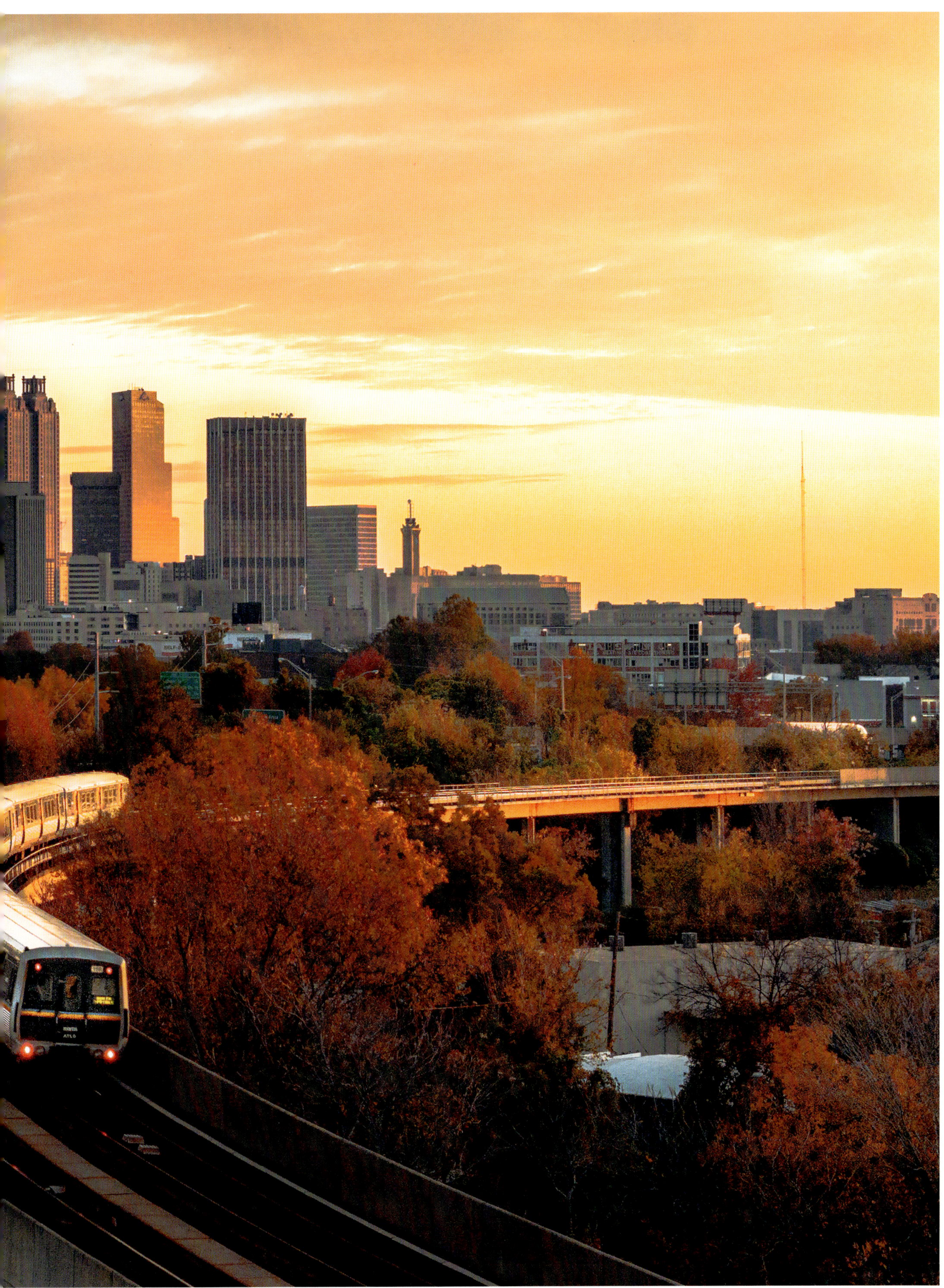

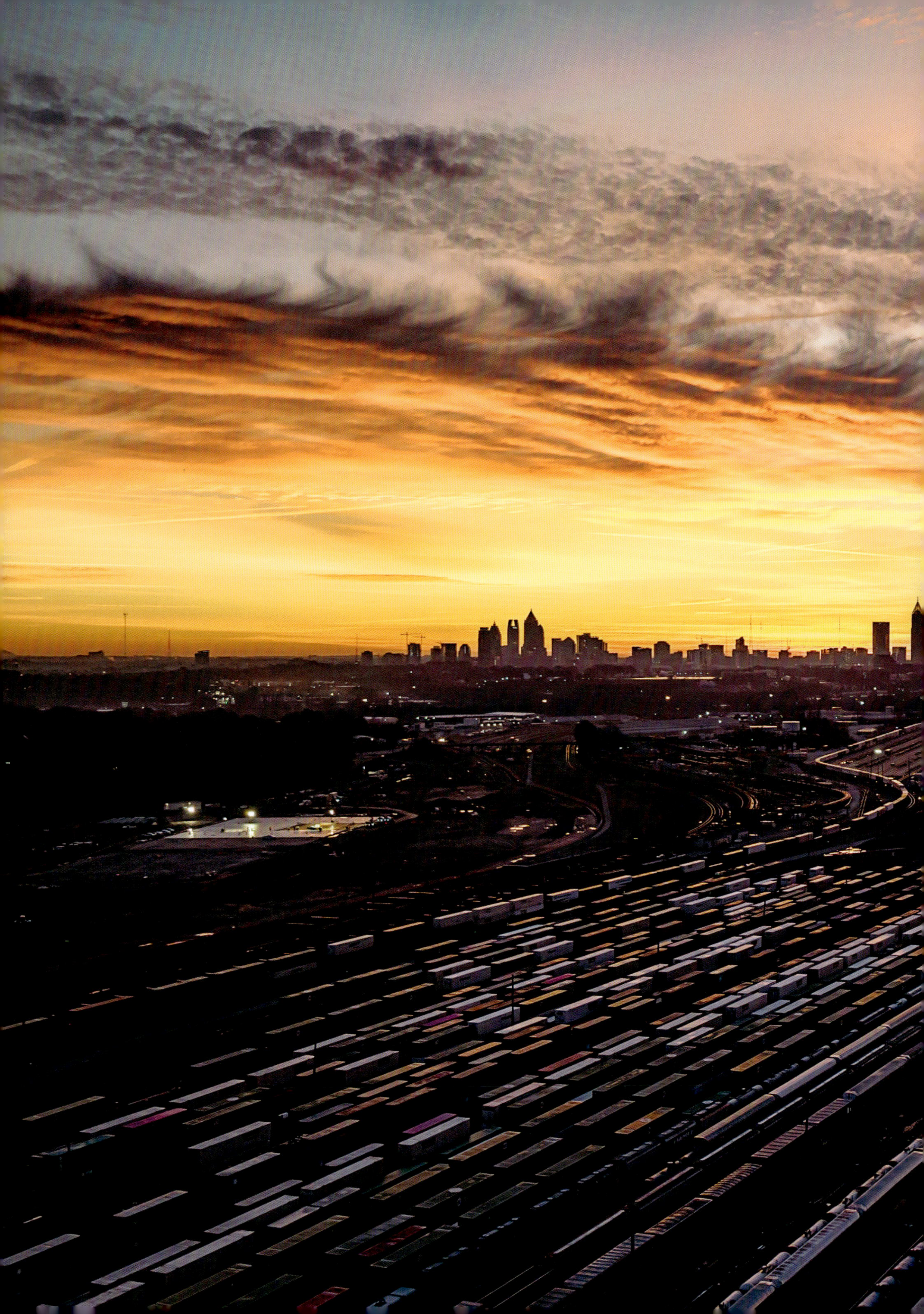

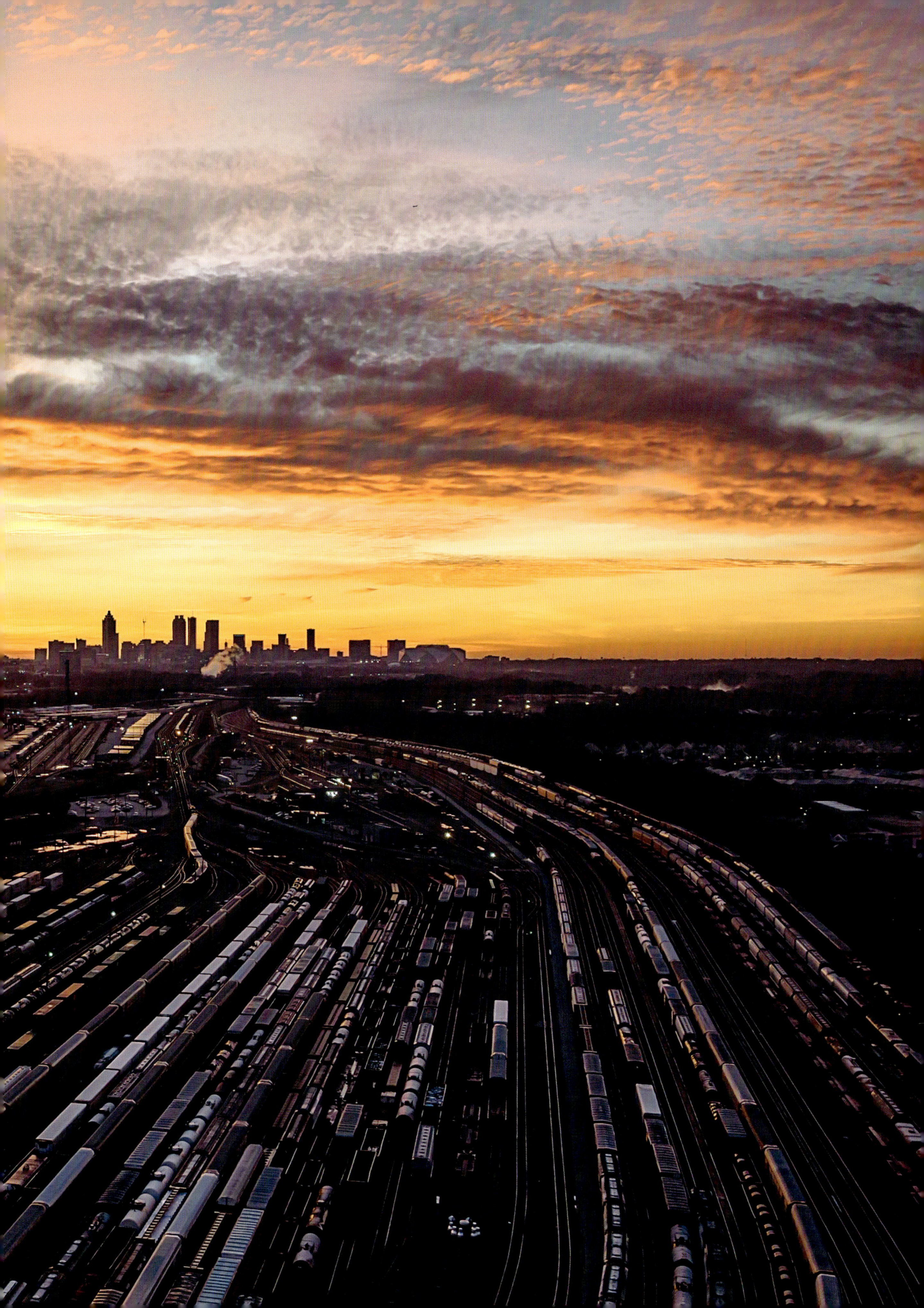

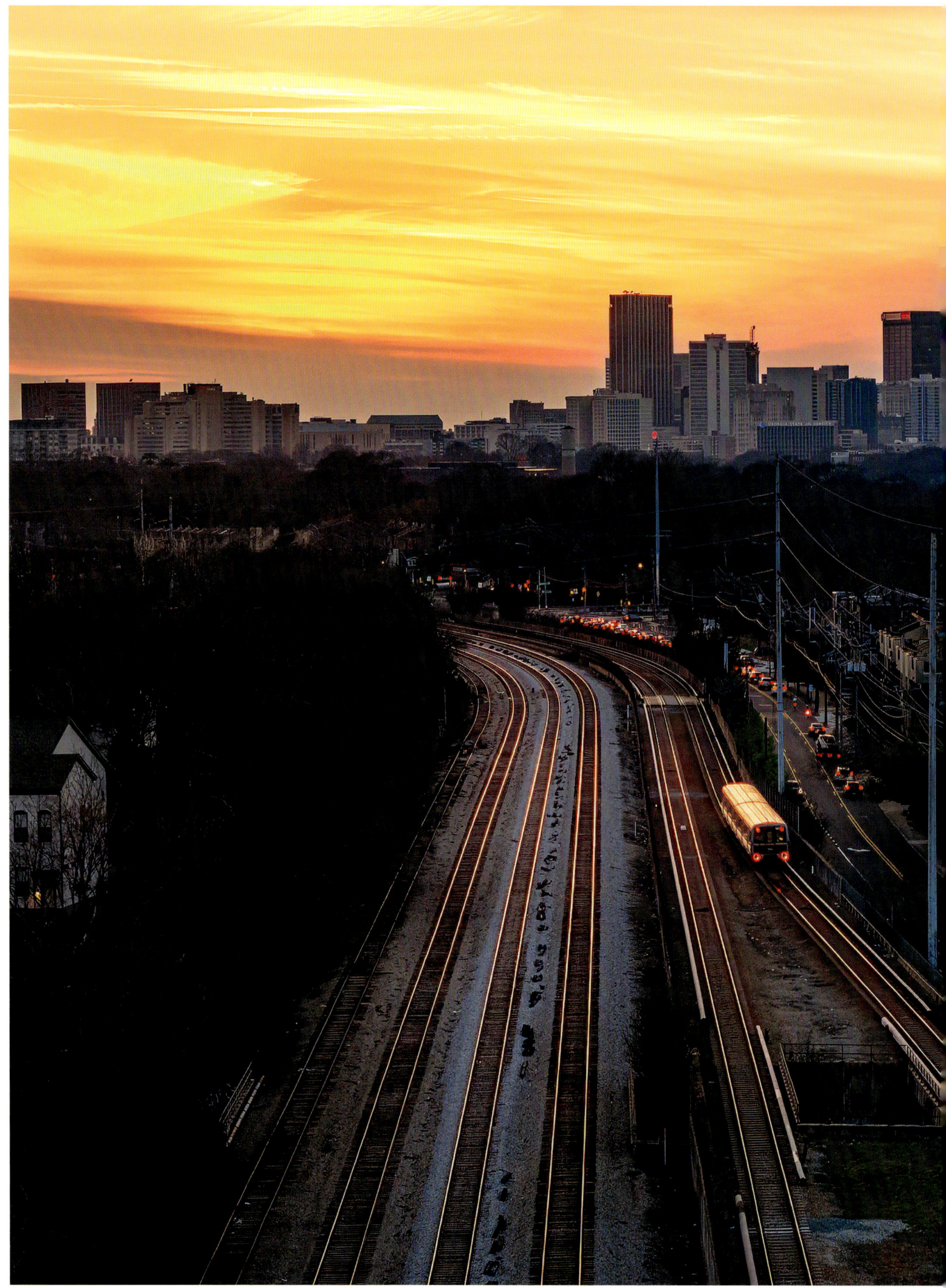

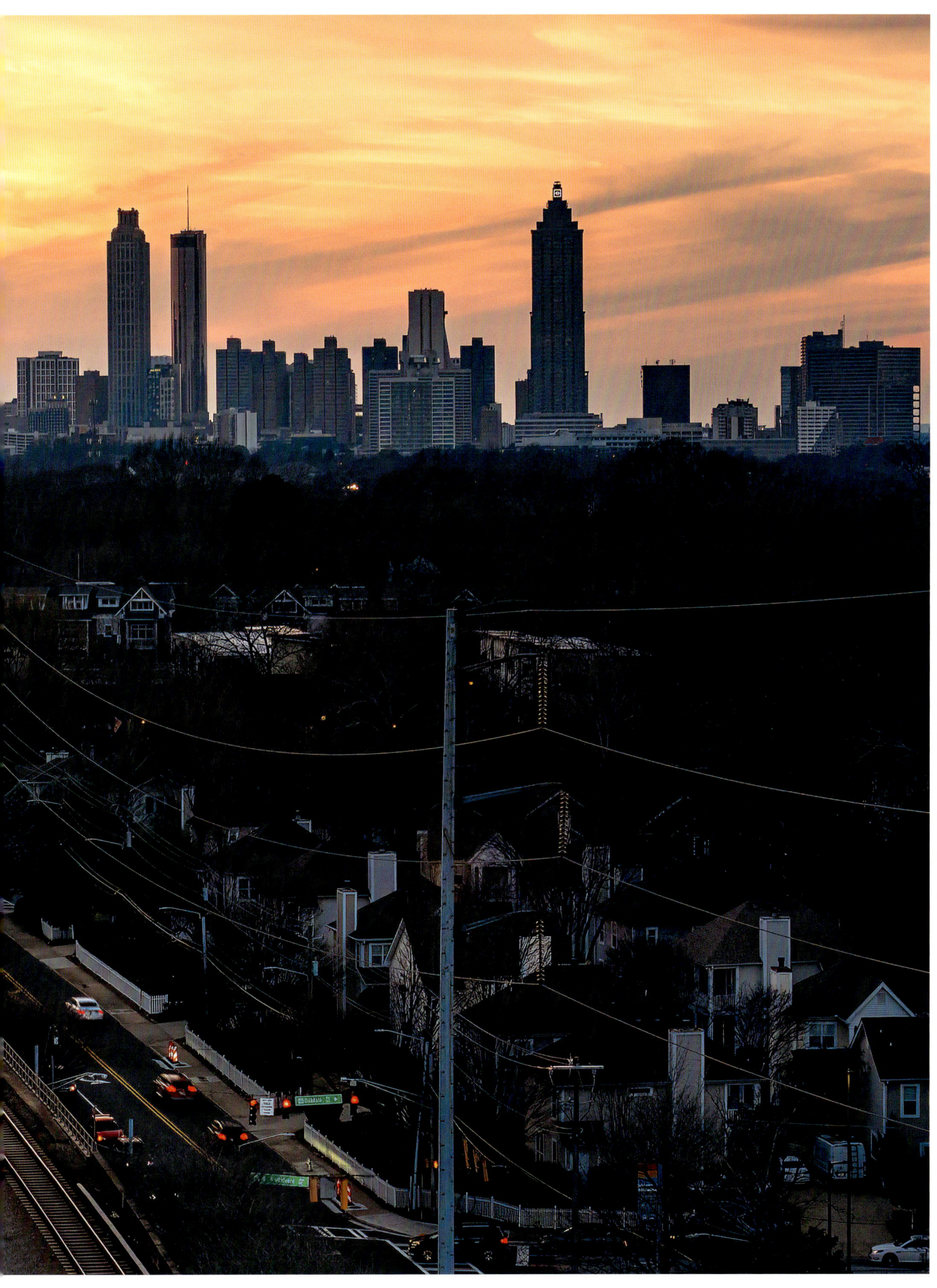

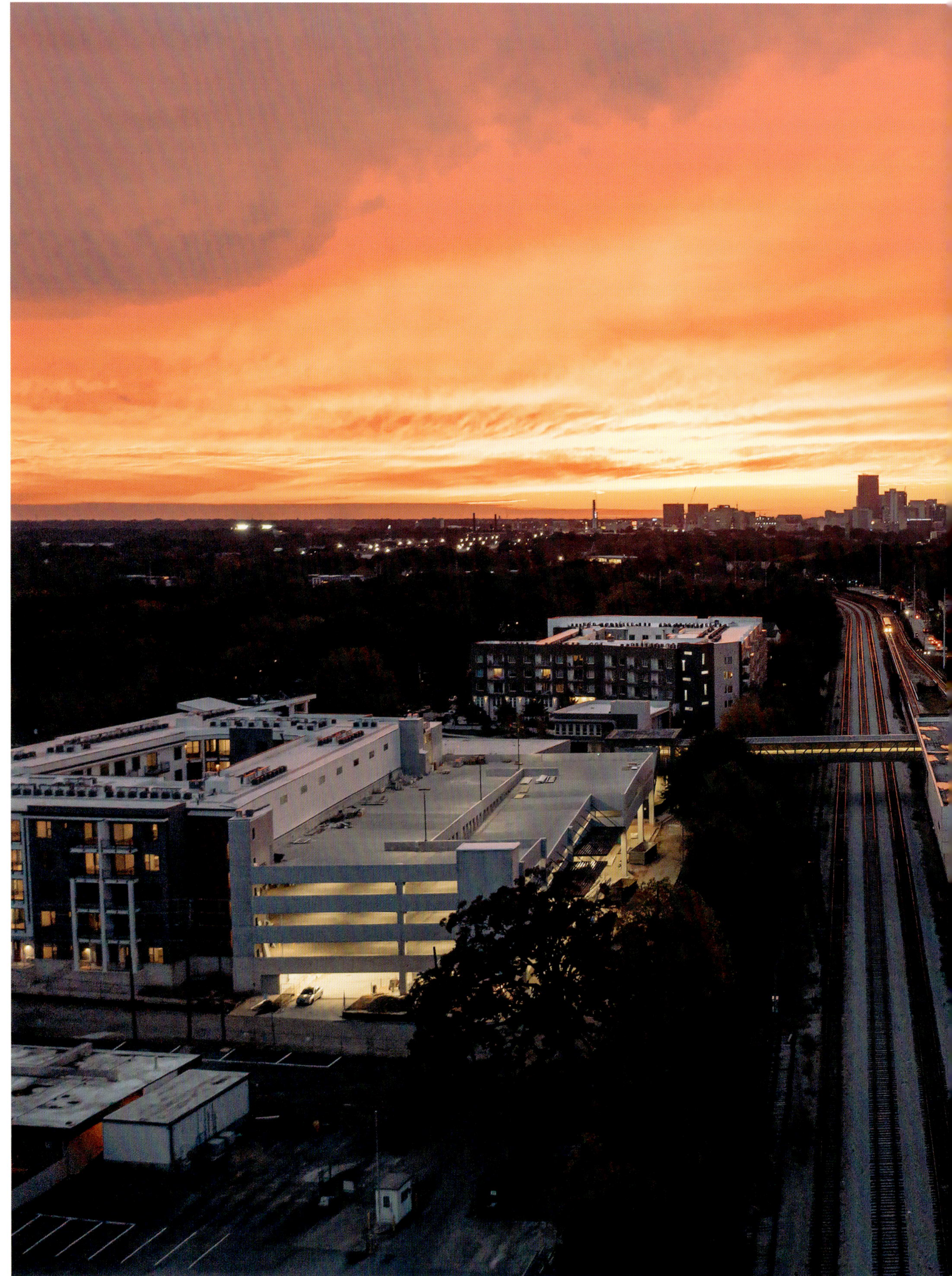

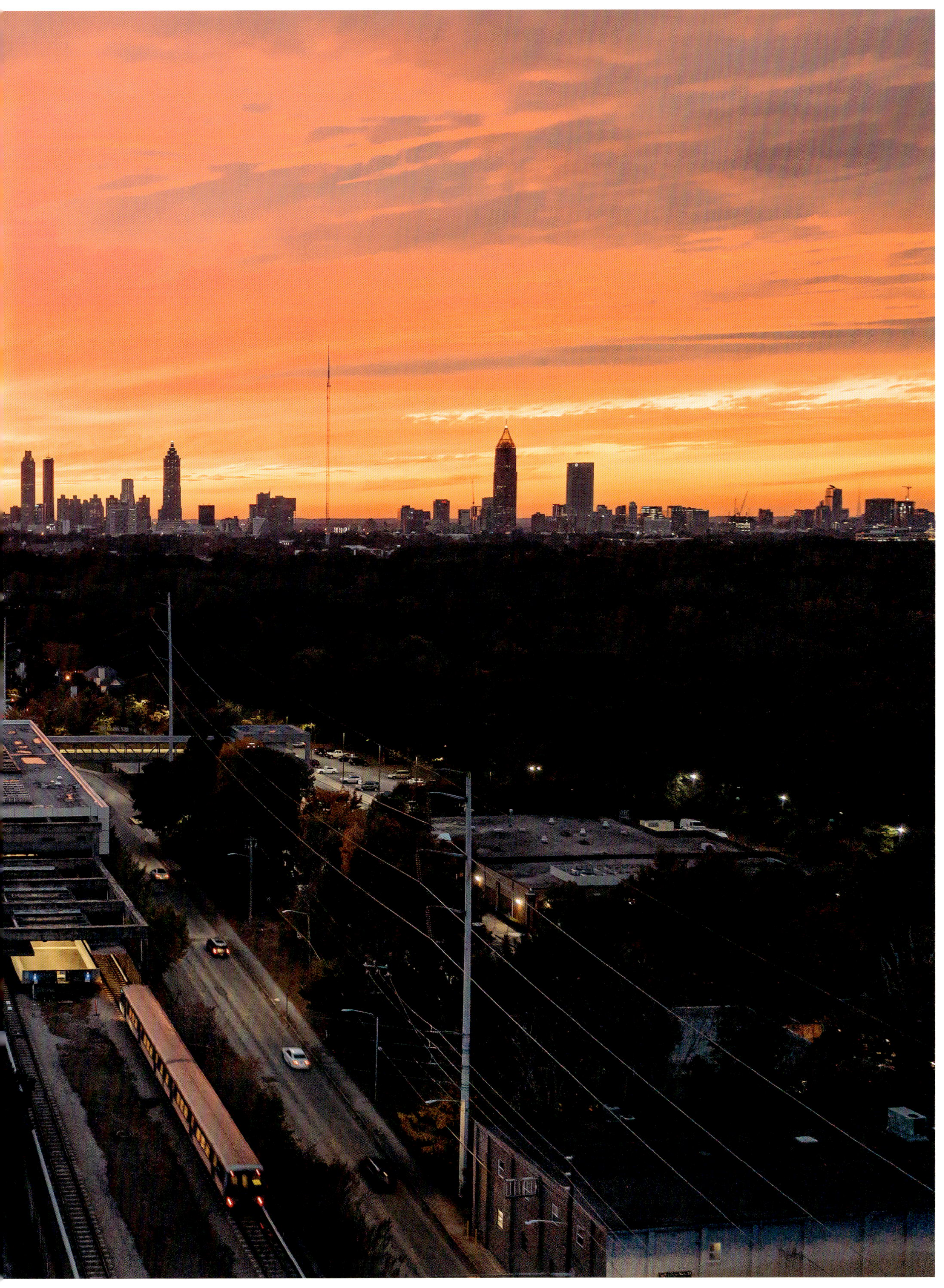

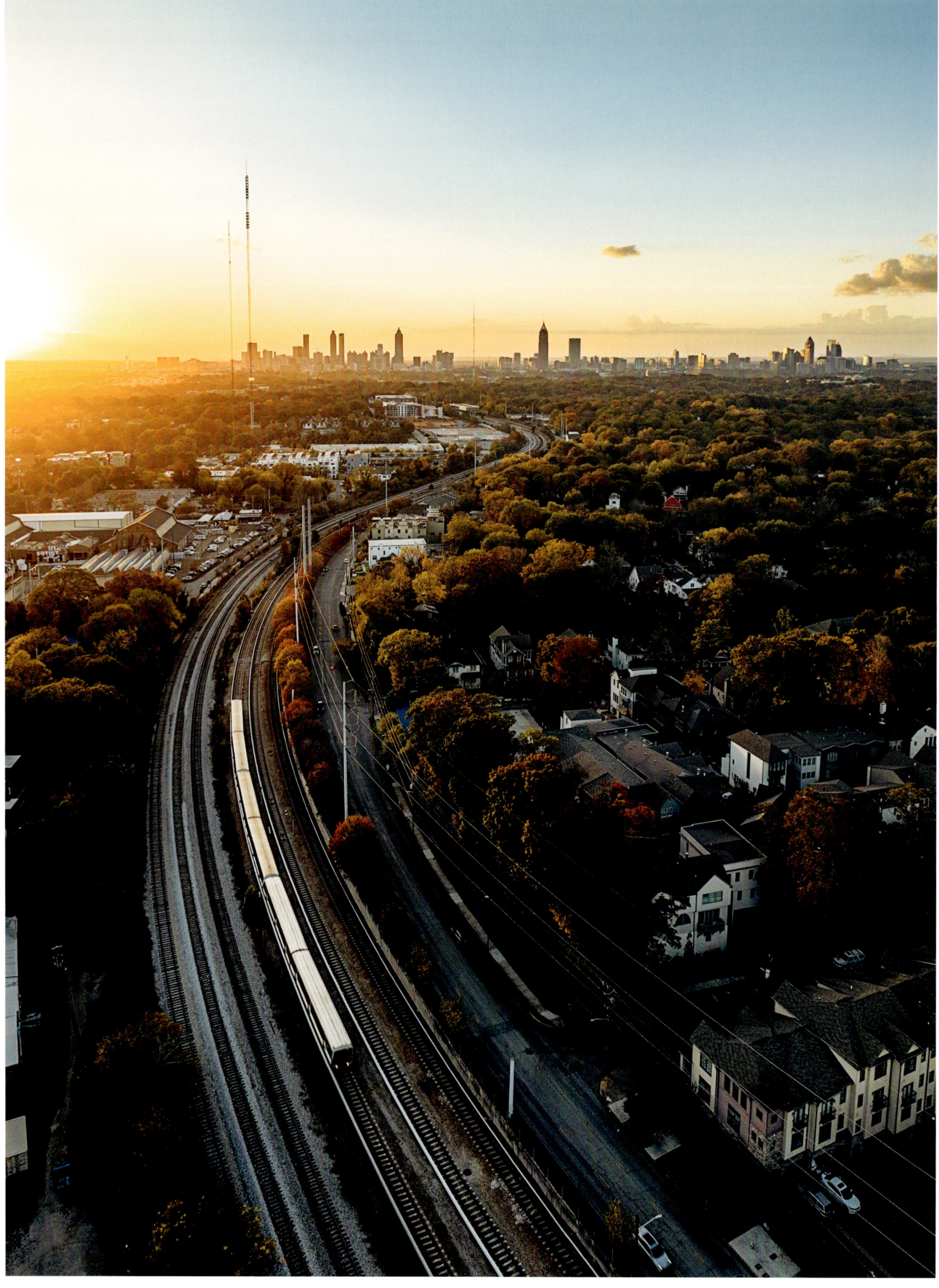

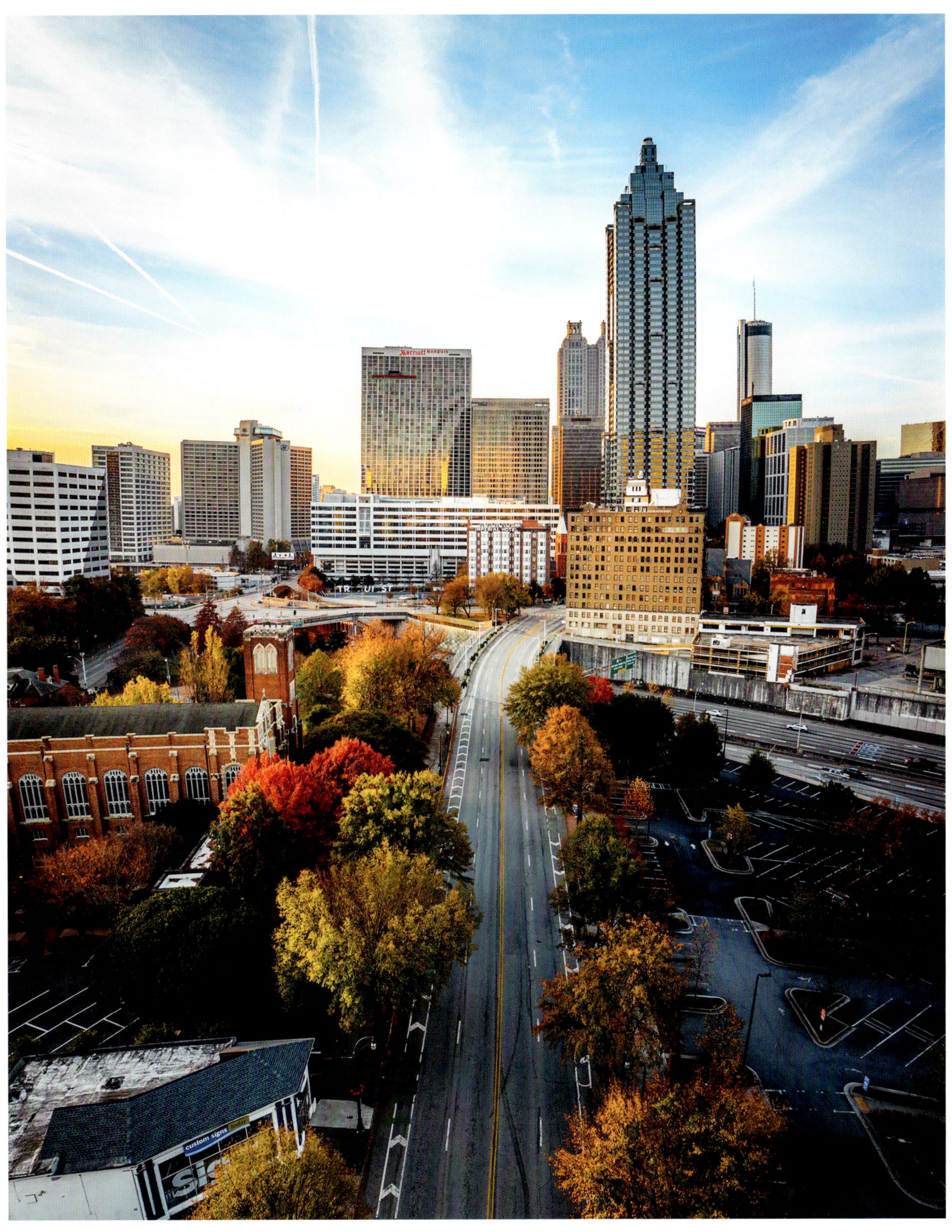

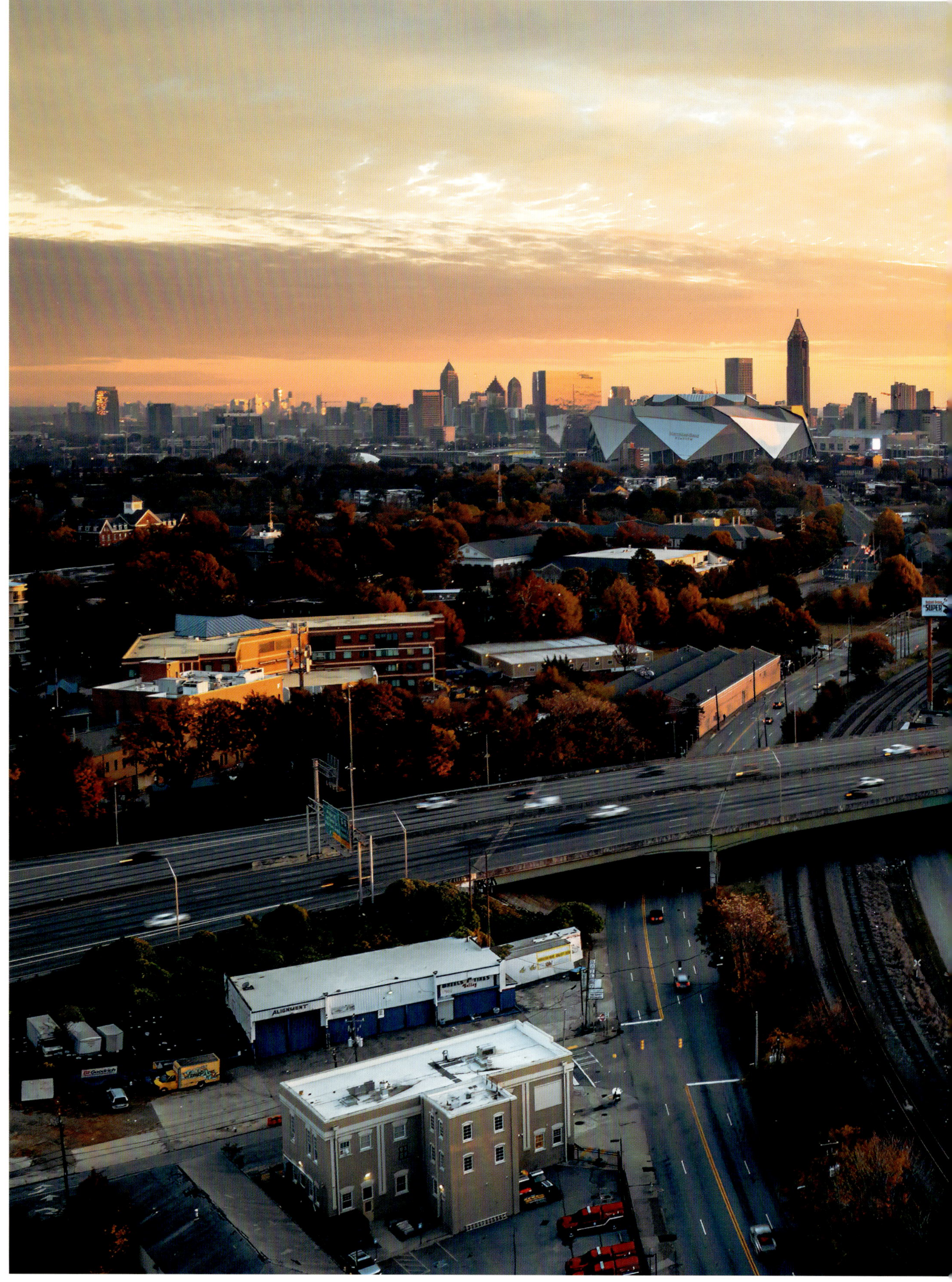

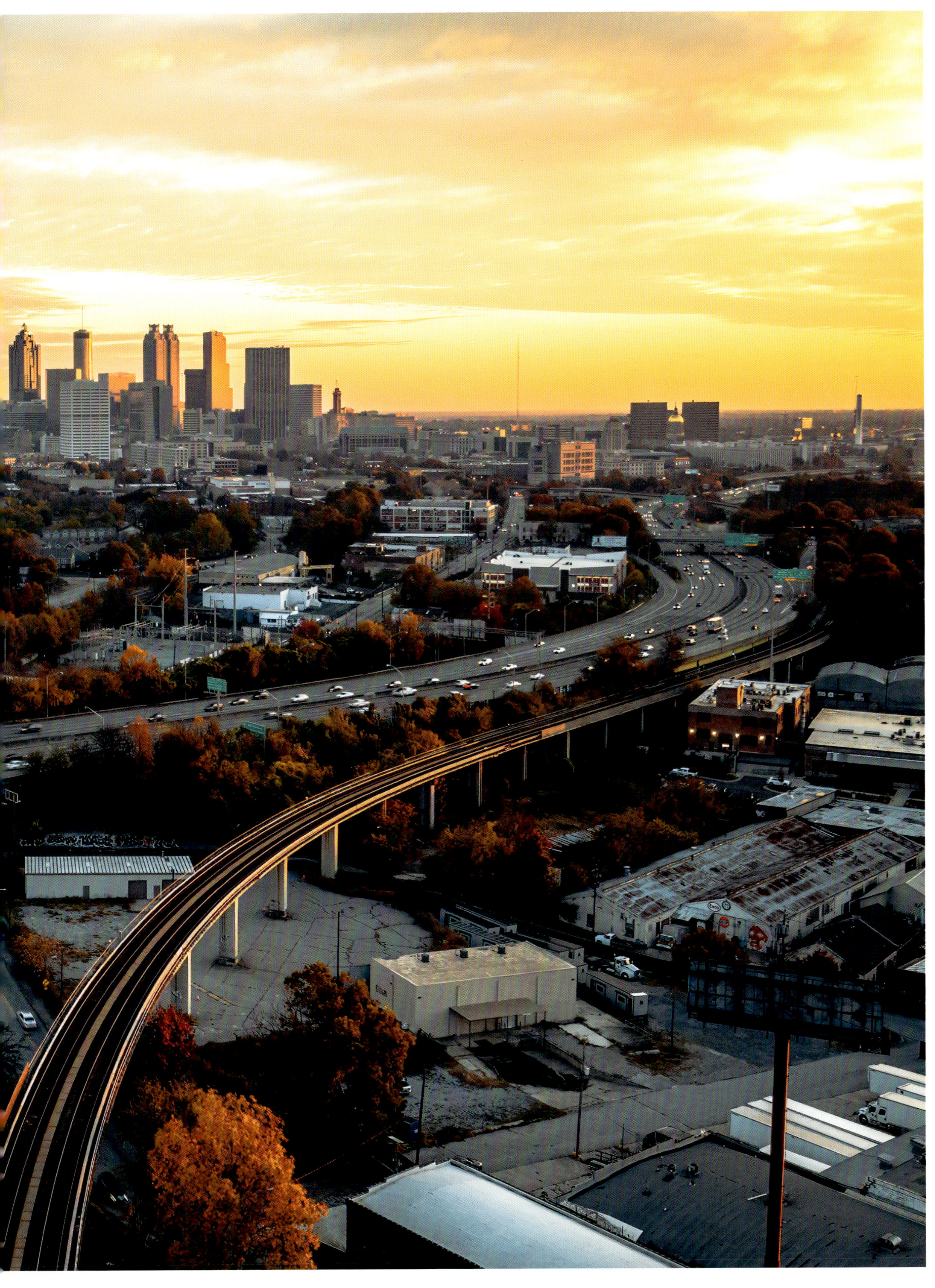

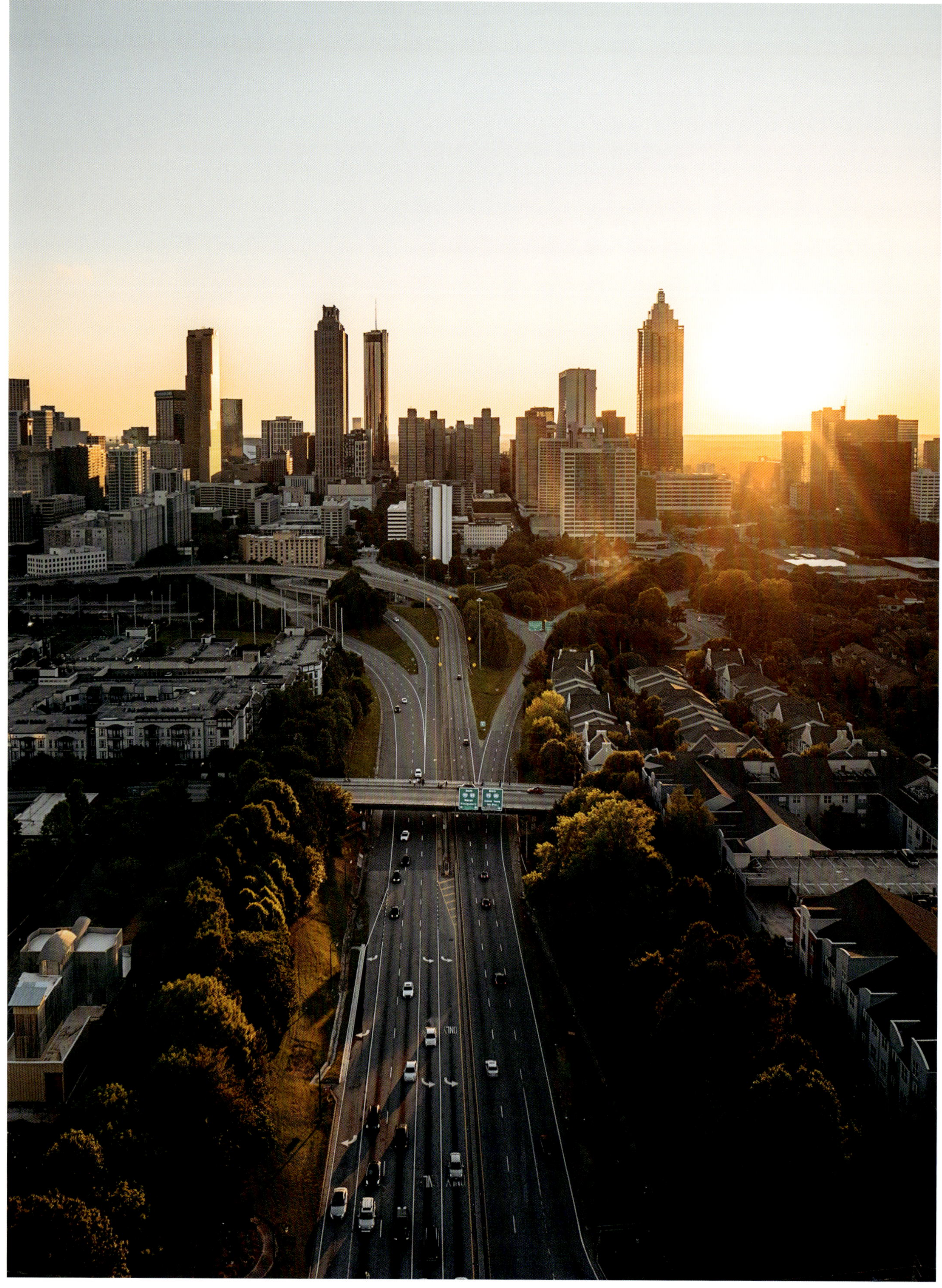

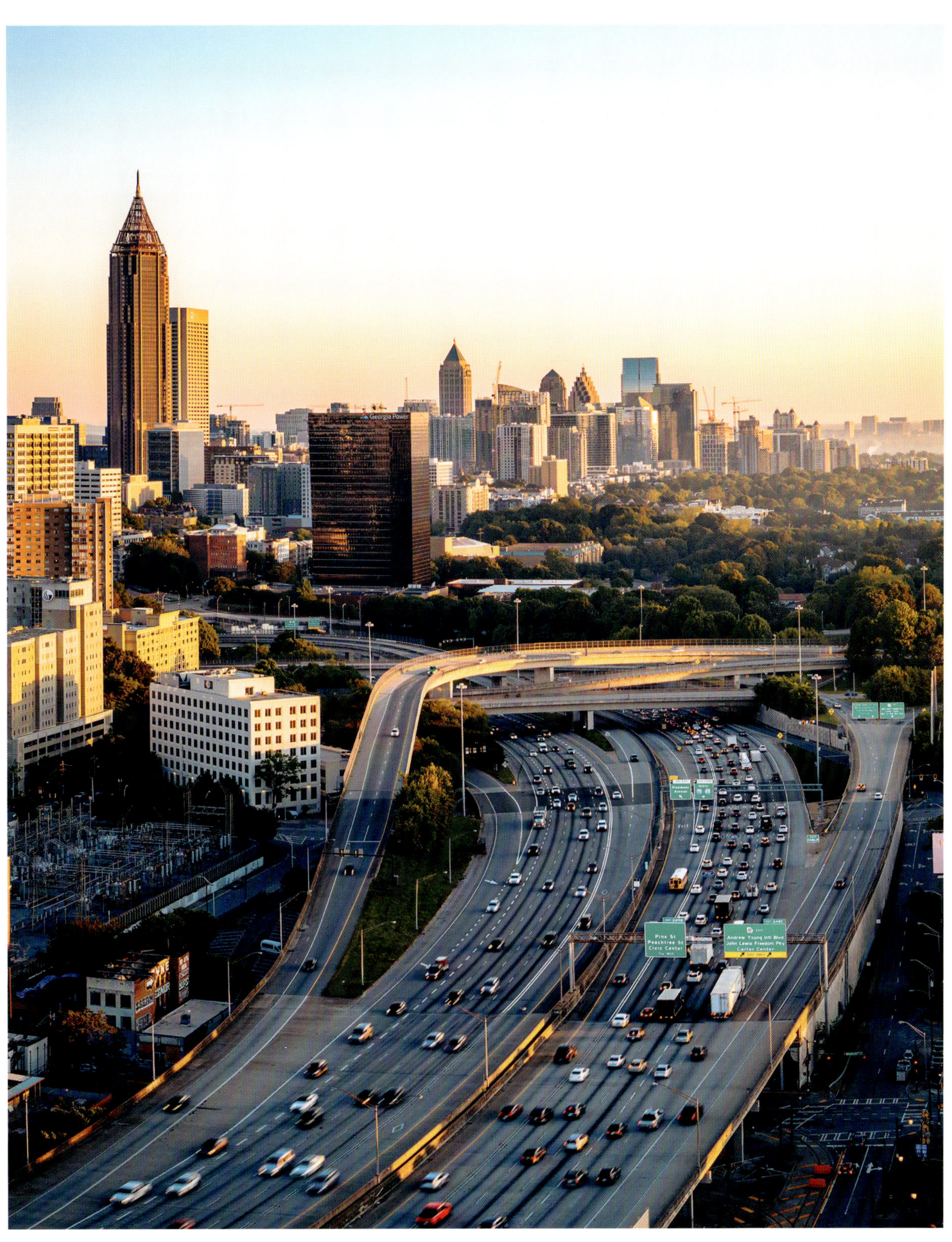

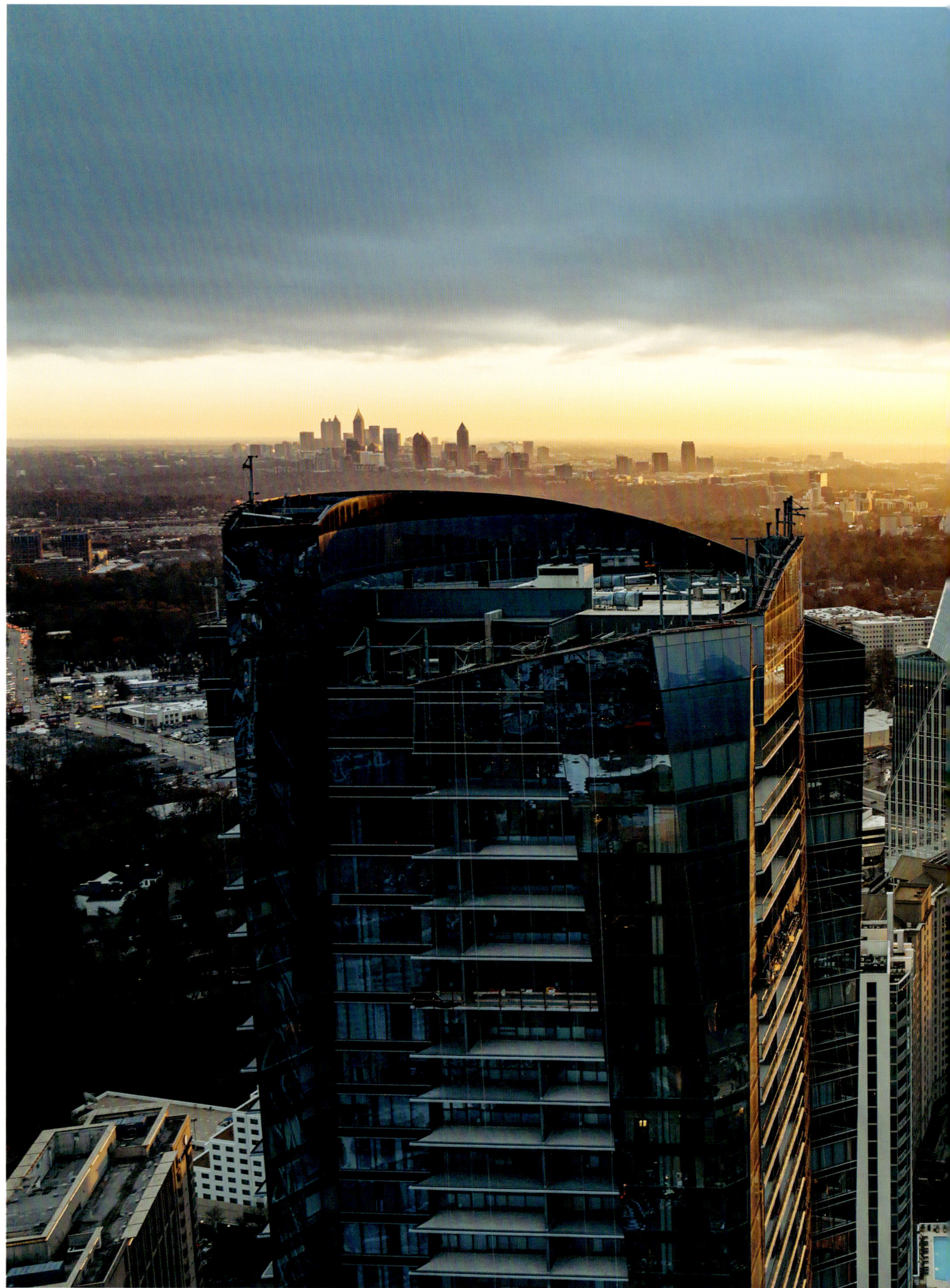

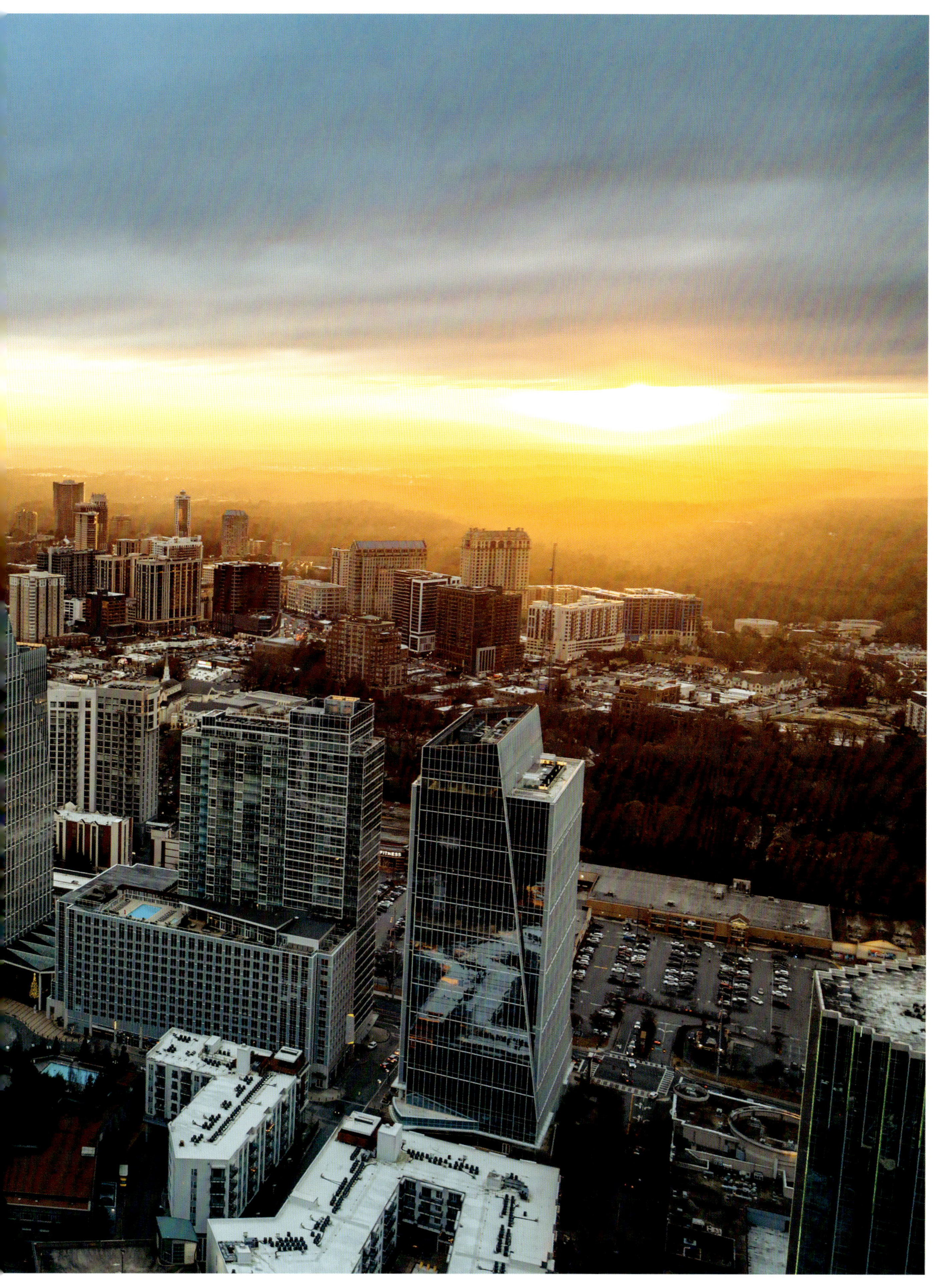

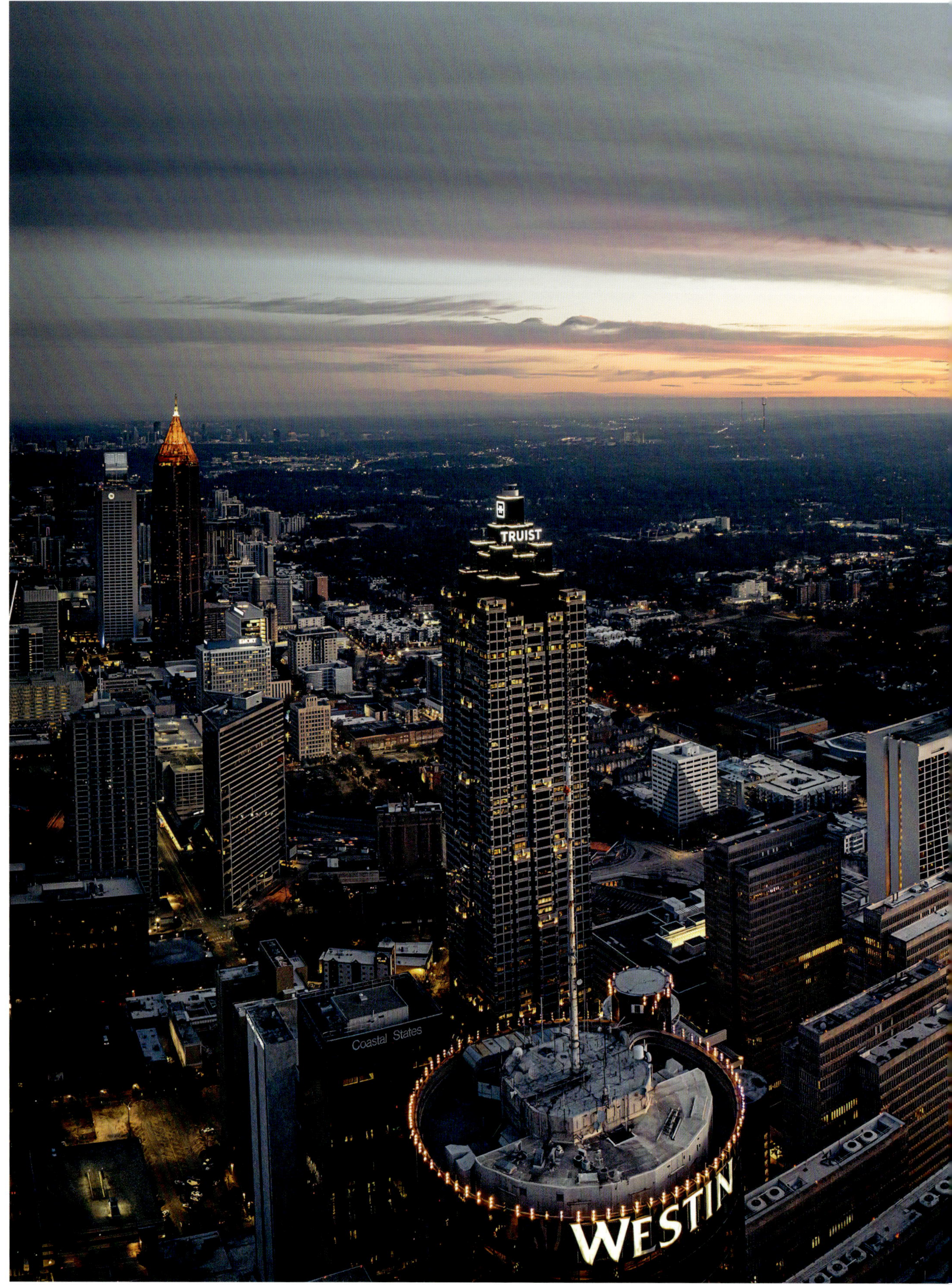

TRUIST
Coastal States
WESTIN

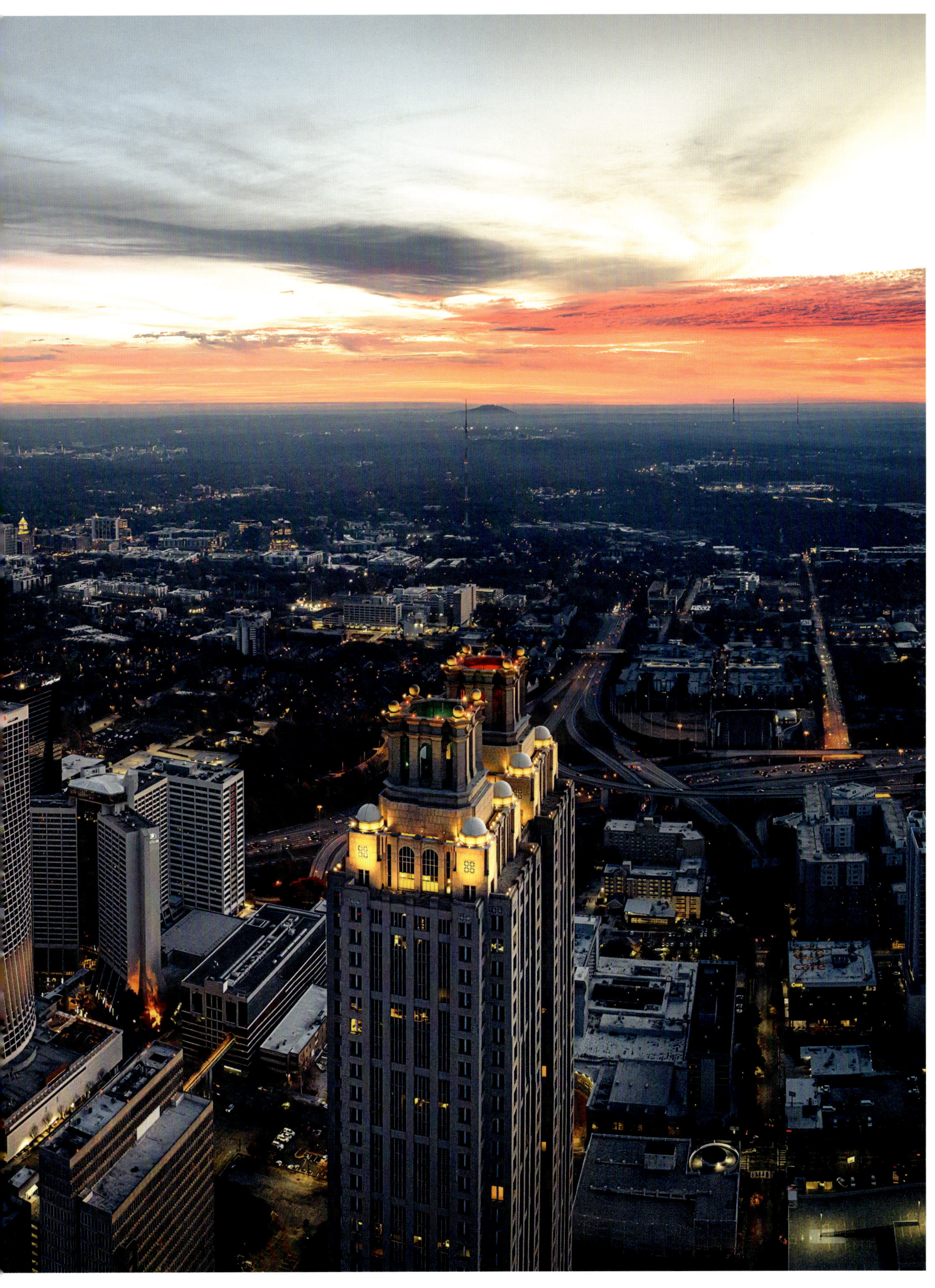

A History of Activism ♦ Often referred to as the "cradle of the civil rights movement," Atlanta is a key hub for activism and leadership. Atlanta's civil rights movement dates back to the late 19th and early 20th centuries. Institutions such as Atlanta University and Morehouse College nurtured a generation of African American leaders and Atlanta was home to prominent civil rights leaders, including Martin Luther King Jr., who was born and raised in the city. ♦ Emerging as a central figure in the civil rights movement, King's legacy is preserved in the city's Martin Luther King Jr. National Historical Park. Located in the Sweet Auburn neighborhood, the site includes King's birth home, the Ebenezer Baptist Church, the King Center for Nonviolent Social Change, and the Historic Fire Station No. 6, which houses a museum dedicated to King's legacy. A statue of King with his arms crossed, reflecting his determination in the face of adversity, stands prominently at the entrance to the park. ♦ When future President of the United States Jimmy Carter became Governor of Georgia, he made civil rights a central part of this agenda. Making his inaugural address at the Georgia State Capitol on January 12, 1971, he boldly declared that "the time for racial discrimination is over." In partnership with Atlanta's Emory University, Carter and his wife, Rosalynn, founded The Carter Center, a nonprofit organization that works to advance human rights and alleviate human suffering. ♦ A civil rights leader and close associate of King, Andrew Young became the first African American U.S. Ambassador to the United Nations before serving as Mayor of Atlanta from 1982 – 1990. As mayor, Young prioritized minority business development and worked to position Atlanta as a global, diverse, and inclusive city. He also played a crucial role in Atlanta's successful bid to host the 1996 Olympics and eventually served as co-chairman of the Games. ♦ Located near the Martin Luther King Jr. National Historic Site, the International Civil Rights Walk of Fame recognizes individuals who sacrificed and struggled to advance civil and human rights. A parade of granite markers features the footstep impressions of icons such as Rosa Parks, Desmond Tutu, Andrew Young, John Lewis, and others. ♦ Atlanta's rich history of activism, leadership, and progress toward racial equality and social justice is still visible today, and the legacy of the civil rights movement in Atlanta continues to shape the city's identity and values.

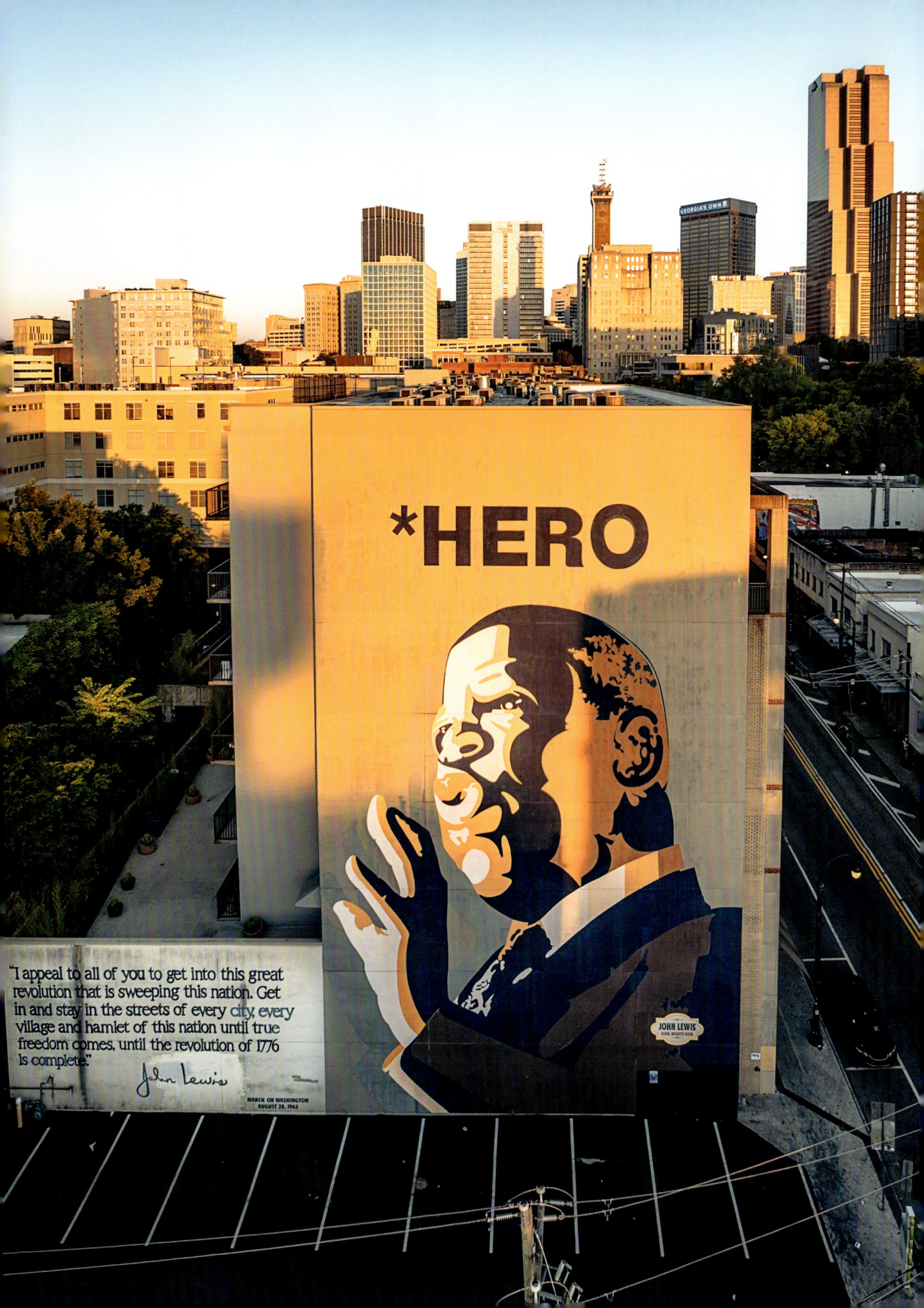

*HERO
"I appeal to all of you to get into this great revolution that is sweeping this nation. Get in and stay in the streets of every city, every village and hamlet of this nation until true freedom comes, until the revolution of 1776 is complete."
John Lewis
MARCH ON WASHINGTON AUGUST 28, 1963
JOHN LEWIS
CIVIL RIGHTS ICON
GEORGIA'S OWN

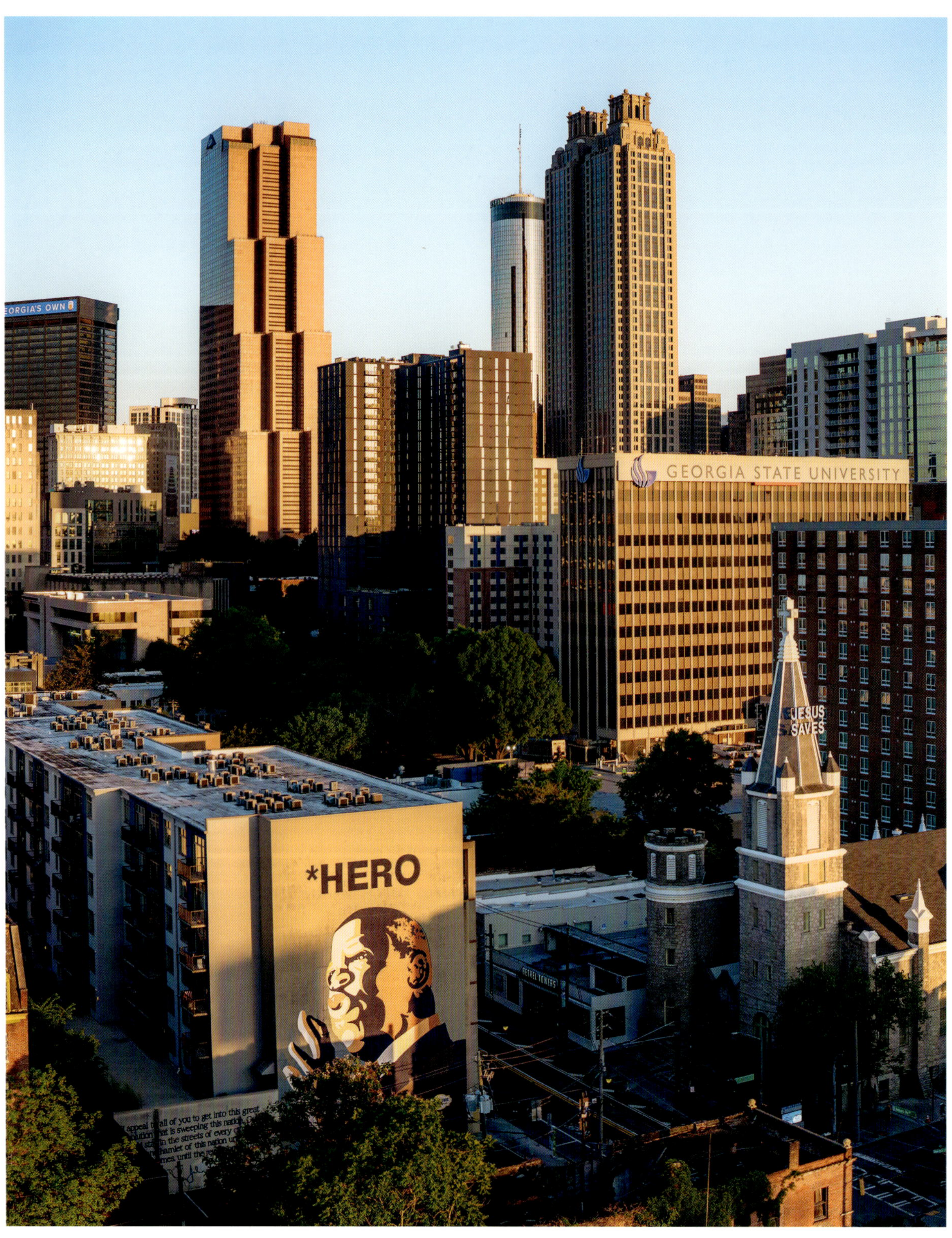

*HERO
I appeal to all of you to get into this great
revolution that is sweeping this nation. Get
in the streets of every city
hamlet of this nation un
mes until the
GEORGIA STATE UNIVERSITY
GEORGIA'S OWN
JESUS SAVES
BETHEL TOWERS

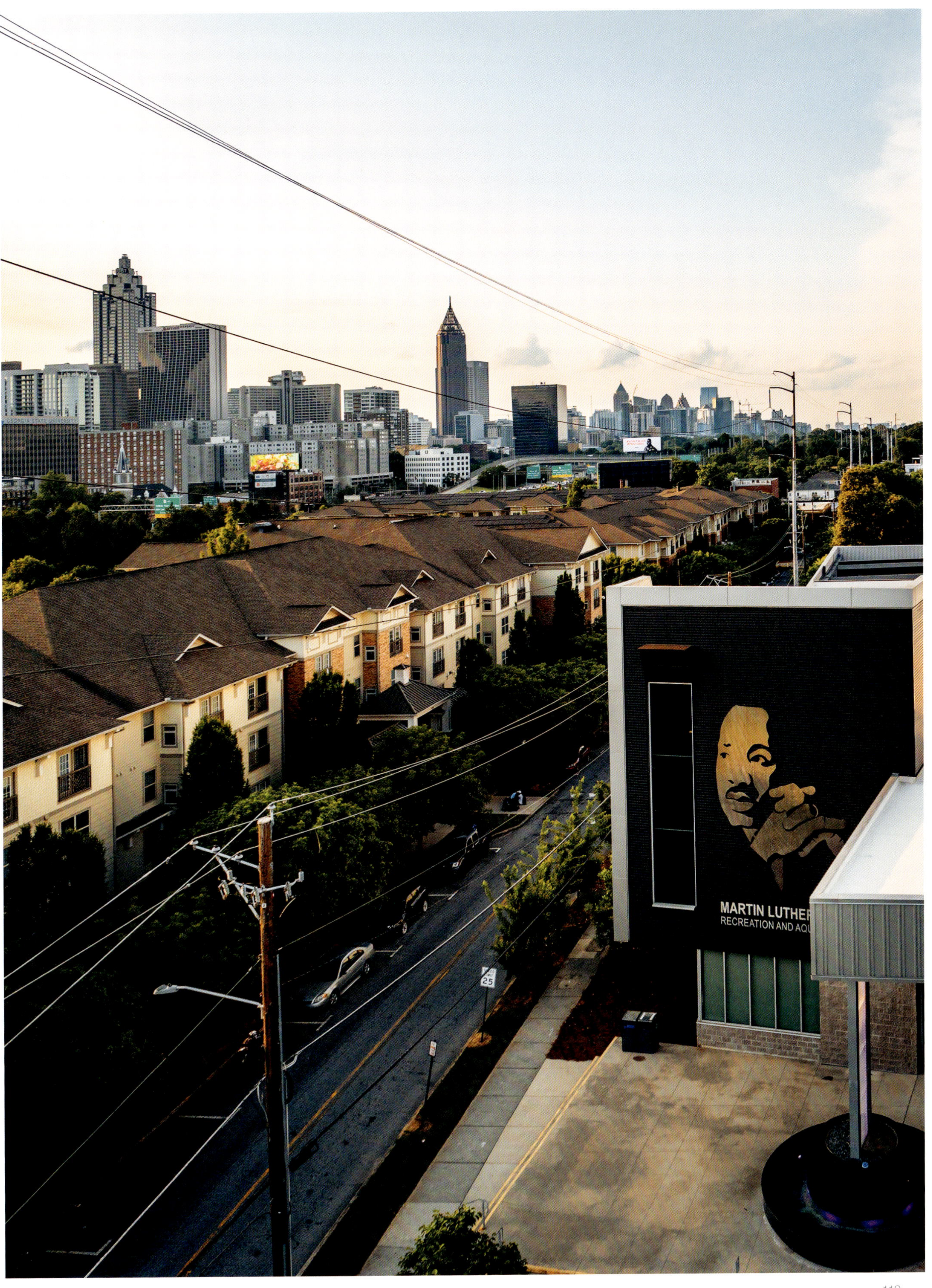
MARTIN LUTHER
RECREATION AND AQU
25

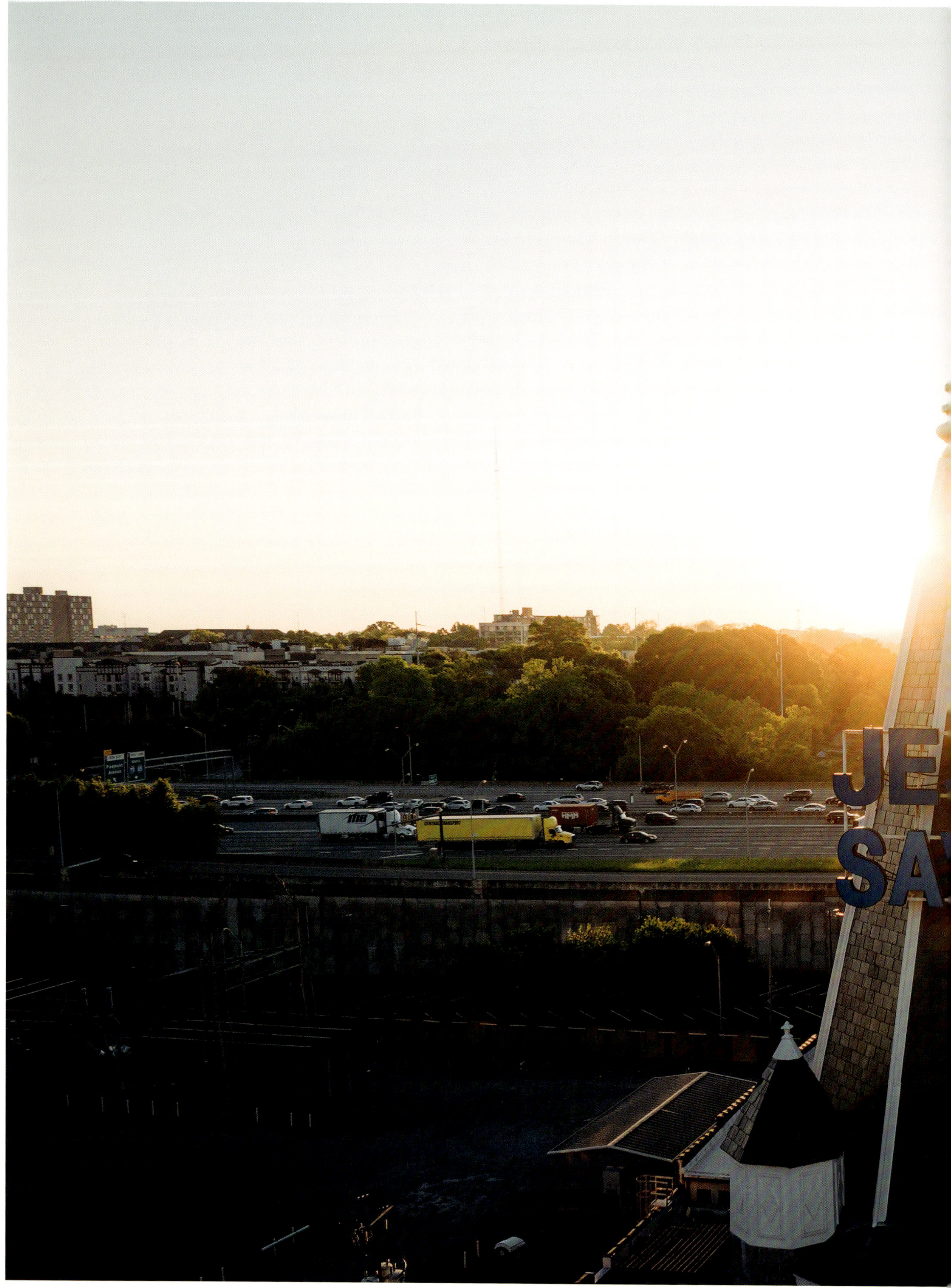
Paghmr
Avenue
JE
SA
MB
CENTRAL TRANSPORT
HMR

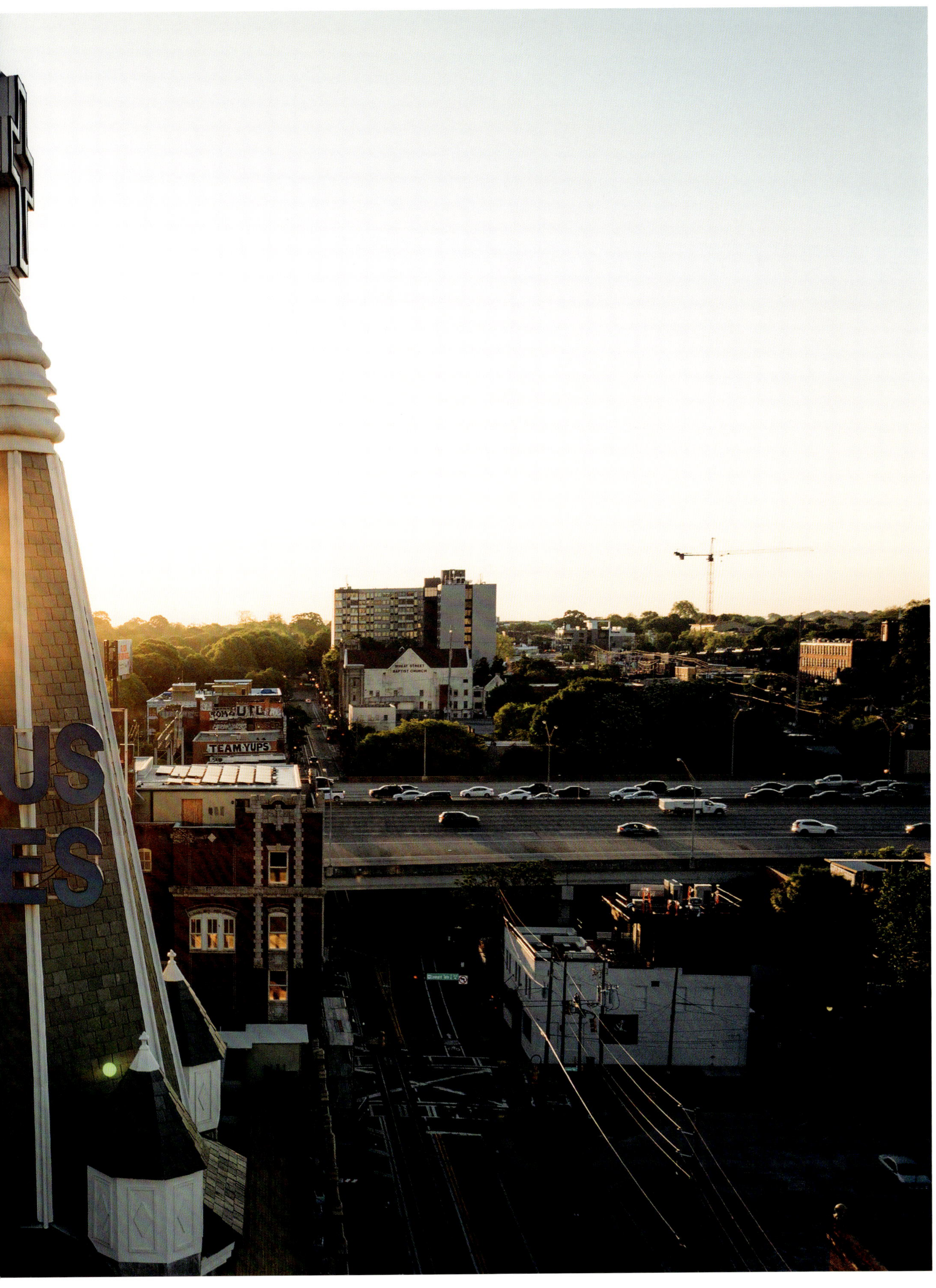

US
ES
TEAM·YUPS
WHEAT STREET
BAPTIST CHURCH

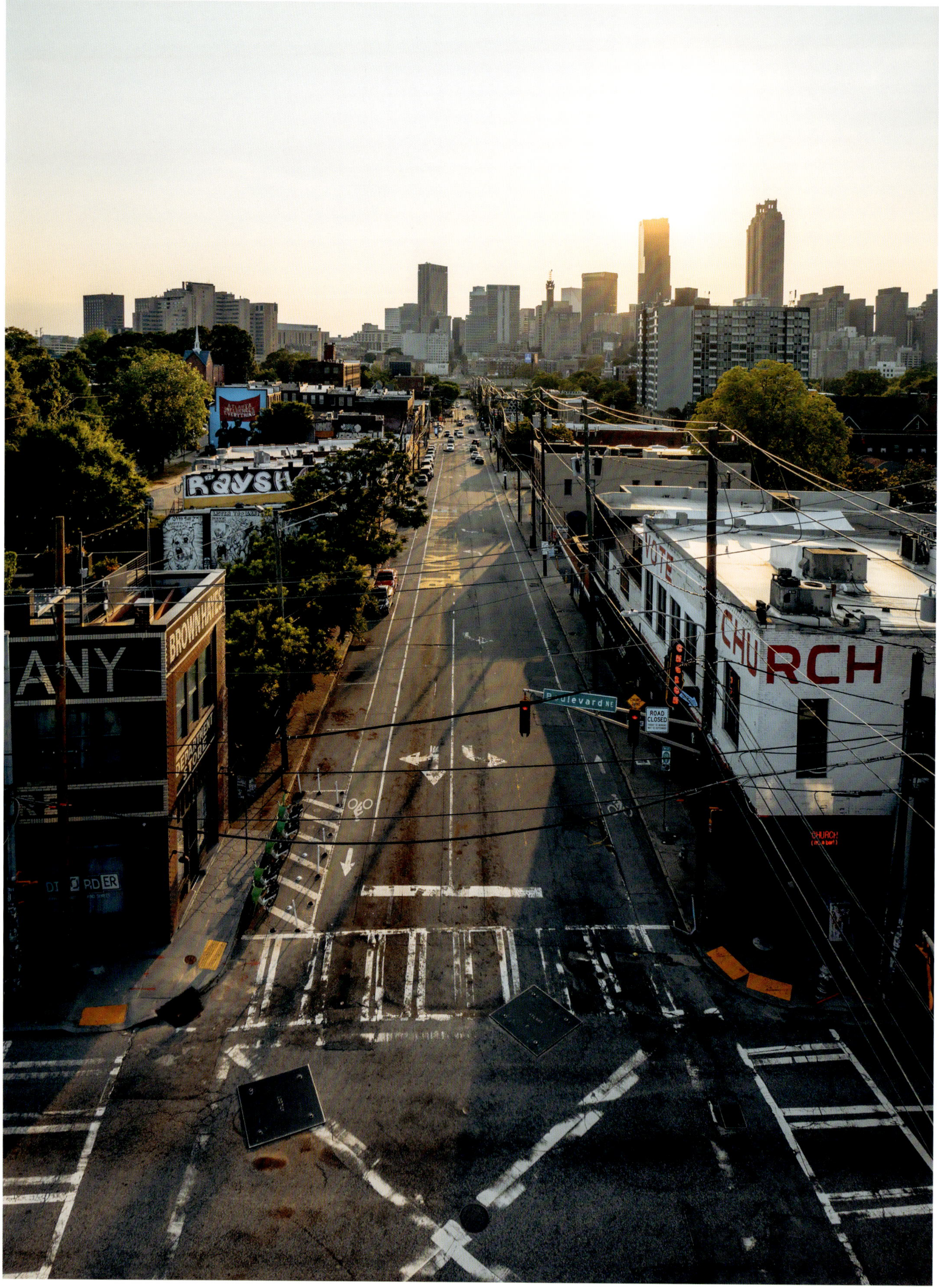
EVERYTHING
R a y SH
BROWN HAT
ANY
DI ORDER
VOTE
CHURCH
CHICAGO
Boulevard NE
ROAD
CLOSED
CHURCH
(it's a bar)

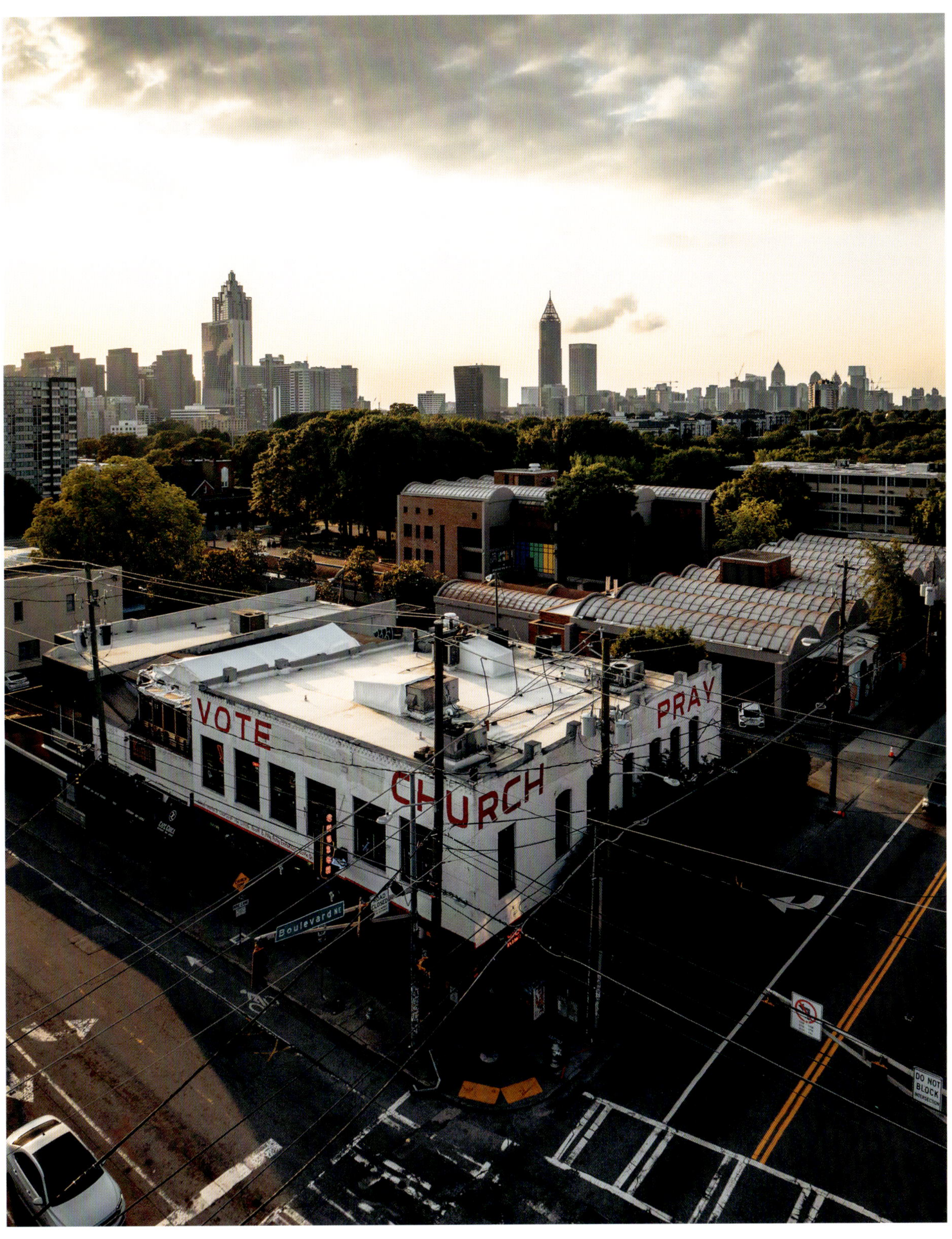

VOTE
PRAY
CHURCH
Boulevard NE
DO NOT BLOCK

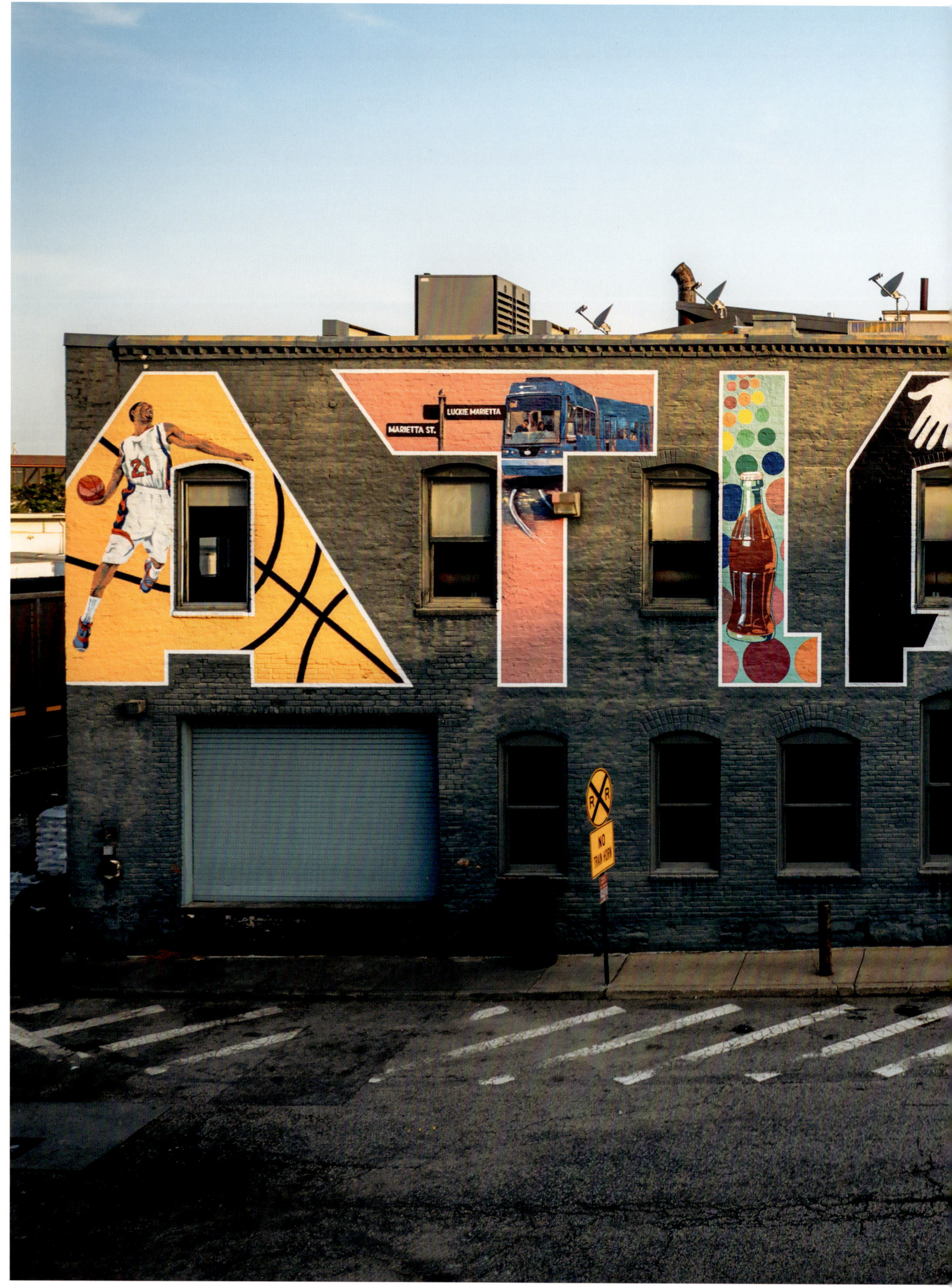
21
MARIETTA ST.
LUCKIE MARIETTA
NO
TRAIN HORN
R R

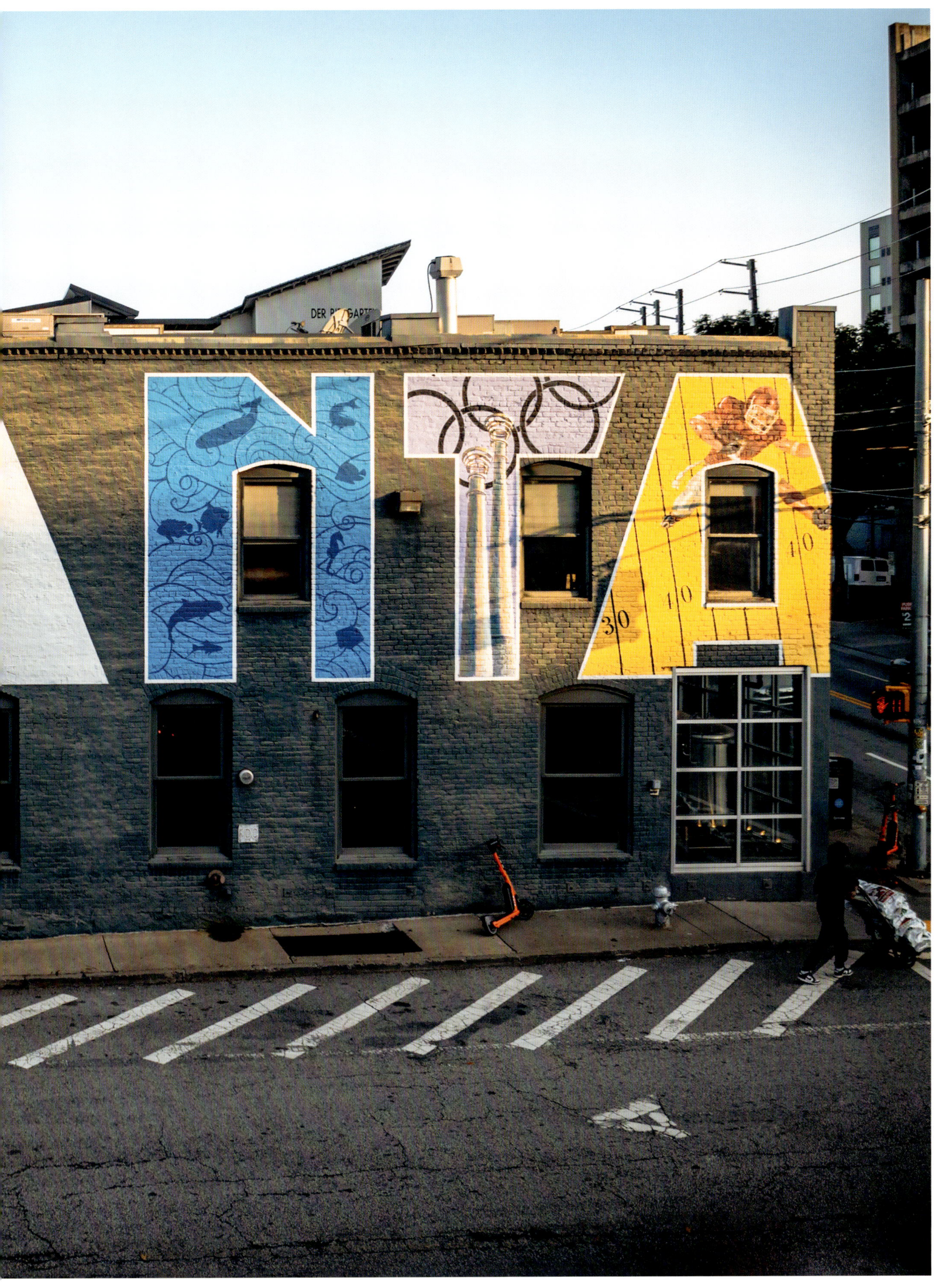

DER BIERGARTEN
NTA
30
10
10

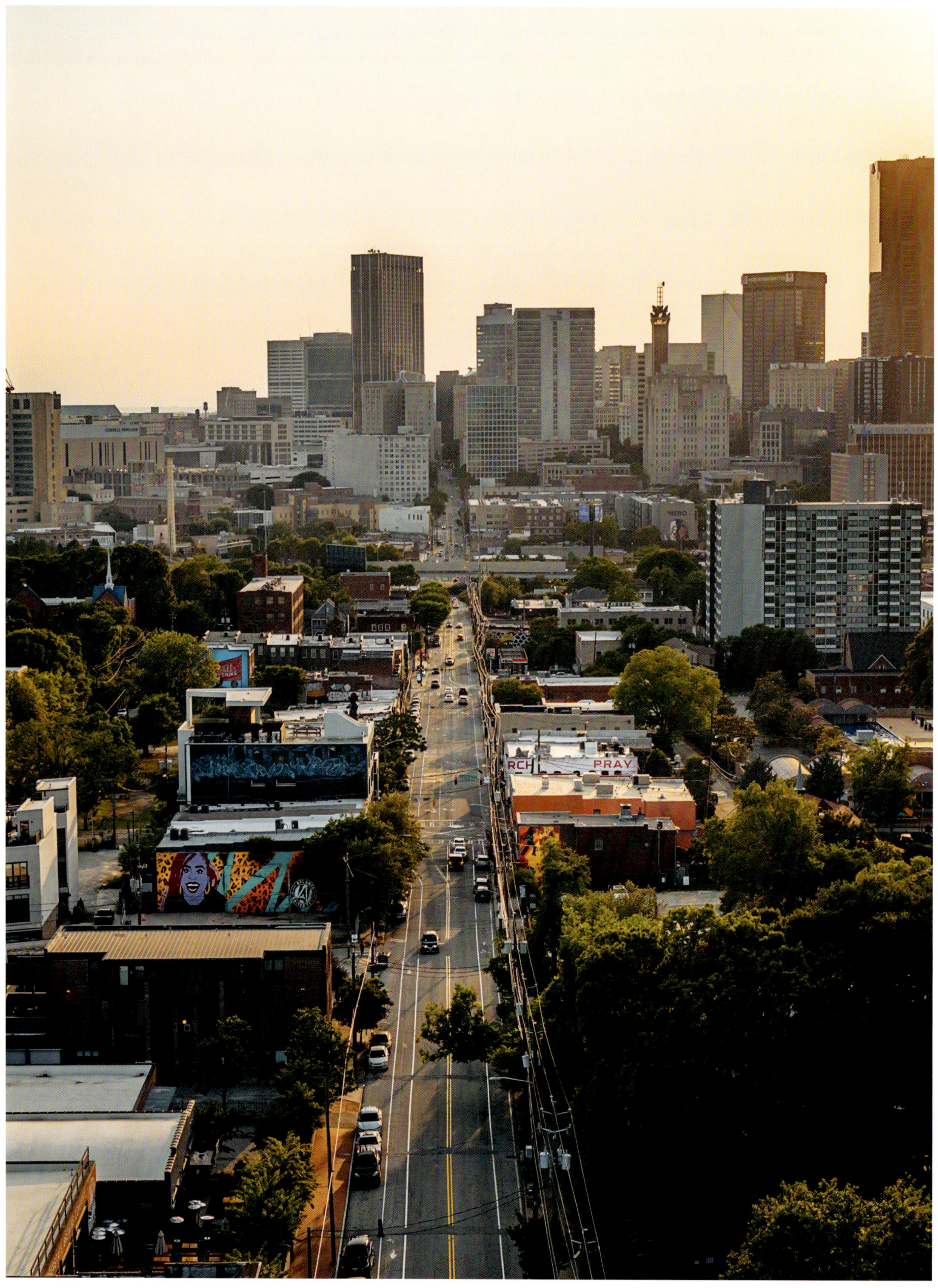

RCH
PRAY
HERO
GEORGIA ST

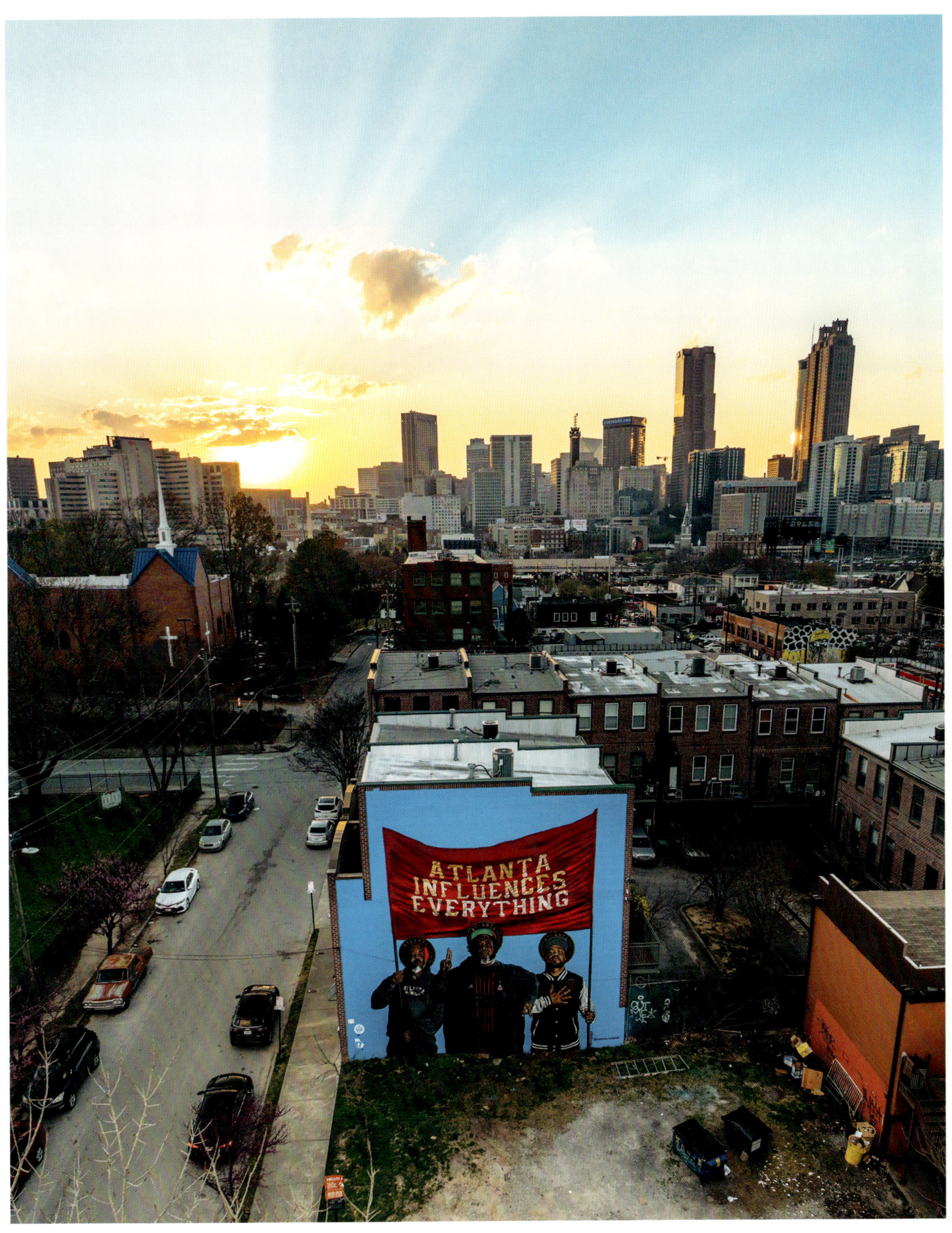
ATLANTA
INFLUENCES
EVERYTHING

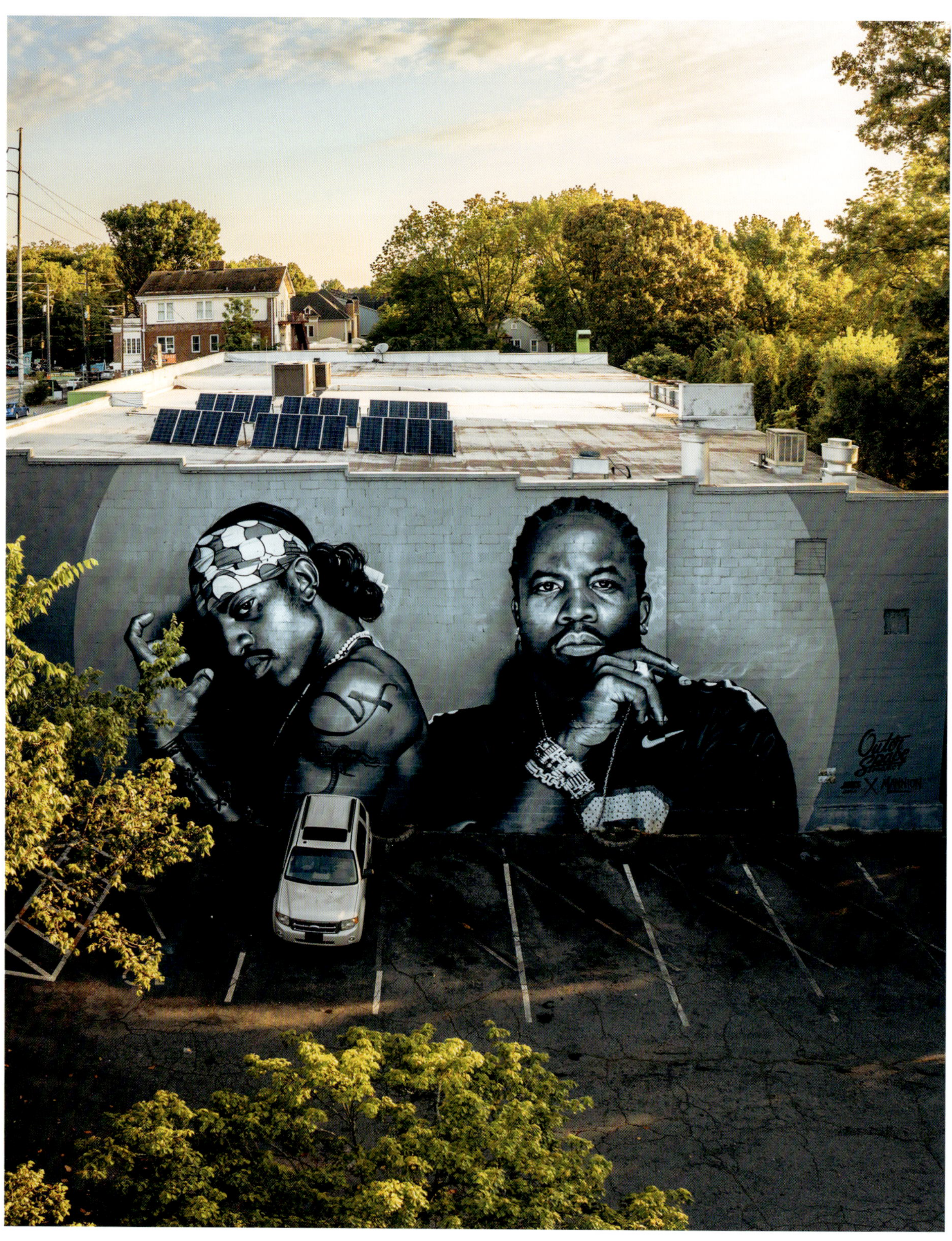

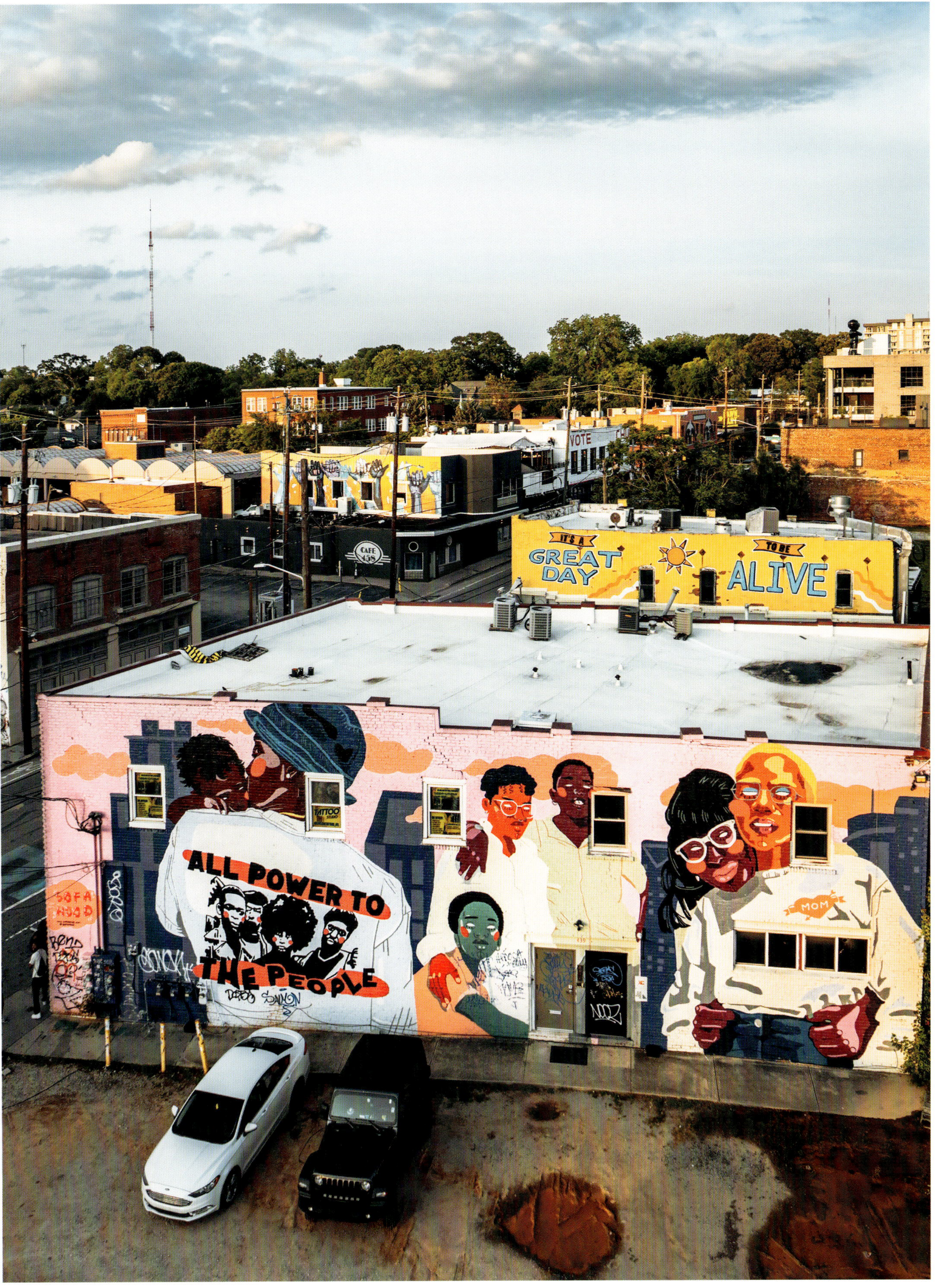
VOTE
IT'S A
GREAT
DAY
TO BE
ALIVE
CAFE
ALL POWER TO
THE PEOPLE
MOM
SOFA
HOOD

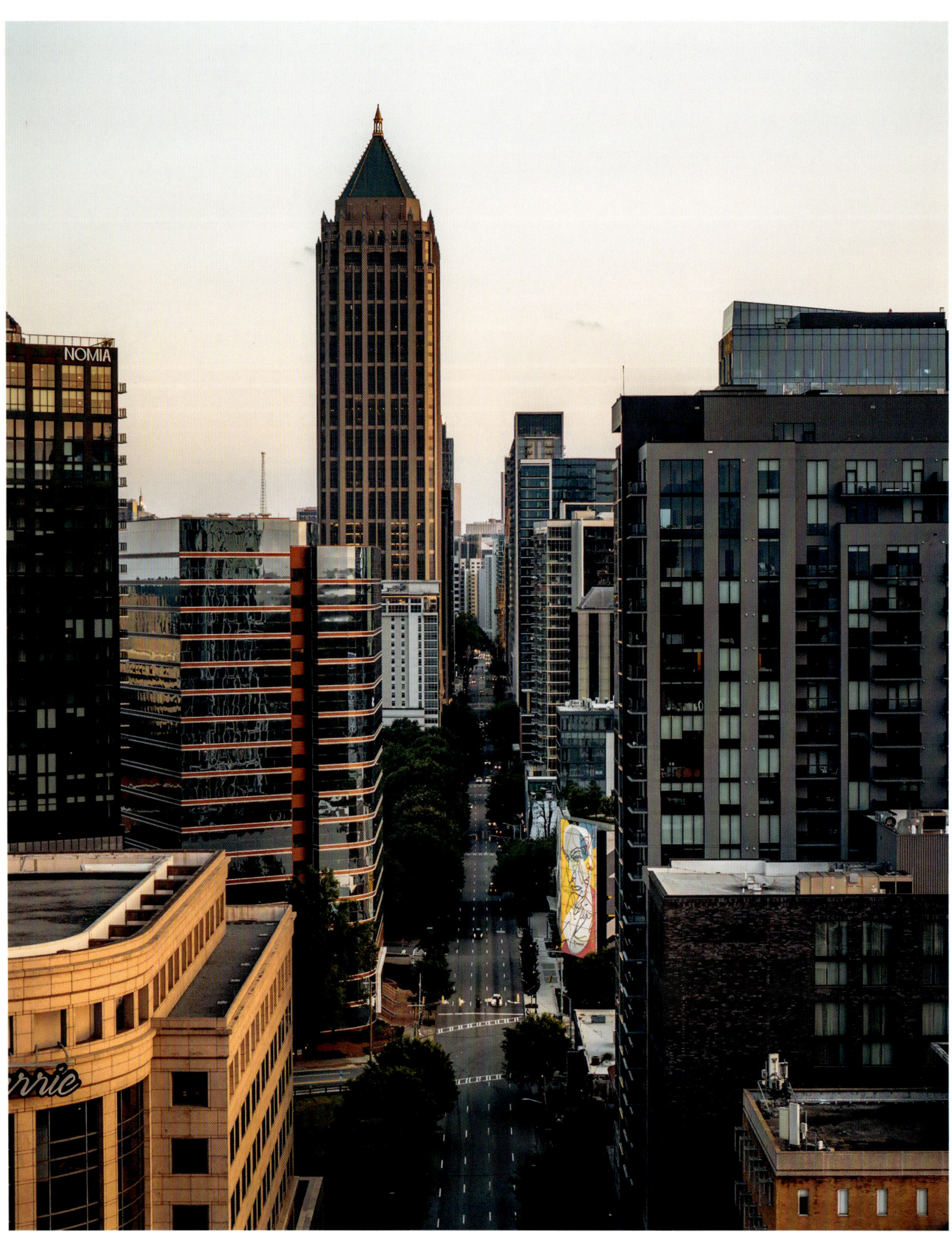

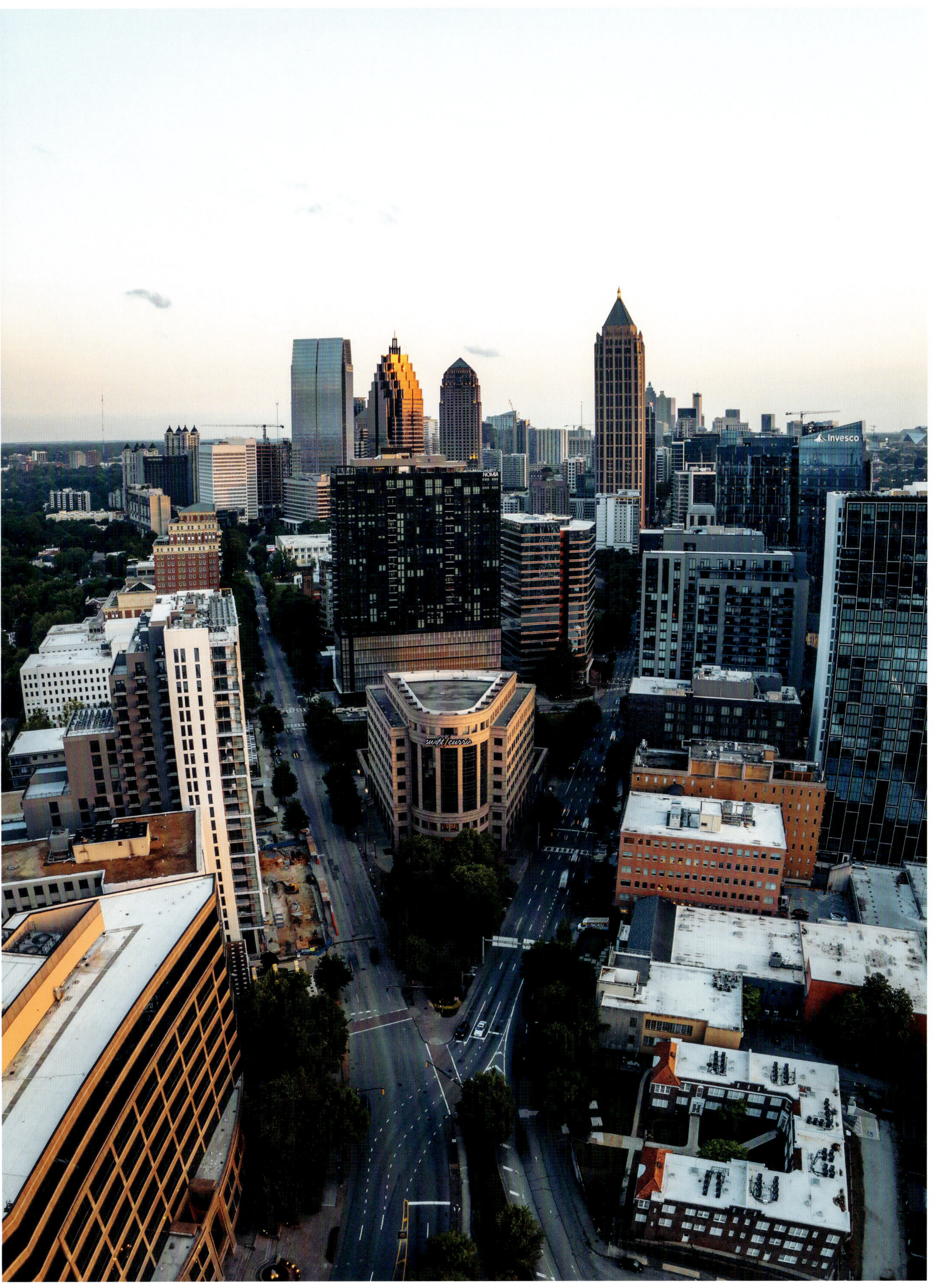

NOMA
swift currie
Invesco

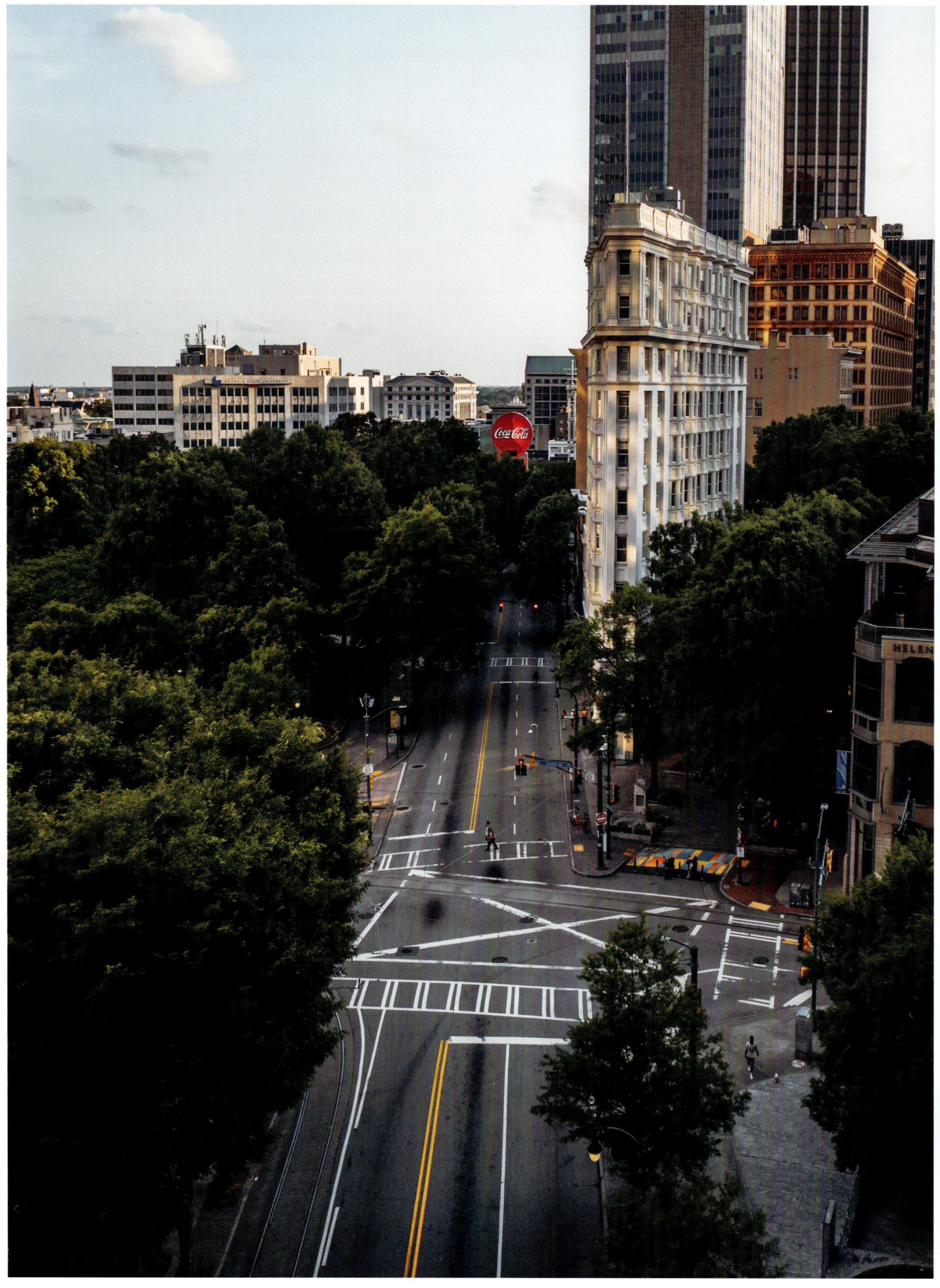

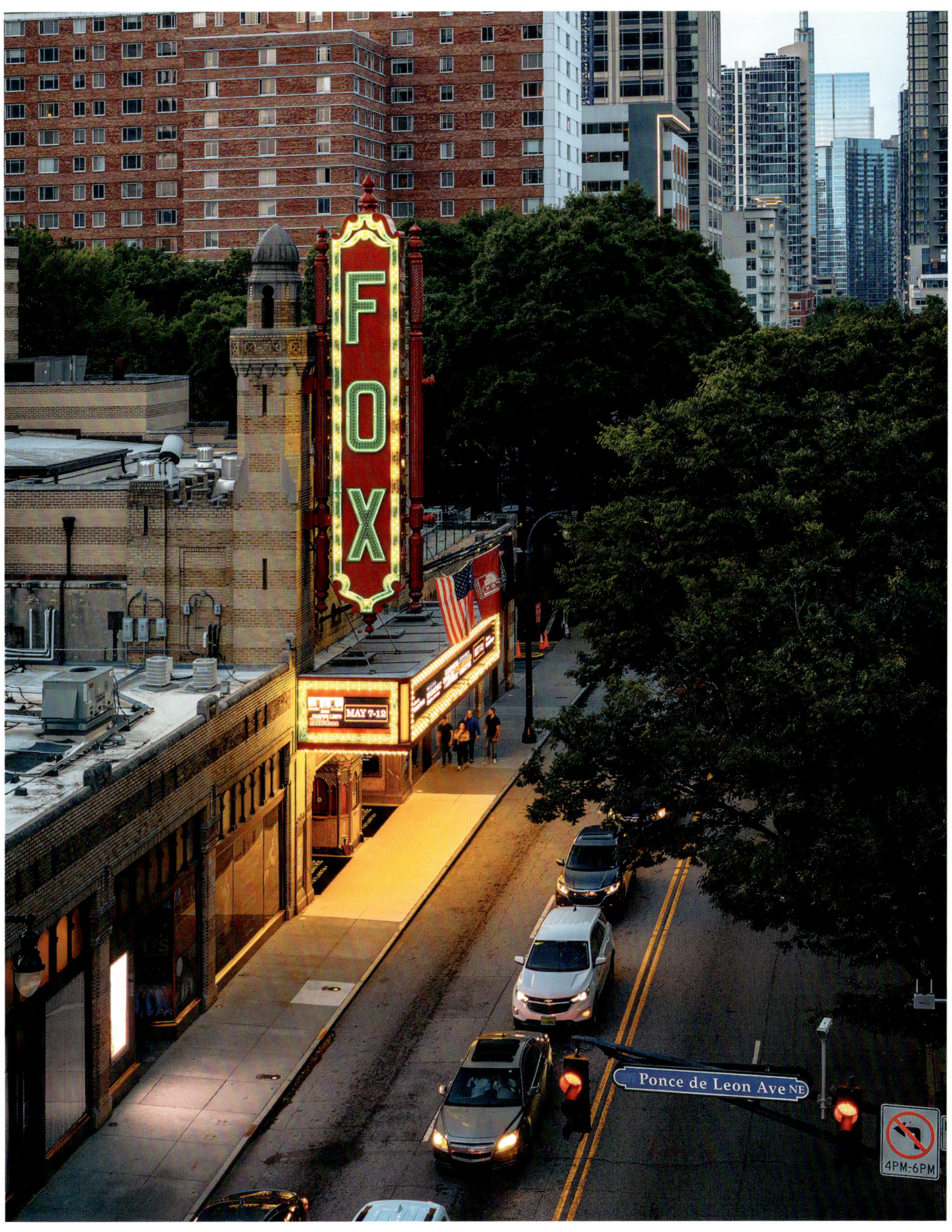

FOX
MAY 7-12
Ponce de Leon Ave NE
4PM-6PM

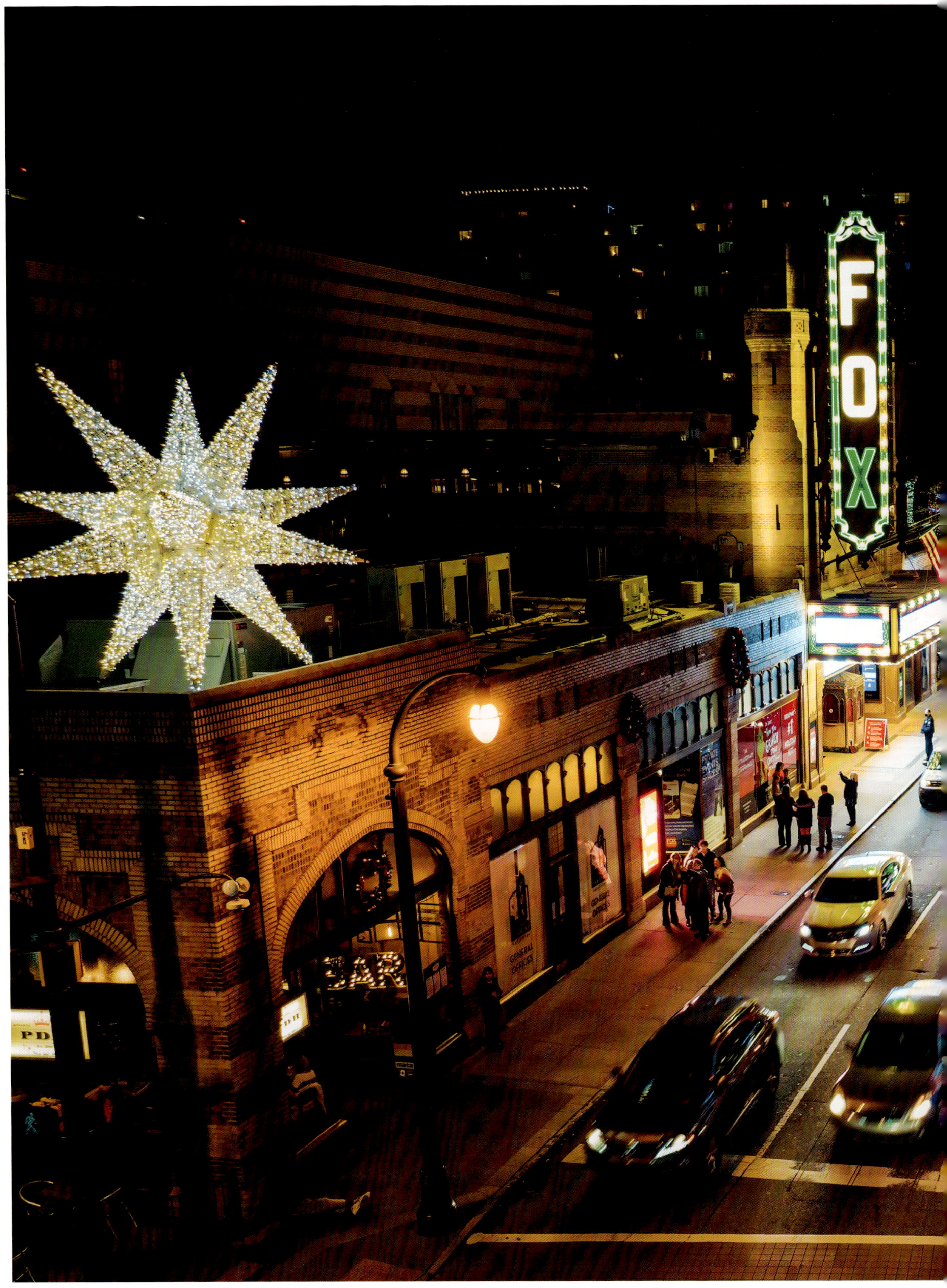
FOX
BAR

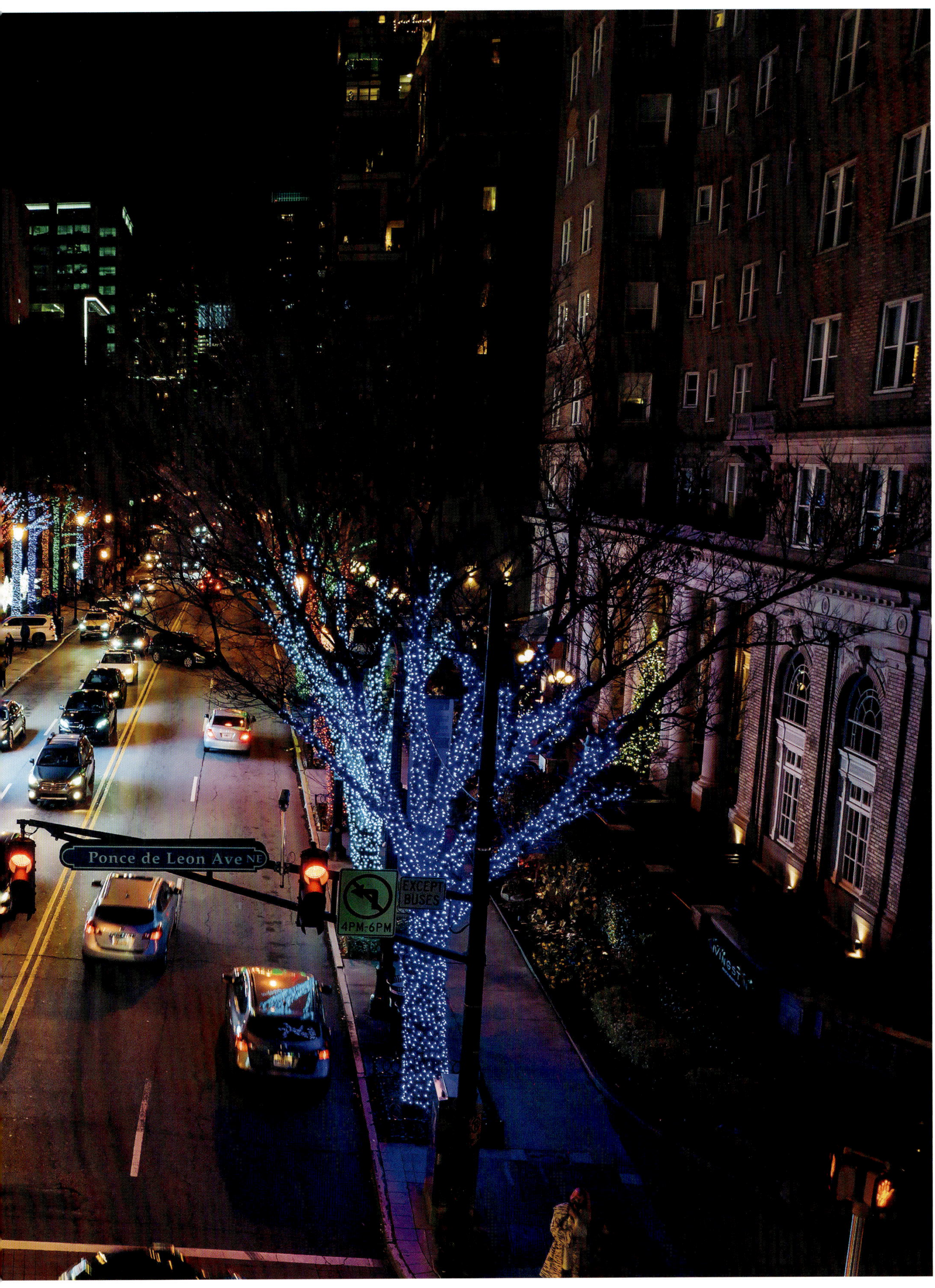

Ponce de Leon Ave NE
EXCEPT BUSES
4PM-6PM

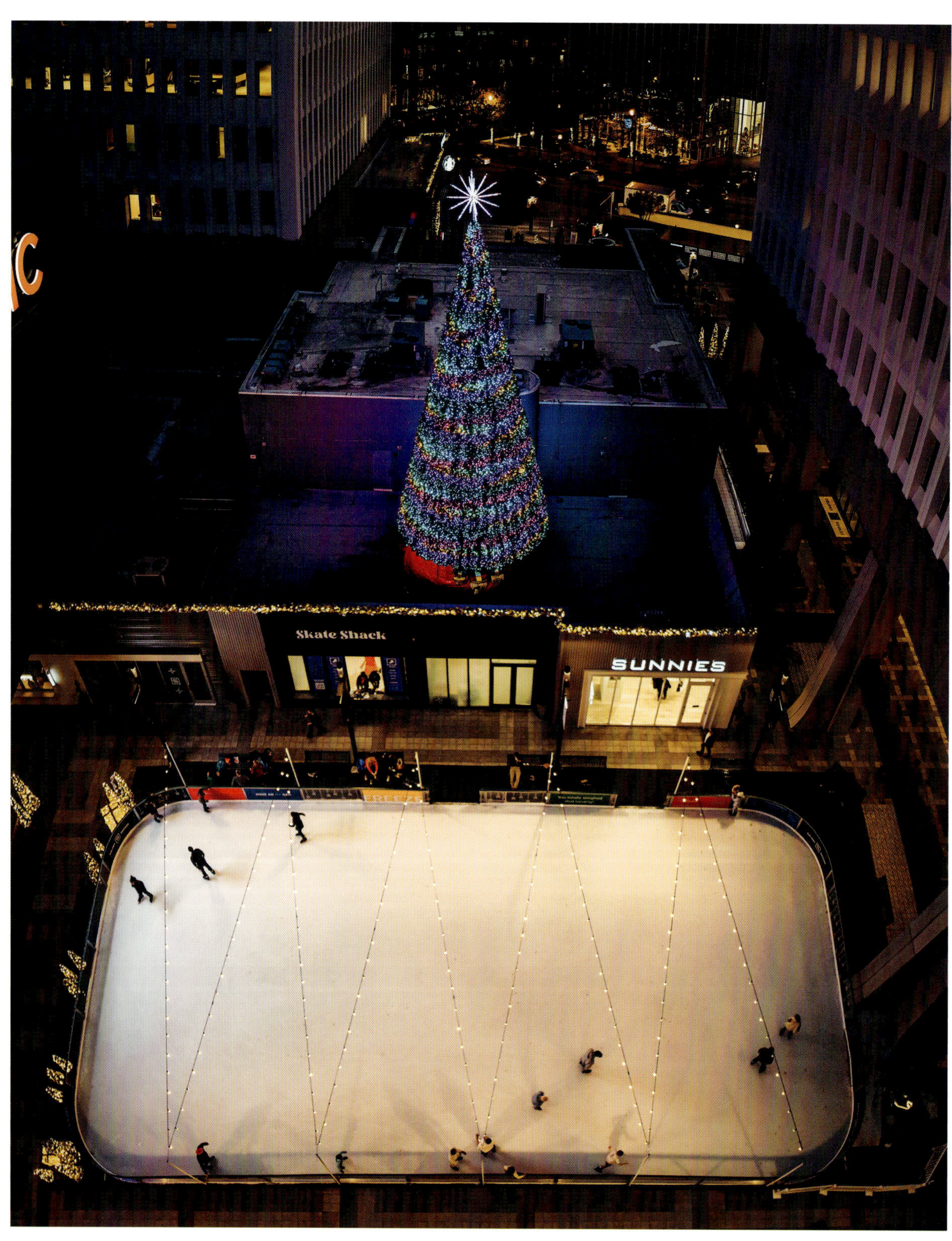

Skate Shack
SUNNIES

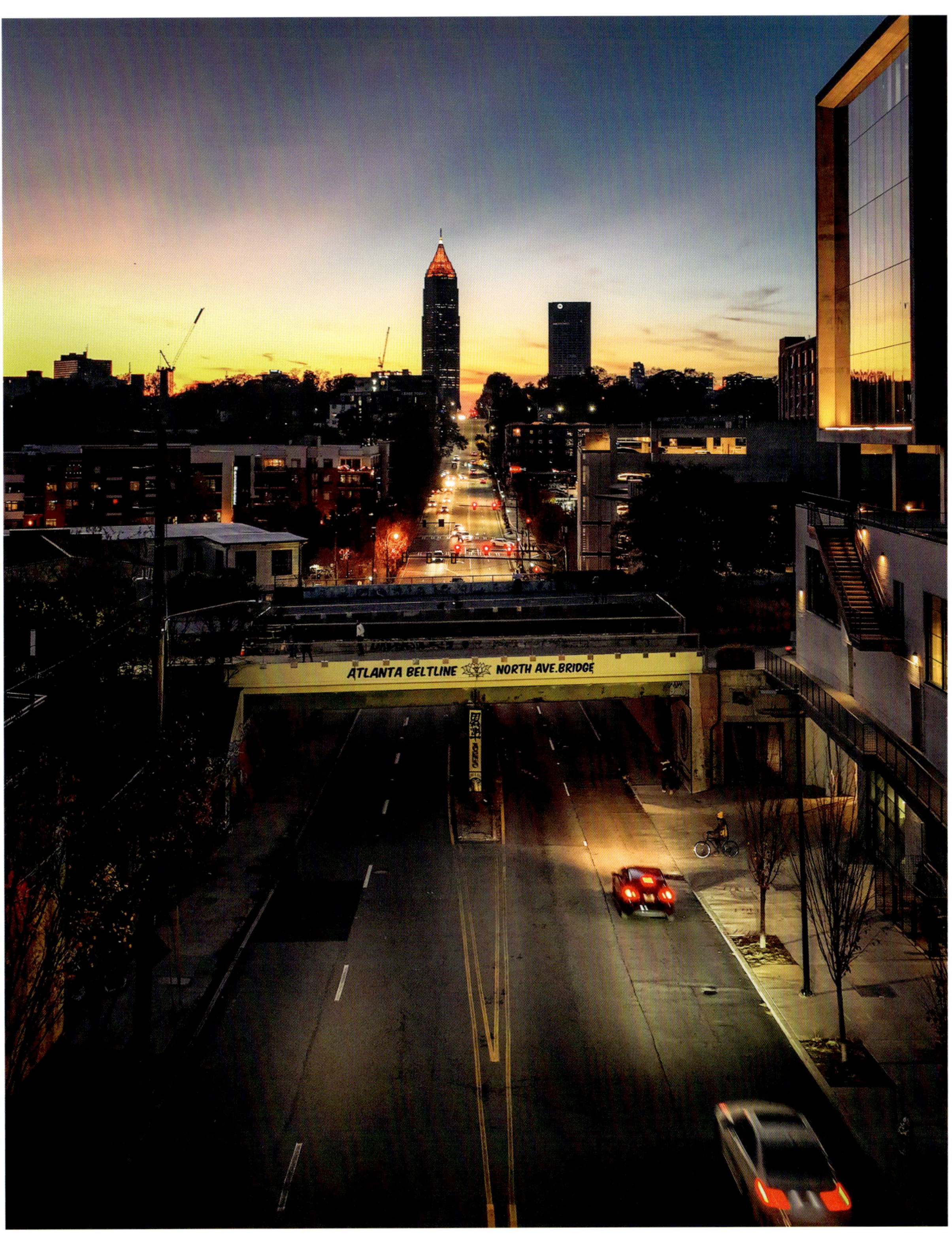

ATLANTA BELTLINE   NORTH AVE. BRIDGE

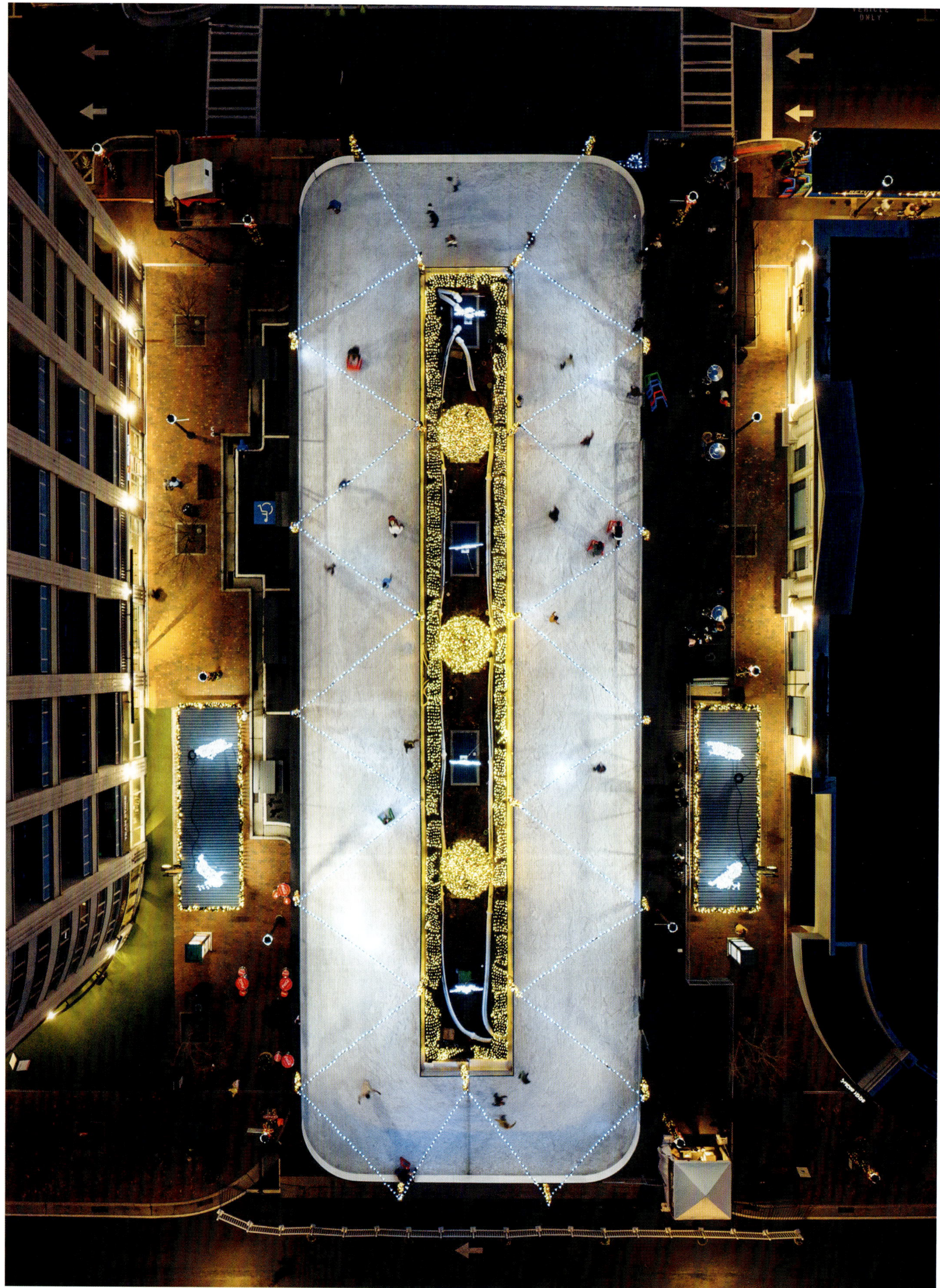

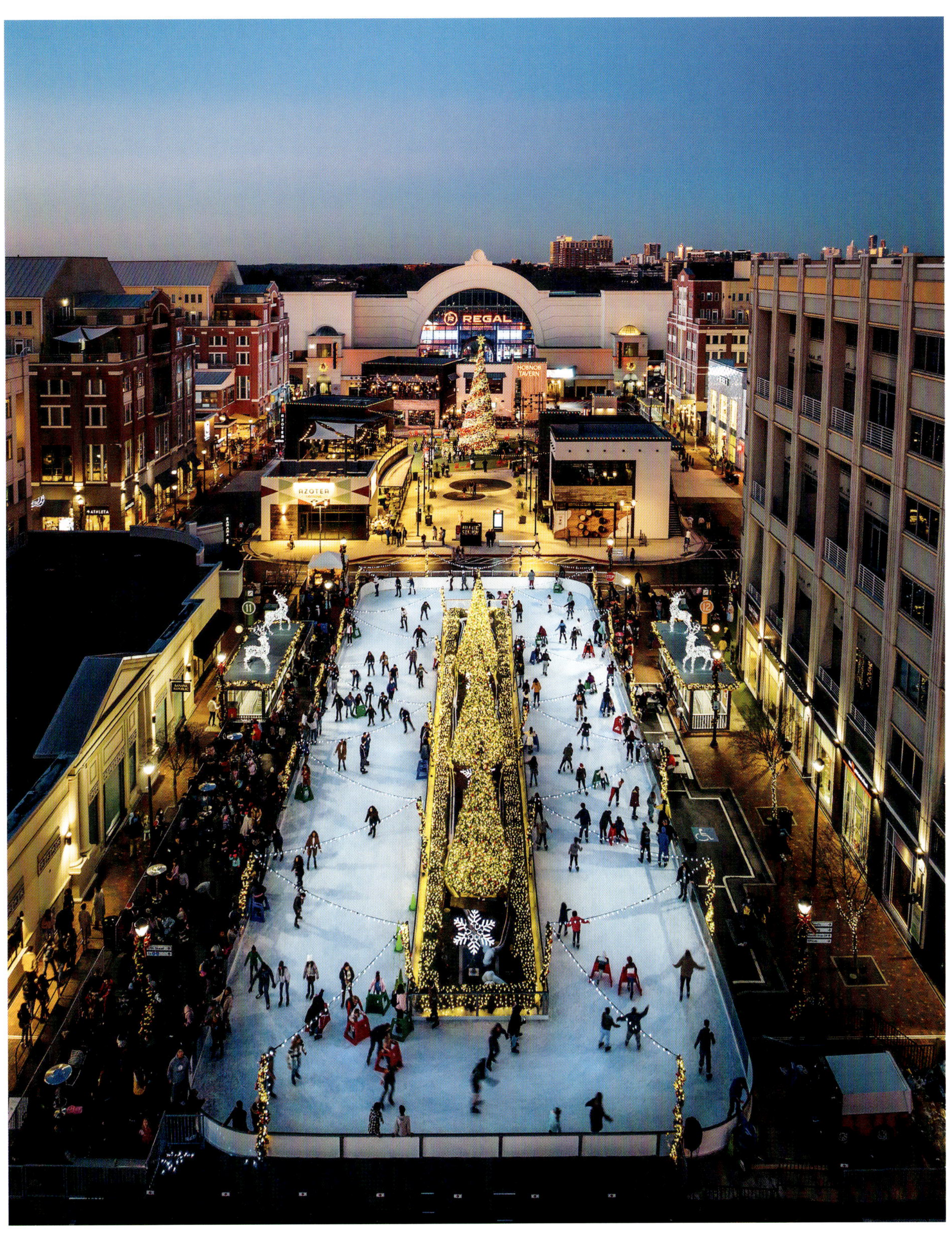

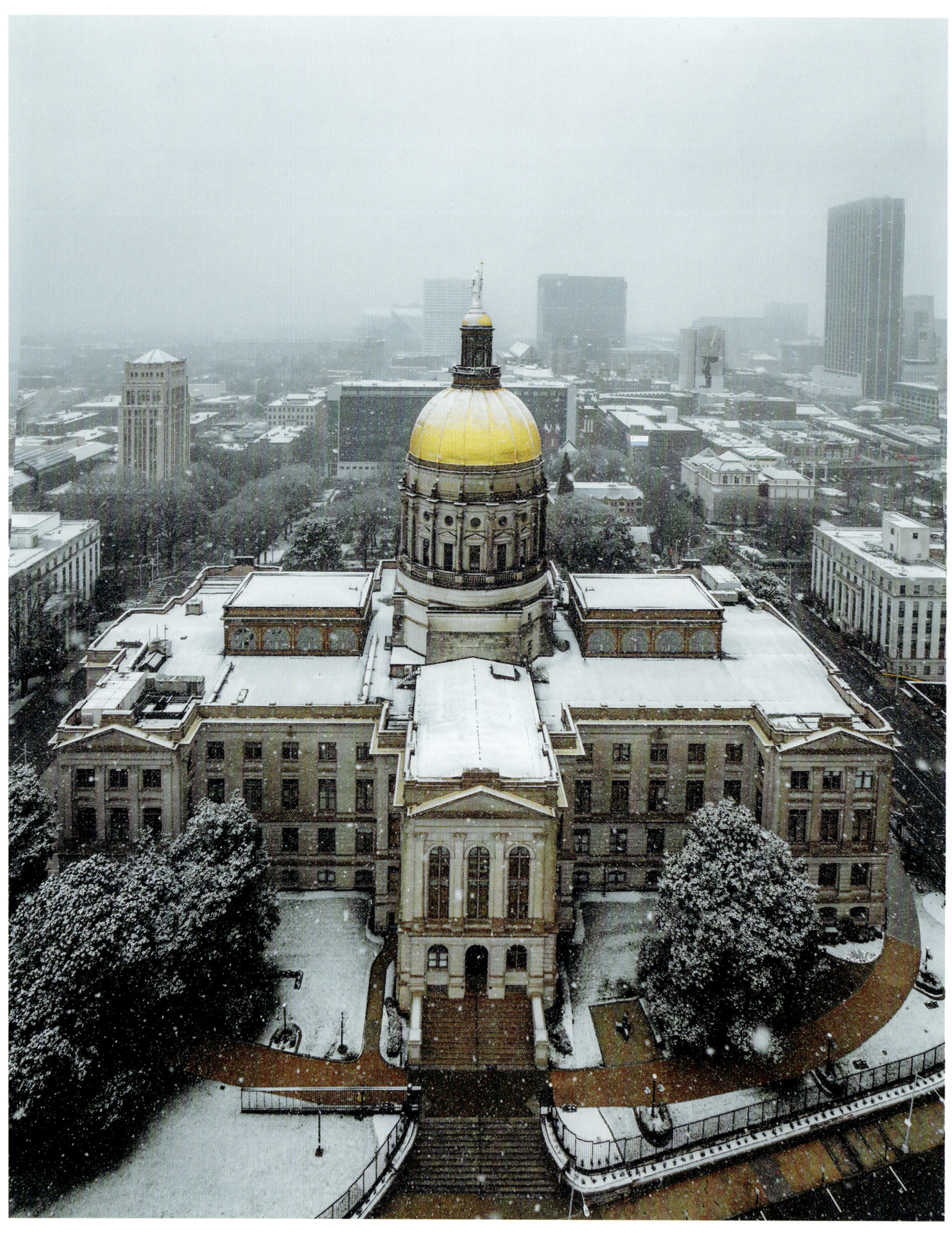

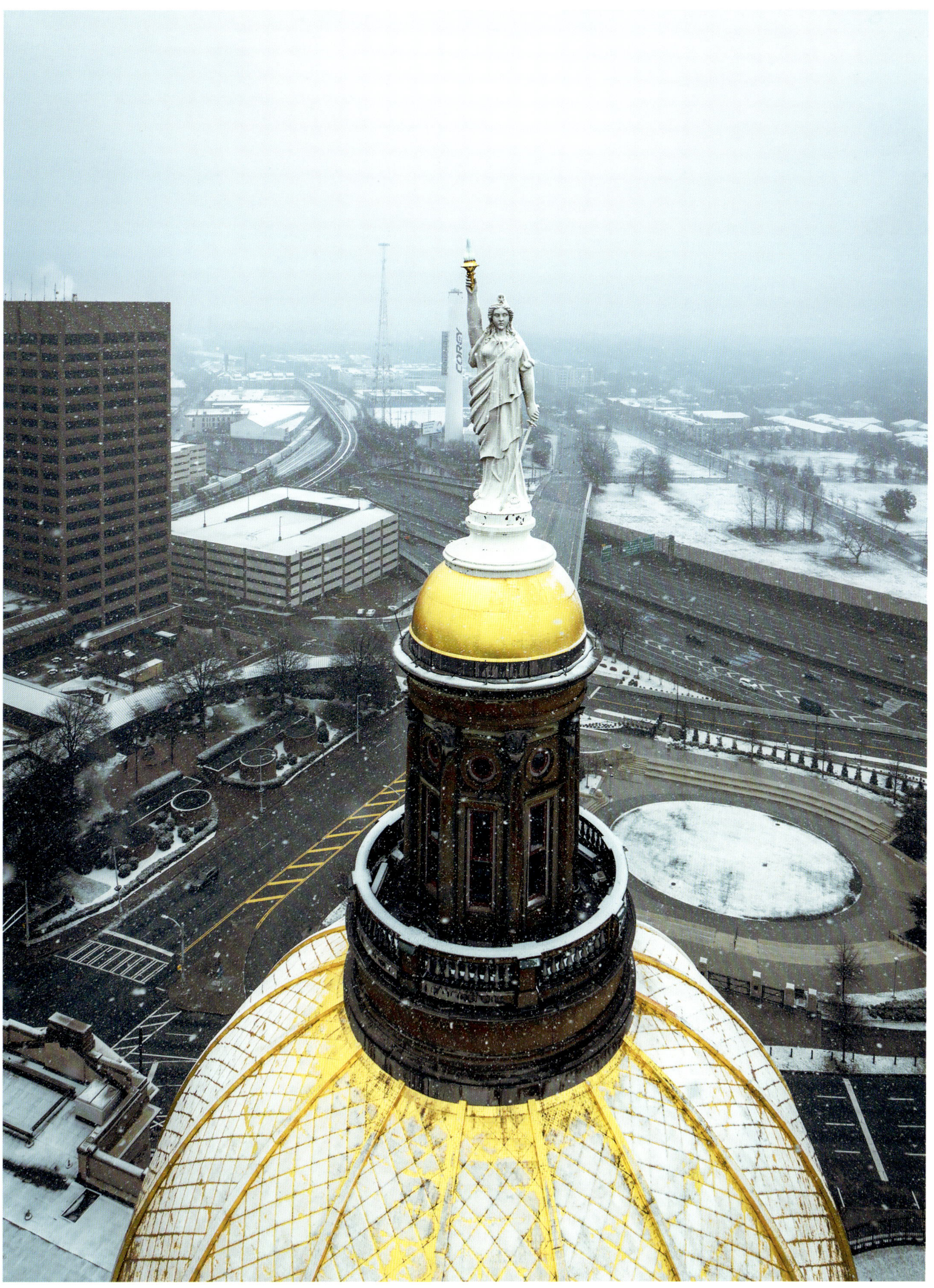

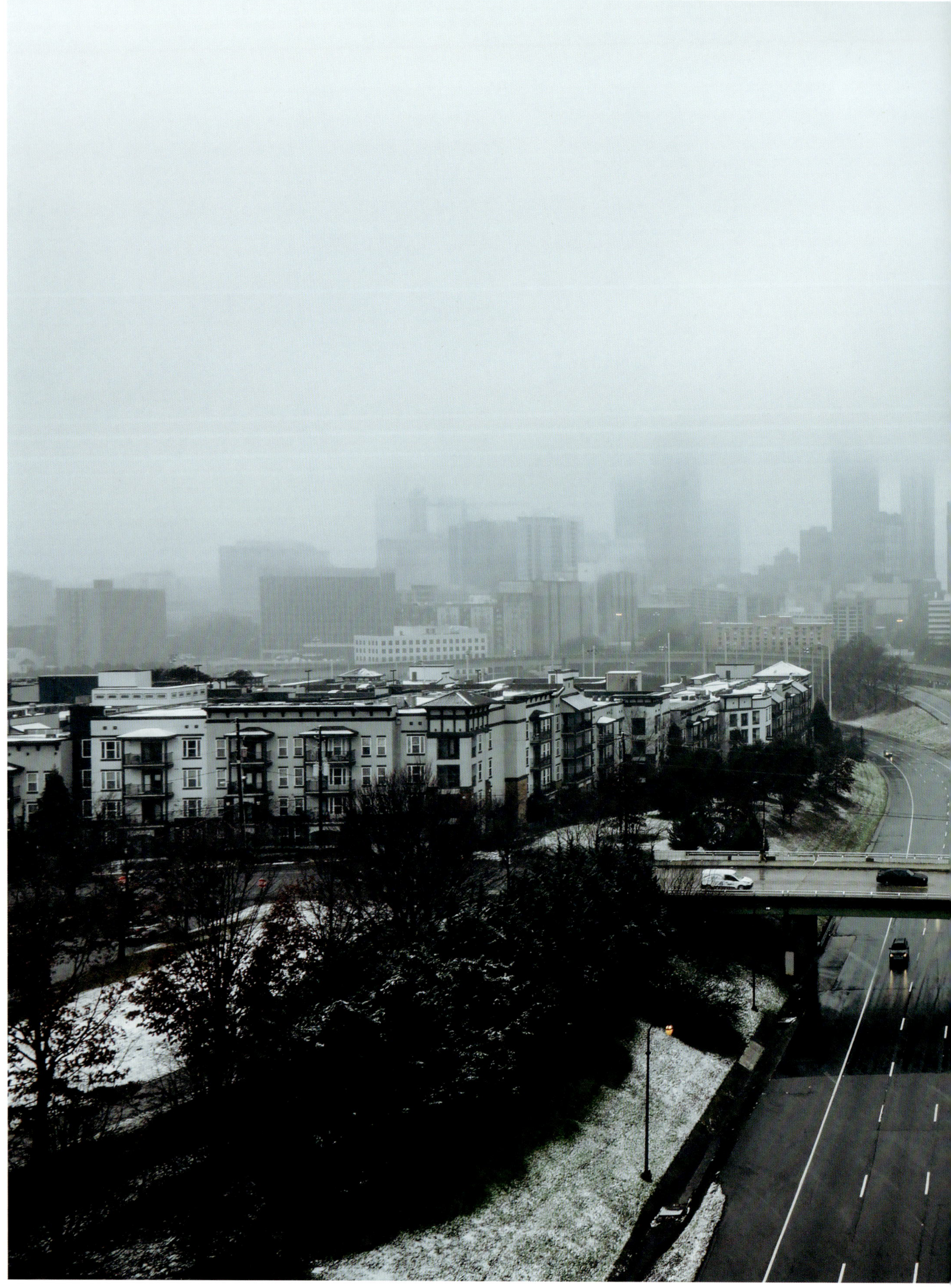

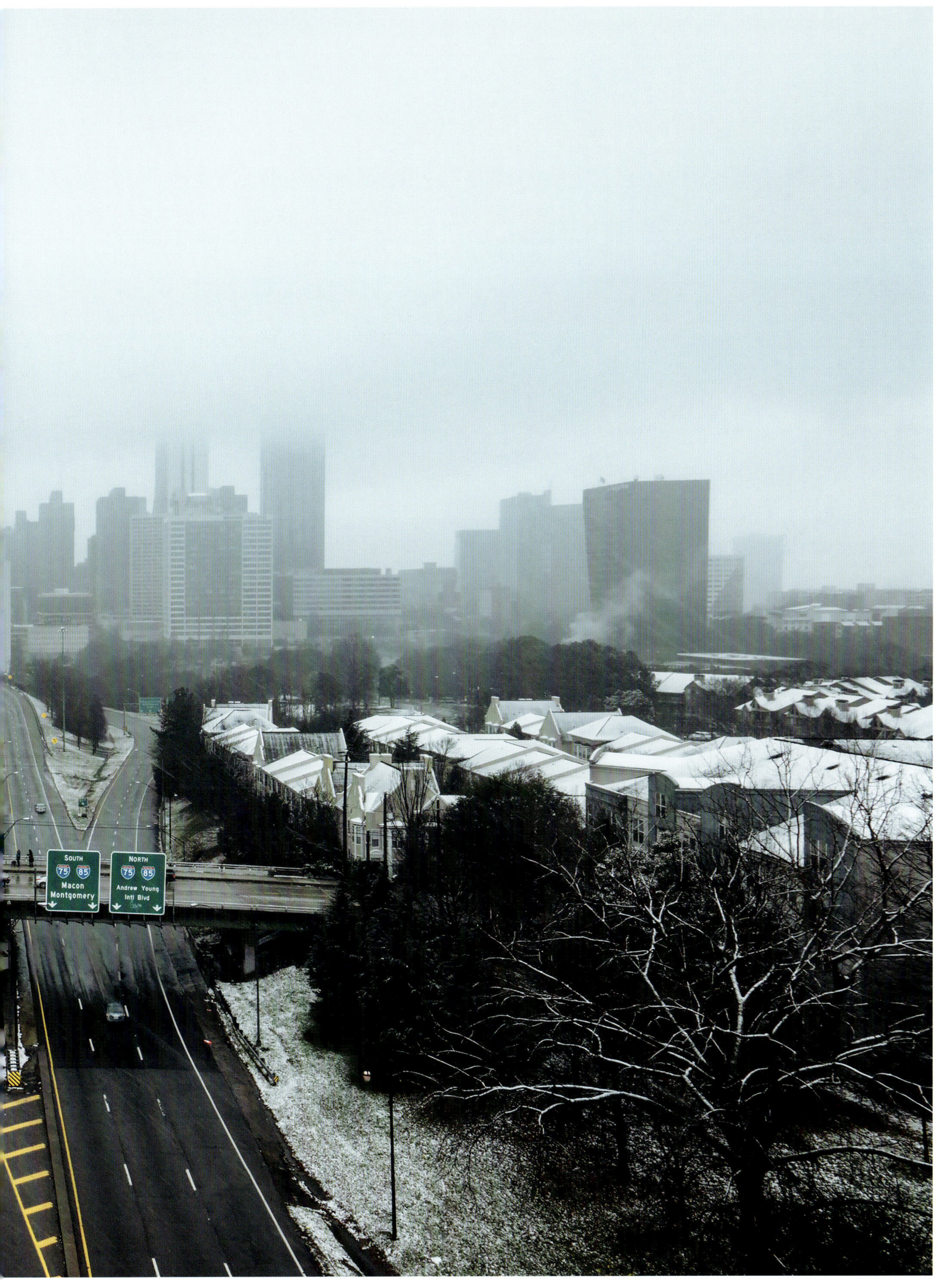

SOUTH
75 85
Macon
Montgomery
NORTH
75 85
Andrew Young
Intl Blvd

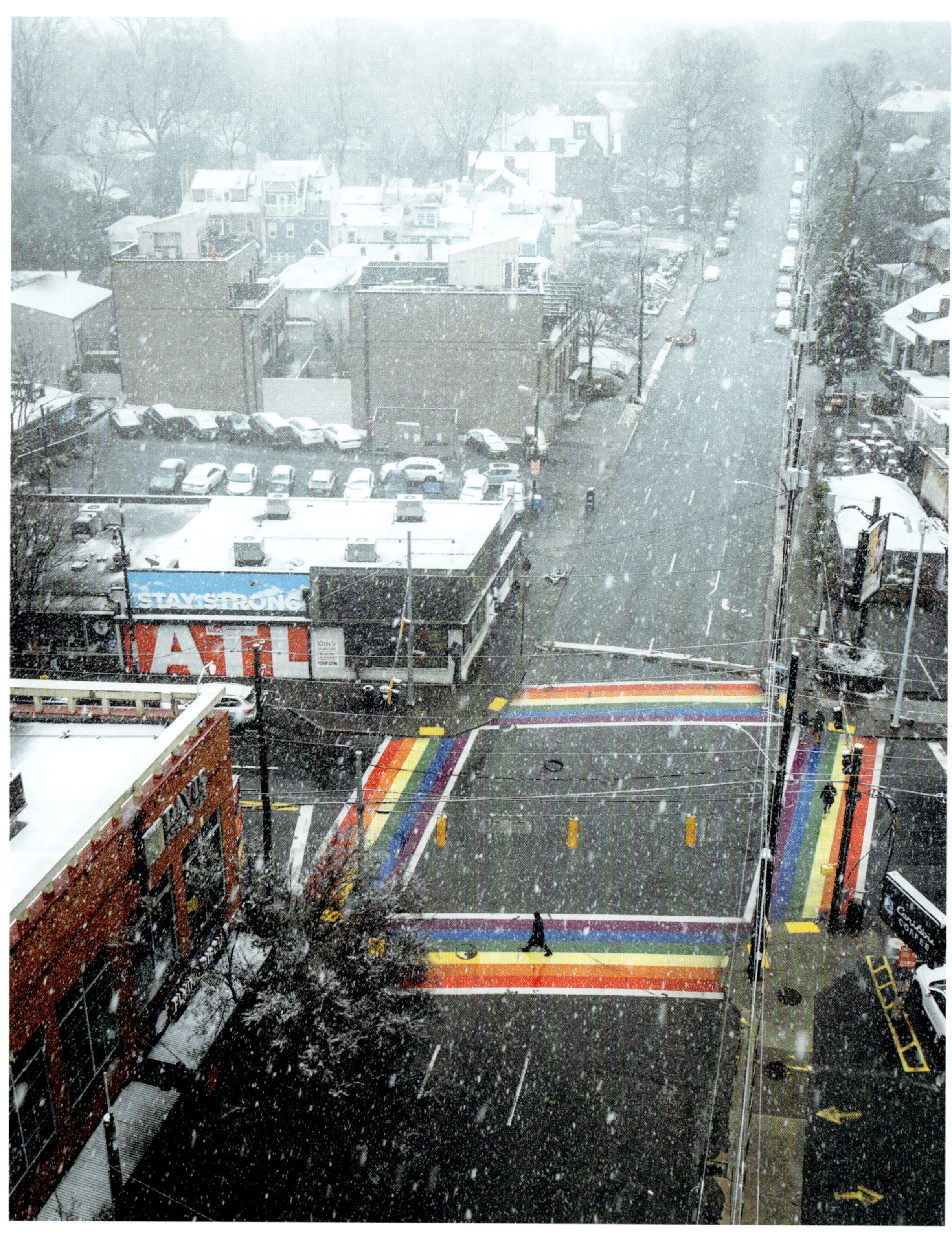
STAY STRONG
ATL

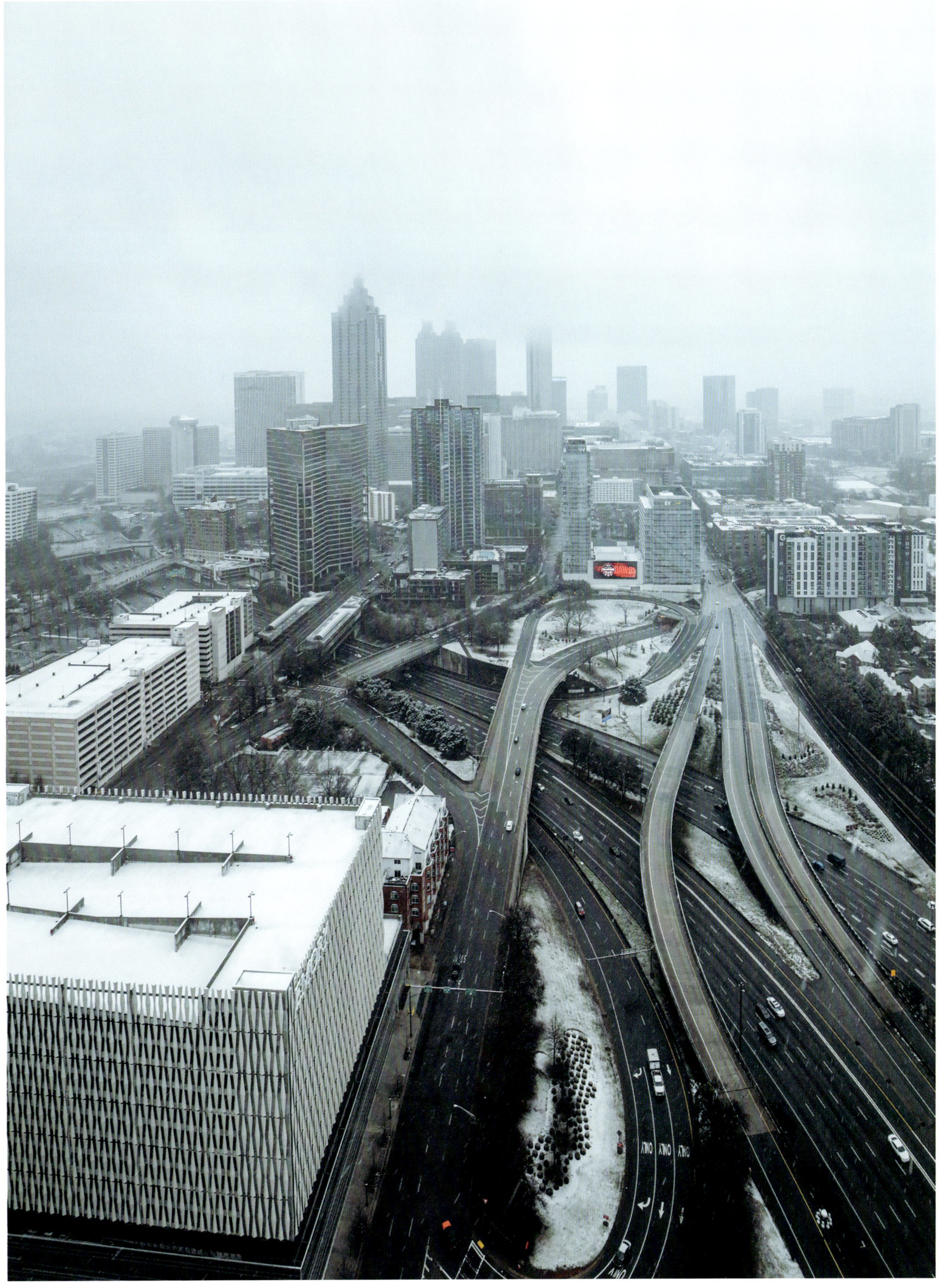

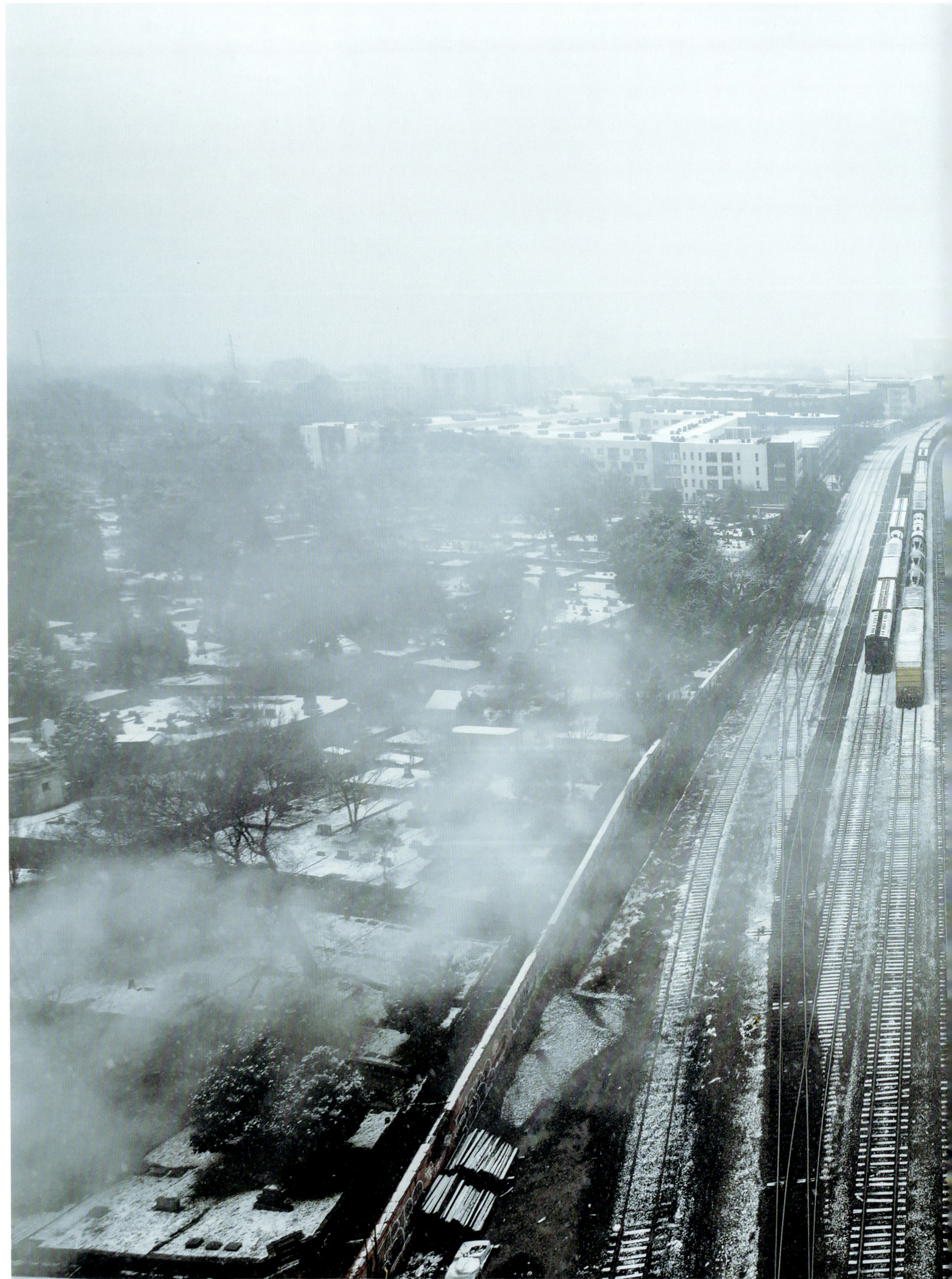

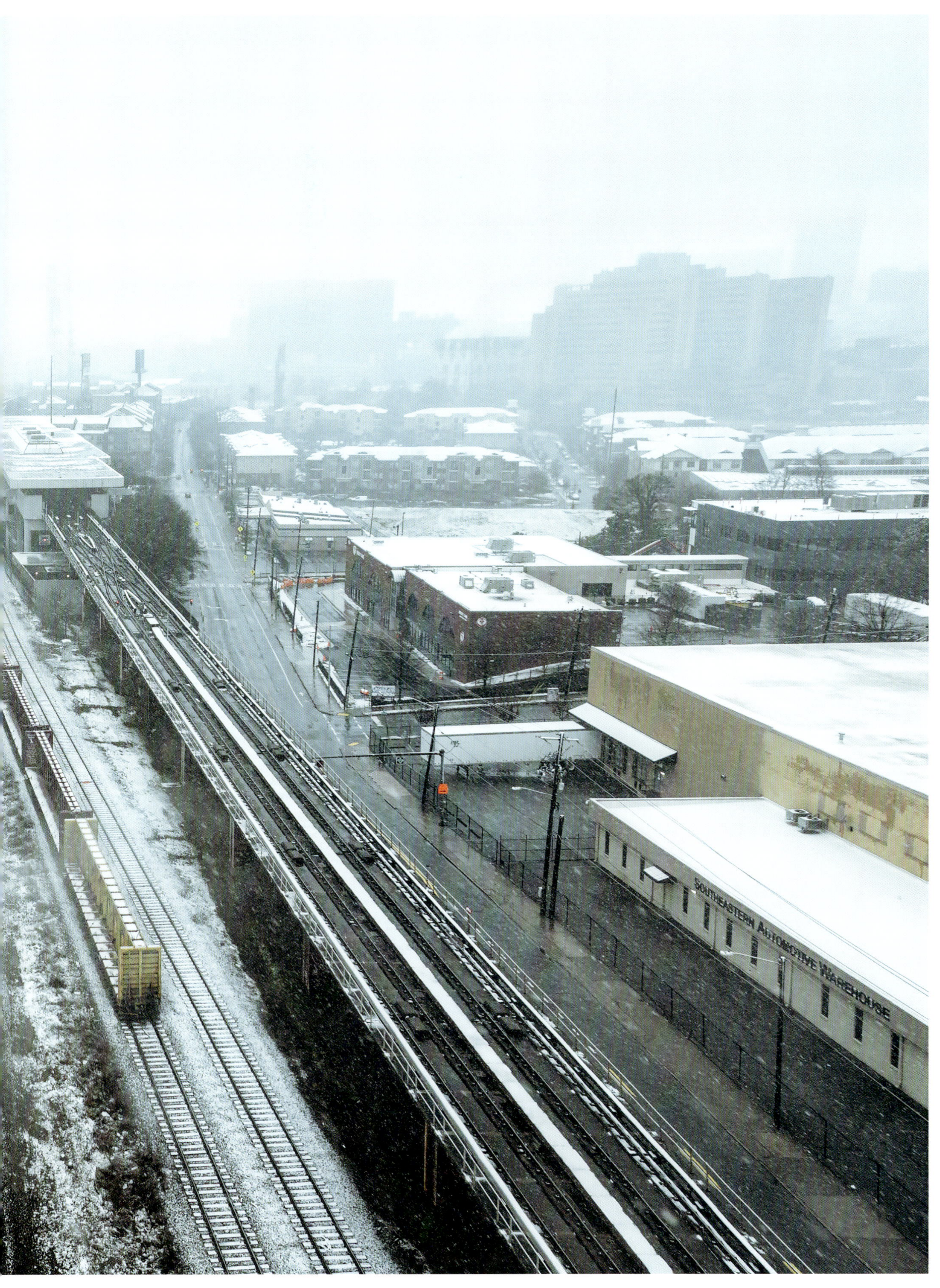
SOUTHEASTERN AUTOMOTIVE WAREHOUSE

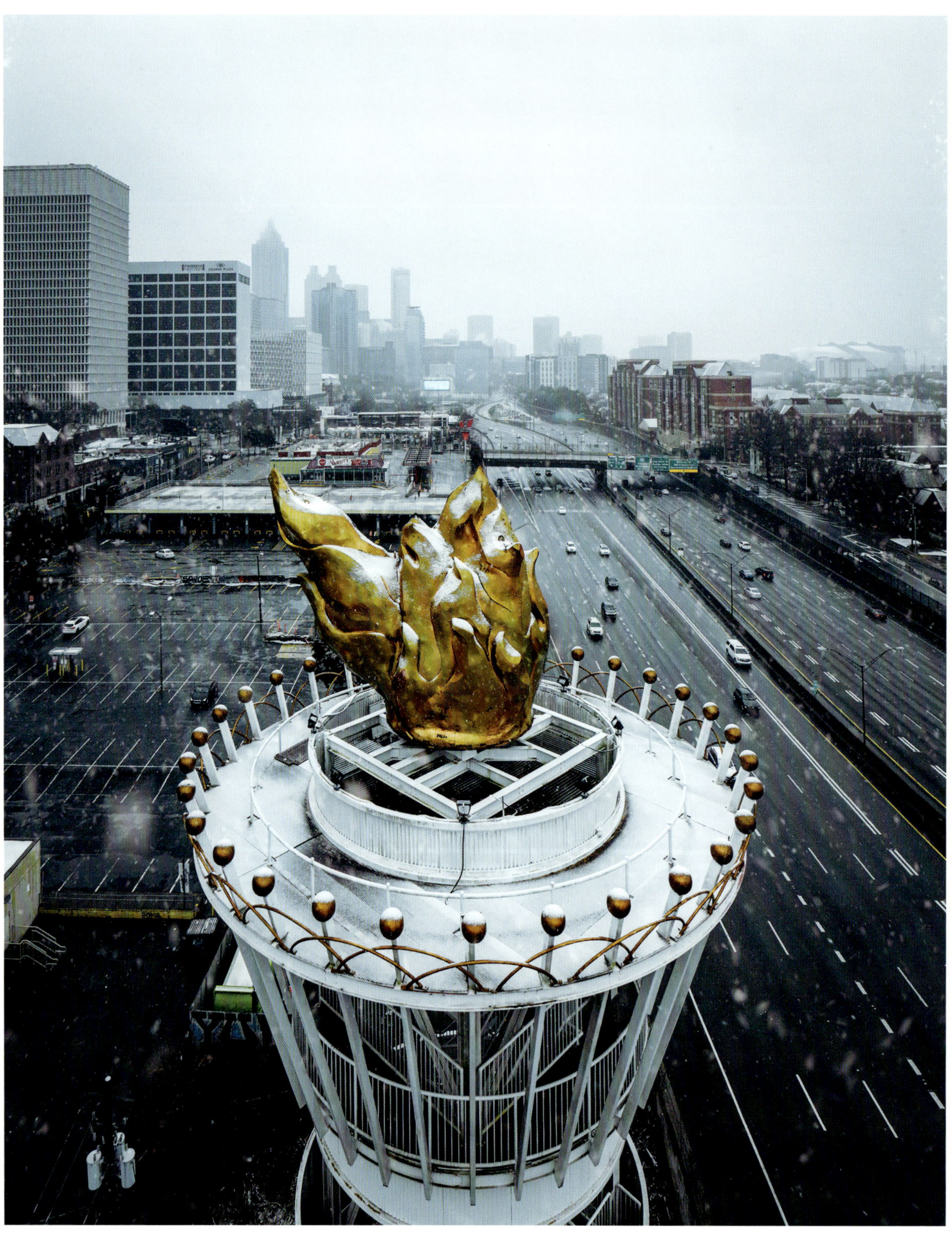

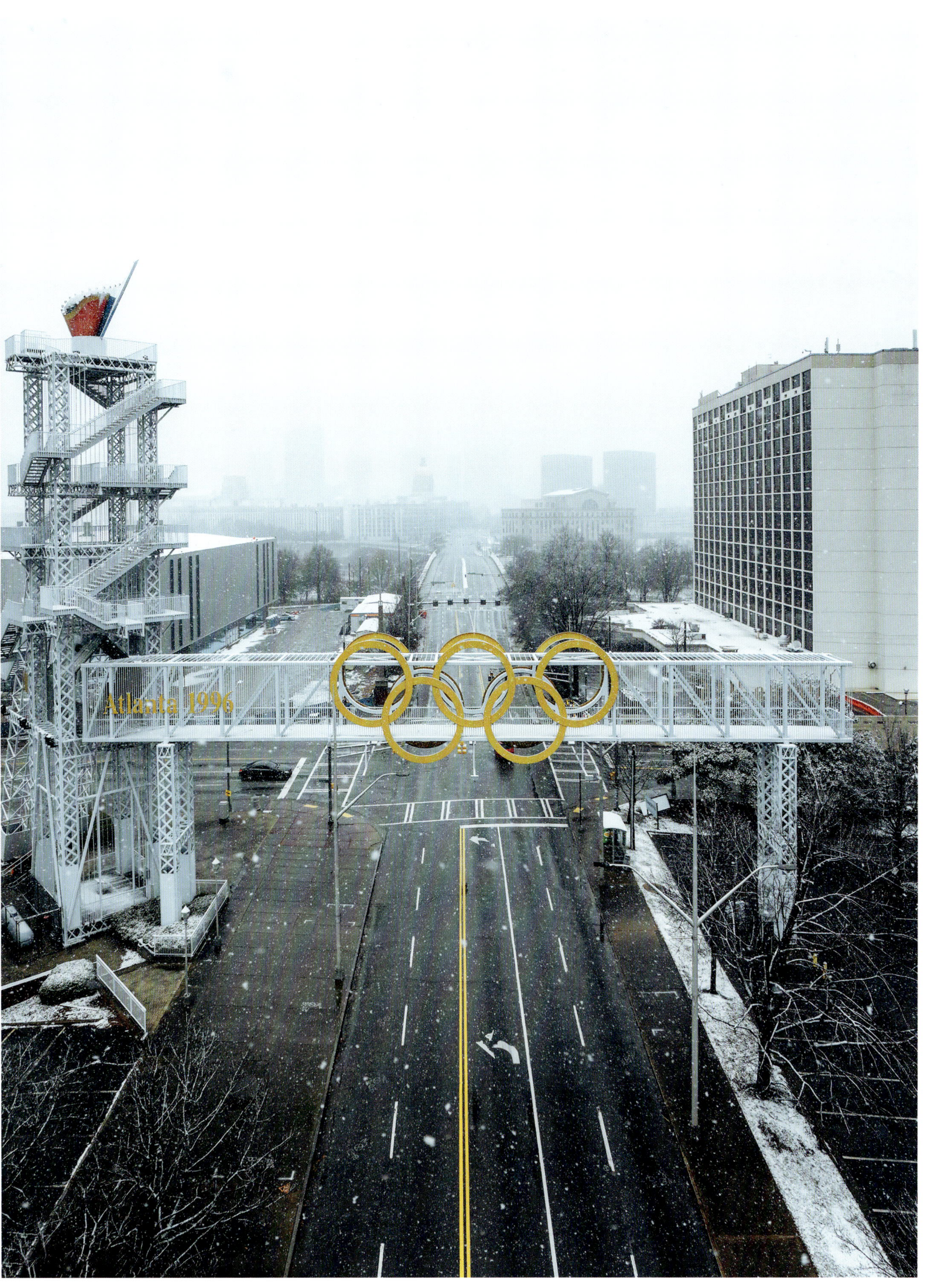

Atlanta 1996

Revitalization ♦ When Atlanta became the fourth U.S. city to host the Olympic Games with the 1996 Summer Olympics, the 100th anniversary of the modern Olympic Games, it underwent a dazzling transformation that redefined the cityscape and revitalized once-neglected parts of the city. ♦ Atlanta utilized both new and existing venues for the Games. One of the notable new constructions, Centennial Olympic Park served as a central gathering place for visitors and hosted various events, including the Festival of the American South, a multicultural expression of southern life. Once an overlooked area, Centennial Olympic Park was transformed into a vibrant green space with its iconic Fountain of Rings. After the Games, a significant portion of the park was redesigned for daily public use, and today Centennial Olympic Park is a bustling space for concerts, festivals, and outdoor activities. ♦ Another structure built specifically for the Olympics, Centennial Olympic Stadium served as the main stadium for the Games, hosting the opening and closing ceremonies, as well as track and field events. The stadium was converted into the baseball park Turner Field, which opened in 1997, home to the Atlanta Braves until the conclusion of their 2016 season. ♦ The Olympic Village, initially home to thousands of athletes, was reimagined after the Olympics as dormitories for Georgia State University. This clever repurposing not only addressed student housing needs but also injected vitality into nearby neighborhoods. The influx of real estate investment during this period spurred a construction boom, with new residential and commercial properties reshaping the city's skyline. ♦ In addition to making sports history, the Atlanta Olympics attracted millions of visitors from around the world, leaving a lasting impact on the city. The international attention attracted new businesses, once-abandoned neighborhoods were reimagined and redeveloped, and Atlanta's transportation infrastructure saw needed improvements. The legacy of the 1996 Olympic Games is woven into the fabric of Atlanta, shaping its present and future.

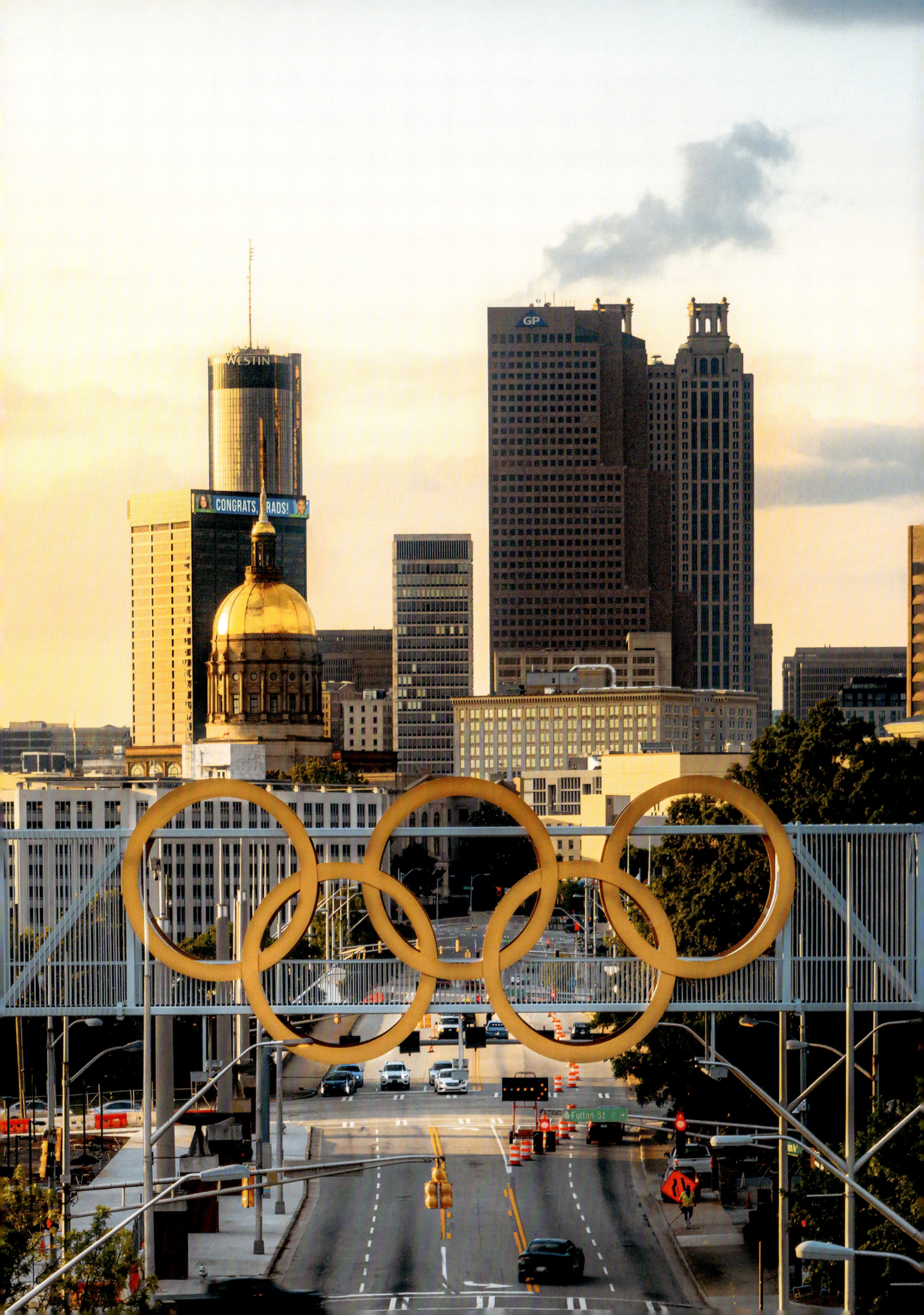

WESTIN
CONGRATS, GRADS!
GP
Fulton St

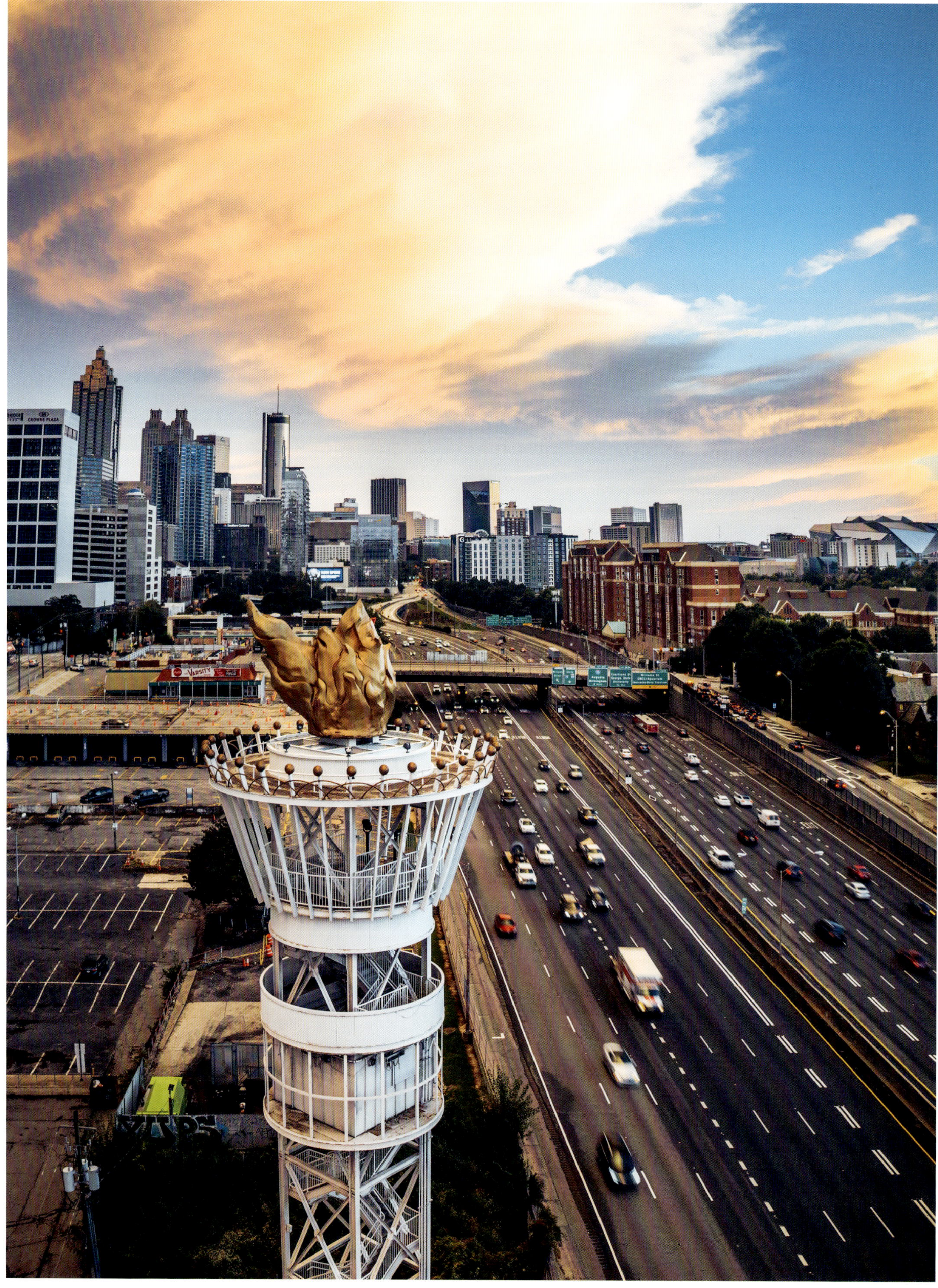

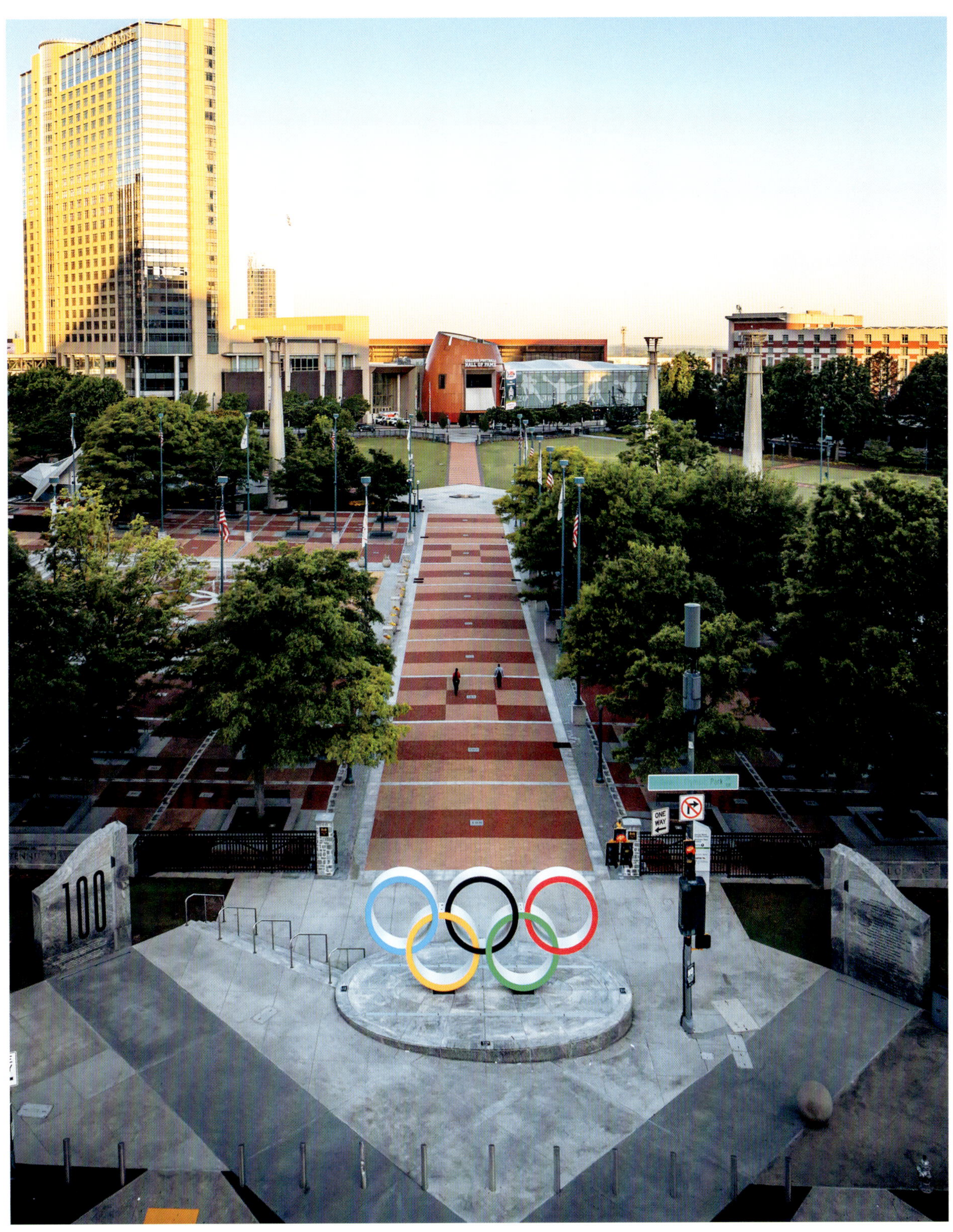

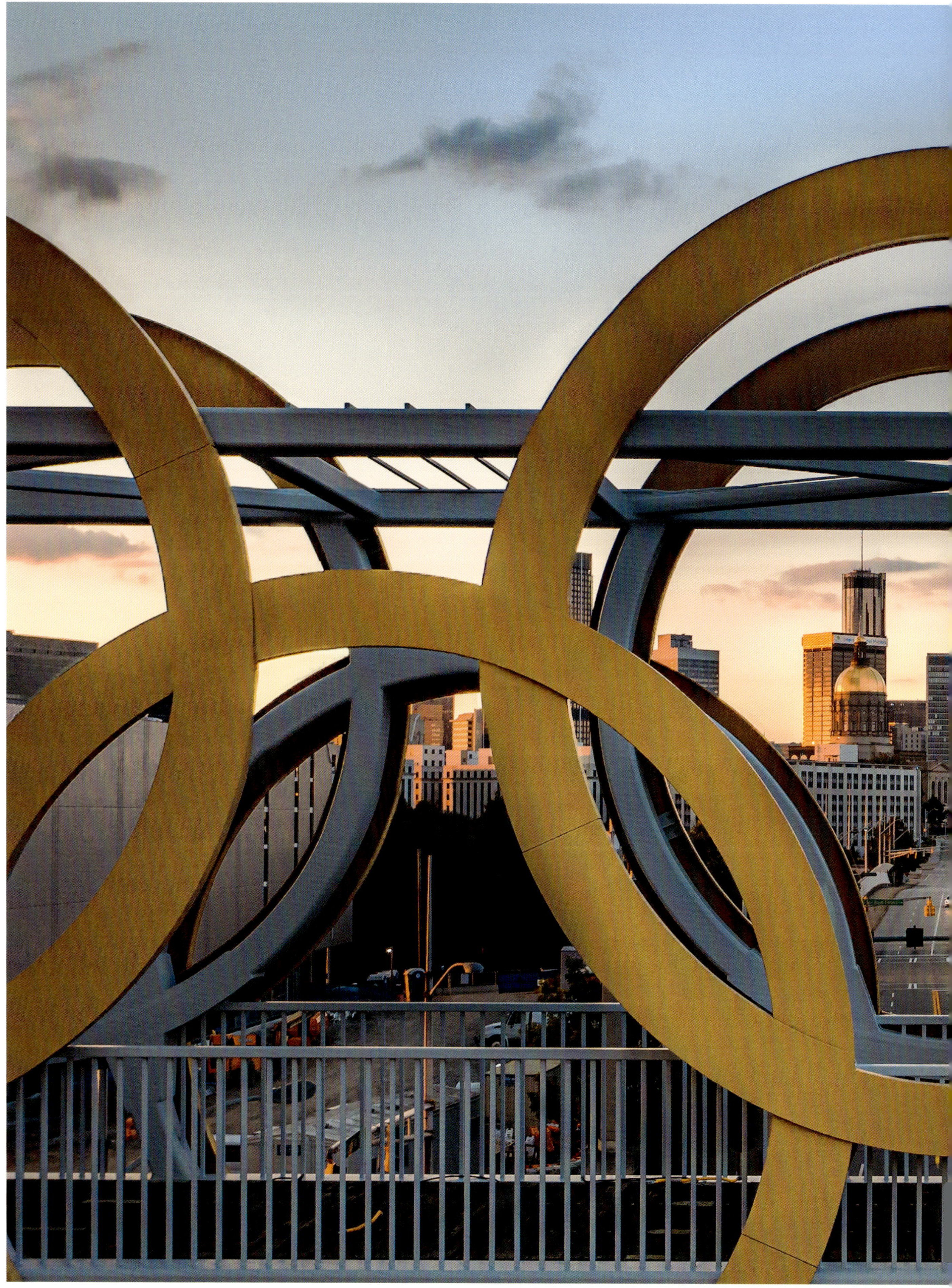

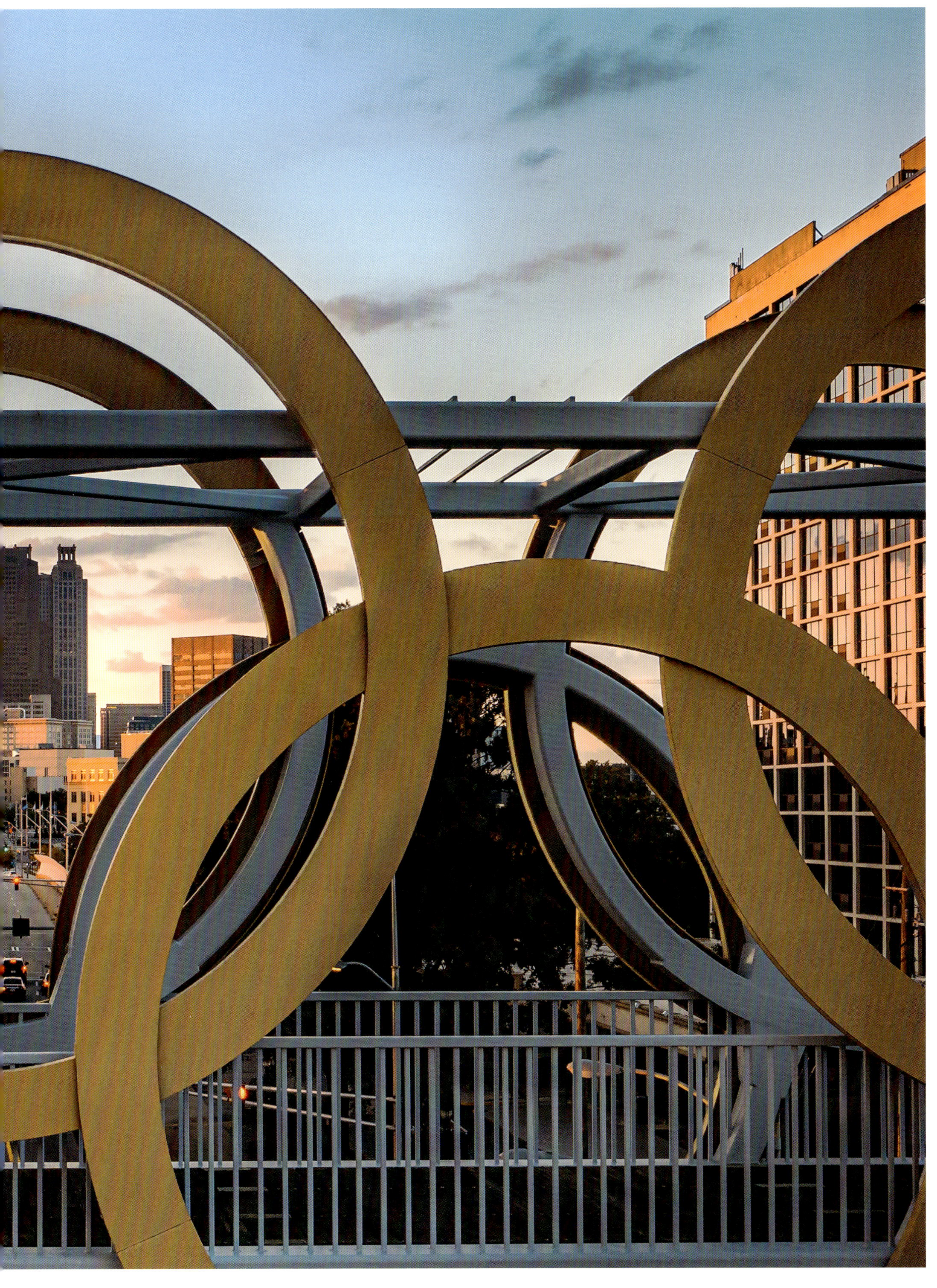

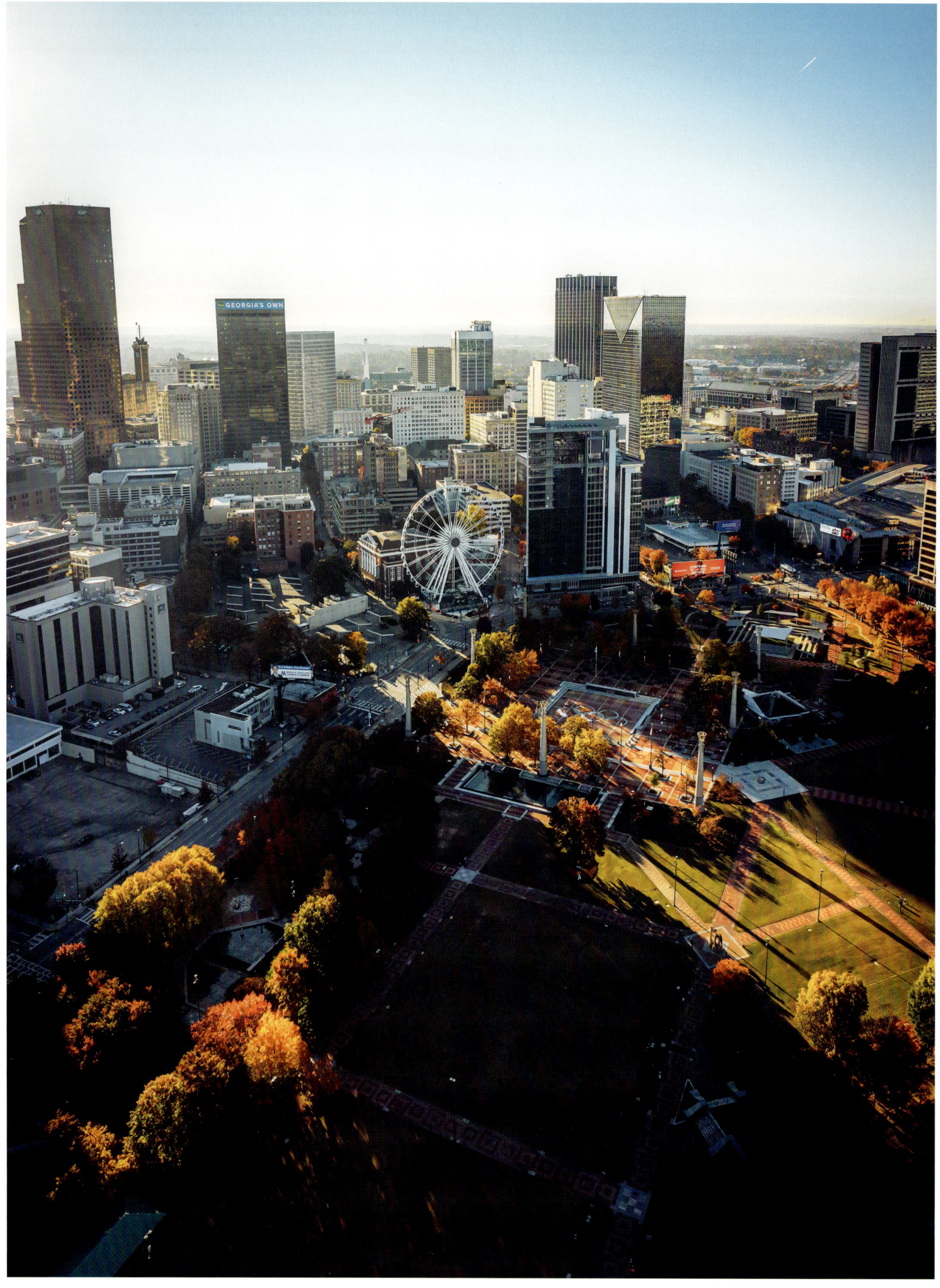

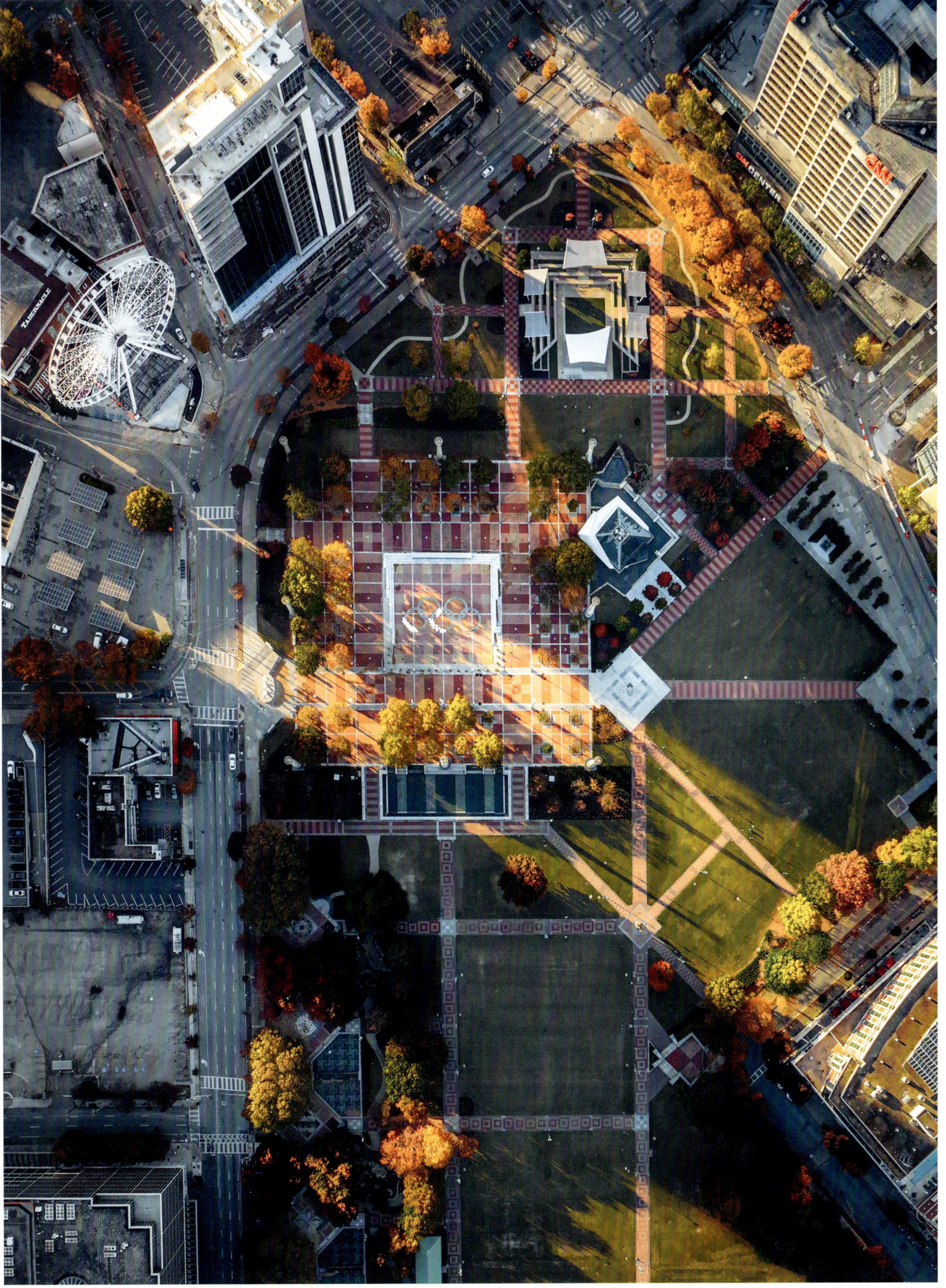

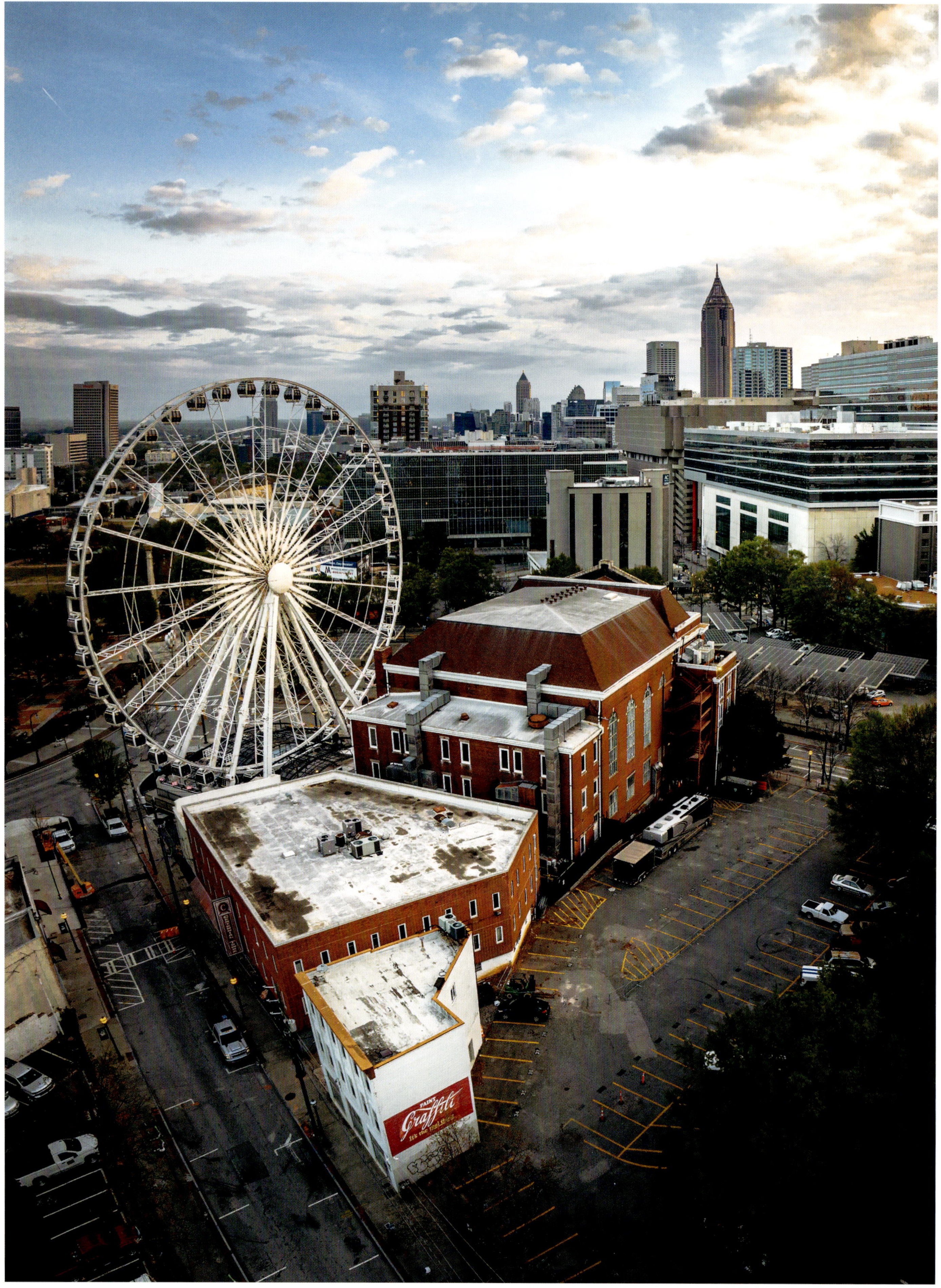
Graffiti

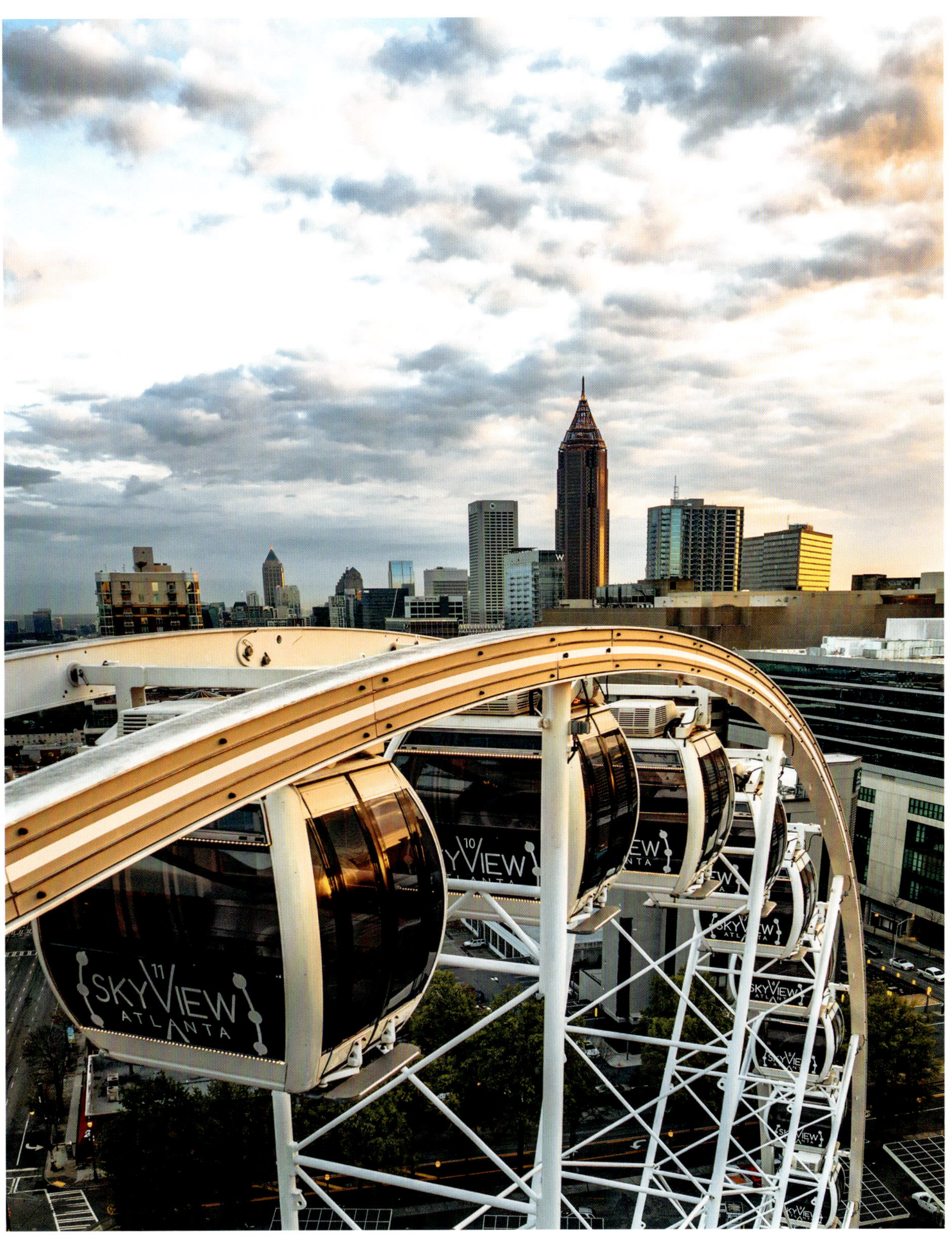

SKYVIEW
ATLANTA
SKYVIEW
ATLANTA

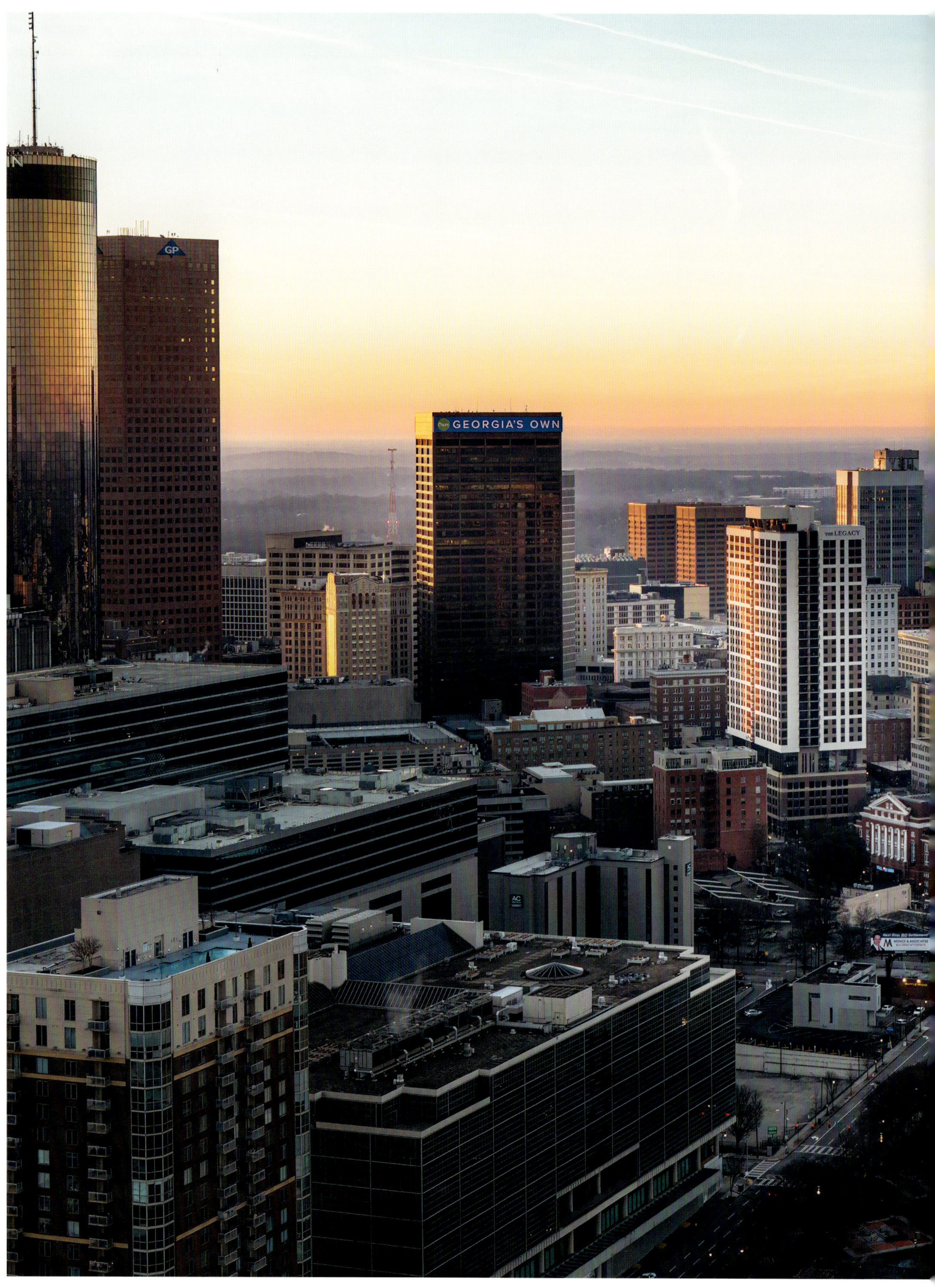

GEORGIA'S OWN
GP
THE LEGACY
AC

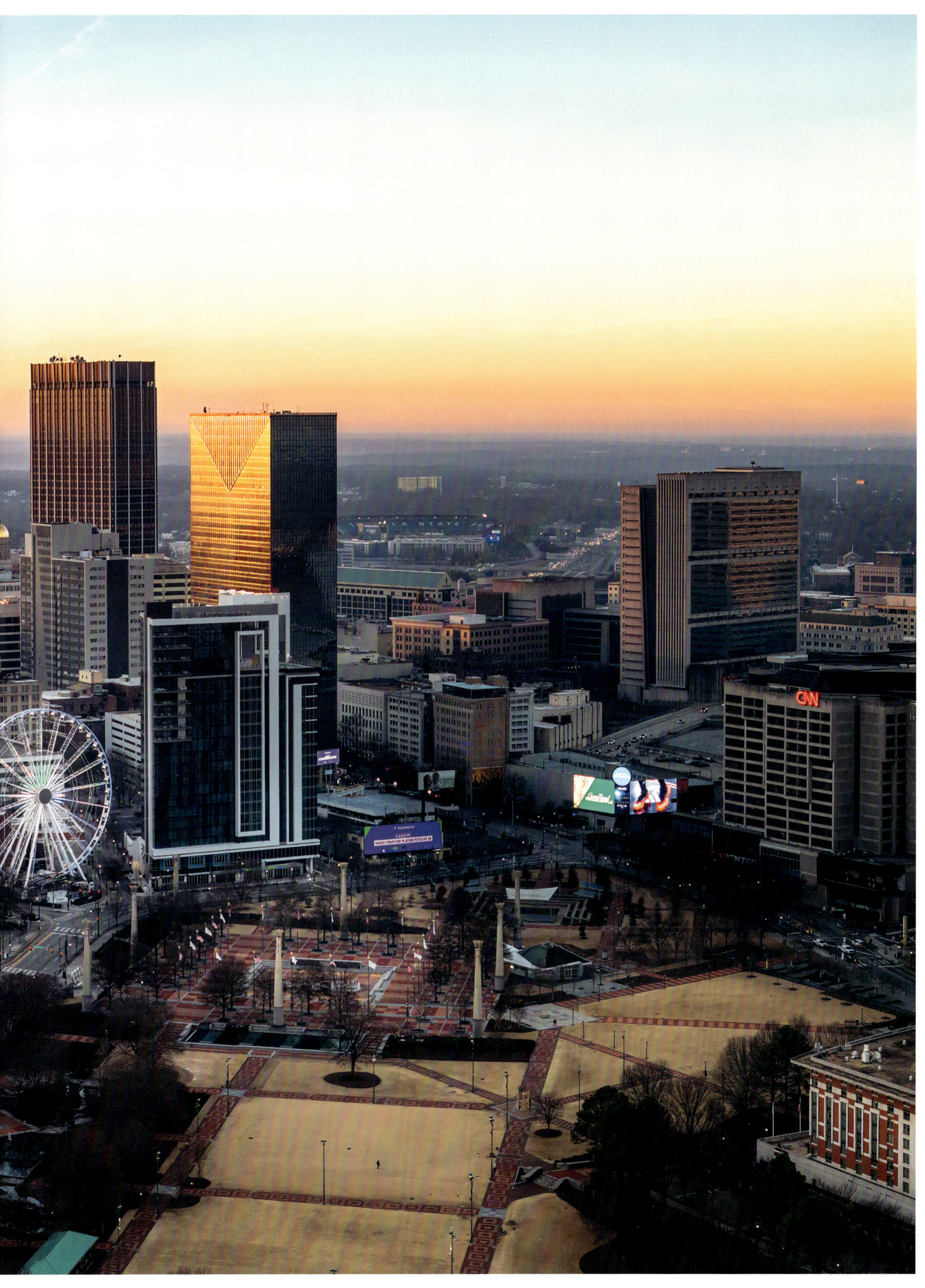

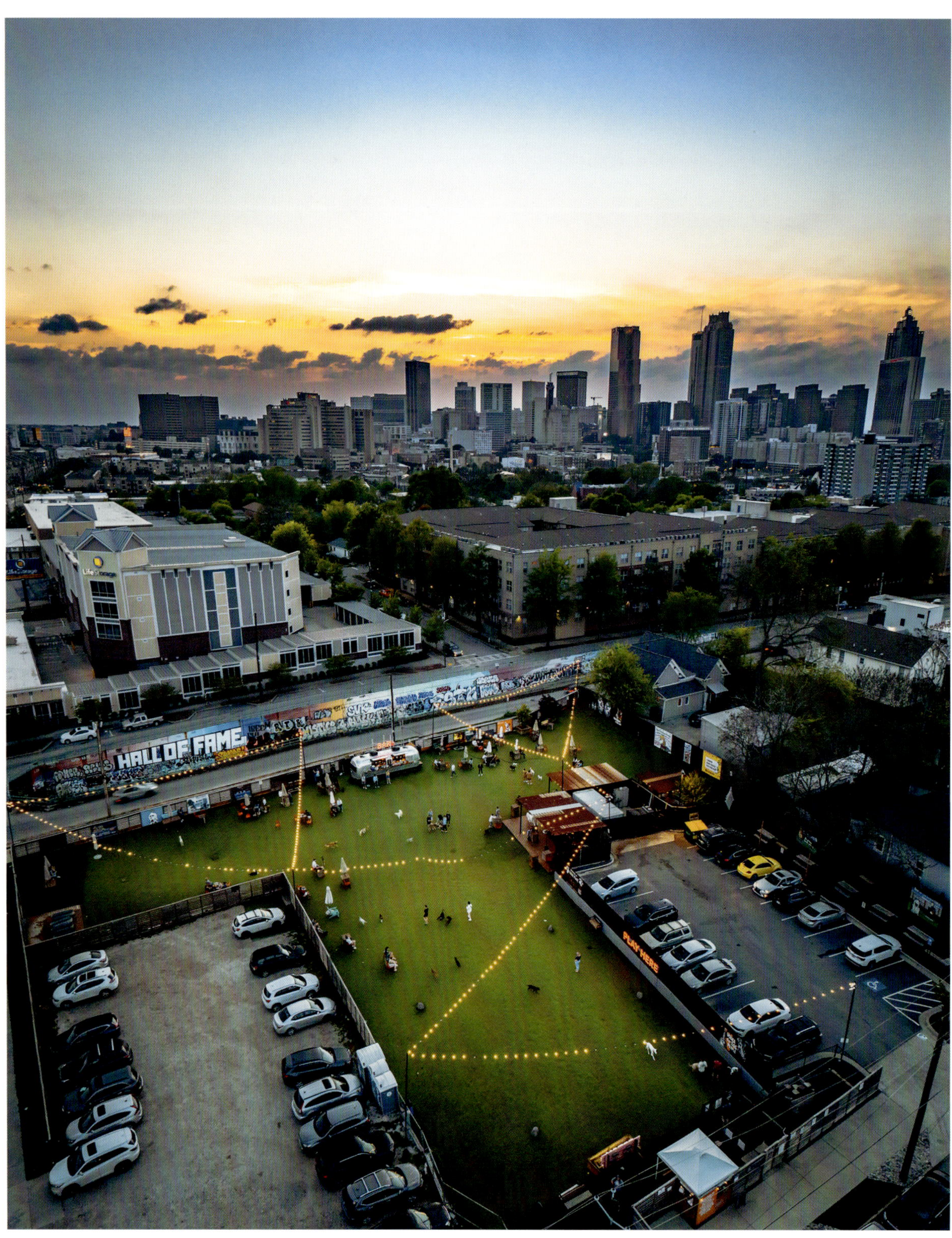

HALL OF FAME
PLAY HERE

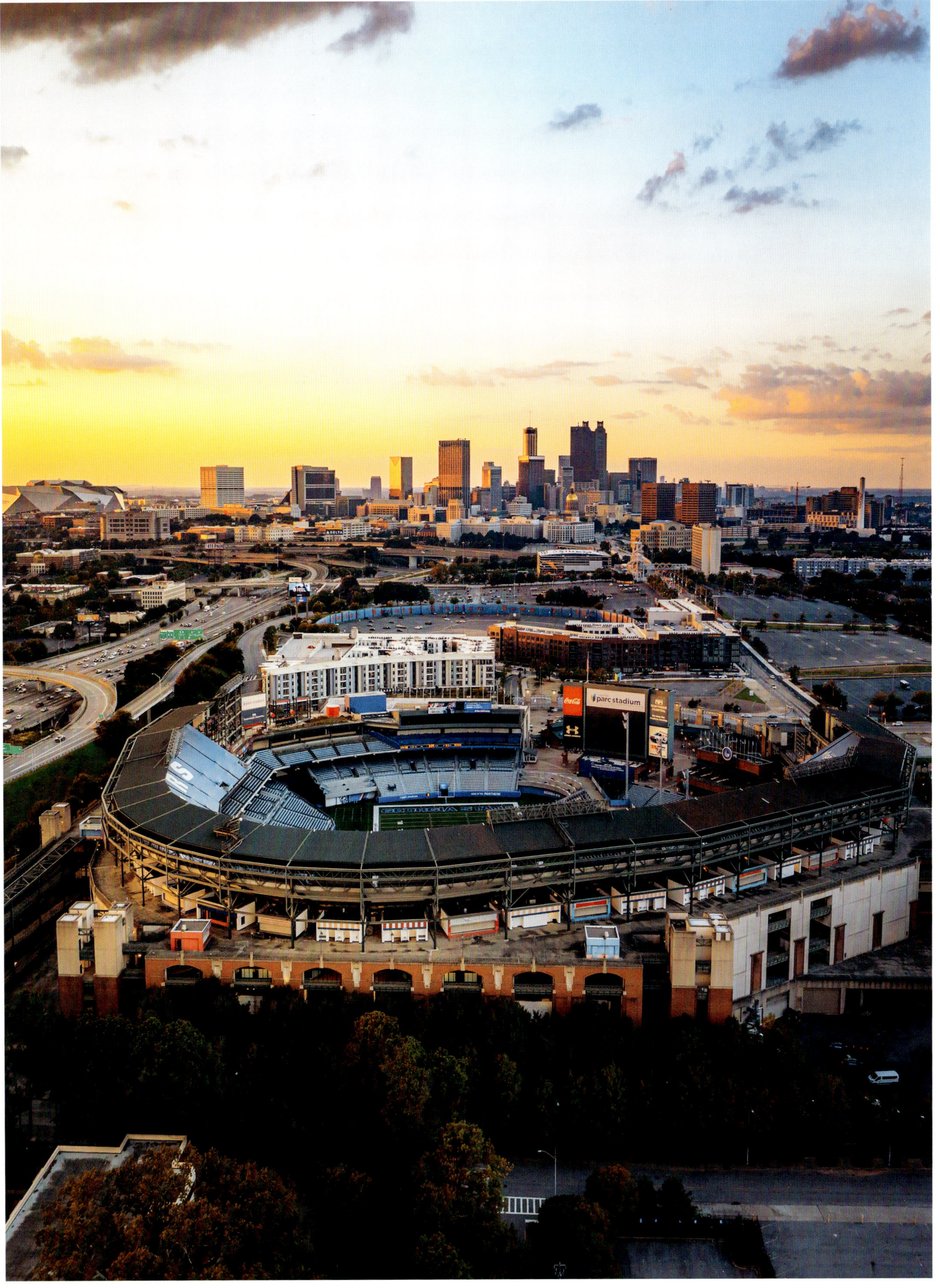
Coca-Cola
parc stadium

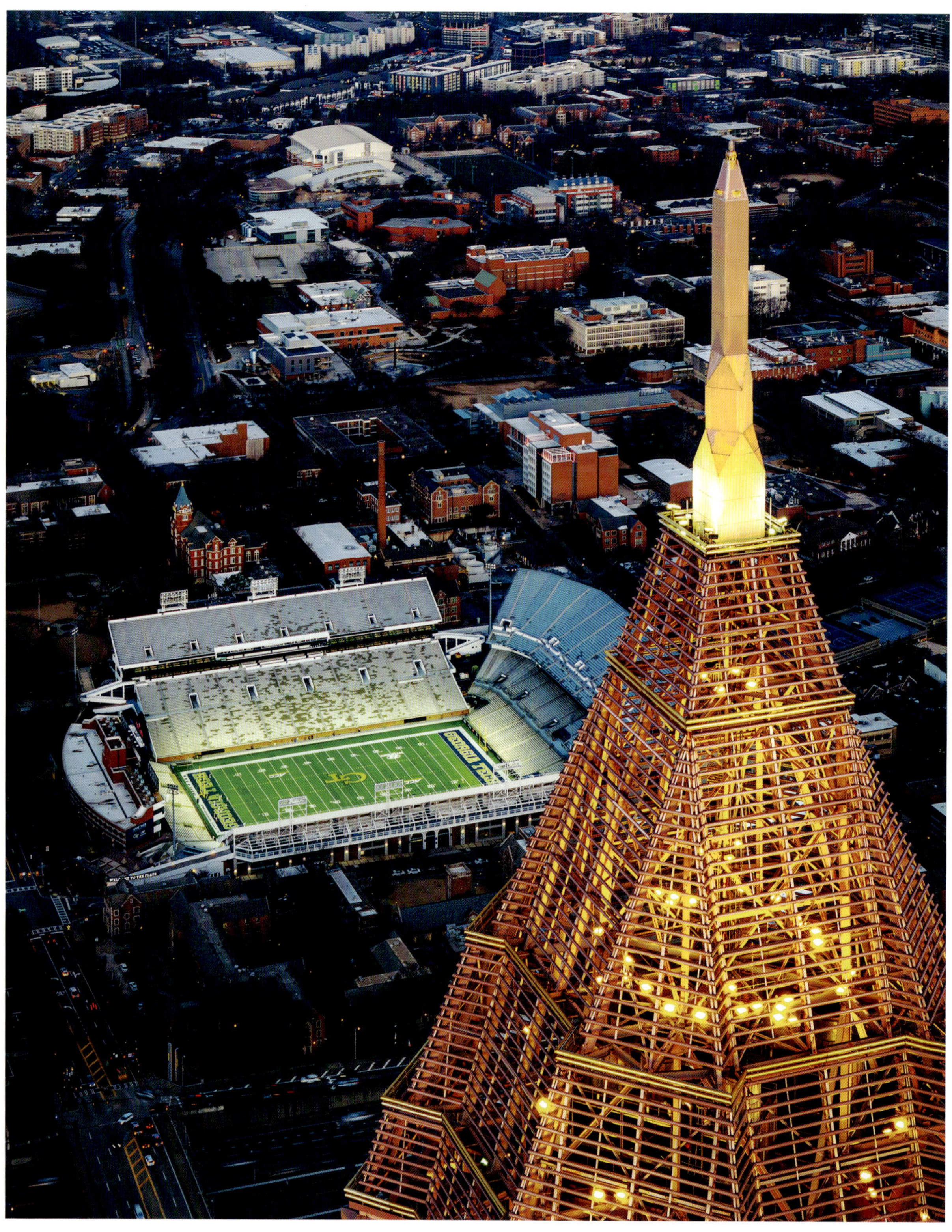

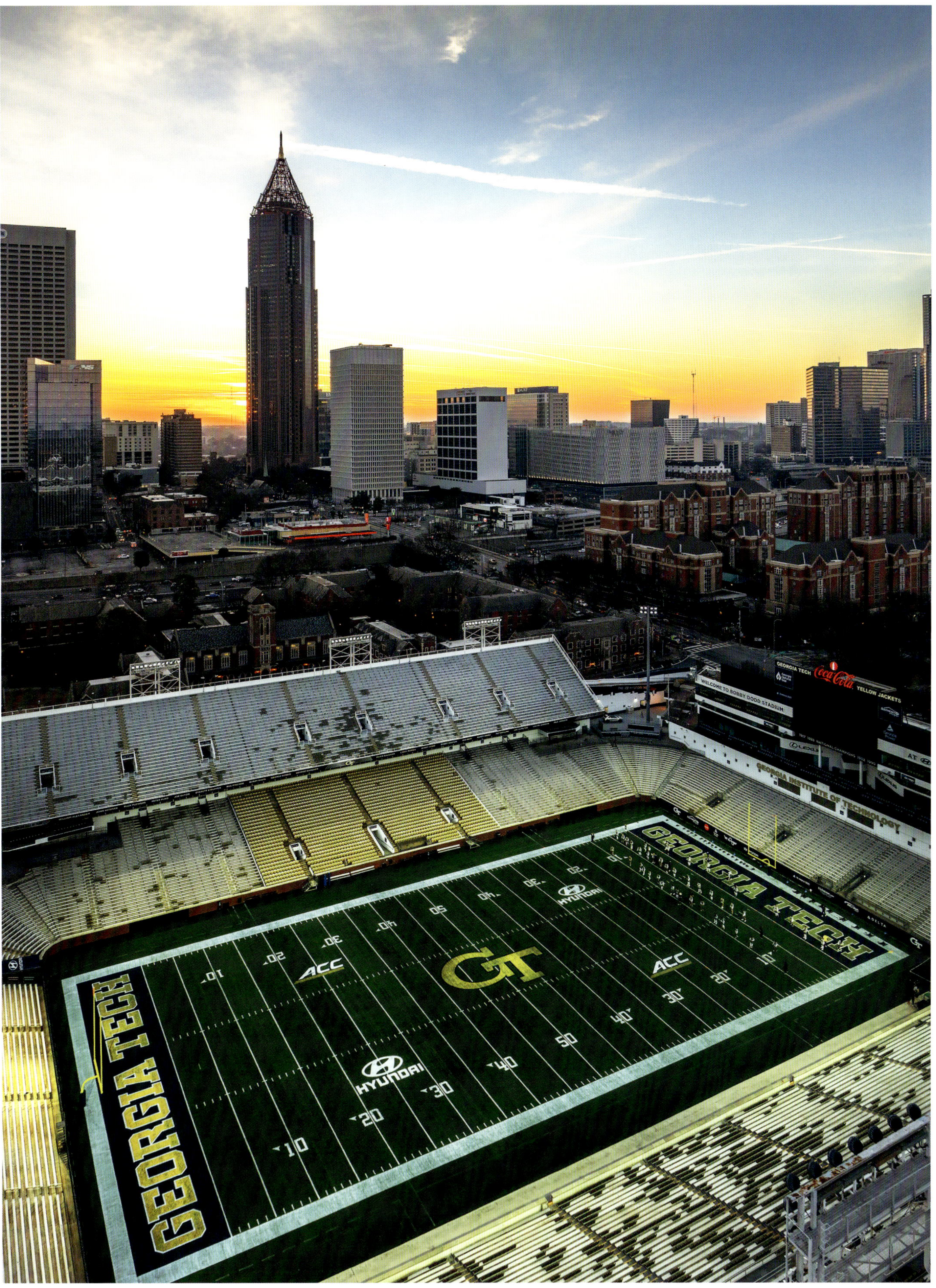

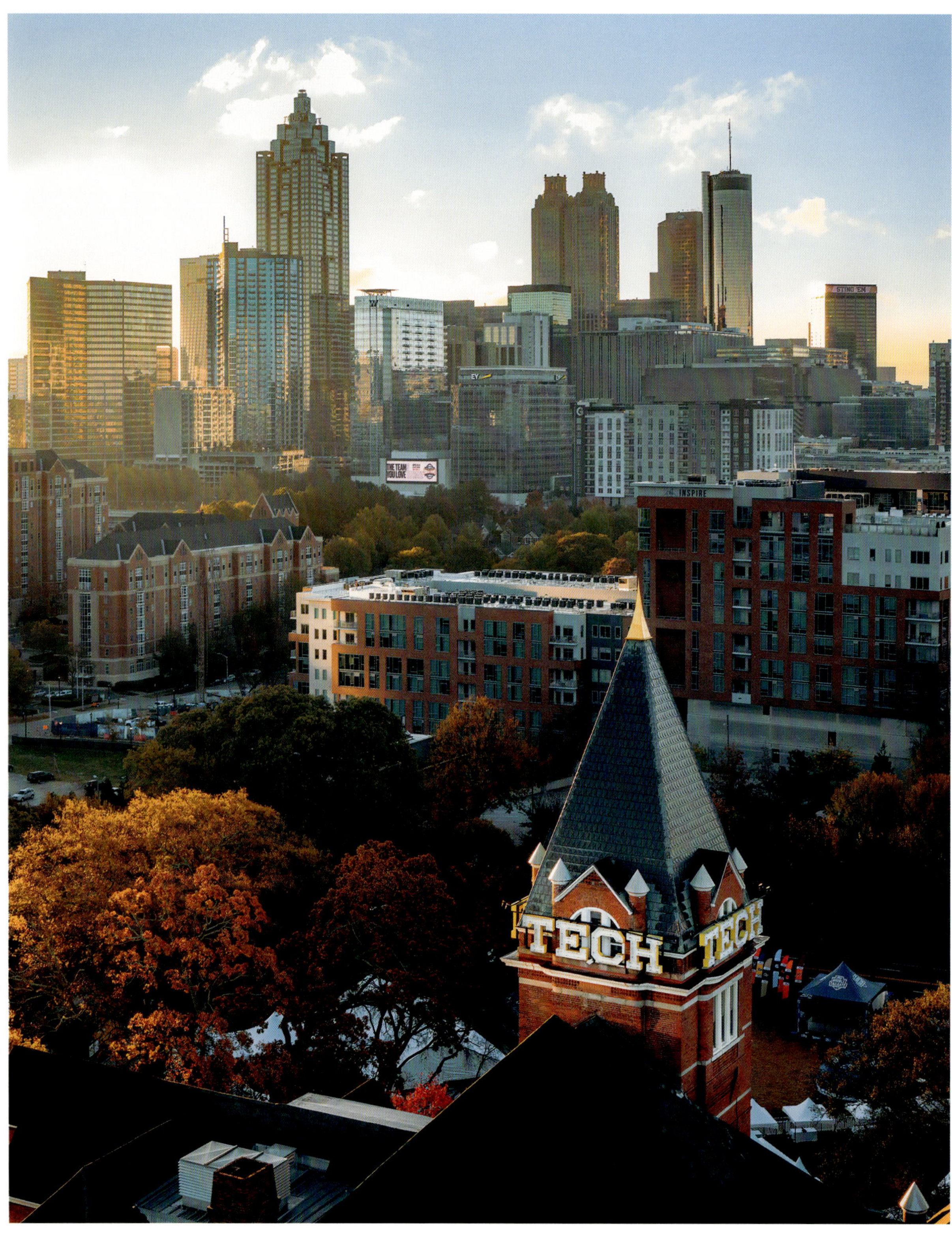

TECH
TECH
INSPIRE

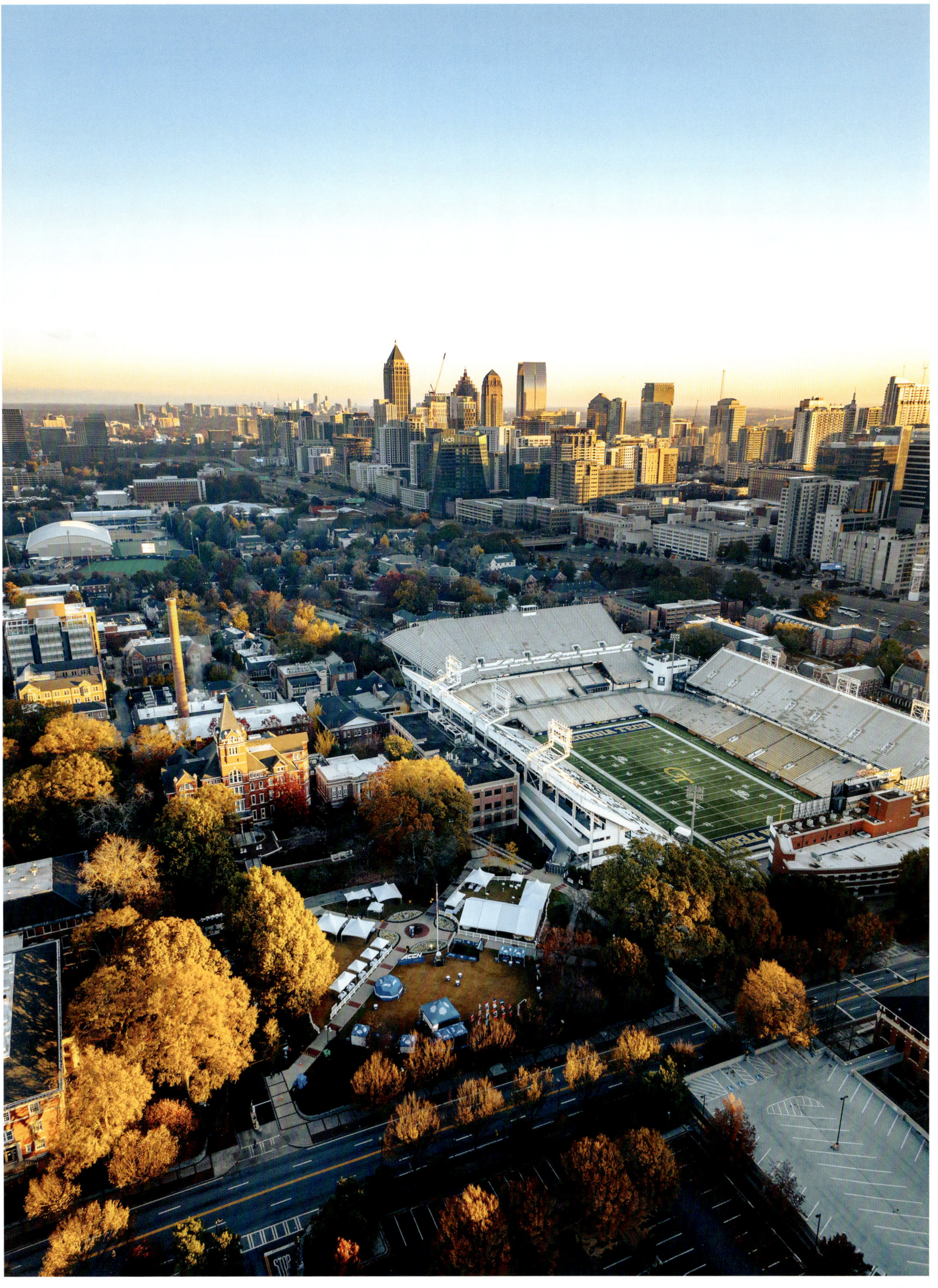

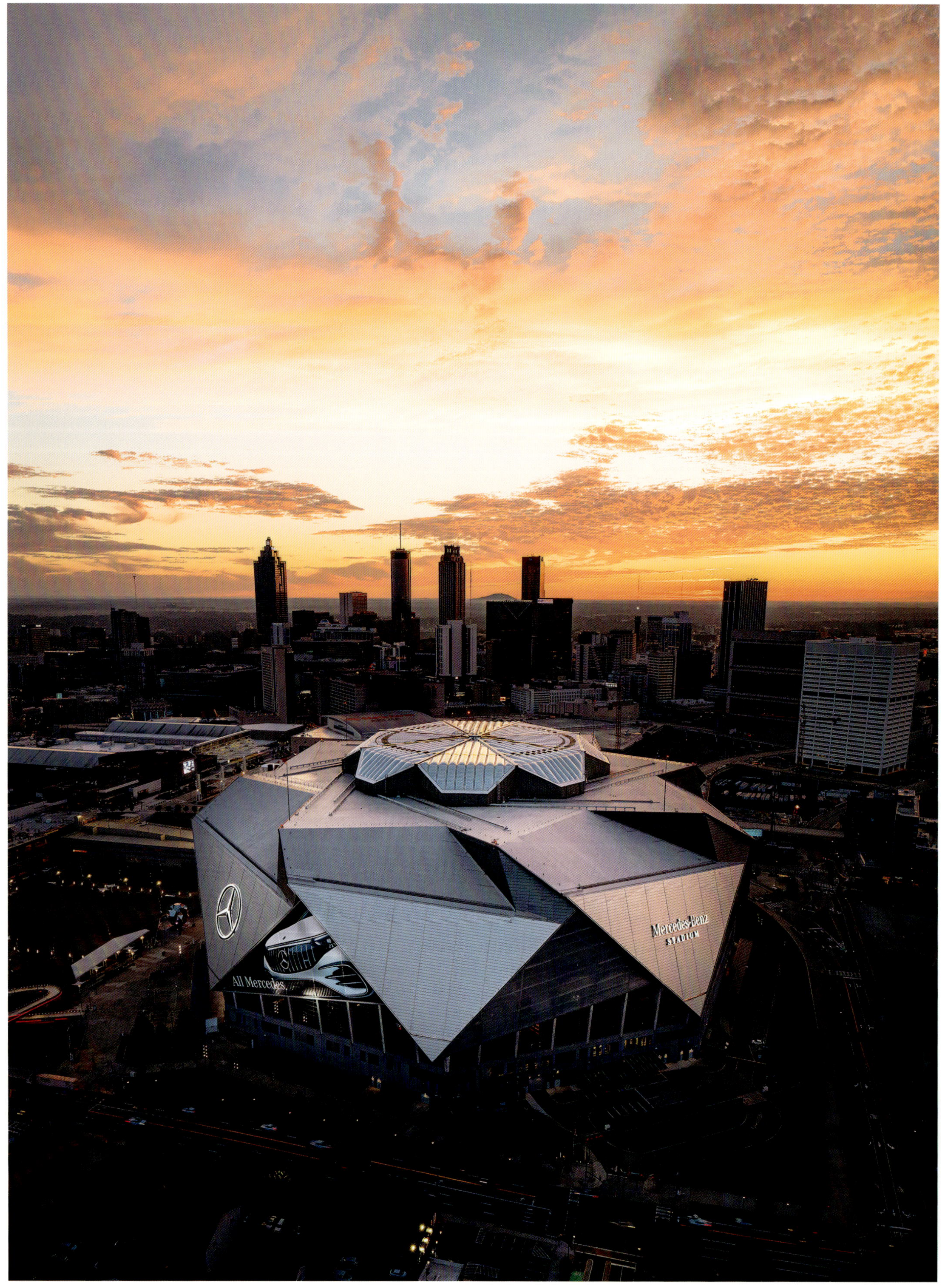

Mercedes-Benz
STADIUM
All Mercedes.

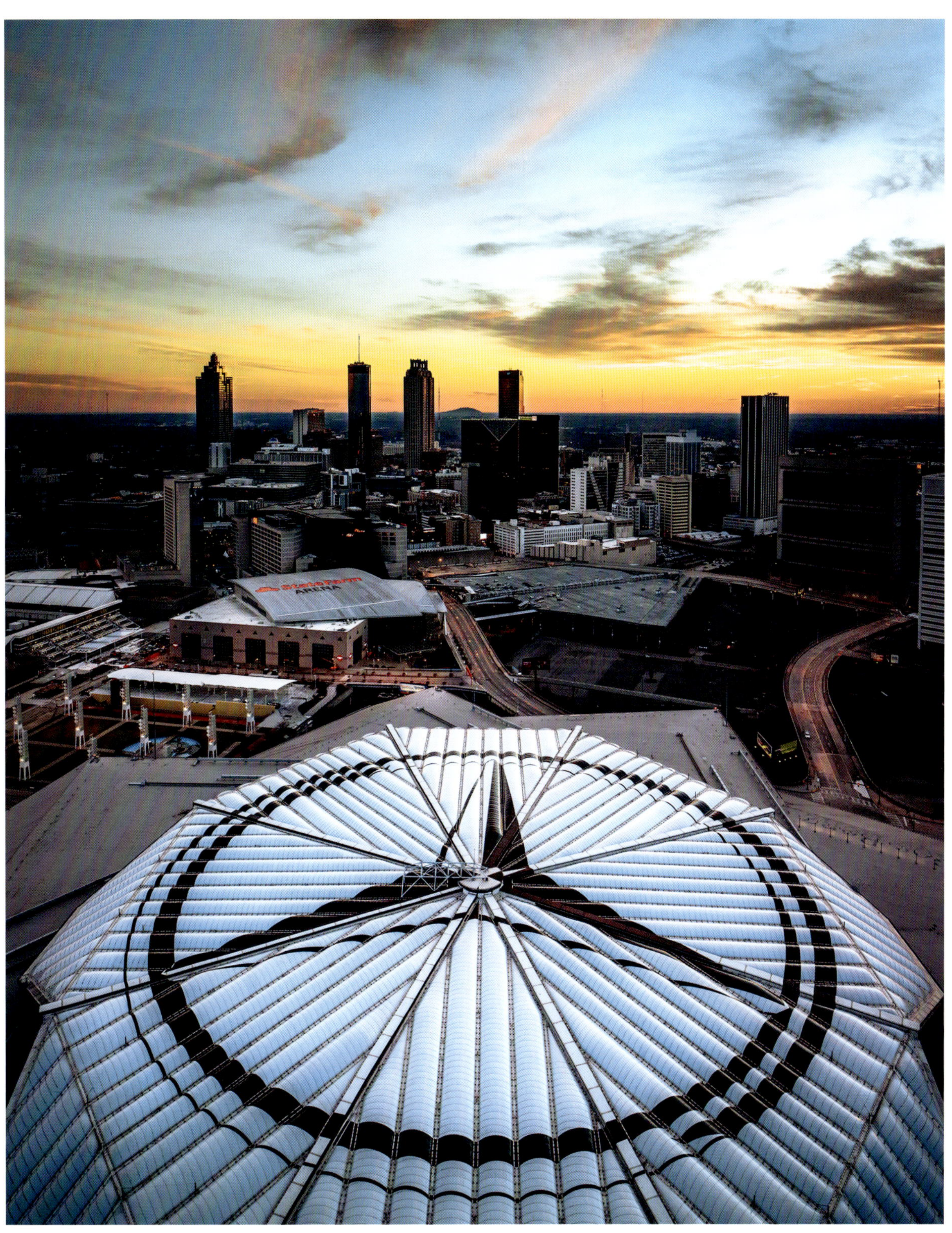

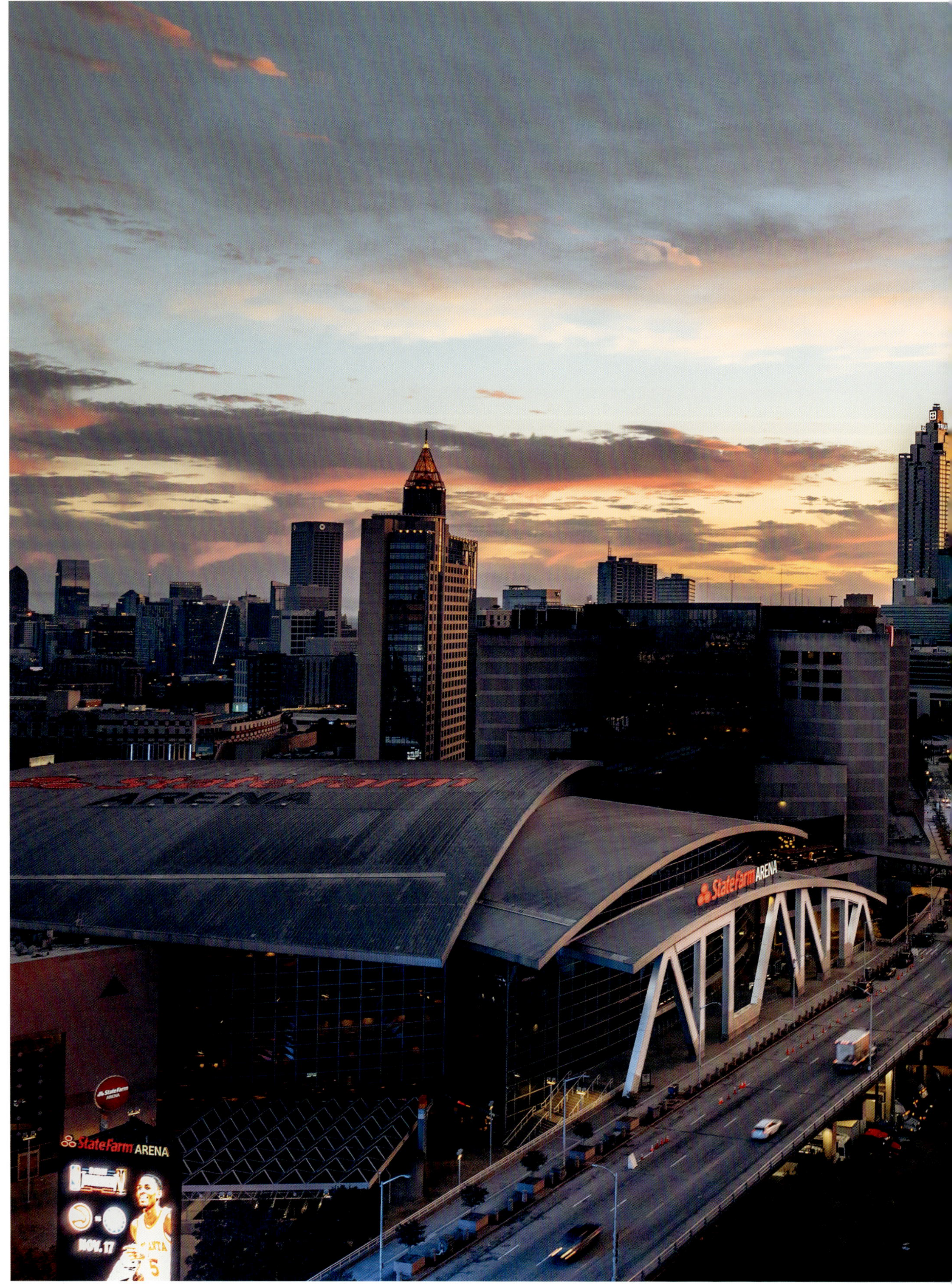
State Farm ARENA
ATLANTA
State Farm ARENA
State Farm ARENA
NOV. 17

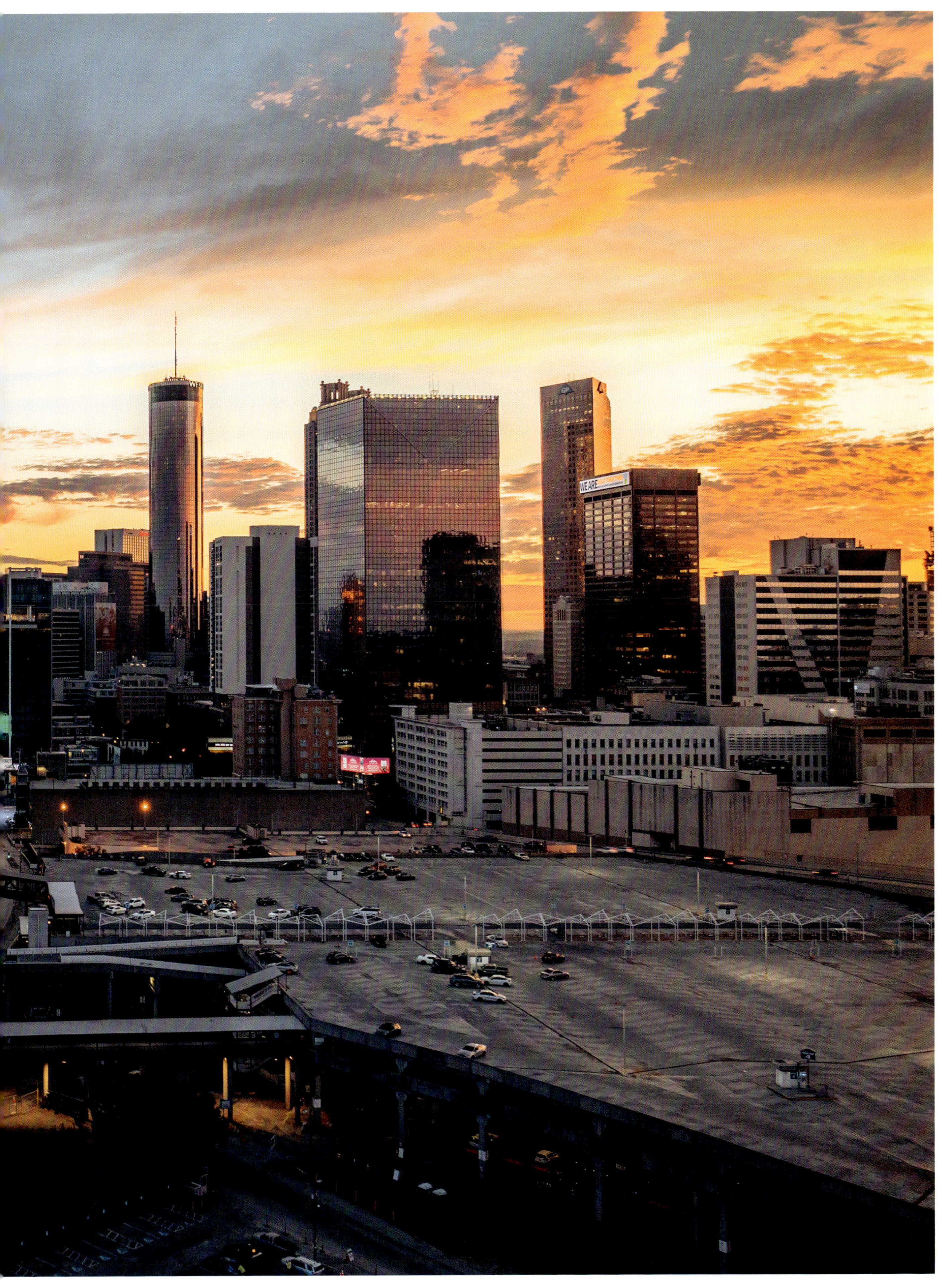
WE ARE

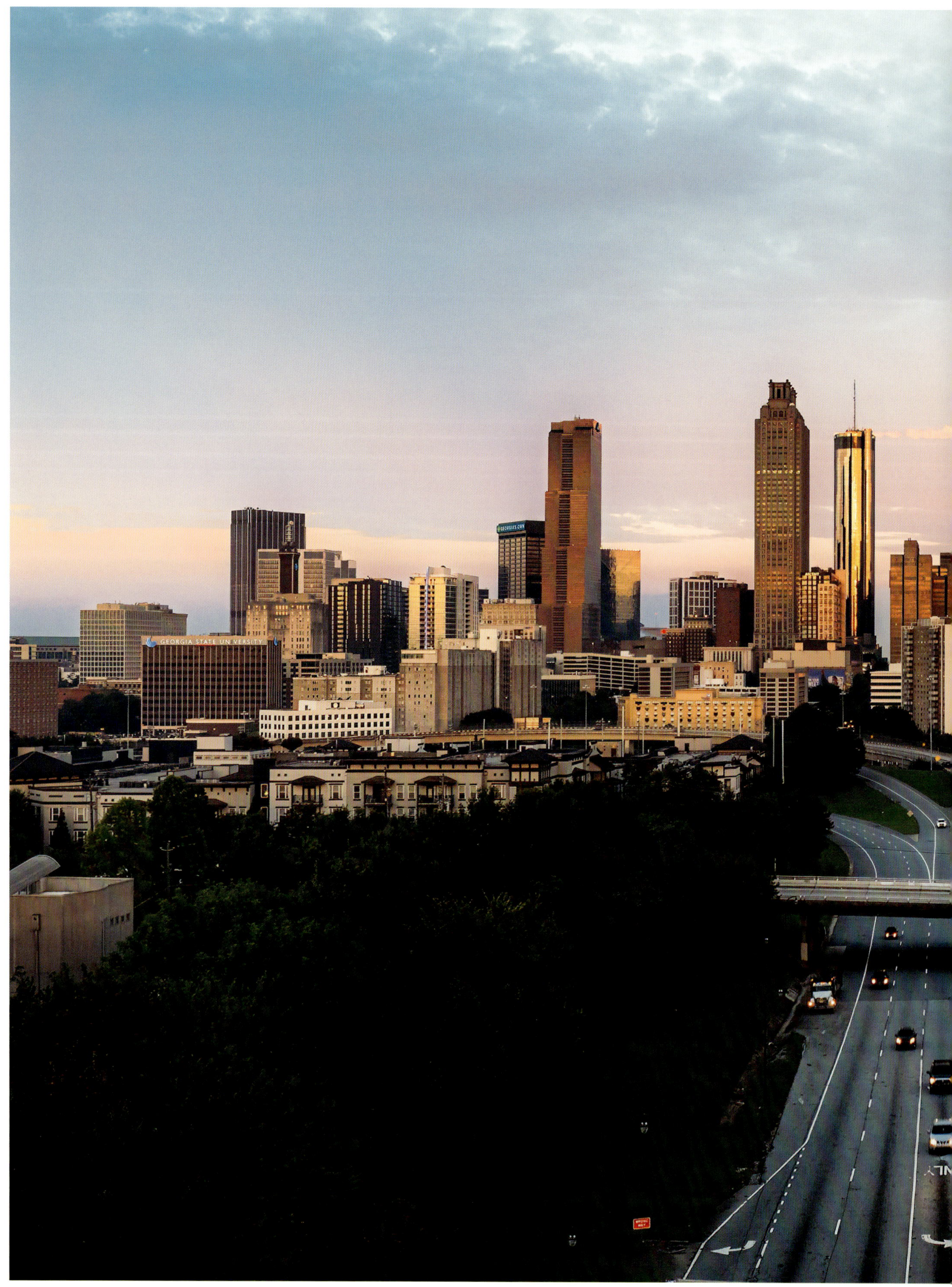

GEORGIA STATE UNIVERSITY

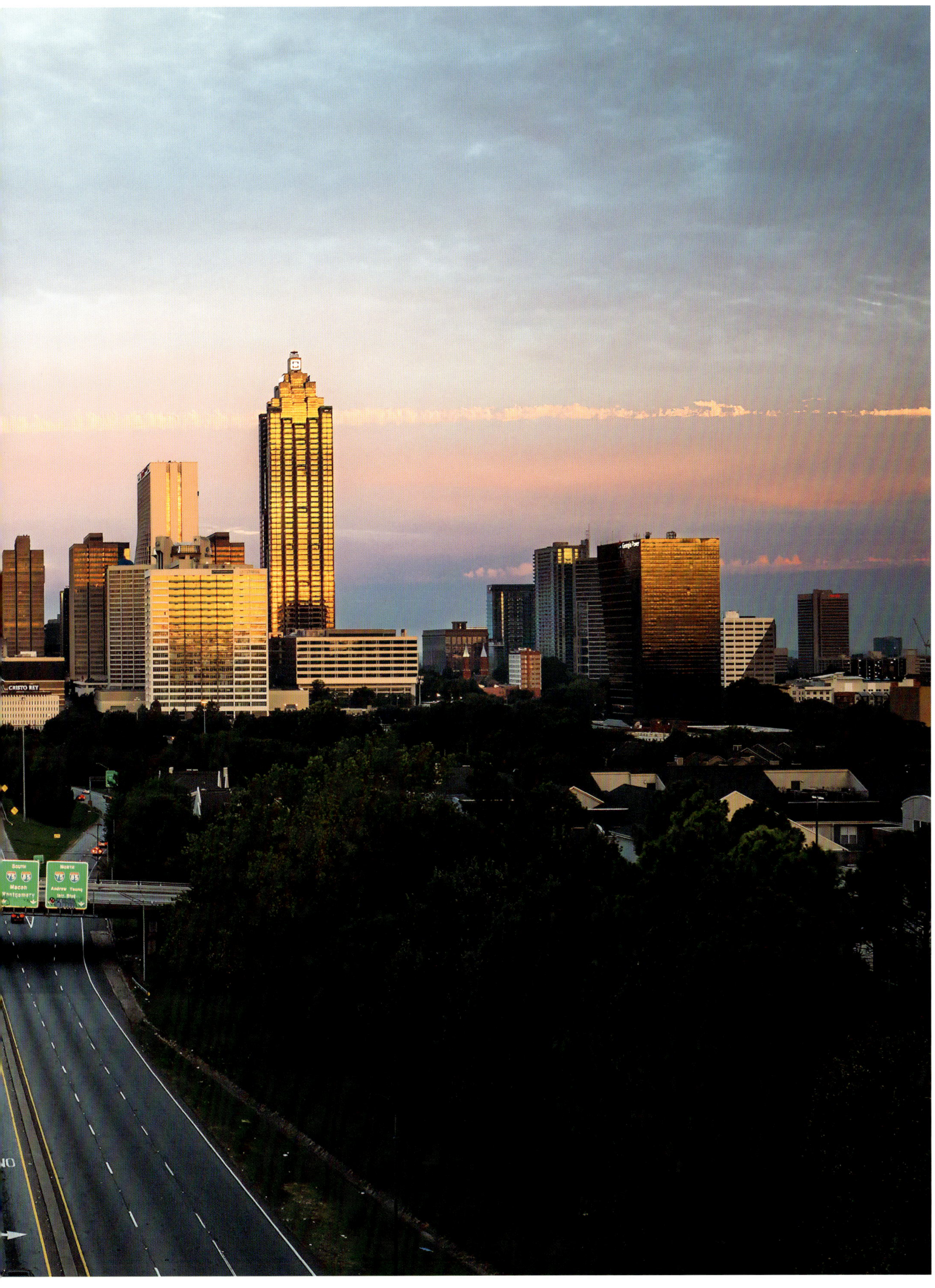

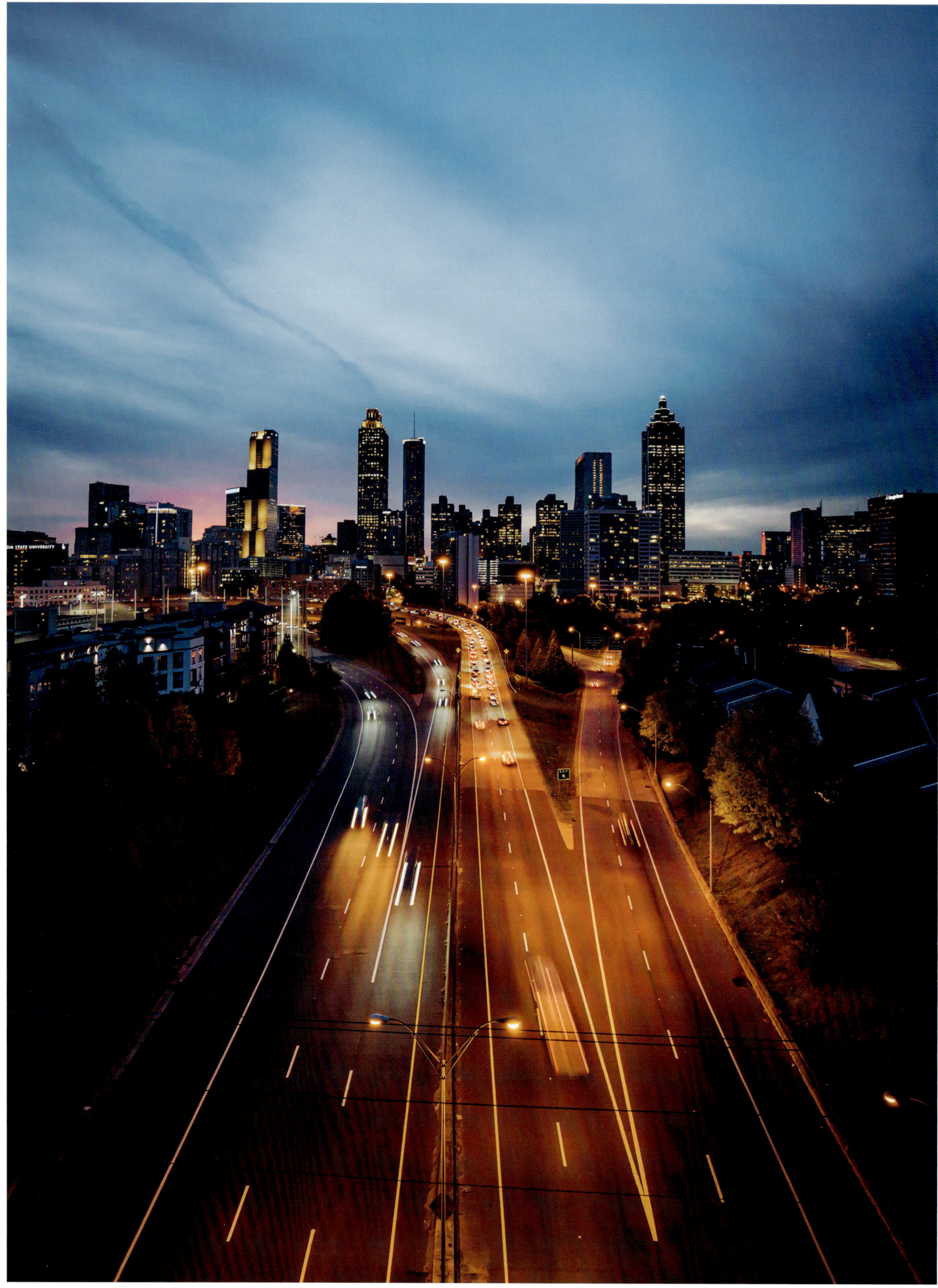

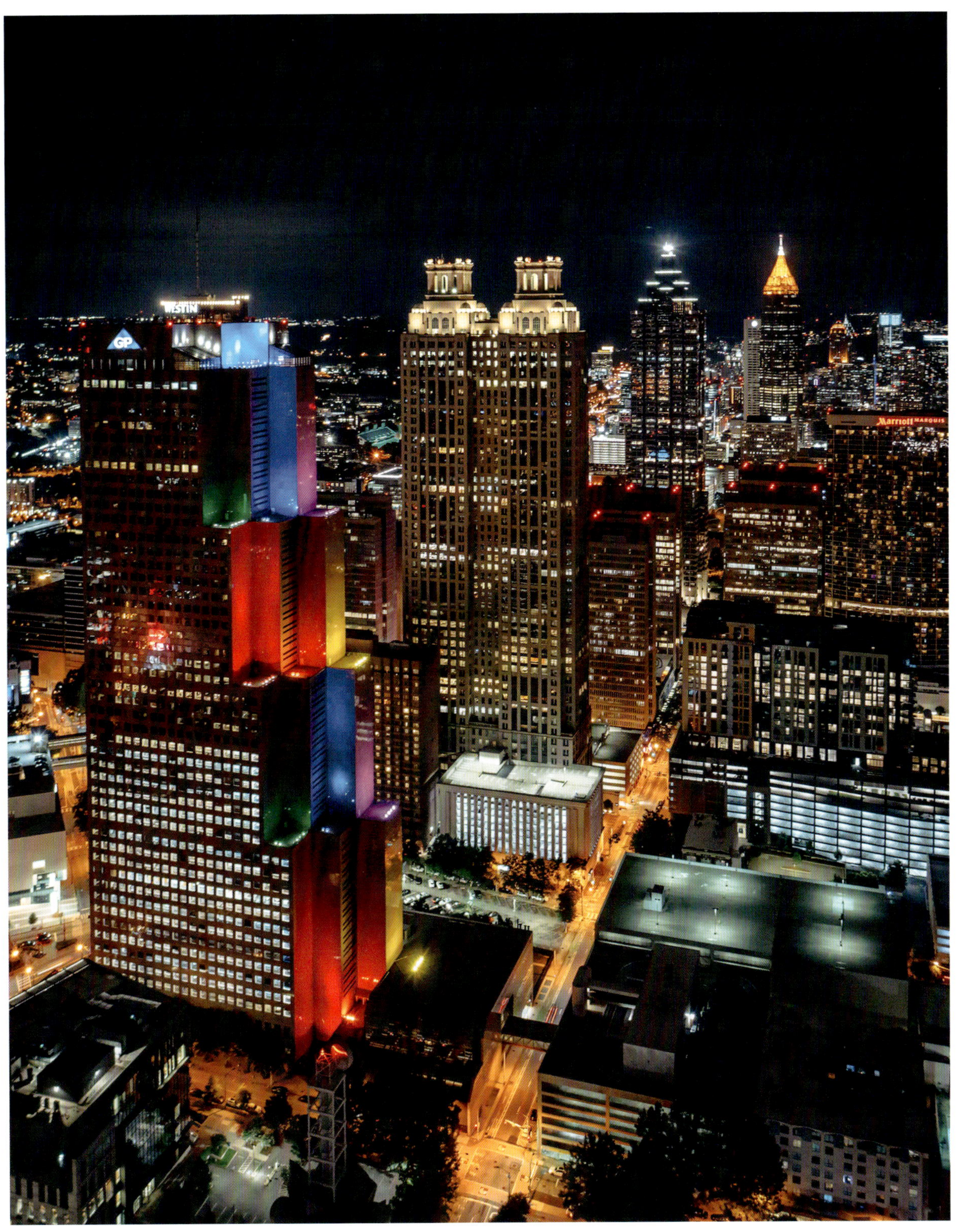

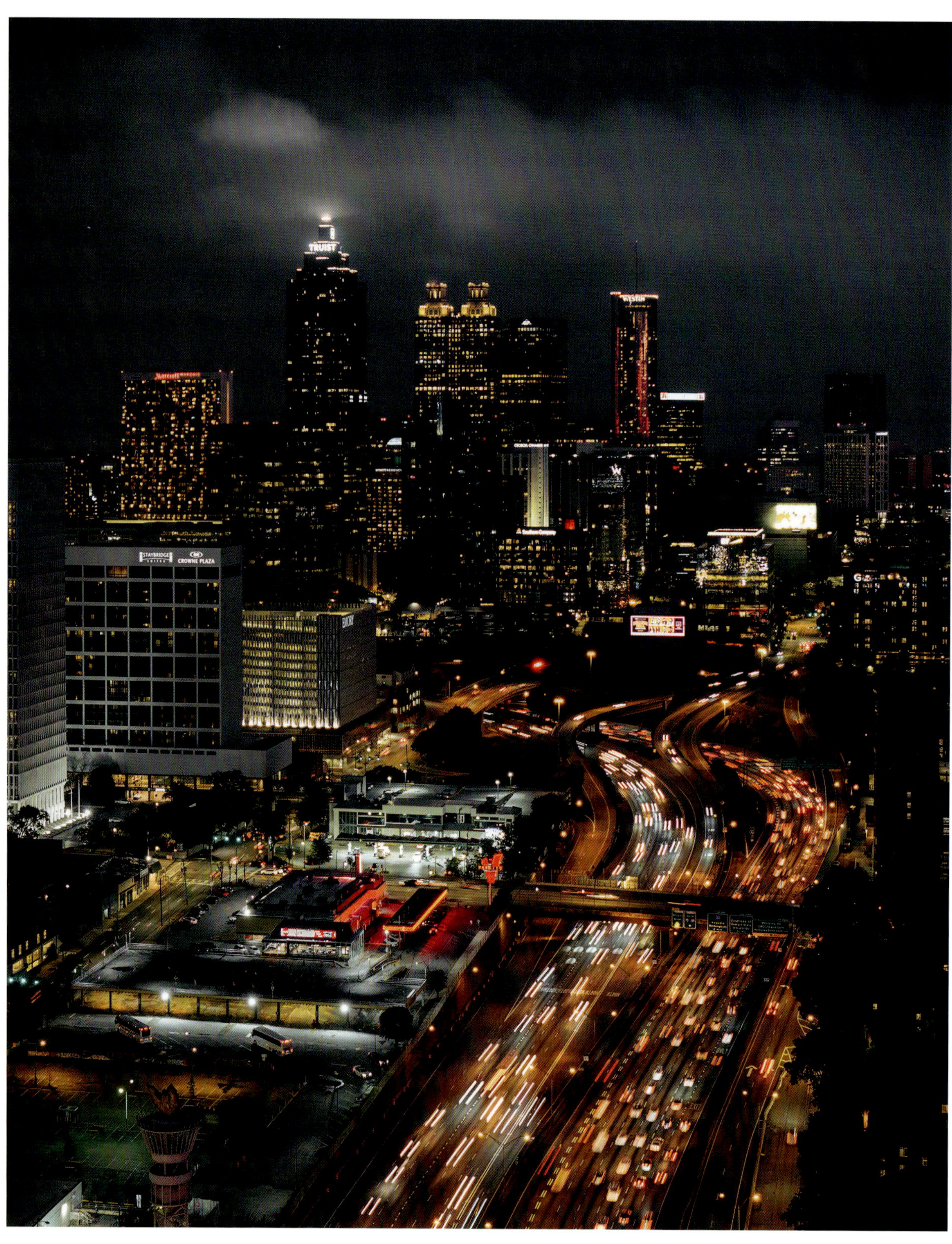

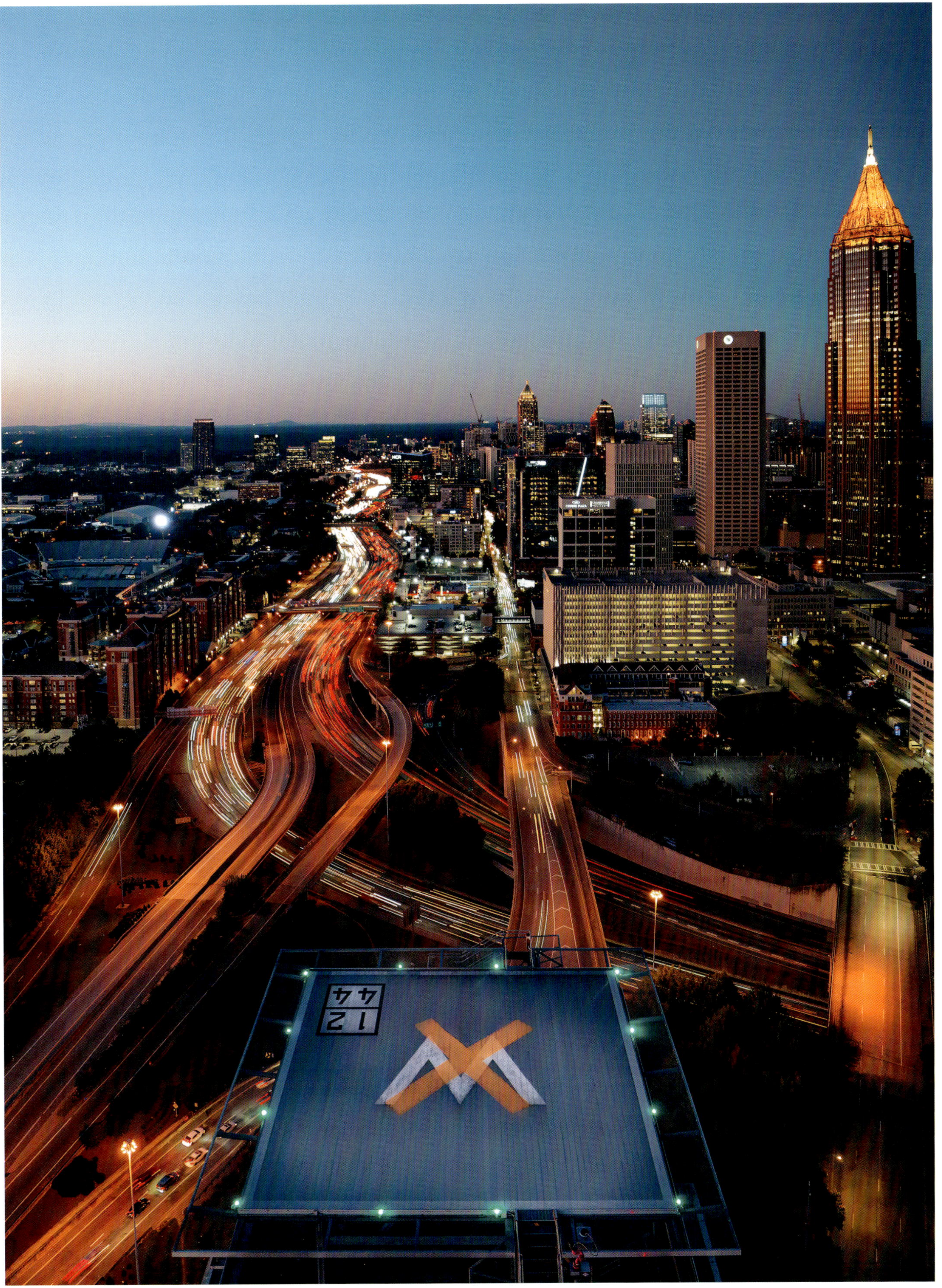

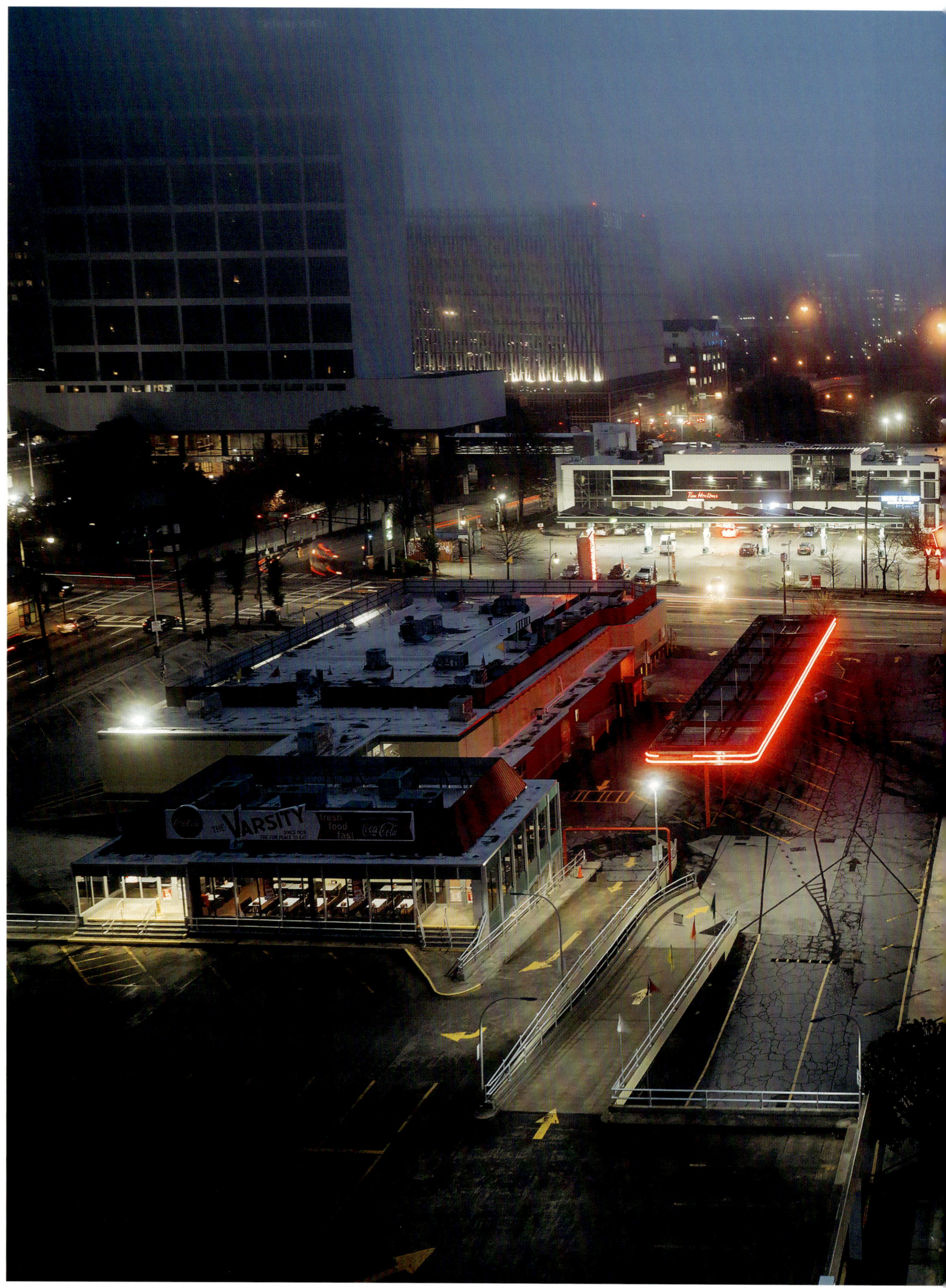
THE VARSITY
Coca-Cola
fresh food fast!
Coca-Cola
Tim Hortons

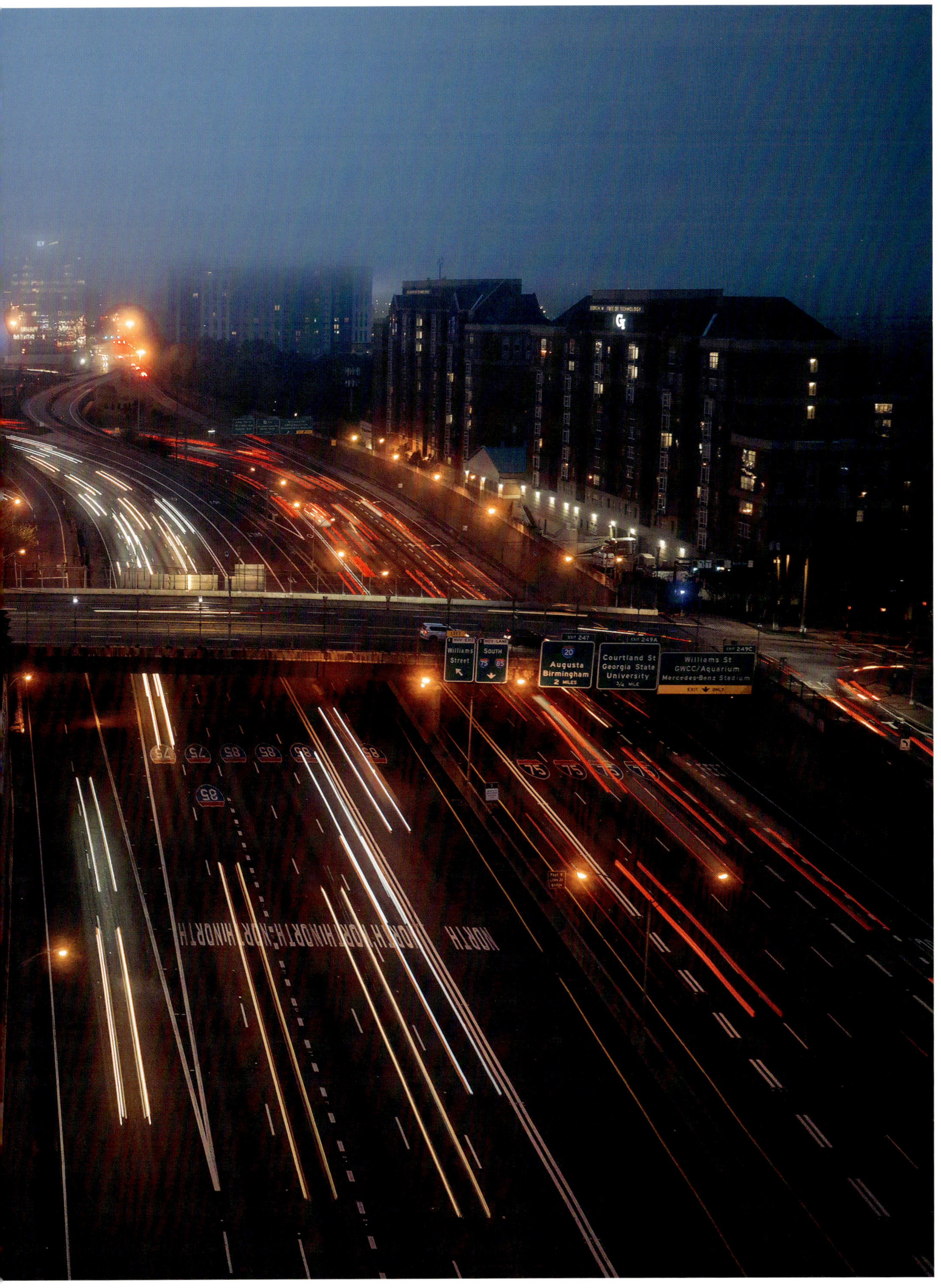
Williams Street
SOUTH
75 85
EXIT 247
20
Augusta
Birmingham
2 MILES
EXIT 249A
Courtland St
Georgia State
University
3/4 MILE
EXIT 249C
Williams St
GWCC/Aquarium
Mercedes-Benz Stadium
EXIT ONLY
NORTH

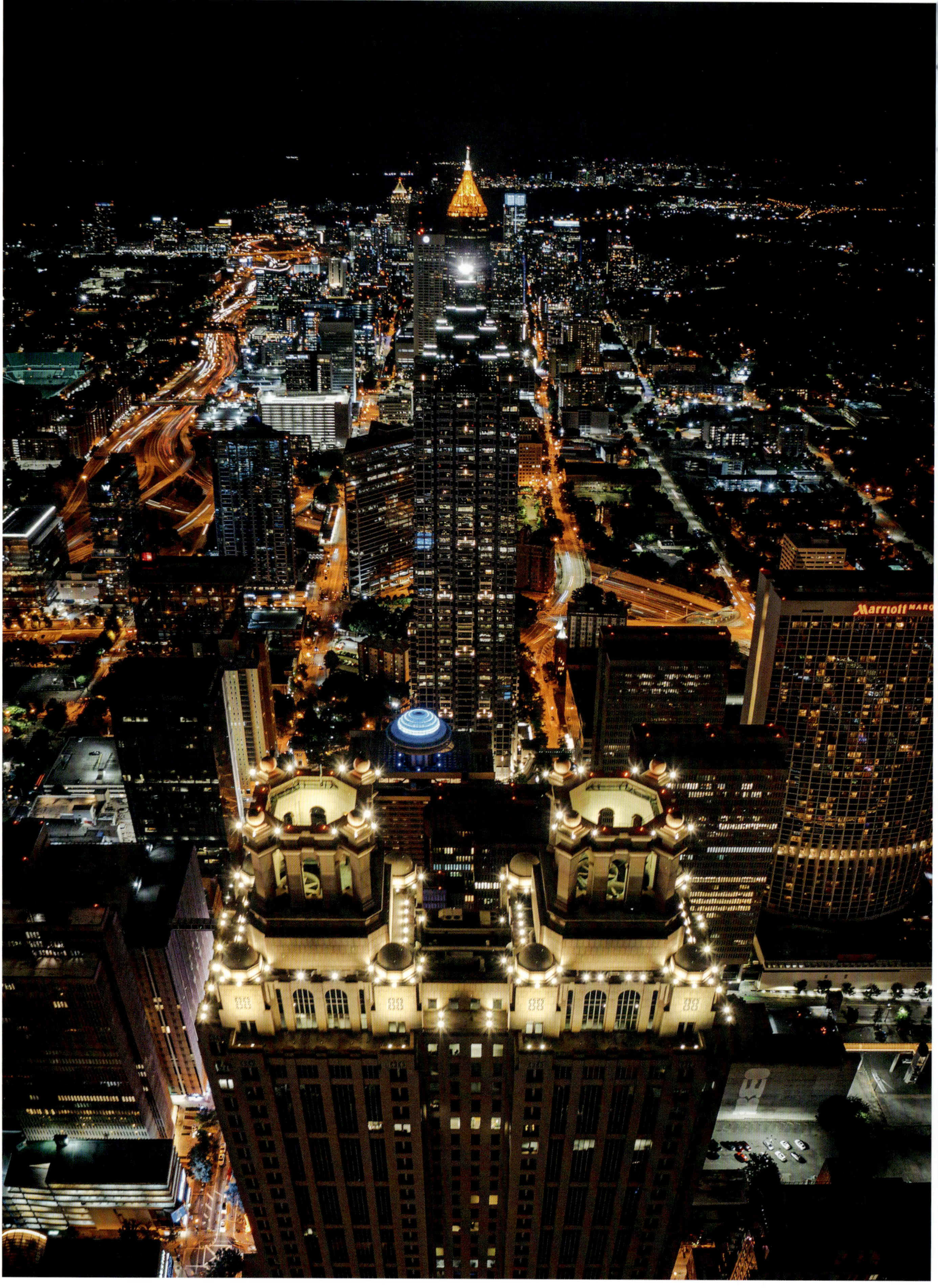
Marriott

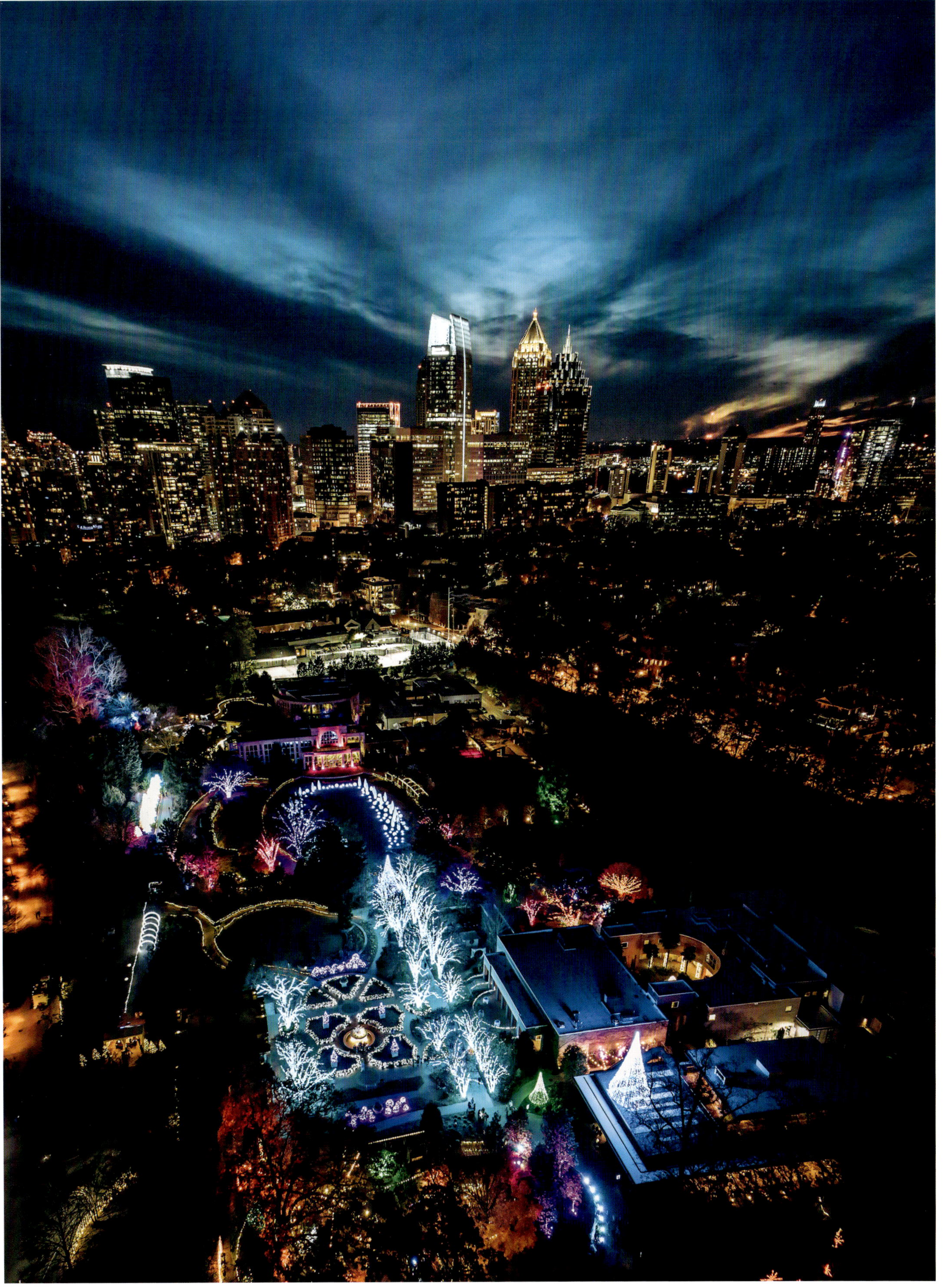

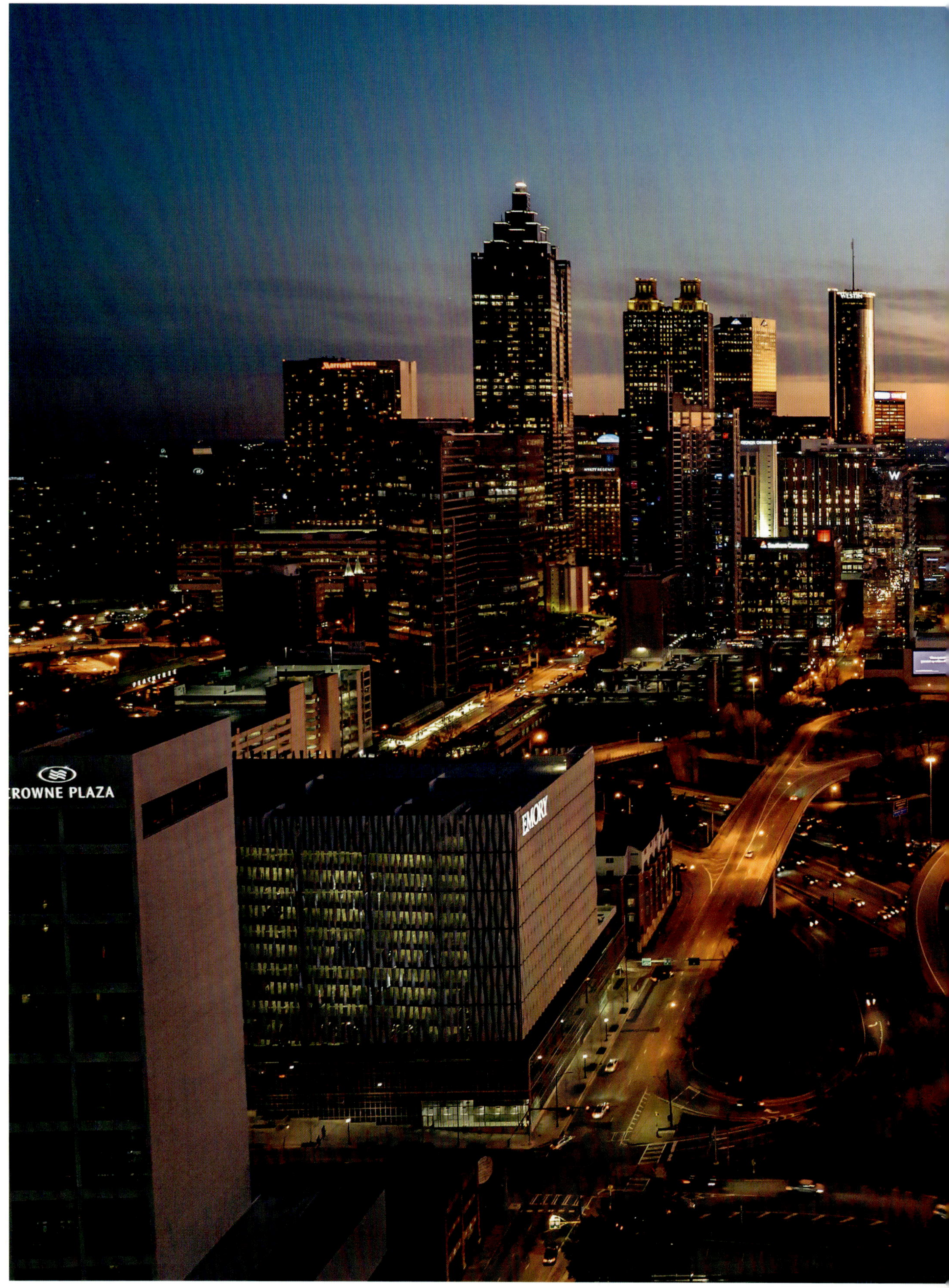
CROWNE PLAZA
EMORY
Marriott MARQUIS
WESTIN
W

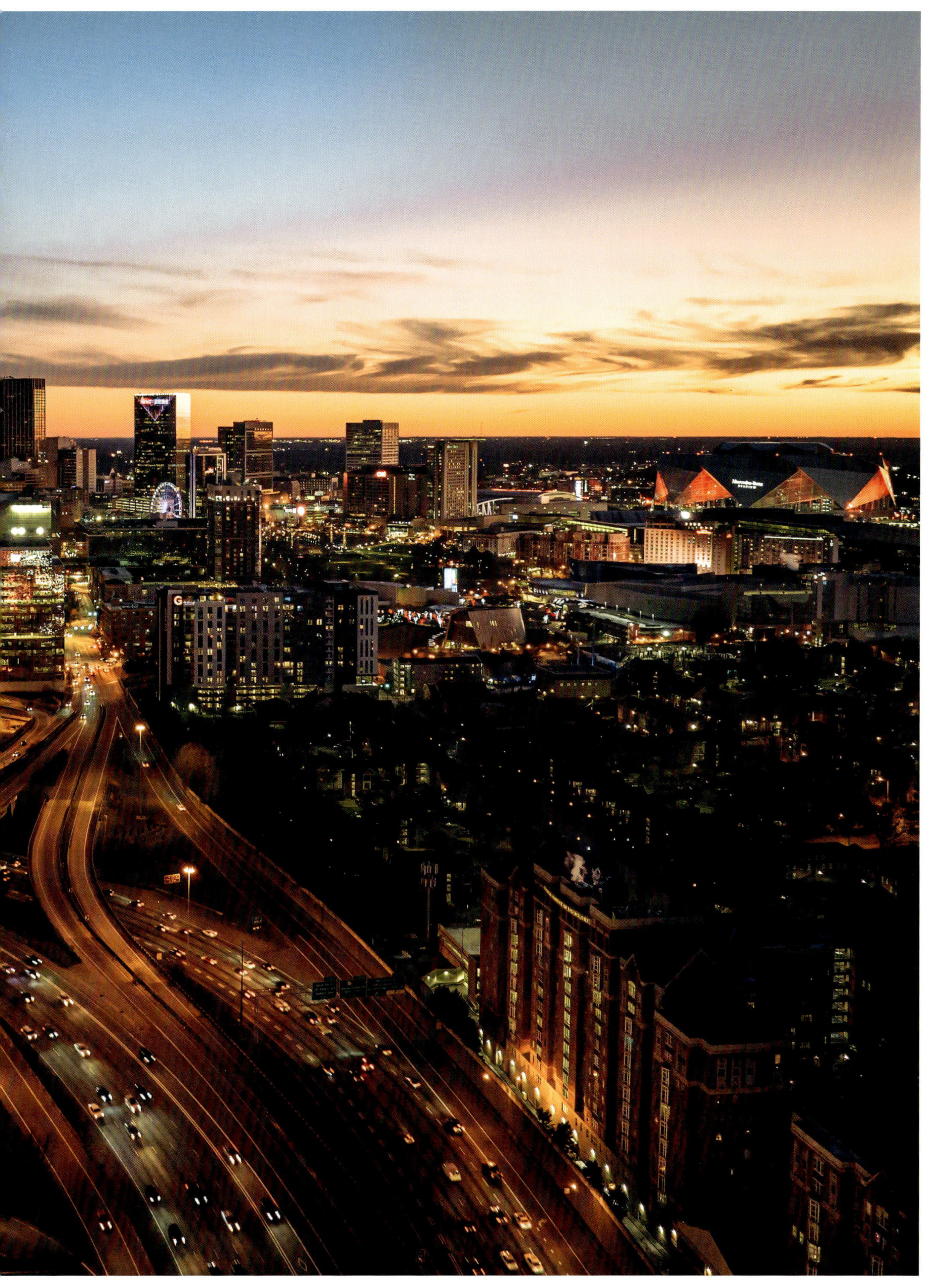

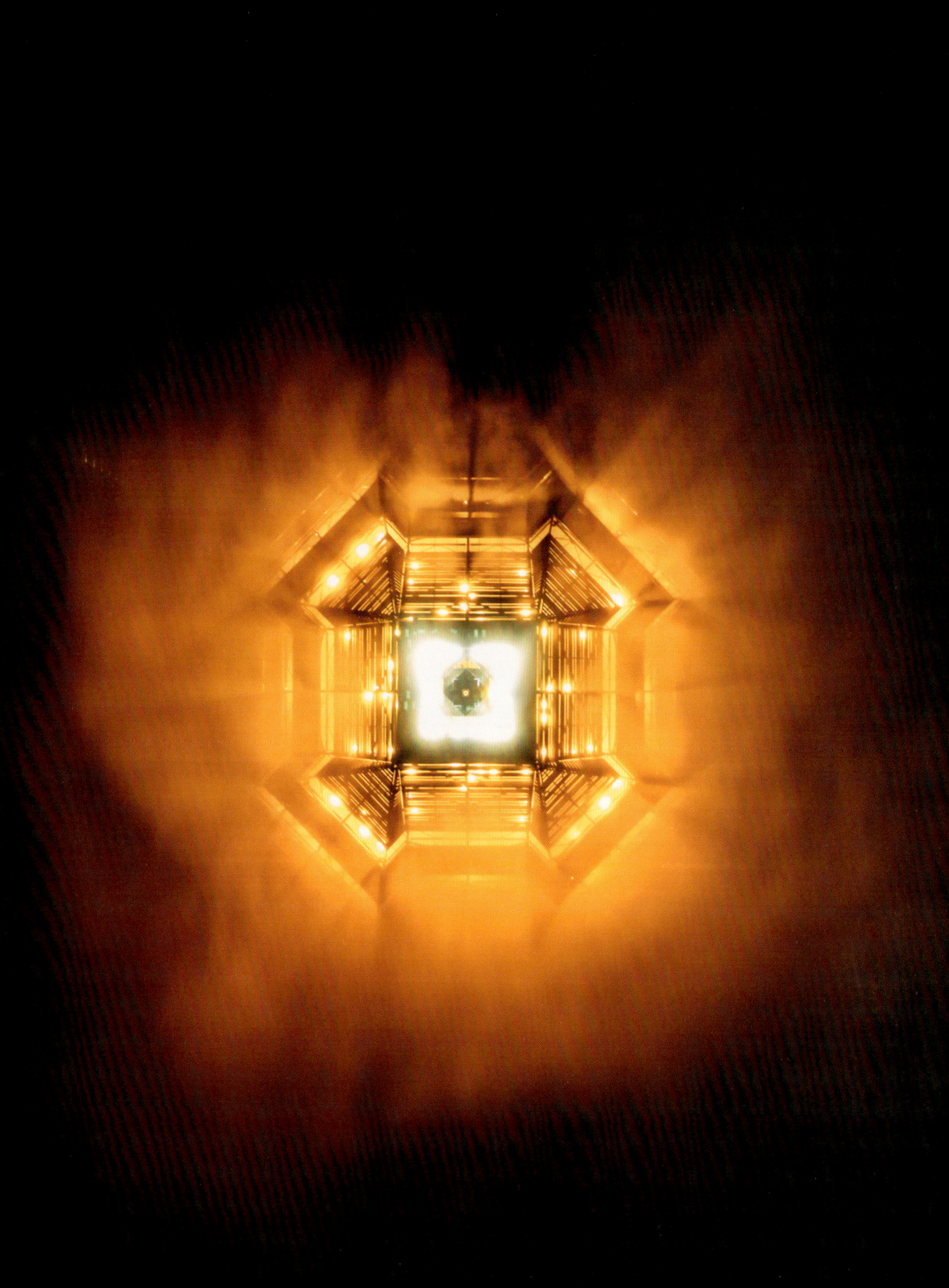

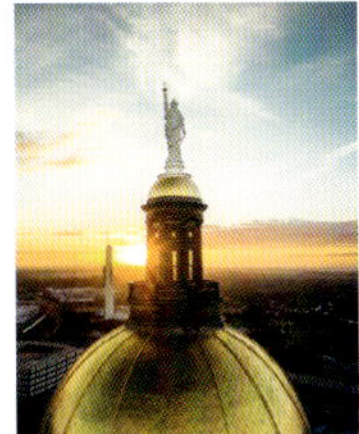

Front Cover
View of Georgia
State Capitol dome

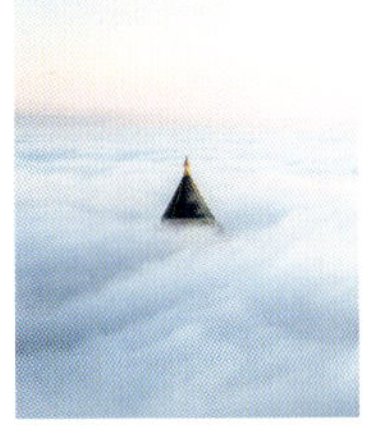

2 View of One
Atlantic Center

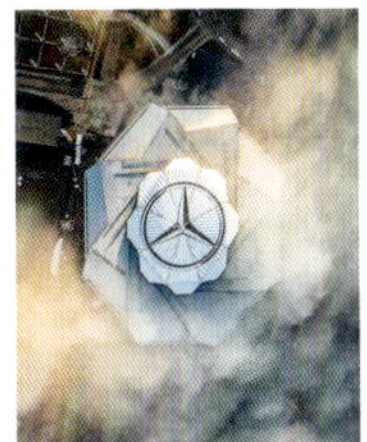

4 Looking down on
Mercedes-Benz Stadium

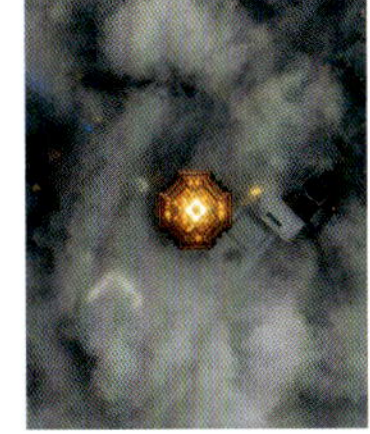

7 Looking down on
Bank of America Plaza

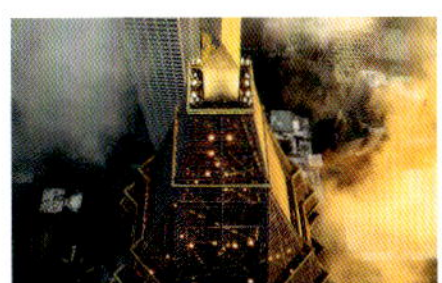

8-9 View of Bank
of America Plaza

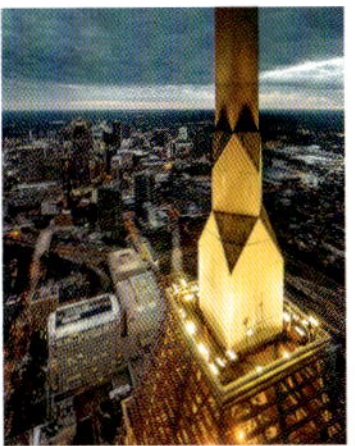

10 View of Bank
of America Plaza

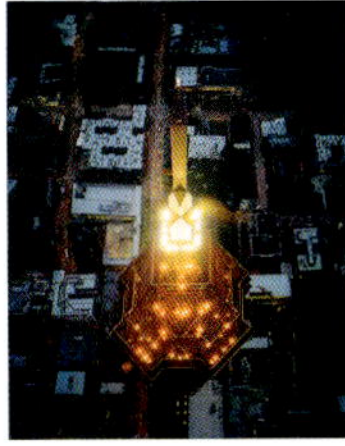

11 View of Bank
of America Plaza

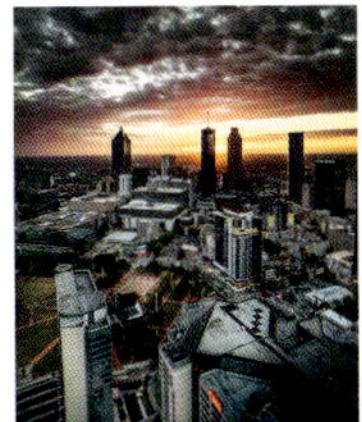

12 View of Downtown
Atlanta

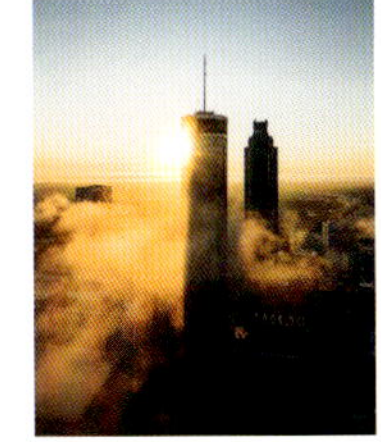

13 View of Westin
Peachtree Plaza and
191 Peachtree Tower

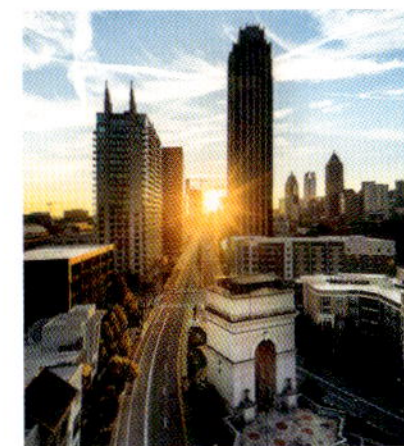

14 View of Atlantic
Station and the Millennium
Gate Museum

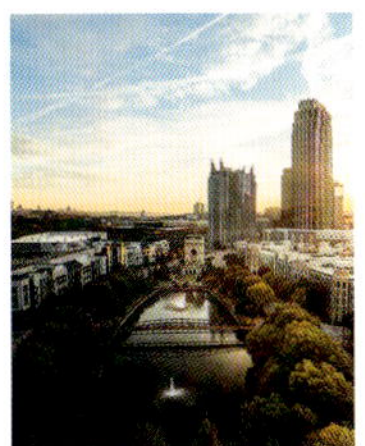

15 View of Atlantic
Station Pond

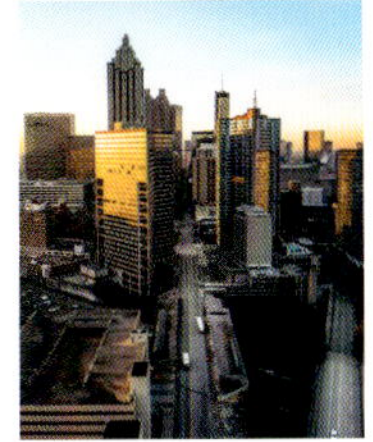

16 View of West
Peachtree Street and
Downtown Atlanta

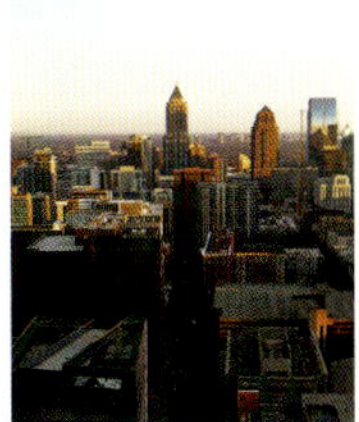

17 View of West
Peachtree Street

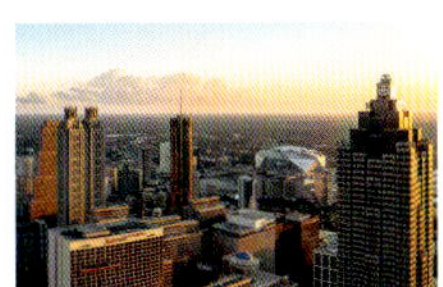

18-19 View of Atlanta
skyline

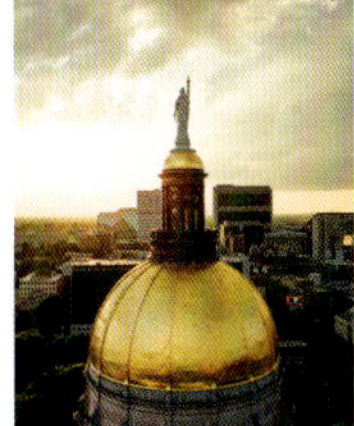

20 View of Georgia
State Capitol dome

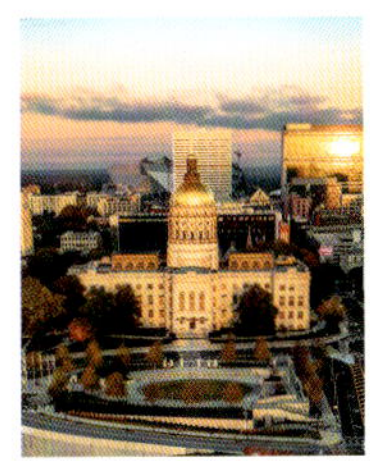

21 View of Georgia
State Capitol

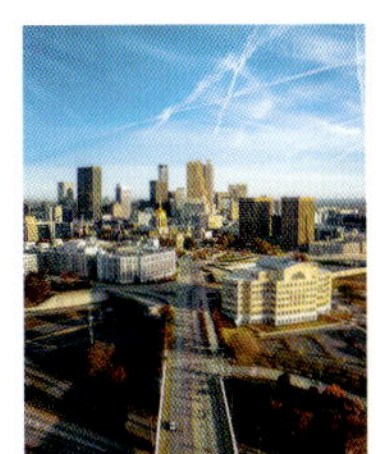

22 View of Capitol Avenue

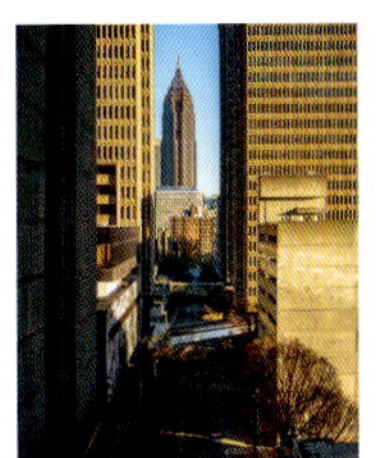

23 View of Peachtree Street

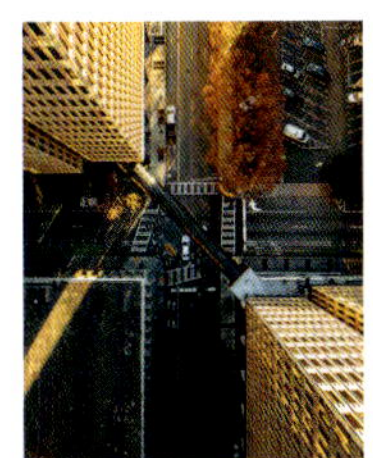

24 Looking down on
Peachtree Center

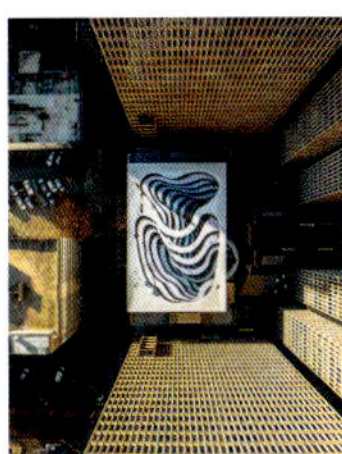

25 View of "Paradigm
Shift" mural at the
Peachtree Center

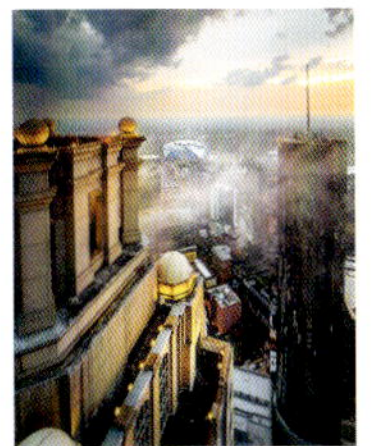

26 View of 191 Peachtree Tower,
Westin Peachtree Plaza, and
Mercedes-Benz Stadium

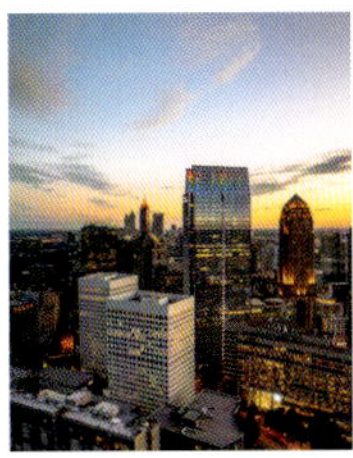

27 View of Symphony Tower

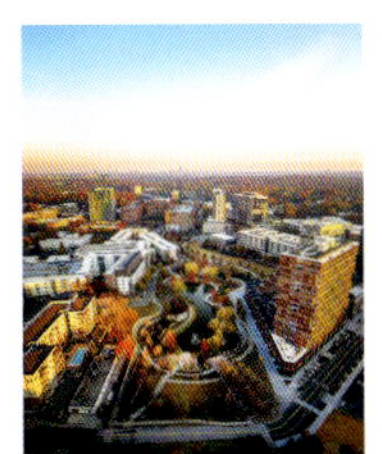

28 View of Historic
Fourth Ward Park

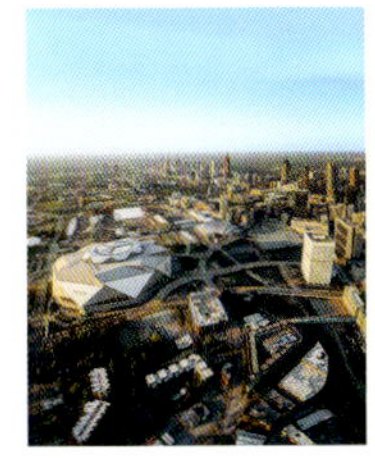

29 View of The Gulch

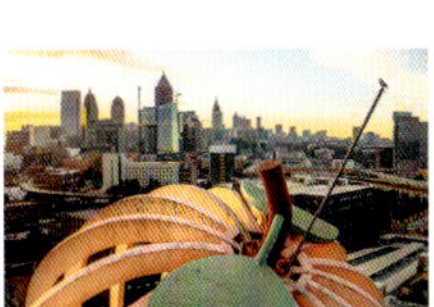

30-31 View of peach sculpture
and Atlanta skyline

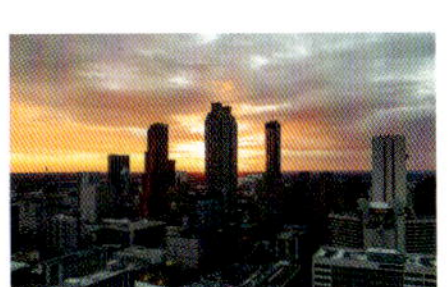

32-33 Sunrise view
of Atlanta skyline

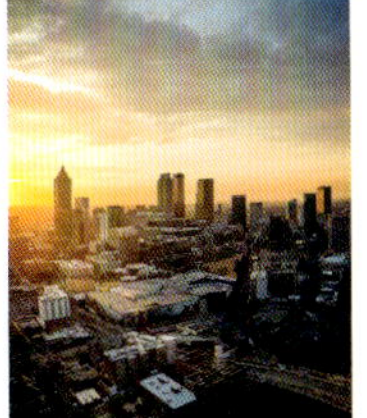

34 Sunrise view
of Atlanta skyline

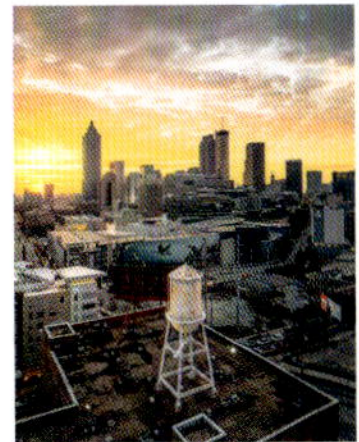

35 Sunrise view of
Downtown Atlanta

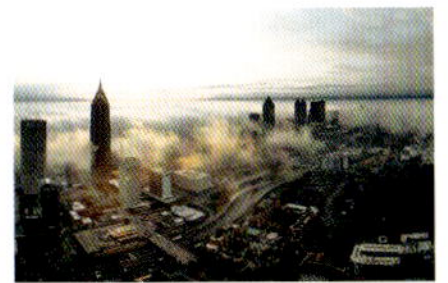

36-37 View of Midtown
and Downtown Atlanta

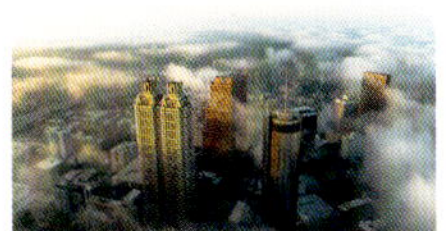

38-39 View of
Downtown Atlanta

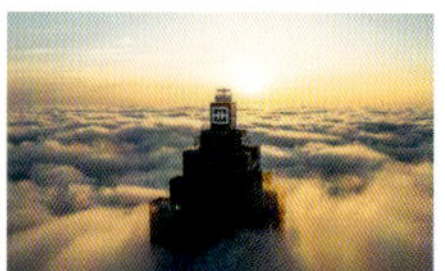

40-41 View of Truist Building

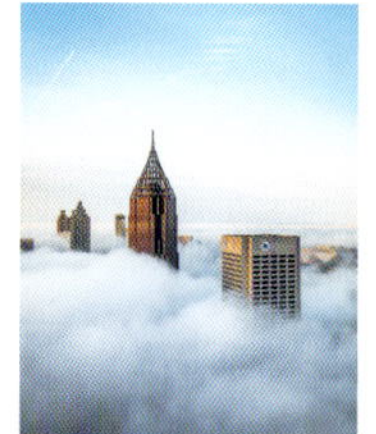

42 View of Midtown Atlanta

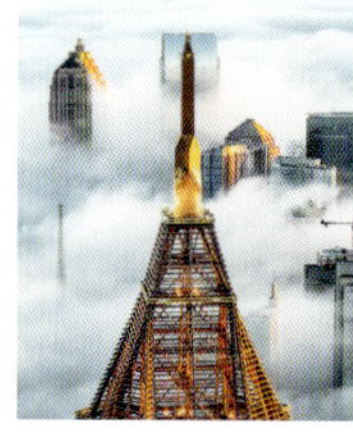

43 View of Bank of America Plaza spire and Midtown Atlanta

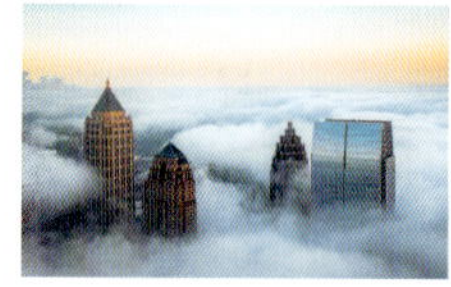

44-45 View of Midtown Atlanta

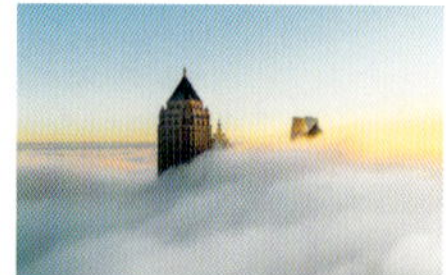

46-47 View of One Atlantic Center

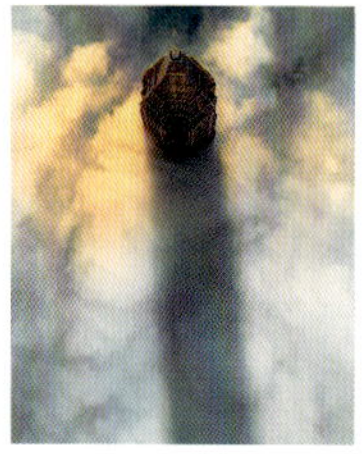

48 Looking down at Bank of America Plaza

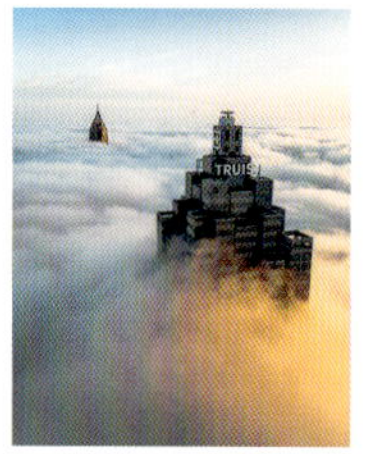

49 View of Truist Building and Bank of America Plaza

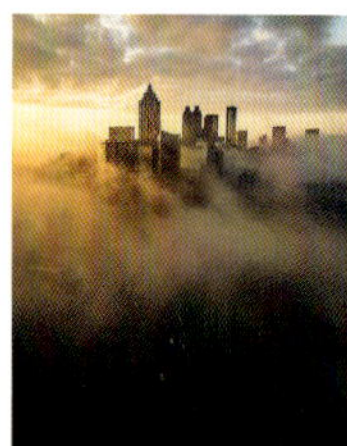

50 View of Downtown Atlanta Skyline

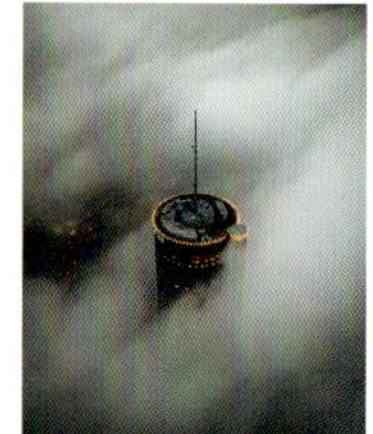

51 View of Westin Peachtree Plaza

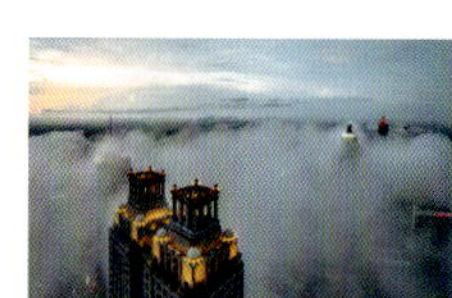

52-53 View of 191 Peachtree Tower

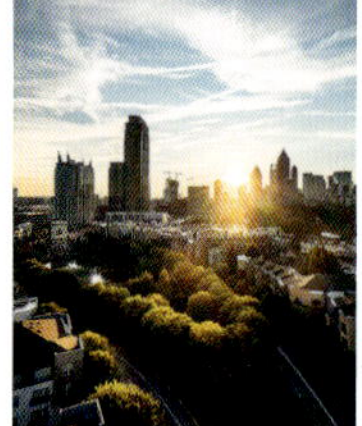

54 View of Atlantic Station

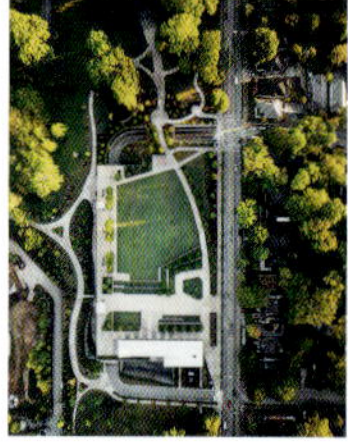

56 Looking down on Grant Park Gateway

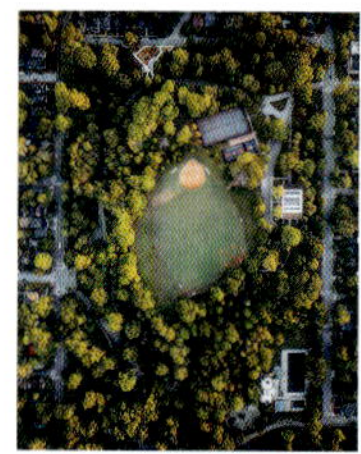

57 Looking down on Grant Park

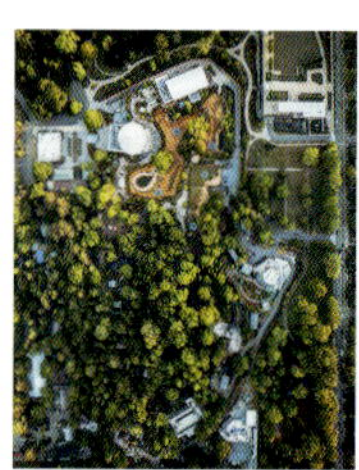

58 Looking down on Zoo Atlanta and Grant Park

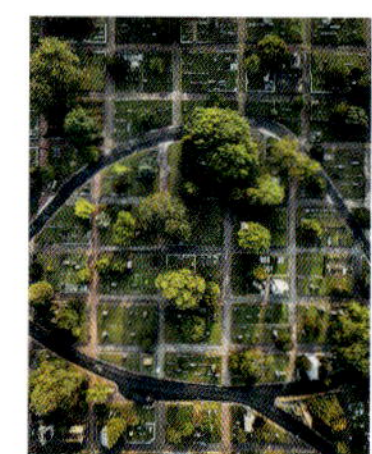

59 Looking down on Oakland Cemetery

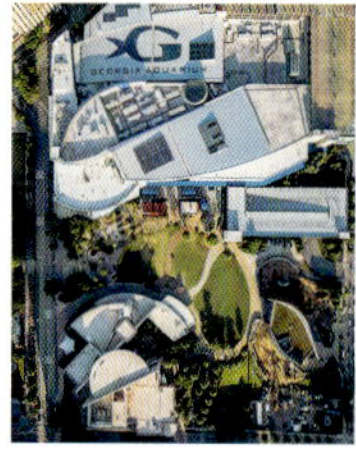

60 Looking down on Georgia Aquarium and Pemberton Place

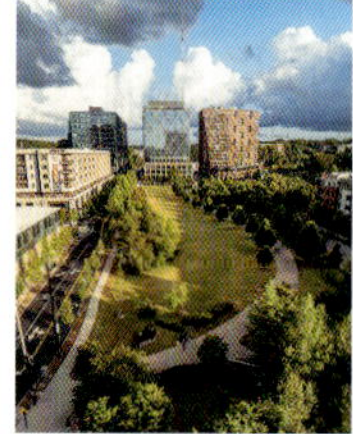

61 View of Historic Fourth Ward Park

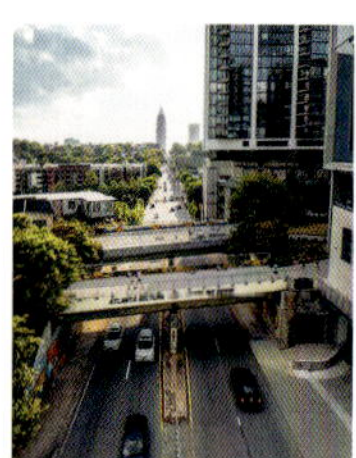

62 View of North Avenue BeltLine bridge

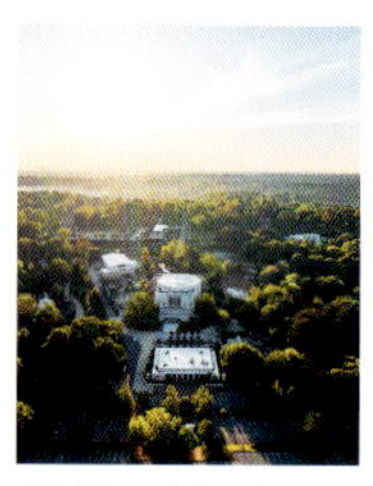

63 View of Zoo Atlanta

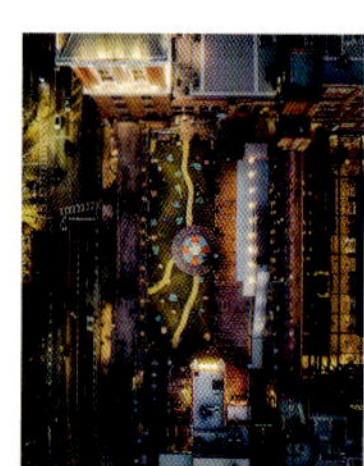

64 Looking down on Ponce City Market

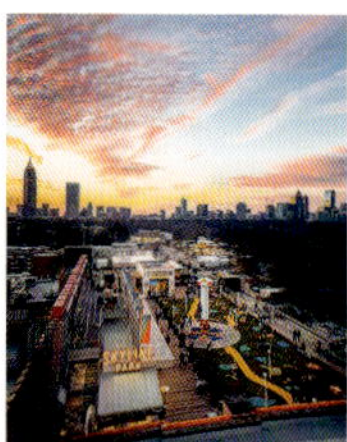

65 View of Skyline Park, Ponce City Market

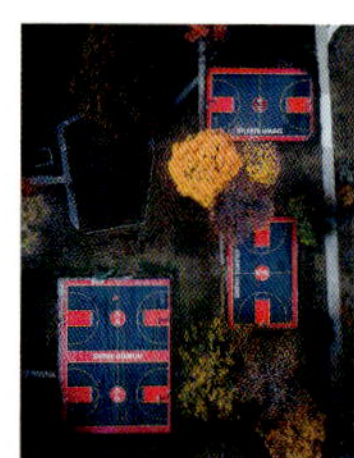

66 Looking down Central Park basketball courts

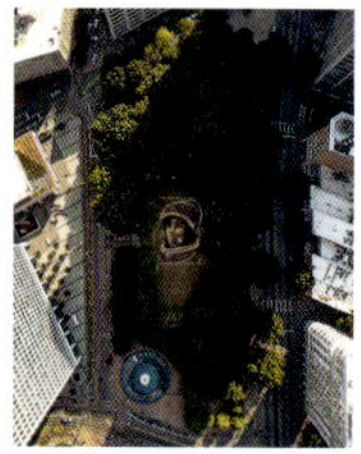

67 Looking down on Woodruff Park

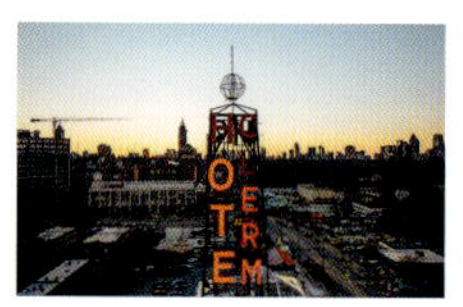

68-69 View of Hotel Clermont

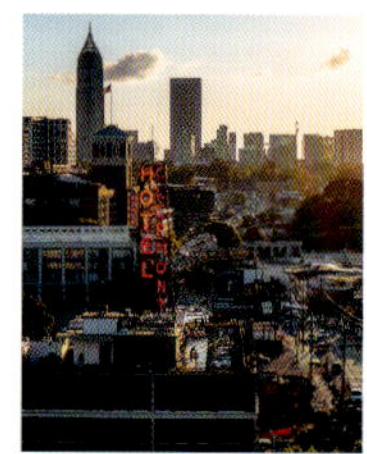

70 View of Ponce de Leon Avenue

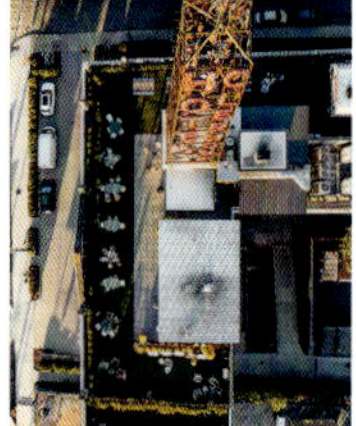

71 Looking down on Hotel Clermont

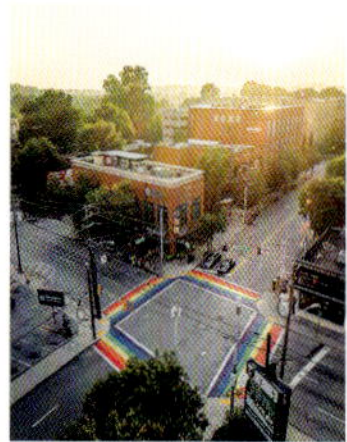

72 View of The Rainbow Sidewalks at 10th Street and Piedmont Avenue

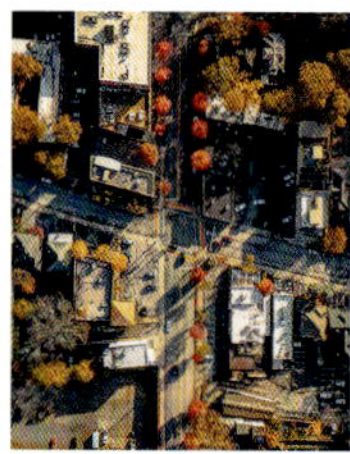

73 Looking down on The Rainbow Sidewalks at 10th Street and Piedmont Avenue

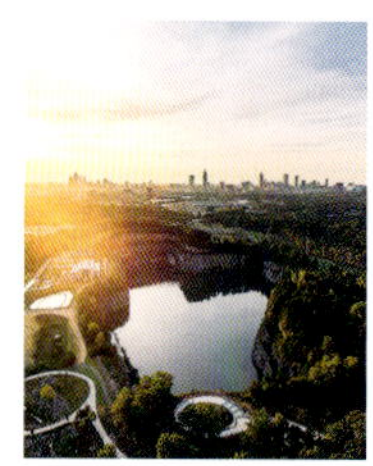

74 View of Westside Reservoir Park

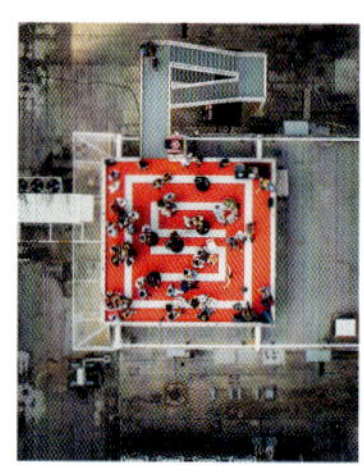

75 Looking down on Colony Square

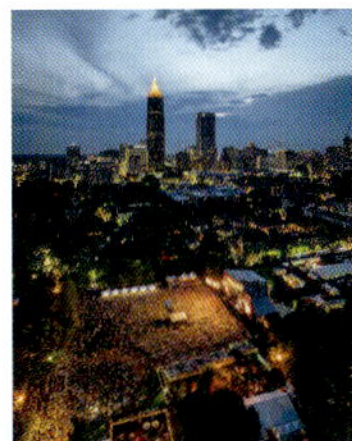

76 Shaky Knees Music Festival, Central Park

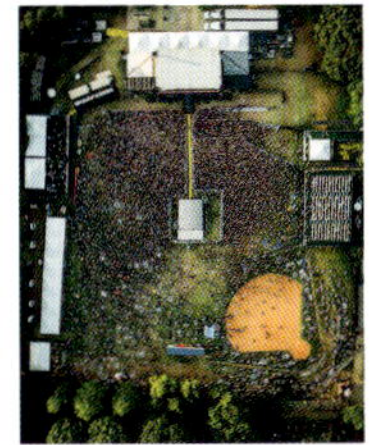

77 Shaky Knees Music Festival, Central Park

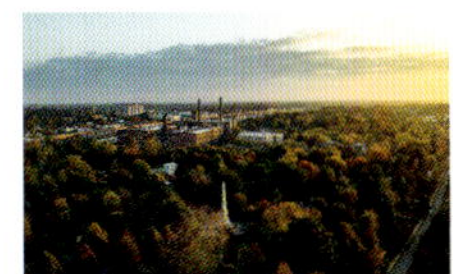

78-79 View of Oakland Cemetery

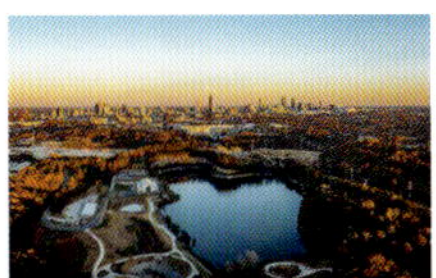

78-79 View of Westside Reservoir Park

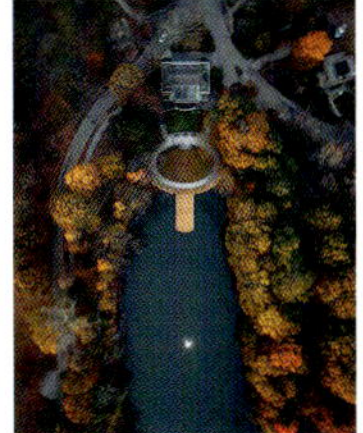

82 View of Lake Clara Meer, Piedmont Park

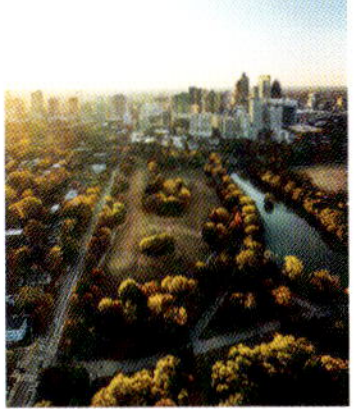

83 View of Piedmont Park

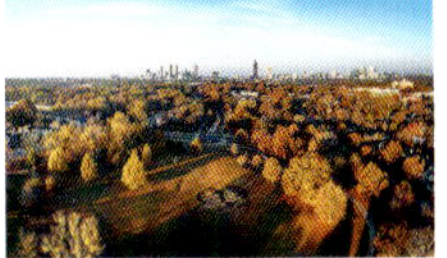

84-85 View of Freedom Park

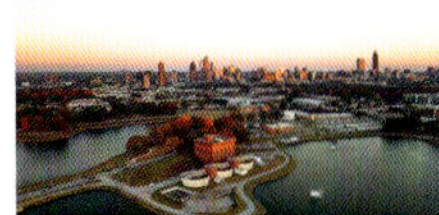

86-87 View of Atlanta City Water Works Reservoir Number One

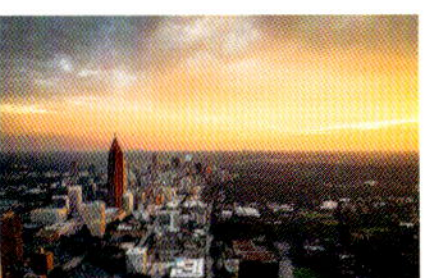

88-89 View of Midtown Atlanta

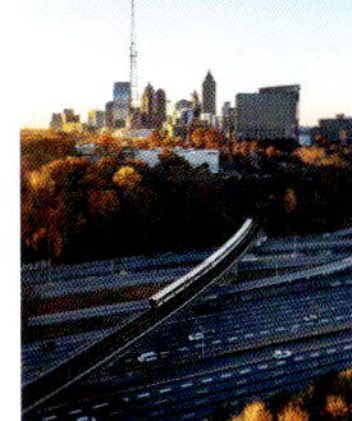

91 View of Midtown Atlanta skyline

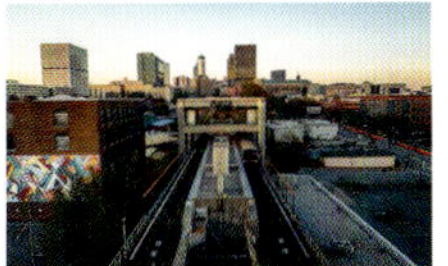

92-93 View of Garnett MARTA Station, Downtown Atlanta

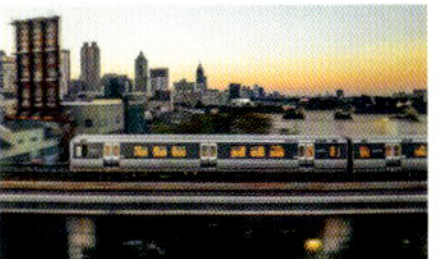

94-95 View of MARTA train, Midtown Atlanta

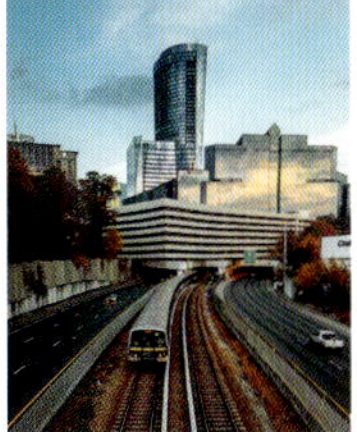

96 View of MARTA train, Buckhead

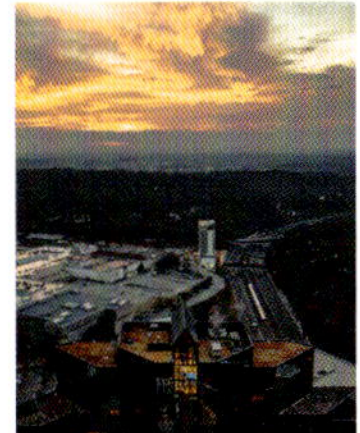

97 View of Buckhead

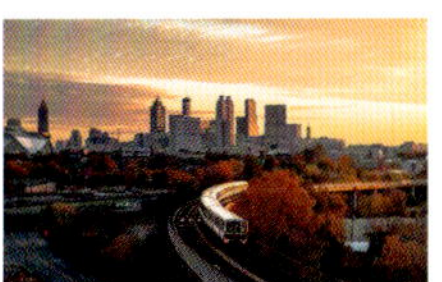

88-89 View of West End MARTA Station

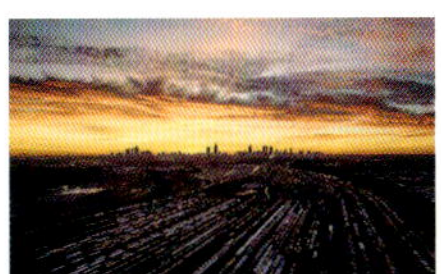

100-101 View of Norfolk Southern-Inman Yard

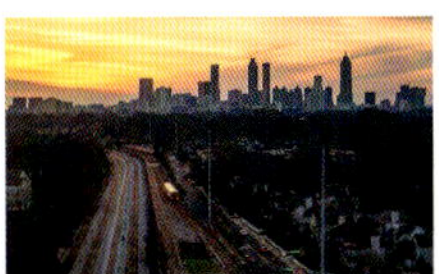

102-103 View of Candler Park MARTA Station

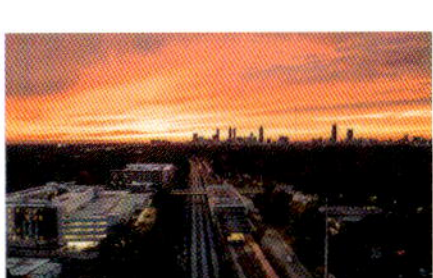

104-105 View of Candler Park MARTA Station

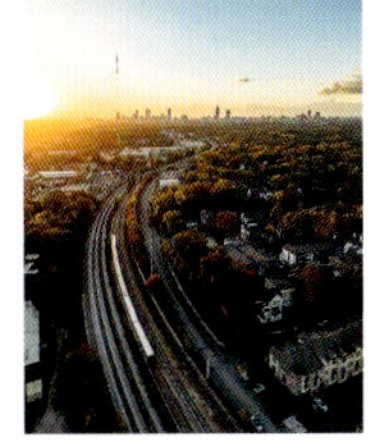

106 View of MARTA train, Kirkwood

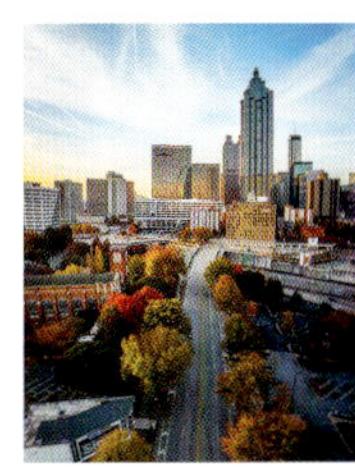

107 View of Peachtree Road and Downtown Atlanta

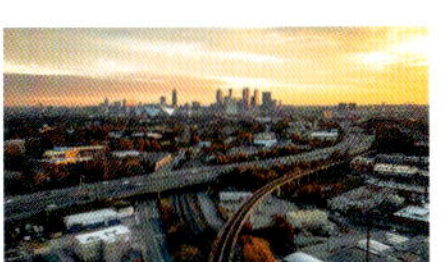

108-109 View of Georgia State Capital

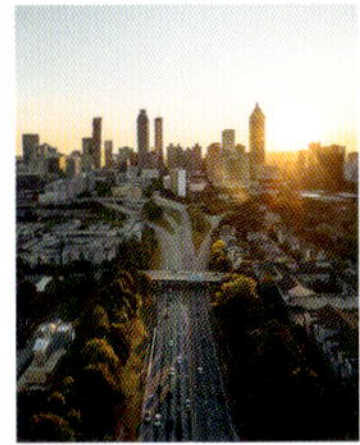

110 View of Jackson Street Bridge

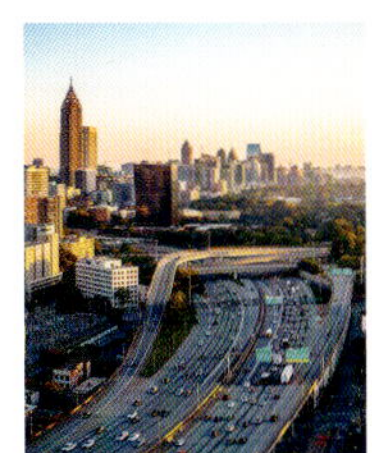

111 View of the Downtown Connector

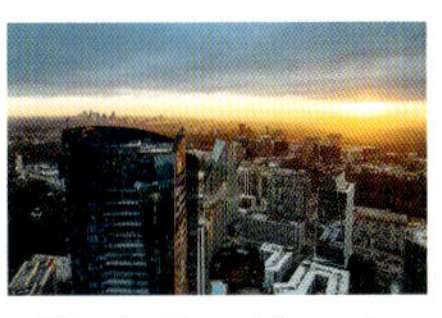

112-113 View of Sovereign building, Buckhead

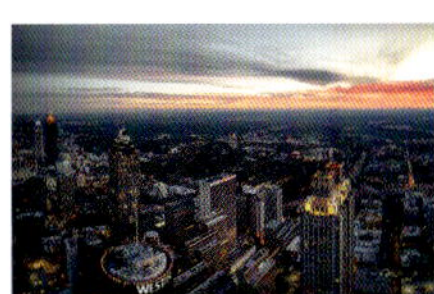

114-115 View of Downtown Atlanta

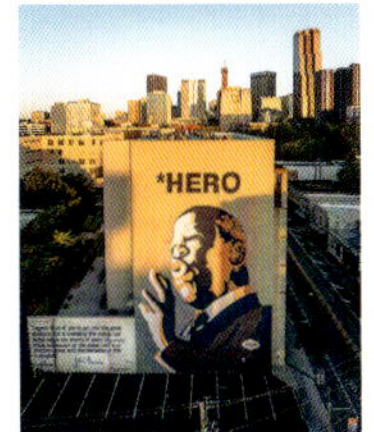

117 View of mural, Auburn Avenue & Jesse Hill Jr. Drive

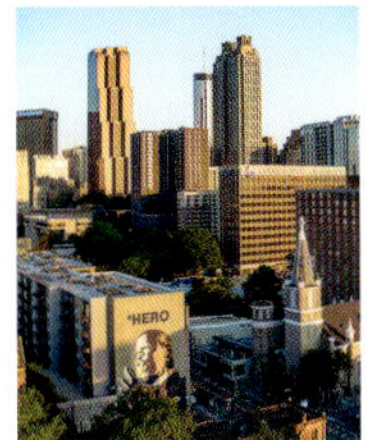

118 View of Auburn Avenue and Big Bethel A.M.E Church

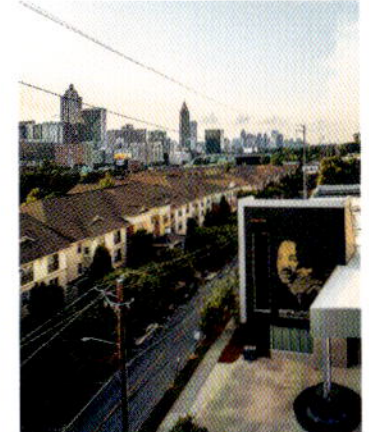

119 View of Martin Luther King Jr Recreation and Aquatic Center

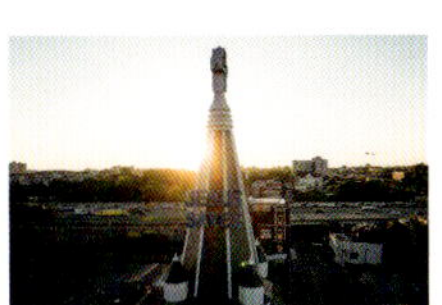

120-121 View of Big Bethel A.M.E Church

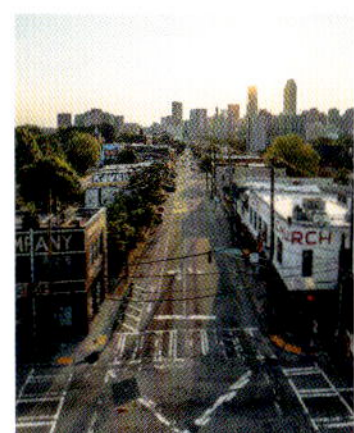

122 View of Edgewood Avenue

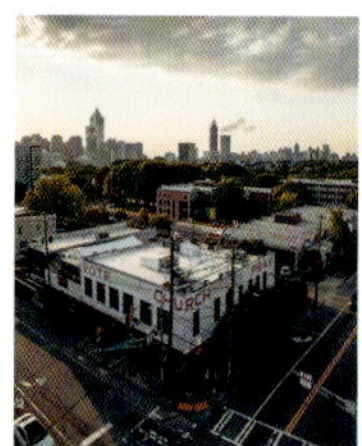

123 View of Sister Louisa's Church of the Living Room and Ping Pong Emporium

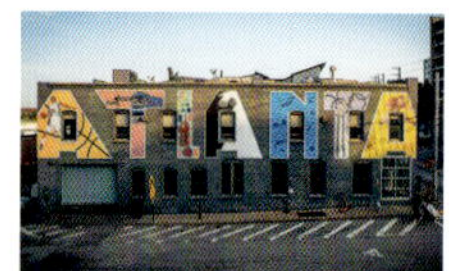

124-125 View of mural, Marietta Street NW

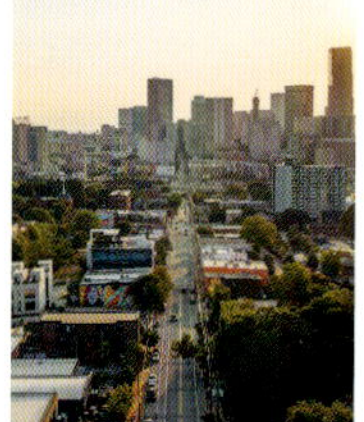

126 View of Edgewood Avenue

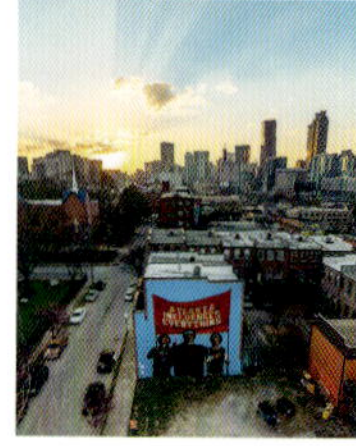

127 View of mural, Chamberlain Street SE

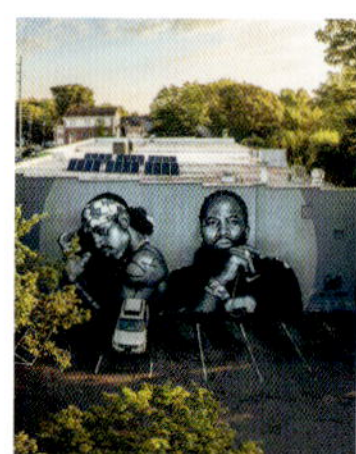

128 View of mural, Moreland Avenue NE

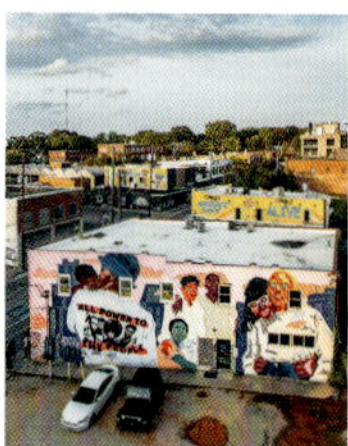

129 View of mural, Edgewood Avenue

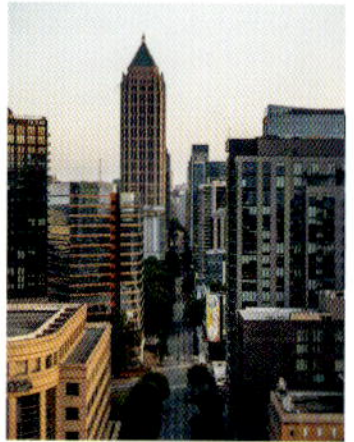

130 View of Midtown Atlanta

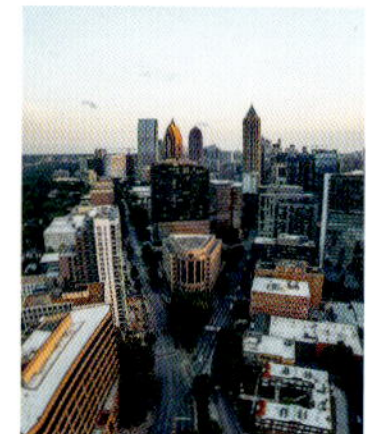

131 View of 1420 Peachtree Street

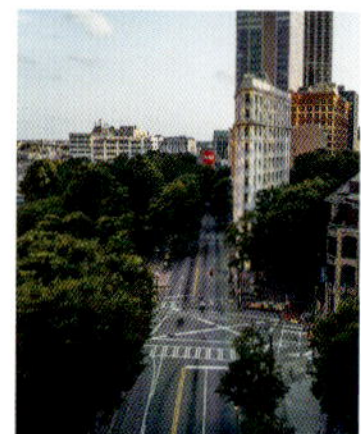

132 View of the Flatiron Building

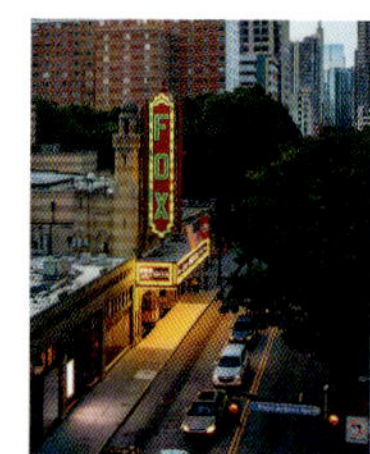

133 View of the Fox Theatre

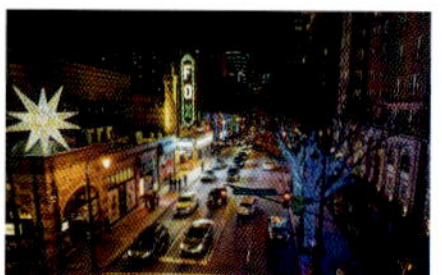

134-135 View of the Fox Theatre

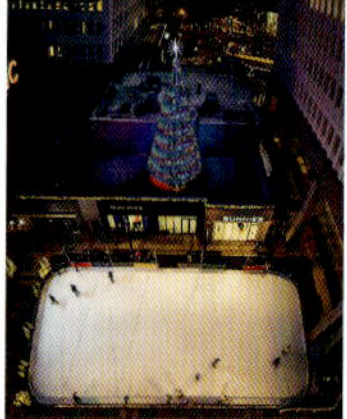

136 Looking down on Colony Square ice rink

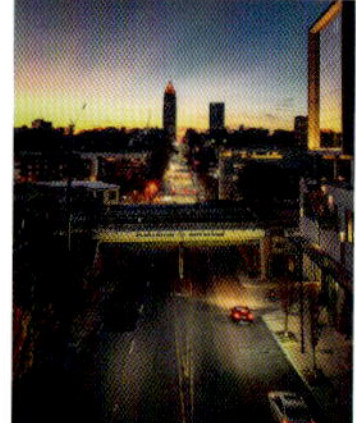

137 View of North Avenue BeltLine bridge

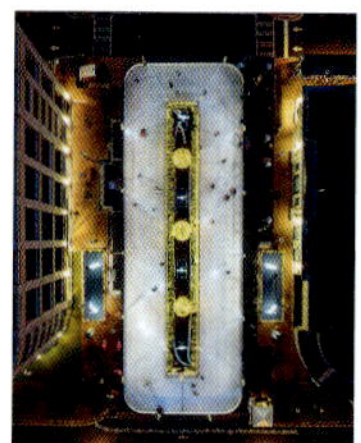

138 Looking down on Atlantic Station skating rink

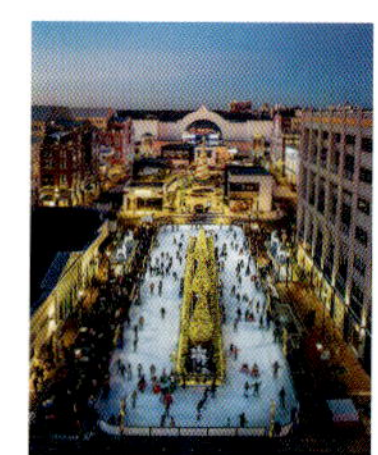

139 View of Atlantic Station skating rink

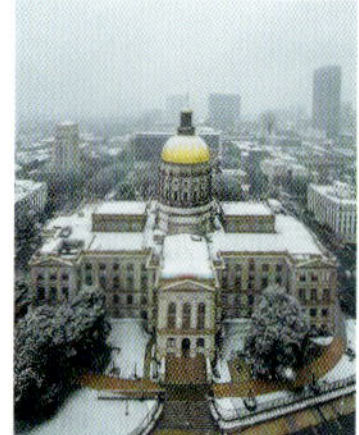

140 View of Georgia State Capitol

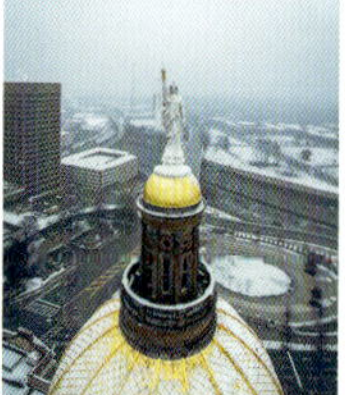

141 View of Georgia State Capitol dome

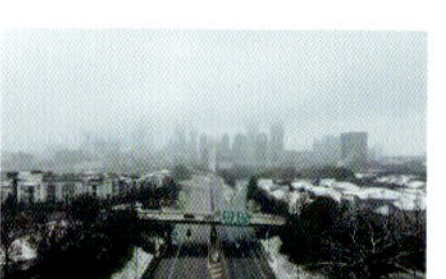

142-143 View of Jackson Street Bridge

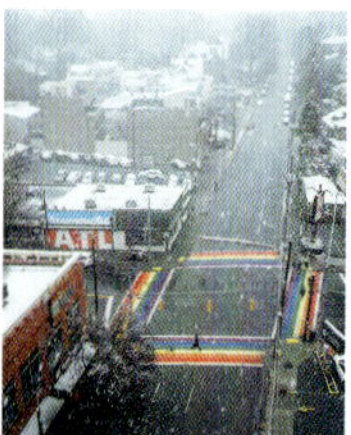

144 View of The Rainbow Sidewalks at 10th Street and Piedmont Avenue

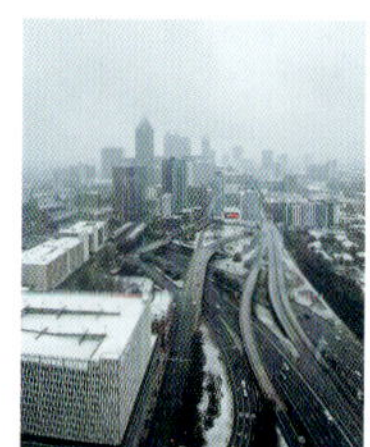

145 View of the Downtown Connector

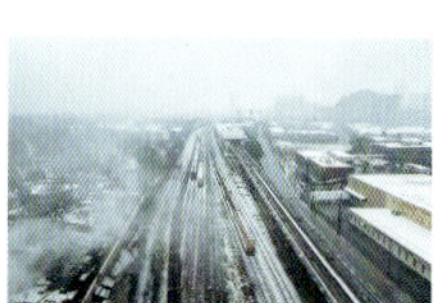

146-147 View of King Memorial MARTA Station

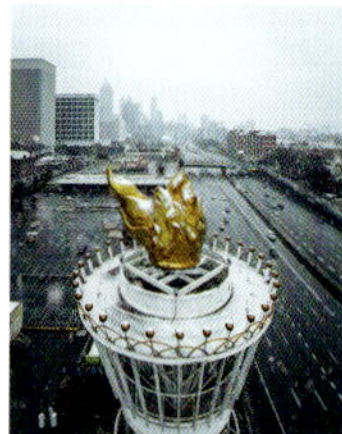

148 View of Olympic Torch Tower

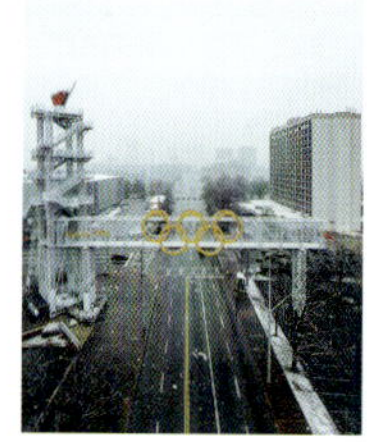

149 View of Atlanta Olympic Cauldron Tower and Rings

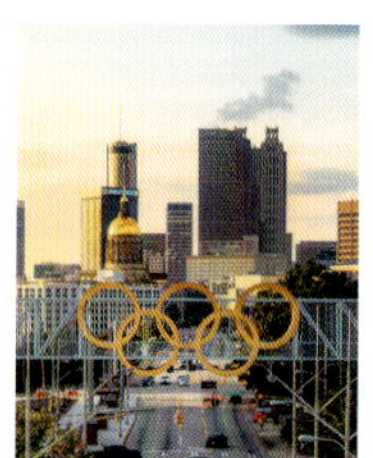

151 View of Olympic Rings overlooking Downtown Atlanta

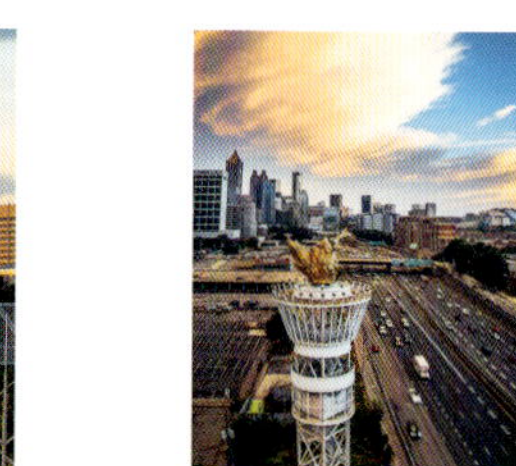

152 View of Olympic Torch Tower

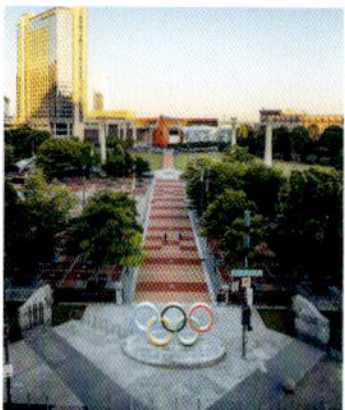

153 View of Centennial Olympic Park

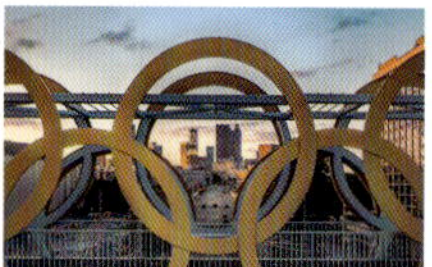

154-155 View of Olympic Rings overlooking Downtown Atlanta

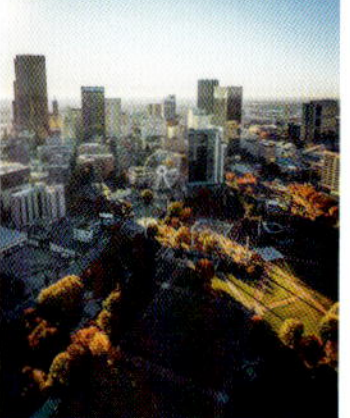

156 View of Centennial Olympic Park

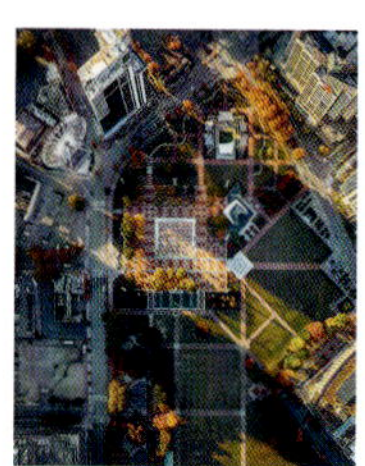

157 View of Centennial Olympic Park

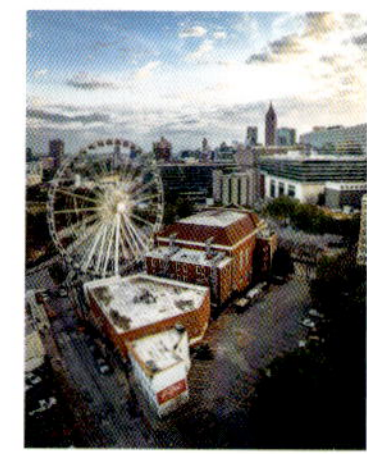

158 View of The Tabernacle and the SkyView Atlanta

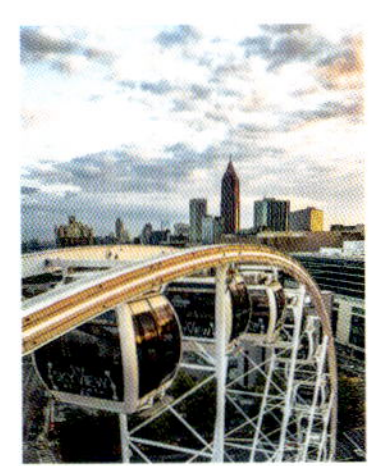

159 View of SkyView Atlanta

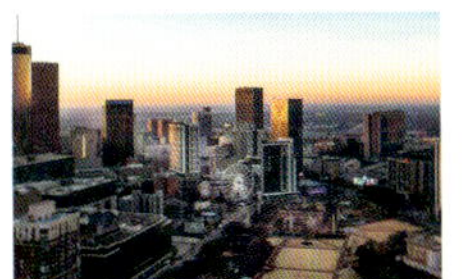

160-161 View of Centennial Olympic Park and Downtown Atlanta

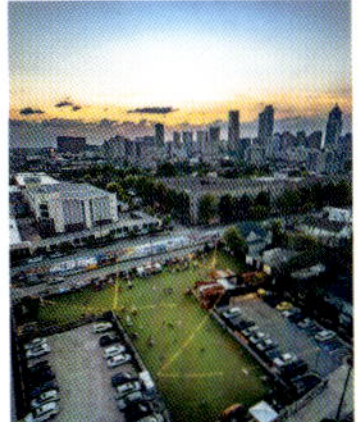

162 View of Fetch Park, Edgewood

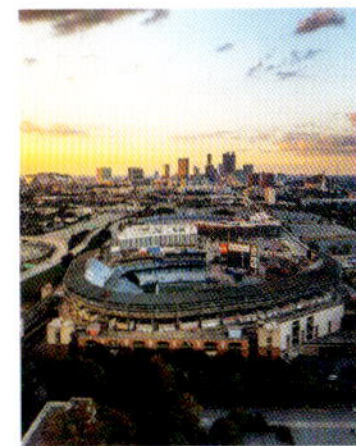

163 View of Center Parc Stadium

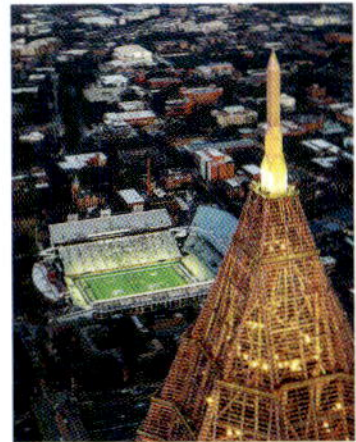

164 View of Bank of America Plaza and Bobby Dodd Stadium

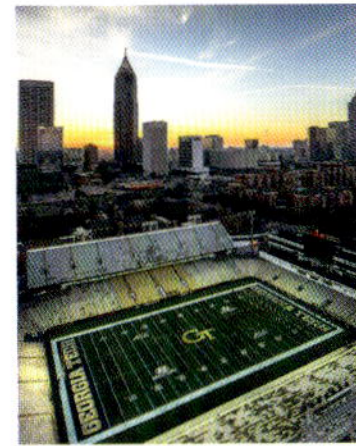

165 View of Bobby Dodd Stadium

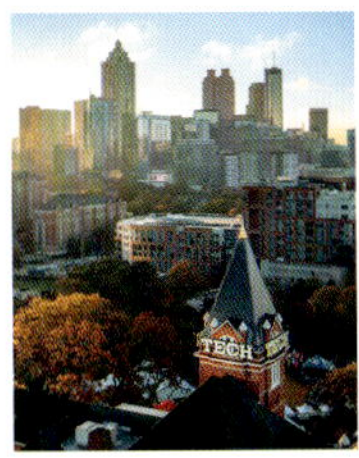

166 View of Georgia Tech Tower

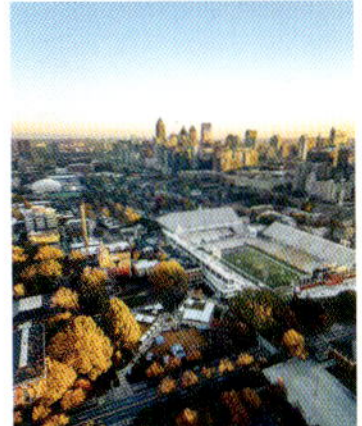

167 View of Georgia Tech Campus

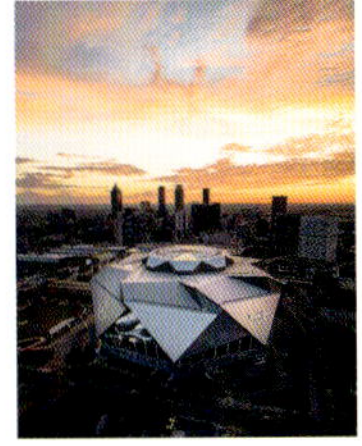

168 View of Mercedes-Benz Stadium

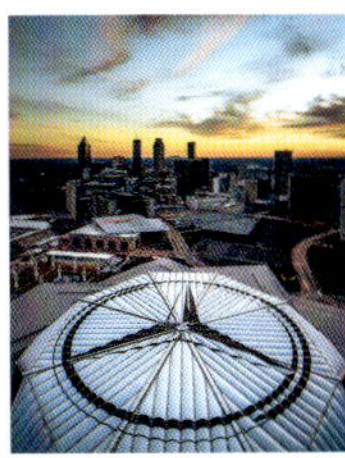

169 View of Mercedes-Benz Stadium

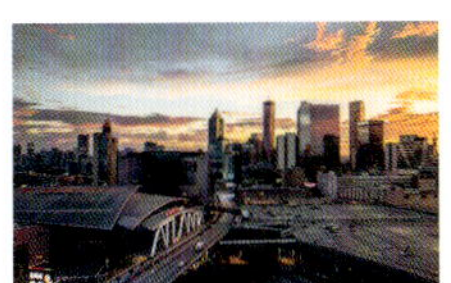

170-171 View of State Farm Arena

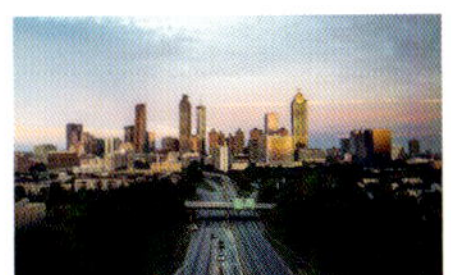

172-173 View of Jackson Street Bridge

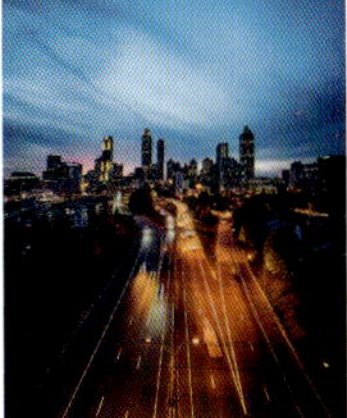

174 View of Jackson Street Bridge

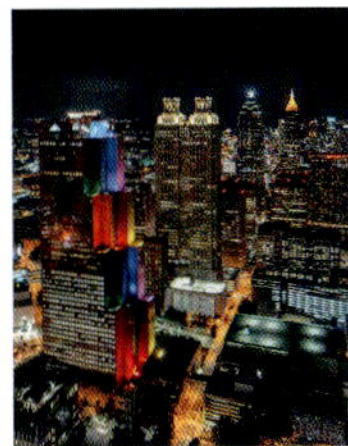

175 View of Downtown Atlanta skyline

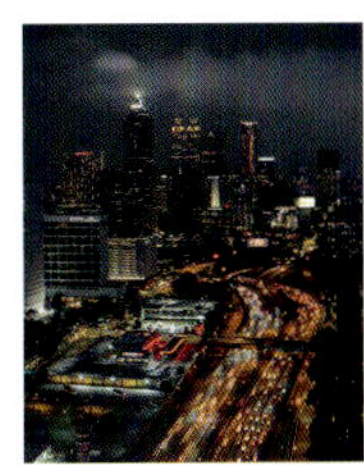

176 View of Atlanta skyline

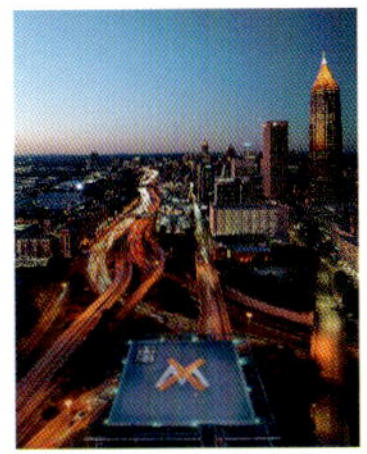

177 View of W Hotel looking towards Midtown Atlanta

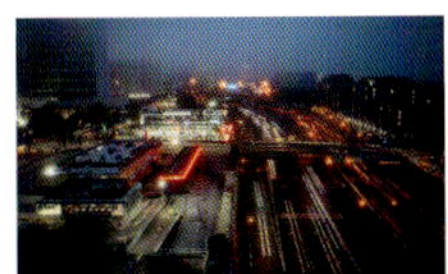

178-179 View of The Varsity, Midtown Atlanta

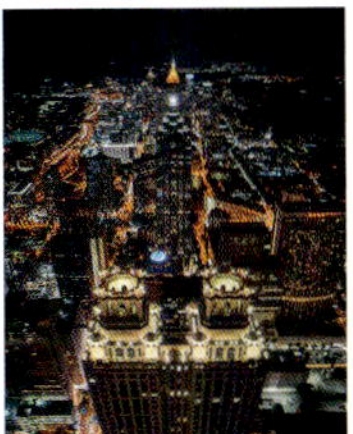

180 View of 191 Peachtree Tower

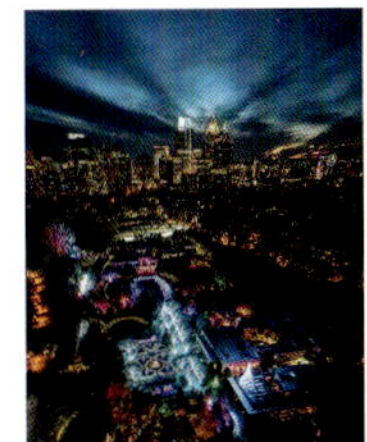

181 View of Atlanta Botanical Gardens

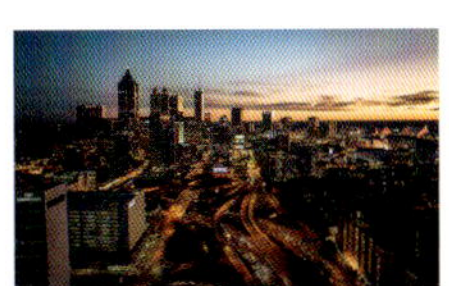

182-183 View of Downtown Atlanta

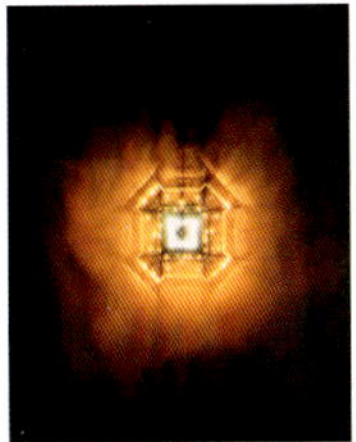

184 Looking down on Bank of America Plaza

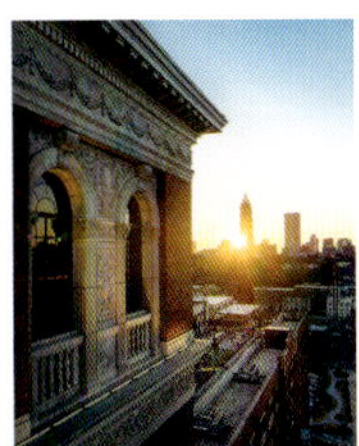

192 View of Ponce City Market

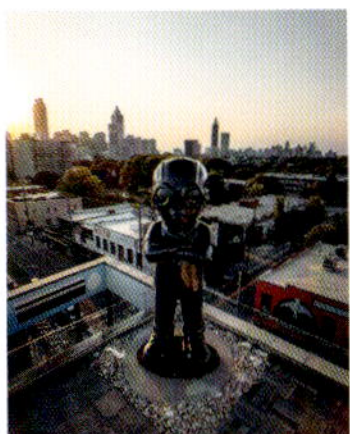

194 View of statue, Marietta Street NW

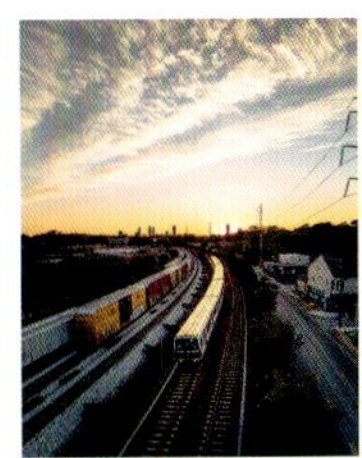

196 View of MARTA, Candler Park

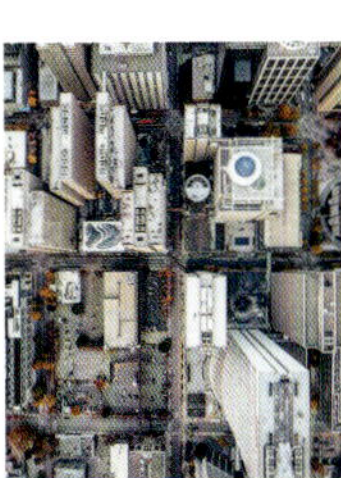

198 Looking down on Downtown Atlanta

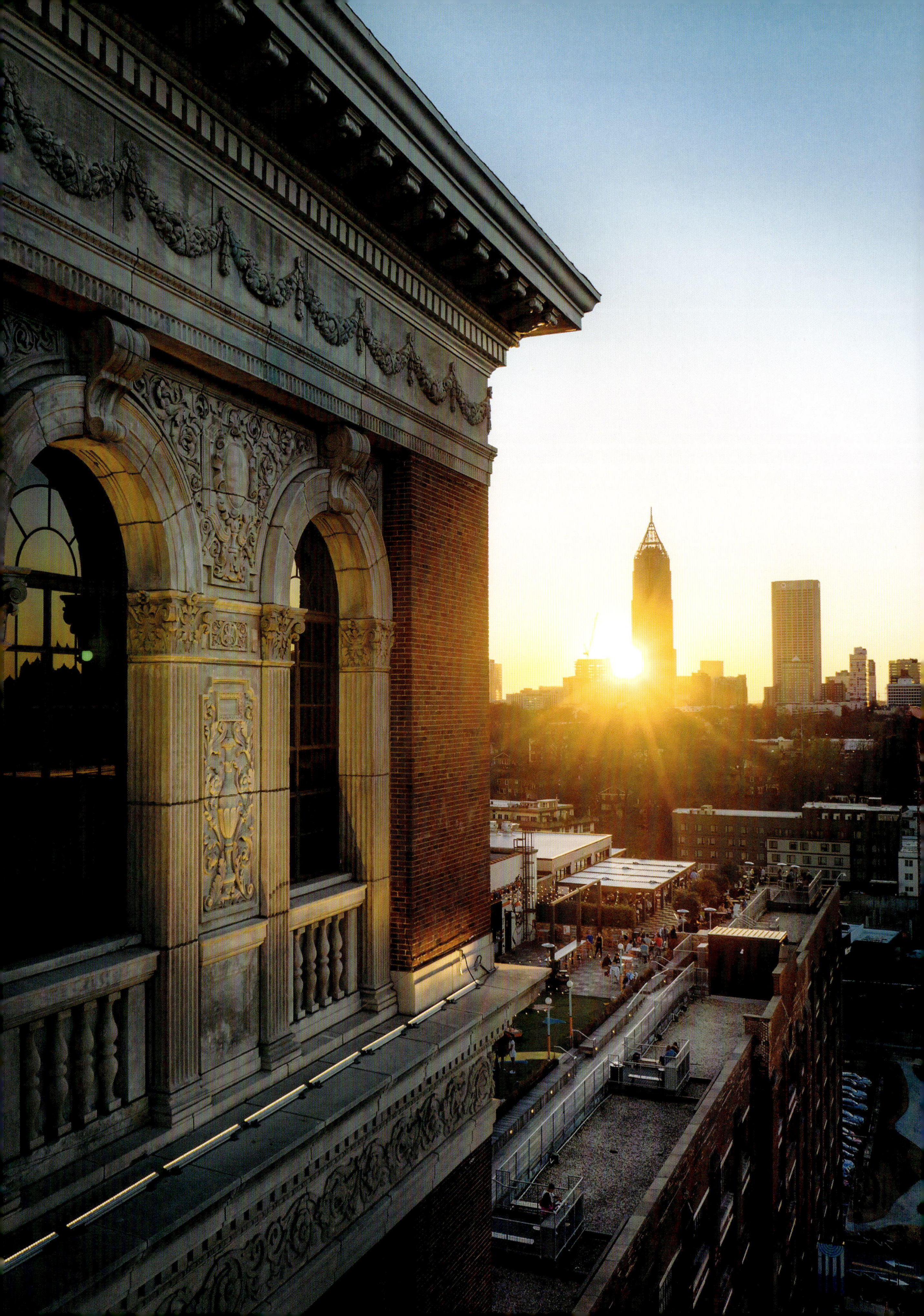

ACKNOWLEDGMENTS

I am so thankful to all my friends and family for their unwavering support throughout my photography career. Your belief in me and your encouragement have been the driving forces behind my passion. Thank you for standing by me and for being my biggest cheerleaders. I am truly blessed to have such amazing people in my life.

A special thank you to my mother for always being there for me, and to my beautiful girlfriend, Courtney, for always pushing me to pursue what I love.

Luis Gaud

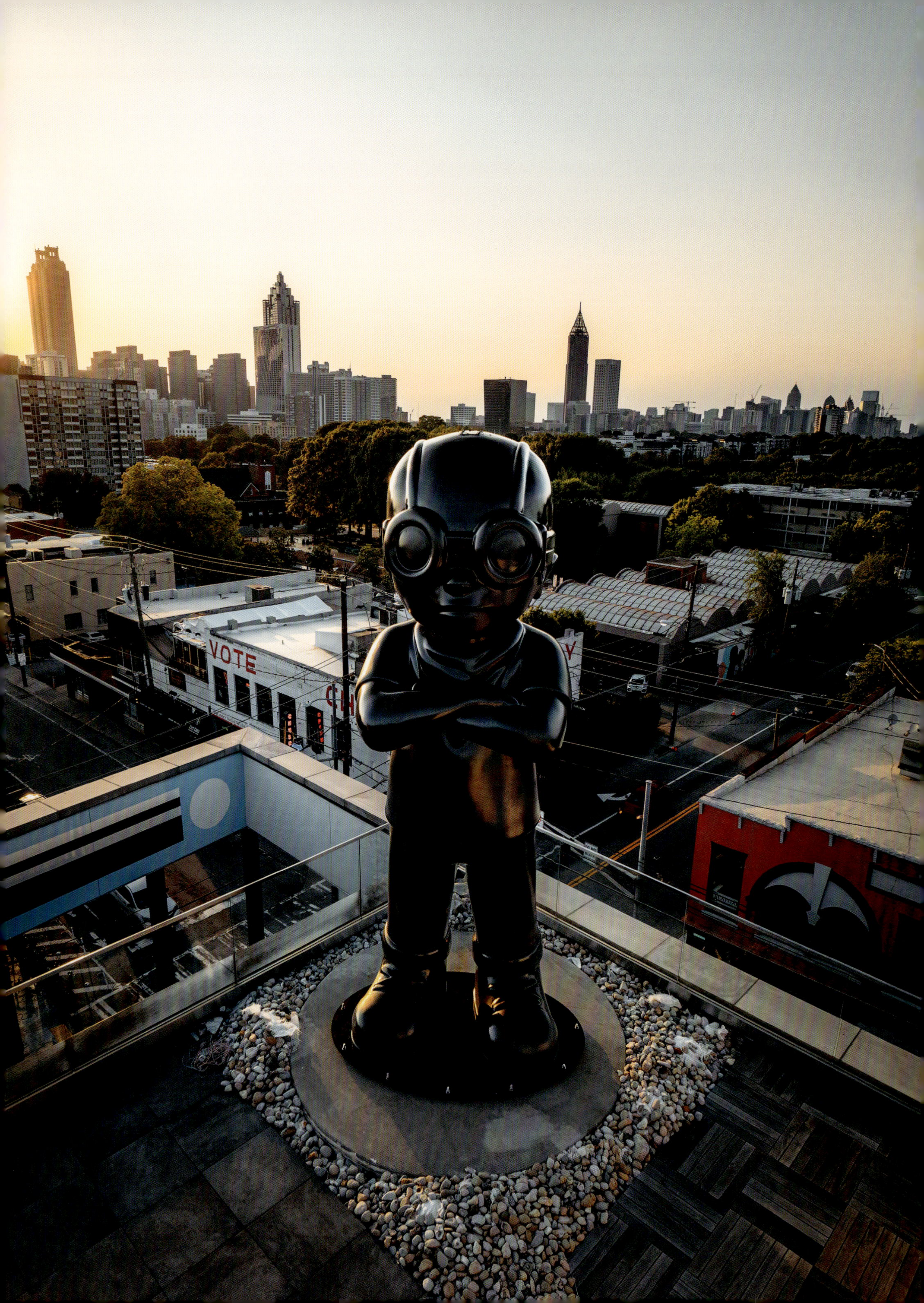

Luis Gaud is an Atlanta-based aeiral photographer. During the 2020 pandemic, social distancing forced Gaud to change his style of photography. He began capturing Atlanta from above, gaining a unique perspective on the city.

Gaud's photographs have been used by the state of Georgia and the city of Atlanta tourism boards, as well as by local media and the city of Atlanta's official social media accounts. *Above & Across Atlanta* is his first book.

@jerrito1

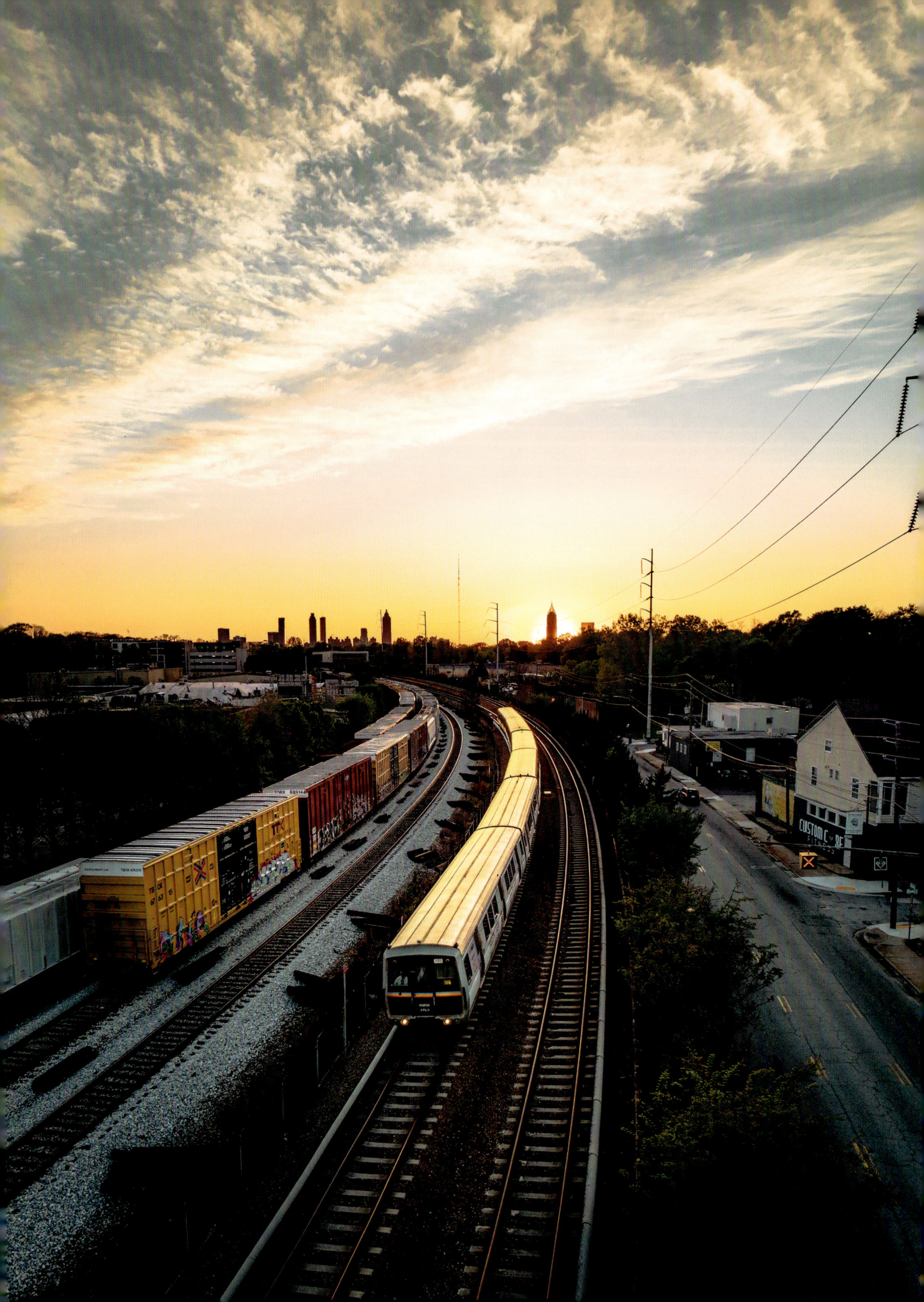
CUSTOM C RE
FITNESS

ABOUT THE EDITORS

+ MICHELLE FITZGERALD
Michelle Fitzgerald is a fierce advocate
for books and is passionate about sharing
them with the widest audience possible.
A veteran of the book publishing industry,
she is the Associate Publisher at Trope
Publishing Co. and served as editor on *New
York* and *Paris*, titles in Trope's City Edition
series, as well as *Above & Across Chicago*.

+ JACK VAN BOOM
Jack is a Chicago-based designer and artist.
A graduate of the School of the Art Institute
of Chicago, he is a designer at Trope
Publishing Co. and served as editor on
New York, part of Trope's City Edition series.

LCCN: 2024938889
ISBN: 978-1-951963-29-3

Printed and bound in China
First printing, 2024

The photographs from *Above &
Across Atlanta* are available for
purchase. For inquiries, email
the gallery at info@trope.com

+ INFORMATION:
For additional information
on our books and prints,
visit TROPE.COM

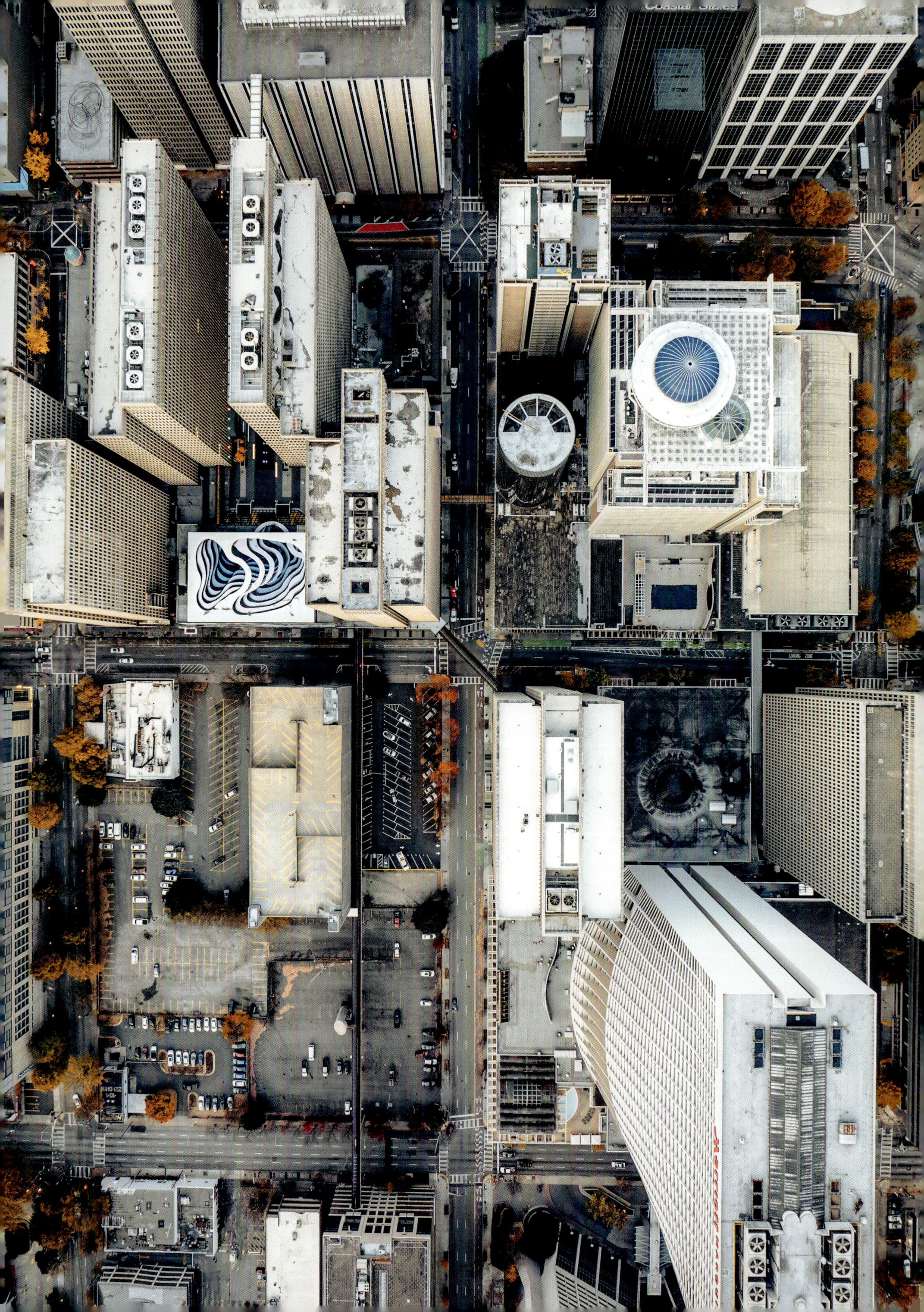